Download Forms on Nolo.com

You can download the forms in this book at:

 www.nolo.com/back-of-book/SMBU.html

We'll also post updates whenever there's an important change to the law affecting this book—as well as articles and other related materials.

More Resources from Nolo.com

 Legal Forms, Books, & Software
Hundreds of do-it-yourself products—all written in plain English, approved, and updated by our in-house legal editors.

 Legal Articles
Get informed with thousands of free articles on everyday legal topics. Our articles are accurate, up to date, and reader friendly.

 Find a Lawyer
Want to talk to a lawyer? Use Nolo to find a lawyer who can help you with your case.

Praise for *The Small Business Start-Up Kit*

"Peri Pakroo has created the perfect legal resource for small business owners who want to create a strong, viable and ethical business. It will save you time, energy and legal fees!"

PAMELA SLIM, author, *Escape from Cubicle Nation* **and**
Body of Work

"Peri walks you through many of the most intimidating aspects of running a small business with solid, tested strategies for success."

DAMIAN TAGGART, Chief Business Development Officer,
Meow Wolf

*"*The Small Business Start-Up Kit *not only helped me launch my multifaceted business both practically and successfully, it helped me appropriately prepare for that launch (and guided me through those first several months of confusion, uncertainty, and excitement). Peri generously offers her experience and expertise to readers as she clearly addresses everything from choosing the right business name to paying taxes to hiring employees. I could not have opened my art gallery or formalized my freelance services without this book, nor would I dare embark on any other business ventures without it!"*

NANCY ZASTUDIL, Owner/Director, The Necessarian, LLC
(DBA Central Features Contemporary Art)

"Covers a wide range of topics, from selecting a marketable name to small business laws, taxes and contracts."

MIAMI HERALD

"Answers important questions, including whether to incorporate and how to price merchandise."

REAL SIMPLE MAGAZINE

11th Edition

The
Small Business
Start-Up Kit

Peri H. Pakroo, J.D.
Edited by Elizabeth Gjelten

ELEVENTH EDITION	FEBRUARY 2020
Editor	ELIZABETH GJELTEN
Cover Design	SUSAN PUTNEY
Book Design	SUSAN PUTNEY
Production	SUSAN PUTNEY
Proofreading	SUSAN CARLSON GREENE
Index	RICHARD GENOVA
Printing	BANG PRINTING

ISSN: 2325-3673 (print)
ISSN: 2331-8139 (online)

ISBN: 978-1-4133-2723-6 (pbk)
ISBN: 978-1-4133-2724-3 (ebook)

This book covers only United States law, unless it specifically states otherwise.

Please note

We believe accurate, plain-English legal information should help you solve many of your own legal problems. But this text is not a substitute for personalized advice from a knowledgeable lawyer. If you want the help of a trained professional—and we'll always point out situations in which we think that's a good idea—consult an attorney licensed to practice in your state.

Acknowledgments for the Latest Edition

It's a great feeling to shepherd this latest edition of my book out into the world. As a self-employed person and small business owner, I constantly have what feels like a million different projects on my plate. This is my choice, of course, and like many self-employed folks I'm allergic to routine; I thrive on variety and the challenge of creative problem-solving. Still (and I think this is also true of many self-employed folks), managing the whirl of new projects and ventures can be a tiring dance. Having one constant—which for me is writing and advising clients about self-employment—is almost like a delicious resting pose. It has become the downward dog of my work life: actual work, but work in which I can settle in and relax and find new depth and strength the more I do it. I'm very thankful to have found a career path that I love and that fits me well, and I'm so very gratified that it helps other people pursuing their own path as well.

I especially want to thank Marcia Stewart for being my editor for the past several years and editions of this and my other books. Marcia, your keen eye and smart ideas always improve my work. Thank you for your attention, clarity, and patience. I feel truly lucky to work with you.

I'd also like to thank Patricia Allaire who helped me immeasurably with anxiety issues I suffered with after my daughter's health crisis a few years ago. As a self-employed person, it is tempting to muddle on in isolation, in large part because it is possible to do so when you set your own hours and don't need to interact with co-workers. I'm so glad I found Patricia who helped me learn more about how anxiety works and how to lessen its grip. Just a few months of targeted work have served me incredibly well for the last couple years, and I'm so thankful for it.

Thanks again to my loves, Turtle, Jila, and Jasper. You are my anchors and I love you beyond words.

P.S. Many other people have helped with the previous editions of this book. See the Acknowledgments below for details.

The Acknowledgments below are almost current (I updated them just a couple years ago), but I felt inspired to add this brief update to celebrate the eighth edition of this book, which was originally published in 2000. Nine editions! This is an exciting milestone. I'm hugely thankful this book keeps on going and continues to help readers pursue their ideas, their projects, and their dreams.

In the past few years, a number of people have entered my life who have helped me in important ways with their support, friendship, creativity, and just all-around awesomeness. Sage Harrington, thank you for everything: child care, research help, podcast jingles, tiny dogs, playing and singing, and just being you. You have been a lifeline through some very tough times; thank you. Matt Corson, thank you for your awesome songs and for pushing me to learn new things. It's a joy to be in your band and I'm glad you can out-boss me (sometimes). Chris Burnett, thank you for roping me into your podcasting kingdom; it has been a super-fun ride! Huge thanks to everyone involved with Pyragraph.com, especially Lex Gjurasic, Eva Avenue, Adam Rubinstein, David Dabney, and Turtle O'Toole. I'm incredibly proud of what we've accomplished, and all of it was under insane circumstances. Immeasurable thanks to the many doctors and nurses who have helped my girl and my family during a very intense medical experience over the past year-plus: Dr. Mark Unverzagt, Dr. Michael Grimley, Kathleen Novak, Dr. David Margolis, Lynette Anderson, Dr. John Bucuvalas, Jennifer Willoughby, and Dr. Lucille McLoughlin, among many others. Debbie Weissman, you have also been an absolute lifesaver with your love, friendship, and support; thank you. Endless love and thanks to my entire family, especially Turtle, Jila, and Jasper. Your love keeps me going.

—PHP 2016

As I write these Acknowledgments it has been exactly 10 years to the day that I have been self-employed full time. I'm so incredibly grateful to all the people who have helped and supported me, both directly and indirectly, as I've kept on blazing my own path these past 10 years. I'm a company of one, but I'm backed by a most excellent crew of family, friends, and collaborators who help me in innumerable ways, including providing advice, knowledge, moral support, and love. This crew is also hugely important in helping me continue to develop and update this book, as each time a new edition comes around I have a couple years' worth of new adventures in self-employment to draw from. So an updated round of thanks is in order.

I thank my lucky stars for my husband, Turtle O'Toole. He has always been incredibly supportive and helpful in everything—from lending an ear to my ideas (ranging from good to bad to loco), to shooting beautiful photos and video for my projects, to just about anything else necessary to keep our collective balls in the air. And now, he's added the role of heroic dad to our two little kids without skipping a beat. Thanks and huge love to you Turtle for every last bit of all of it.

My super-darlings Jila and Jasper give me daily (often hourly) inspiration, motivation, and a tether to everything that's true, pure, and important. Thank you Jila for doing such a great job these days of letting Mama talk on the phone, and thank you Jasper for your power to cut through any cloud of stress with your sunshine smile.

My parents, Kay and Reza Pakroo, have always believed I could do anything, which is an amazing foundation to have when you're charting your own course. Thanks so much for that, Mom and Dad.

My sister Zara Pakroo put up with a bossy big sister for years, which deserves thanks in itself. But I also want to thank you, Z, for helping me figure out how to put a lid on it sometimes. I try; really I do.

My family on the O'Toole side is an incredibly generous, supportive bunch of folks and I feel very lucky to be part of the family. Thanks especially to Kay O'Toole and Bob and Bebe O'Toole for all your support, encouragement, and generosity over the years.

I've had some excellent Nolo editors over the years with the previous new editions of this book, but working with Marcia Stewart for the last few years has really spoiled me. Thank you so much Marcia for your excellent ideas, your amazing attention to detail, and your overall energy and attitude that always leaves me feeling inspired after we talk on the phone. You have really helped me improve my work and I'm so very grateful for that. Thanks also to prior Nolo editors Beth Laurence and Cathy Caputo for their ace help with previous editions including some fairly major revisions that really improved the books. And big thanks to the awesome Nolo production team, including Susan Putney, Terri Hearsh, Emily Dunn, and Jaleh Doane for creating such attractive, clean, easy-to-read books. Most writers (myself included) know the awful feeling of seeing their hard work all mucked up with ugly production, so I'm particularly appreciative to have these books look so great.

Heartfelt and loving thanks to Jake Warner for getting me started writing books way back when I was a fresh, young, and very green editor at Nolo. You're such an inspiration Jake, and I feel really lucky to have worked for you.

I have deep love and appreciation for my longtime friend David Dabney, whom I can always count on to lend an ear about anything from a nasty client to money troubles to problems with *Photoshop* or *WordPress*. It can be tricky to balance friendships with doing business, but with Dave it's easy and has been for years. Thanks Dave for everything, but mostly for being my friend.

Thanks also to Clare Zurawski, Agnes Noonan, and the whole team at WESST for giving me such excellent opportunities to support small businesses in my local community, and for the many ways you've supported me. I'm thankful for the wonderful work you do and for being able to be a part of it.

Stacey Stickler and Laura Taylor, you rock my world and I love you. Love also to Inga Muscio (you never fail to inspire me); Samantha Campostrini-Medeiros (your bravery and compassion are astounding); Lex Gjurasic (how I wish you hadn't moved so far); and Christina Kennedy (your open heart, photos, music, and friendship have truly fed me this last year). Huge love to Debbie Weissman; thanks to you we have family in New Mexico. And to Kayte Blanke: We wish you lived closer and love you dearly. Thanks and love also to Emily Cooney for your loving care.

—PHP 2012

Dedication

I dedicate this book to my grandmother Eunice Michaelson Jones—
a spitfire if ever there was one.

About the Author

Peri Pakroo (www.peripakroo.com) is a business author and coach,
specializing in creative and smart strategies for self-employment and small
business. She has started, participated in, and consulted with start-up
businesses for more than 20 years. She is the founder, publisher, and editor
of Pyragraph (www.pyragraph.com), an online career magazine for artists,
musicians, designers, filmmakers, writers, and other creative workers
worldwide.

Peri received her law degree from the University of New Mexico School
of Law in 1995, and a year later began editing and writing for Nolo,
specializing in small business and intellectual property issues. She is the
author of the top-selling Nolo titles *The Women's Small Business Start-Up
Kit, The Small Business Start-Up Kit* (national and California editions),
and *Starting & Building a Nonprofit,* and has been featured in numerous
national and local publications including *Entrepreneur, Real Simple,
Investor's Business Daily,* and *BusinessWeek.* For several years Peri taught
adult education courses at WESST (www.wesst.org) in Albuquerque, a
nonprofit whose mission is to facilitate entrepreneurship among women
and minorities in the state of New Mexico. She is active in supporting
local, independent businesses and is a co-founder of the Albuquerque
Independent Business Alliance.

Table of Contents

Your Small Business Start-Up Companion

You don't have an MBA. Hell, you've never taken a business class. You spent your college years studying literature and art history, and periodically dropping out to travel the world. And now you find yourself thinking about going into business for yourself—maybe as a photographer, an owner of a café, or the founder of a software company. "Me, a businessperson?" you skeptically wonder. You keep trudging to work each morning, but as the hours tick by, you find yourself fantasizing more and more about kissing your 9-to-5 job goodbye. You jot down some notes, work out some kinks in your plan and continue to wonder whether it just might fly....

Unfortunately, most people who have toyed with business ideas this way never get to find out whether they would have worked or not. For a variety of practical, financial, and psychological reasons, most folks just don't take the leap from idea to reality. Certainly in some cases this might be a good thing. Having consulted with prospective start-ups for many years, I know full well that not all business ideas are good ones. But I find it such a shame when a would-be entrepreneur with terrific ideas gets thwarted or hung up on issues that really don't have to be terminal.

Folks new to the world of small business commonly report they get stuck because they don't know how to do things like write a business plan, do market research, price their goods or services, make financial projections or reports, manage staff, or draft a contract. The truth is, none of these tasks involve rocket science. Each can be done—and done effectively—with a simple, systematic approach. That's what this book offers: an easy-to-understand, step-by-step approach to all the important tasks an entrepreneur needs to tackle.

As Conditions Change, the Elements of Success Are the Same

While so many aspects of business are subject to relentless change—technology and global economic conditions are two particularly volatile factors—the good news for those just starting a business is that the elements of success remain pretty constant. Businesses tend to succeed when they (1) offer products or services that customers want; (2) do so with efficient operations, savvy marketing, and consistent sales efforts; and (3) have solid financial management. Period.

Some of you may be saying "Sure, that *sounds* easy, but I have no idea how to actually *do* any of those things!" The good news is you're not alone, and learning how to break down the essentials of what makes a business successful is actually not terribly complicated. For example:

- Don't know whether enough customers actually want your product or service? Start small and grow slowly based on what you learn is popular with customers. Prioritize doing simple, inexpensive market research, perhaps using free online surveys.
- Don't know how to manage a retail store or a small services firm? Break down your activities into systems, write out procedures and checklists, and consider using technology (like project management software) to help streamline operations.
- Don't know how to create a website or use social media? Consider adding someone with these skills to your team, either as an employee or independent contractor.
- Hate doing sales? Consider bringing on a sales-oriented partner, manager, or independent contractor.

- Don't know how to track your money or prepare financial reports? Read up on the basics (as in this book), occasionally hire a bookkeeper for some hands-on learning sessions, and use software that makes generating reports easy.

The chapters in this book focus on these and other important business tasks and systems, breaking them down into simple steps that are easy to get started. Even if you feel like a fish out of water in the "business world," you'll have a clearer idea of the key inner workings of a successful small business—and how to set one up yourself—once you read through this book.

Systems Facilitate Success

Mind you, I don't mean to imply that starting a successful business is easy. I know there are a million different details to work out—how you'll produce your product or service, how much you'll charge, what marketing strategies to use, how to manage your cash flow—and you need to nail all of this down before you stand to make a dime. You'll likely find that very few, if any, other businesspeople have done exactly what you're setting out to do, so you'll have to answer a lot of questions on your own (or with your partners). It can be scary and lonely—and while exhilarating, it's almost always stressful.

However, instead of feeling overwhelmed, take heart in the fact that there are some tried-and-true methods to radically boost your chances of success. Perhaps the most powerful of these is to establish systems for important tasks like managing finances, marketing your products or services, hiring staff, and so on. From simple systems like checklists and procedures put in writing, to complex software used to manage projects or clients, thoughtful systems can make a huge difference in how a business runs.

When efficient systems are in place—for example, you have clear, step-by-step procedures for entering receipts into your bookkeeping software, planning the year's marketing initiatives, or performing annual reviews for employees—valuable mental time is freed up. When you and your managers aren't constantly reinventing the wheel with your operations, you can think about really important things, like what industry changes are on the horizon, what trends are happening with customer tastes, or how to distinguish your company from its competition.

Because I'm by nature a linear thinker (for better or for worse), you'll find that I've tackled the topics in this book by breaking them down and presenting them in as systematic a way as possible. The more that you can systematize your business, the better you'll be positioned for success. I encourage you to try to envision your business like a machine with various moving parts. Successful businesses manage to keep those parts moving with a minimum of direction from owners or supervisors—and well-established systems are the best way to achieve this.

Why This Book Is a Must for Start-Ups

Unlike many other small business guides, this one won't spend your precious time quizzing you on whether you really want to start a business after all. If you need more help deciding whether or not entrepreneurship is for you, you should probably buy a different book. If, on the other hand, you want a book that cuts to the chase and explains systematically what you need to do to plan and launch a business officially and legally, this book is for you. It's organized so you can skip around to whatever topics you're grappling with at the time; you don't need to read the book from cover to cover. If you are already knowledgeable about a topic or you've already taken care of a particular task, you can either skip those chapters or use them as a guide to evaluate what you've already done.

Take the Leap

One of the main ideas to take away from this book is that there's nothing mysterious or even terribly complex about the process of starting your own business. Whether you've drafted a highly specific business plan with the help of accountants and consultants or you've scratched it out on a cocktail napkin, the process of fleshing out that idea, refining it, and turning it into a legitimate business is the same. That's the process I cover in the following chapters.

This book will help you build an efficient operation that, over time, will free you from day-to-day business tasks so you can focus your energies on big-picture strategic development, which is at the heart of the role of business owner. As easy as it is to get mired in operational details, it's essential to find some breathing room on a regular basis so that you can step back, evaluate market conditions, spot opportunities and threats, and take action to keep your business on a profitable course. You'll need confidence to make important business decisions—and you'll need guts, too. You may well find that some of the questions burning in your mind have no clear answer, because no one has asked those particular questions or tried those ideas before. You probably wanted to start a business in the first place so that you could call your own shots—but this can often be quite a heavy burden. You may not believe it now, but some days you'll probably find yourself wishing you had a boss.

You'll need to learn to trust yourself, both when you feel optimistic and when you suspect that one of your ideas is less than brilliant. You'll also have to develop a sense for when you need help and learn to be judicious in taking the advice of people around you. Part of the art of controlling your own destiny is accepting the wisdom of others while maintaining your own focus and direction. It's not always an easy balance to maintain, but you'll undoubtedly get better at it as you gain experience in running your own show. The bottom line: Think hard, keep your mind open—and fight like hell to make your ideas a reality.

Take the leap.

Stephen Parr, owner and director of Oddball Film and Video, a stock film and video footage company in San Francisco, California (www.oddballfilms.com):
I started making video art in the 1970s. After a while I started collecting all these weird bits of film because it was cheaper than shooting it myself. I gathered all kinds of old, found footage, like military training films, educational films, home movies, and all kinds of other images, and put them together into montages, which I screened in nightclubs as background visuals. I was showing them all over— nightclubs in New York, Chicago, San Francisco—and I made some money by selling the tapes to the clubs.

Then I started getting calls from companies in Silicon Valley that produce industrial videos, like training films and promotional programs for corporate trade shows. Video game companies were calling, too. Companies like Sega, Sun Microsystems, and Silicon Graphics wanted to pay me for my footage. Friends thought I should go into business selling the stock footage I had collected, but I didn't know if I could make a living doing it. I didn't know anything about the stock footage business. There were a few companies doing it, but they were in New York or LA, and they seemed really huge.

But since I liked working with images and since the business had already started to take off on its own, I decided to formalize it. I wanted an interesting company name that conveyed what I did. We came up with Oddball. It's a word that people don't really use anymore, more of a '40s or '50s expression—an oddball is someone kind of weird, unbalanced, or unusual, you know?

At the most basic level, my business involves finding, organizing, and preserving historical footage. And then distributing it. Our clients include ad agencies; news organizations; documentary and feature filmmakers; industrial, corporate, and music video producers; educational film- makers; and anyone who needs offbeat and unusual images. In one way, we're like a library: We archive and license historical visual information.

These days, I spend most of my time trying to organize and publicize my business. And I spend a lot more time trying to obtain films than actually looking at them. Still, what I do at Oddball is an extension of the work I've been doing since the 1970s. I guess it became a business the day I decided I wasn't going to do anything else.

More Small Business Products from Nolo

Nolo's website (www.nolo.com) offers books, software, online legal forms, a lawyer directory, and free legal information to help businesses solve specific legal problems. Here are some of the most popular business titles. You'll find more online, including an online LLC formation service.

Business Plans and Financing

How to Write a Business Plan
by Mike P. McKeever
Explains in detail how to write a business plan, whether for your own purposes or to attract money from lenders or investors—including how to evaluate the profitability of your business idea; estimate operating expenses; and determine assets, liabilities, and net worth.

Commercial Leases

Negotiate the Best Lease for Your Business
by Janet Portman
A guide to the ins and outs of finding a space for your business, negotiating a lease, and solving problems that arise from it.

Business Operations

Quicken Legal Business Pro
A software package containing more than 100 contracts, legal forms, and worksheets, along with the complete text of six of Nolo's bestselling business titles: *The Legal Guide for Starting & Running a Small Business*, *The Manager's Legal Handbook*, *How to Write a Business Plan*, *Contracts: The Essential Business Desk Reference*, *Deduct It! Lower Your Small Business Taxes*, and *The Essential Guide to Federal Employment Laws*.

Forms of Ownership

Form Your Own Limited Liability Company
by Anthony Mancuso
Offers instructions and forms to create an LLC in your state, as well as a full explanation of LLCs and how they work.

Incorporate Your Business: A Step-by-Step Guide to Forming a Corporation in Any State
by Anthony Mancuso
Ready to incorporate your business? This do-it-yourself guide provides everything you need to get the job done—without a lawyer.

LLC or Corporation? Choose the Right Form for Your Business
by Anthony Mancuso
Explains the legal and tax differences between LLCs and corporations.

Nolo's Guide to Single-Member LLCs
by David M. Steingold
Provides an overview of how to form and run a single-member LLC, including unique tax and liability issues.

Form a Partnership: The Complete Legal Guide
by Denis Clifford and Ralph Warner
Describes the legal and practical issues of creating a partnership—including financial and tax liabilities, contributions and distributions, and changes in ownership.

More Small Business Products from Nolo (continued)

Business Buyout Agreements: Plan Now for All Types of Business Transitions
by Bethany Laurence and Anthony Mancuso
Explains how to protect your business interests by drawing up a "premarital" agreement between you and your business owners that sets out a plan for what happens if you or a co-owner leaves the company. A must for any new business with more than one owner.

Intellectual Property

Trademark: Legal Care for Your Business & Product Name
by Stephen Fishman
The information and forms you need to choose a distinctive trademark, register it, and fight infringers.

Tax

Deduct It! Lower Your Small Business Taxes
by Stephen Fishman
Take all the business tax deductions you're due! Write off travel expenses, meals, and much more.

Home Business Tax Deductions: Keep What You Earn
by Stephen Fishman
The complete guide to the tax deductions your home business can claim—including your home office costs.

Tax Savvy for Small Business
by Frederick W. Daily
Offers plain-English explanations of tax laws and rules on business deductions, plus tax info on LLCs, partnerships, corporations, and more.

Workplace Laws

The Employer's Legal Handbook
by Fred S. Steingold
All the basics of employment law in one place—including safe hiring and firing practices, wages, hours, employee benefits, taxes and liability, discrimination, and sexual harassment.

The Manager's Legal Handbook
by Lisa Guerin and Sachi Barreiro
A quick reference to employment law from a manager's perspective, combining legal information and practical ideas.

Working With Independent Contractors
by Stephen Fishman
Explains all the tricky IRS rules and provides downloadable forms and instructions for hiring independent contractors.

Get Updates, Forms, and More at This Book's Companion Page on Nolo.com

You can download any of the forms and worksheets in this book at:

www.nolo.com/back-of-book/SMBU.html

When there are important changes to the information in this book, we'll post updates on this same dedicated page (what we call the book's companion page). See Appendix B, "How to Use the Downloadable Forms on the Nolo Website," for a complete list of forms and resources available on Nolo.com.

Choosing a Legal Structure

You probably already have a rough idea of the type of legal structure your business will take, whether you know it or not. That's because, in large part, the ownership structure that's right for your business—a sole proprietorship, partnership, LLC, or corporation—depends on how many people will own the business and what type of services or products it will provide, things you've undoubtedly thought about quite a bit.

For instance, if you know that you will be the only owner, then a partnership is obviously not your thing. (A partnership by definition has more than one owner.) And if your business will engage in risky activities (for example, trading stocks or repairing roofs), you'll want not only to buy insurance, but also to consider forming an entity that provides personal liability protection (a corporation or a limited liability company), which can shield your personal assets from business debts and claims. If you plan to raise capital by selling stock to the public or want to give your employees stock options, then you should form a corporation.

If you've considered these issues, then you'll be ahead of the game in choosing a legal structure that's right for your business. Still, you'll need to consider the benefits and drawbacks of each type of business structure before you make your final decision.

Limited Liability

One basic distinction that you'll probably hear mentioned lots of times is the difference between businesses that provide their owners with "limited liability" and those that don't. Corporations and LLCs both provide owners with limited personal liability. Sole proprietorships and general partnerships do not.

Limited liability basically means that the creditors of the business cannot normally go after the owners' personal assets to pay for business debts and claims arising from lawsuits. (Liability for business debts is discussed in detail later in this chapter.)

As you read about specific business types in this chapter, you'll see how a decision to form a limited liability entity (a corporation or an LLC, mainly) can dramatically affect how you run your business. On the other hand, sole proprietorships and partnerships (which are somewhat simpler to run than corporations and LLCs) may leave an owner personally vulnerable to business lawsuits and debts.

In all states, the basic types of business structures are:

- sole proprietorships
- partnerships (general and limited)
- limited liability companies (LLCs), and
- corporations.

To help you pick the best structure for your business, this chapter explains the basic attributes of each type.

This chapter will also help you answer the most common question new entrepreneurs ask about choosing a business form: Should I choose a business structure that offers protection from personal liability—a corporation or an LLC? Here's a hint as to what the best advice will be: If you focus energy and money into getting your business off the ground as a sole proprietorship or a partnership, you can always incorporate or form an LLC later.

Sole Proprietorships

SKIP AHEAD

Sole proprietorships are one-owner businesses. Any business with two or more owners cannot, by definition, be a sole proprietorship. If you know that there will be two or more owners of your business, you can skip ahead to "Partnerships," below.

Making the Decision to Go Official

Some of you may be grappling with a more preliminary question than what legal structure you should choose, and wondering whether or not to formalize your business—to go the official route and register your business with the appropriate agencies in your state. For instance, maybe you've been doing freelance graphics work on the side for a number of years, but now you're thinking of quitting your 9-to-5 job to take on graphics work full time.

Generally speaking, anyone with a good-sized or otherwise visible business should bite the bullet and complete all of the necessary registration tasks to become official. Operating under the table can all too easily be exposed, and the government can come after you for fines and penalties, simply for operating without the necessary paperwork. And if you're making a profit, ignoring the IRS is definitely a bad idea. Besides fines and back taxes, you could even face criminal charges and jail time.

On the other hand, tiny, home-based, hobby-type businesses can often operate for quite some time without meeting registration requirements.

If you're braiding hair or screen printing t-shirts or holding an occasional junk sale out of your garage, for instance, you can probably get by without formal business registration—at least for a while. Keep in mind, however, that just because it may be possible doesn't mean it's the best option. Often, formally registering your business can benefit you, the owner, as well, since you can then write off business expenses and reduce your personal taxes. In Chapter 9, we discuss hobby businesses in more depth, including how tax laws deal with businesses that continually lose money.

If you're not sure whether you want to register your business and open it up to the world of government regulations, the information about registration requirements in this book will put you in a better position to make a decision. Chapter 7 walks you through the many governmental requirements that apply to all new businesses, and explains how to go about finding and satisfying any additional requirements that may apply to your specific business.

A sole proprietorship is simply a business that is owned by one person and that hasn't filed papers to become a corporation or an LLC. Sole proprietorships are easy to set up and to maintain—so easy that many people own sole proprietorships and don't even know it. For instance, if you are a freelance photographer or writer, a craftsperson who takes jobs on a contract basis, a salesperson who receives only commissions, or an independent contractor who isn't on an employer's regular payroll, you are automatically a sole proprietor. This is true whether or not you've registered your business with your city or obtained any licenses or permits. And it makes no difference whether you also have a regular day job. As long as you do for-profit work on your own (or sometimes with your spouse—see "Running a Business With Your Spouse," below) and have not filed papers to become a corporation or a limited liability company, you are a sole proprietor.

> ⚠ CAUTION
>
> **Don't ignore local registration requirements.** If you've started a business without quite realizing it—for example, you do a little freelance computer programming, which classifies you as a sole proprietor by default—be aware that you have likely not satisfied the governmental requirements for starting a business. Most cities and many counties require businesses—even tiny home-based sole proprietorships—to register with

them and pay at least a minimum tax. And if you do business under a name different from your own (say, Christina Kennedy does business under the name "Monster Photography"), you usually must register that name—known as a fictitious business name—with your county. In practice, lots of businesses are small enough to get away with ignoring these requirements. But if you aren't in compliance and you are caught, you may be subject to back taxes and other penalties. (See Chapter 7 for an explanation of how to make the necessary filings with the appropriate government offices.)

Pass-Through Taxation

In the eyes of the law, a sole proprietorship is not legally separate from the person who owns it. This is one of the fundamental differences between a sole proprietorship and a corporation or an LLC, and it has two major effects: one related to taxation (explained in this section), and the other to personal liability (explained in the next).

At income tax time, a sole proprietor simply reports all business income or losses on his or her individual income tax return. The business itself is not taxed. The IRS calls this "pass-through" taxation, because business profits pass through the business to be taxed on the business owner's tax return. You report income from a business just like wages from a job, except that, along with Form 1040, you'll need to include Schedule C, on which you'll provide your business's profit and loss

Running a Business With Your Spouse

If you plan to start a sole proprietorship and expect that your spouse may occasionally help out with business tasks, you should be aware of a fuzzy area in federal tax law that you can use to your advantage. The IRS typically allows a spouse to pitch in without pay without risking being classified as an owner or as an employee of the other spouse's business. This situation is sometimes erroneously called a "husband-wife sole proprietorship."

The normal rule is that someone who does work for a business must be (from a legal standpoint) a co-owner, an employee, or an independent contractor. But your spouse can volunteer—that is, work without pay—for your sole proprietorship without being classified as an employee, freeing the business from paying payroll tax.

That saves you money—and, if you have no other employees, also allows you to avoid the time-consuming record keeping involved in being an employer. Similarly, a spouse who is not classified as a partner or an independent contractor won't have to pay self-employment taxes, and your business won't have to file a partnership tax return.

Also consider that under marital property laws that vary from state to state, if a business is started or significantly changed when a couple is married, both spouses may have an ownership interest in the business regardless of whose name is on the ownership document.

If you are concerned about the possible consequences of divorce, read Chapter 15, "Planning for Changes in Ownership." It discusses how divorce and other life events, such as retirement and death, can affect ownership of a business and explains how to plan in advance to accommodate the possibilities. You may also want to check with a lawyer who is experienced in handling marital property issues to see how your business could be affected in the event of a divorce in your particular state.

Finally, if you and your spouse both want to be active partners in a co-owned business—each with an official say in management—you should create a partnership or an LLC or corporation, even though this will mean filing somewhat more complicated tax returns and other business paperwork. If your spouse tries to squeak by as a volunteer in a so-called husband-wife sole proprietorship when you're really working together as a partnership, you run the risk of being audited, having the IRS declare you're a partnership, and socking your spouse with back self-employment taxes.

information. One helpful aspect of this arrangement is that if your business loses money—and, of course, many start-ups do in the first year or two—you can use the business losses to offset any taxable income you have earned from other sources.

EXAMPLE: Rob has a day job at a coffee shop, where he earns a modest salary. His hobby is collecting obscure records at thrift stores and rummage sales. Contemplating the sad fact that he has no extra money to spend at the flea market on Saturday morning, he decides to start selling some of the vinyl gems he's found. Still working his day job, he starts a small business that he calls Rob's Revolving Records.

During his first full year in business, he sees that a key to consistently selling his records is developing connections and trust among record collectors. Unfortunately, while he is concentrating on getting to know potential buyers and others in the business, sales are slow. At year end he closes out his books and sees that he spent nearly $9,000 on records, his website, marketing items such as business cards, and other incidental supplies, while he made only $3,000 in sales. But there is some good news: Rob's loss of $6,000 can be counted against his income from his day job, reducing his taxes and translating into a nice refund check, which he'll put right back into his record business.

CAUTION

Your business can't lose money forever. See the discussion of tax rules for money-losing businesses in Chapter 9.

RESOURCE

Be ready for the day you'll owe taxes. Once your business is underway and turning a profit, you'll have to start paying taxes. (See Chapter 9 for an overview of the taxes that small businesses face.) Taxes can get fairly complicated, however, and you may need more in-depth guidance. For detailed information on taxes for the various types of small businesses, read *Tax Savvy for Small Business*, by Frederick W. Daily (Nolo). This book gives exhaustive information on deductions, record keeping, and audits that will help you reduce your tax bill and stay out of trouble with the IRS.

Personal Liability for Business Debts

Another crucial thing to know about operating your business as a sole proprietor is that you, as the owner of the business, can be held personally liable for business-related obligations. This means that if your business doesn't pay a supplier, defaults on a debt, loses a lawsuit, or otherwise finds itself in financial hot water, you, personally, can be forced to pay up. This can be a sobering possibility, especially if you own (or soon hope to own) a house, a car, or other treasures. Personal liability for business obligations stems from the fundamental legal attribute of being a sole proprietor: You and your business are legally one and the same.

As explained in more detail in the sections that discuss corporations and LLCs, below, the law provides owners of these businesses with "limited personal liability" for business obligations. This means that, unlike sole proprietors and general partners, owners of corporations and LLCs can normally keep their houses, investments, and other personal property even if their businesses fail. In short, if you are engaged in a risky business, you may want to consider forming a corporation or an LLC (although a thorough insurance policy can protect you from most lawsuits and claims against the business if your company is a sole proprietorship or partnership).

CAUTION

Commercial insurance doesn't cover business debts. Commercial insurance can protect a business and its owners from some types of liability (for instance, slip-and-fall lawsuits), but insurance never covers business debts. The only way to limit your personal liability for business debts is to use a limited liability business structure, such as an LLC or a corporation (or a limited partnership or limited liability partnership).

Creating a Sole Proprietorship

Setting up a sole proprietorship is incredibly easy. Unlike starting an LLC or a corporation, you generally don't have to file any special forms or pay any special fees to start working as a sole proprietor. You'll simply declare your business to be a sole proprietorship when completing the general registration requirements that apply to all new businesses, such as getting a business license from your county or city or a seller's permit from your state.

For example, when filing for a business tax registration certificate with your city, you'll often be asked to declare what kind of business you're starting. Some cities require only that you check a "sole proprietorship" box on a form, while other cities have separate tax registration forms for sole proprietorships. Similarly, other forms you'll file, such as those to register a fictitious business name and to obtain a seller's permit, will also ask for this information. (These and other start-up requirements are discussed in detail in Chapter 7.)

Partnerships

Bring two or more entrepreneurs together into a business venture, stir gently, and— poof!—you've got a partnership. By definition, a partnership is a business that has more than one owner and that has not filed papers with the state to become a corporation or an LLC (or a limited partnership or limited liability partnership).

CAUTION

Partnerships and registration requirements. Though businesses with two or more owners are partnerships by default, they still must satisfy various governmental requirements for starting a business. Most cities and many counties require all businesses to register with them and pay at least a minimum tax. And if you do business under a name other than the partners' names, you usually must register that name—known as a fictitious business name—with your county. (See Chapter 7 for an explanation of how to make the necessary filings with the appropriate government offices.)

General Versus Limited Partnerships

Usually, when you hear the term "partnership," it means a general partnership. As discussed in more detail below, general partners are personally liable for all business debts, including court judgments. In addition, each individual partner can be sued for the full amount of any business debt (though that partner can turn around and sue the other partners for their share of the debt).

Another very important aspect of general partnerships is that any individual partner can bind the whole business to a contract or business deal—in other words, each partner has "agency authority" for the partnership. And remember, each of the partners is fully personally liable for a business deal gone sour, no matter which partner signed the contract. So choose your partners carefully.

There are also a couple of special kinds of partnerships, called limited partnerships and limited liability partnerships. They operate under very different rules and are relatively uncommon, so they are only briefly described here.

A limited partnership requires at least one general partner and at least one limited partner. The general partner has the same role as in a general partnership: He or she controls the company's day-to-day operations and is personally liable for business debts. The limited partner contributes financially to the business (for example, by investing $100,000 in a real estate partnership) but has minimal control over business decisions or operations, and normally cannot bind the partnership to business deals. In return for giving up management power, a limited partner gets the benefit of protection from personal liability. This means that a limited partner can't be forced to pay off business debts or claims with personal assets, but can lose an investment in the business. But beware: A limited partner who tires of being passive and starts tinkering under the hood of the business should understand that his or her liability can quickly become unlimited that way. If a creditor can prove that the limited partner took acts that led the creditor to believe that he or she was a general partner, the limited partner can be held fully and personally liable for the creditor's claims.

Another kind of partnership, called a limited liability partnership (LLP) or sometimes a registered limited liability partnership (RLLP), provides all of its owners with limited personal liability. In some states, these partnerships are only available to professionals, such as lawyers and accountants, and are particularly well suited to them. Most professionals aren't keen on general partnerships, because they don't want to be personally liable for another partner's problems—particularly those involving malpractice claims. Forming a corporation to protect personal assets may be too much trouble, and some states won't allow these professionals to form an LLC. The solution is often a limited liability partnership. This business structure protects each partner from debts against the partnership arising from professional malpractice lawsuits against another partner. (A partner who loses a malpractice suit because of personal mistakes, however, doesn't escape liability.)

Pass-Through Taxation

Similar to a sole proprietorship, a partnership (general or limited) is not a separate tax entity from its owners; instead, it's what the IRS calls a "pass-through entity." This means the partnership itself does not pay any income taxes; rather, income passes through the business to each partner, who pays taxes on a share of

profit (or deducts a share of losses) on an individual income tax return (Form 1040, with Schedule E attached). However, the partnership must also file what the IRS calls an "informational return"—Form 1065 —to let the government know how much the business earned or lost that year. No tax is paid with this return—just think of it as the feds' way of letting you know they're watching.

Personal Liability for Business Debts

Since a partnership is legally inseparable from its owners, just like a sole proprietorship, general partners are personally liable for business-related obligations. What's more, in a general partnership, the business actions of any one partner bind the other partners, who can be held personally liable for those actions. So if your business partner takes out an ill-advised high-interest loan on behalf of the partnership, makes a terrible business deal, or gets in some other business mischief without your knowledge, you could be held personally responsible for any debts that result.

EXAMPLE: Jamie and Kent are partners in a profitable landscape gardening company. They've been in business for five years and have earned healthy profits, allowing them each to buy a house, decent wheels, and even a few luxuries—including Jamie's collection of garden sculptures and Kent's roomful of vintage musical instruments. One day Jamie, without telling Kent, orders a shipment of exotic poppy plants that he is sure will be a big hit with customers. But when the shipment arrives, so do agents of the federal drug enforcement agency, who confiscate the plants, claiming they could be turned into narcotics. Soon thereafter, criminal charges are filed against Jamie and Kent, resulting in several newspaper stories. Though the partners are ultimately cleared, their attorneys' fees come to $50,000 and they lose several key accounts, with the result that the business runs up hefty debts. As a general partner, Kent is personally liable for these debts even though he had nothing to do with the ill-fated poppy purchase.

Before you get too worried about personal liability, keep in mind that many small businesses don't face much of a risk of racking up large debts. For instance, if you're engaged in a low-risk enterprise, such as freelance editing, landscaping, or running a small band that plays weddings and other social events, your risk of facing massive debt or a huge lawsuit is pretty small. For these types of small, low-risk businesses, a good business insurance policy that covers most liability risks is almost always enough to protect owners from a catastrophe like a lawsuit or fire. Insurance won't cover regular business debts, however. If you have significant personal assets like fat bank accounts or real estate and plan to rack up some business debt, you may want to limit your personal liability with a different business structure, such as an LLC or a corporation.

Partnership Agreements

By drafting a partnership agreement, you can structure your relationship with your partners pretty much however you want. You and your partners can establish the shares of profits (or losses) each partner will receive, what the responsibilities of each partner will be, what should happen to the partnership if a partner leaves, and how a number of other issues will be handled. It is not legally necessary for a partnership to have a written agreement; the simple act of two or more people doing business together creates a partnership. But only with a clear written agreement will all partners be sure of the important—and sometimes touchy—details of their business arrangement.

In the absence of a partnership agreement, your state's version of the Uniform Partnership Act (UPA) or Revised Uniform Partnership Act (RUPA) kicks in as a standard, bottom-line guide to the rights and responsibilities of each partner. Most states have adopted the UPA or RUPA in some form. In California, for example, if you don't have a partnership agreement, then California's RUPA states that each partner has an equal share in the business's profits, losses, and management power. Similarly, unless you provide otherwise in a written agreement, a California partnership won't be able to add a new partner without the unanimous consent of all partners. (Cal. Corp. Code § 16401.)

In short, it's important to understand that you can override many of the legal provisions contained in the UPA or RUPA if you and your partners have your own written agreement.

 RELATED TOPIC

Businesses with more than one owner should address potential changes in ownership. The partnership agreement provisions discussed in this chapter cover the very basics. Chapter 15 covers what is known as a buy-sell agreement, which establishes rules for what will happen if an owner retires, becomes disabled, dies, gets divorced, or otherwise faces a situation that brings business ownership into question. Buy-sell provisions can exist in a separate document or may be included in partnership agreements or other organizational documents depending on the company structure: operating agreements for LLCs or bylaws for corporations. Read Chapter 15 to become familiar with the ownership issues that can arise when your business is owned by more than one person—and how best to head off problems with a solid agreement.

There's nothing terribly complex about drafting partnership agreements. They're usually only a few pages long and cover basic issues that you've probably thought over to some degree already. Partnership agreements typically include at least the following information:

- name of partnership and partnership business
- date of partnership creation
- purpose of partnership

- contributions (cash, property, and work) of each partner to the partnership
- each partner's share of profits and losses
- provisions for taking profits out of the company (often called partners' draws)
- each partner's management power and duties
- how the partnership will handle departure of a partner, including buyout terms
- provisions for adding or expelling a partner, and
- dispute resolution procedures.

These and any other terms you include in a partnership agreement can be dealt with in more or less detail. Some partnership agreements cover each topic with a sentence or two; others spend up to a few pages on each provision. You need an agreement that's appropriate for the size and formality of your business, but it's not a good idea to skimp on your partnership agreement.

FORM

Take a look at the short sample partnership agreements on the following pages to see how a very basic partnership agreement can be put together. You'll find a downloadable partnership agreement on the Nolo website; see Appendix B for the link to this form and other forms in the book.

The sample partnership agreements included here and on the Nolo website are about as basic as it gets—the bare minimum—and you'll almost surely want to use something more detailed for your business.

Partnership Agreement #1

Alison Shanley and Peder Johnson make the following partnership agreement.

Name and Purpose of Partnership

As of September 22, 20xx, Alison and Peder are the sole owners and partners of the Vermont Fly-Fishing Company. The Vermont Fly-Fishing Company shall be headquartered in Rutland, Vermont, and will sell fly-fishing equipment by mail order.

Contributions to the Partnership

Alison and Peder will make the following contributions to the partnership:

Alison Shanley	cash	$10,000
	desk, miscellaneous office furniture	1,000
	Total contribution:	$11,000
Peder Johnson	cash	$7,000
	computer system	2,000
	Total contribution:	$9,000

Profit and Loss Allocation

Alison and Peder will share business profits and losses in the same proportions as their contributions to the business.

Management of Partnership Business

Alison and Peder will have equal management powers and responsibilities.

Departure of a Partner

If either Alison or Peder leaves the partnership for any reason, including voluntary withdrawal, expulsion, or death, the remaining partner shall become the sole owner of the Vermont Fly-Fishing Company, which shall become a sole proprietorship. The remaining owner shall pay the departing partner, or the deceased departing partner's estate, the fair market value of the departing partner's share of the business as of the date of his or her departure. The partnership's accountant shall determine the fair market value of the departing partner's share of the business according to the partnership's book value.

Mediation of Disputes

Alison and Peder agree to mediate any dispute arising under this agreement with a mutually acceptable mediator.

Amendment of Agreement

This agreement may not be amended without the written consent of both partners.

Alison Shanley	Peder Johnson
Signature _____	Signature _____
Date _____	Date _____
SSN # _____	SSN # _____

Partnership Agreement #2

Christine Wenc, Simon Romero, and Brendan Doherty agree to the terms of the following agreement.

1. **Name of Partnership.** Christine, Simon, and Brendan are partners in the Wenc & Romero Partnership. They created the partnership on July 12, 20xx.

2. **Partnership Purpose.** The Wenc & Romero Partnership will provide public relations services to clients.

3. **Contributions to the Partnership.** Christine, Simon, and Brendan will contribute the following to the partnership:

    Christine: $1,000 cash; one Macintosh computer (value $1,500); and one monitor (value $500).

    Simon: $1,000 cash; one fax machine (value $400); one laser printer (value $1,200).

    Brendan: $500 cash; various office equipment (value $500).

4. **Profits and Losses.** Christine, Simon, and Brendan shall share profits and losses as follows:

    Christine 40%; Simon 40%; Brendan 20%

5. **Partnership Decisions.** Christine, Simon, and Brendan will have the following management authority:

    Christine 2 votes; Simon 2 votes; Brendan 1 vote

    No partner may accept a new client without the agreement of the others.

6. **Additional Terms to Be Drafted.** Christine, Simon, and Brendan agree that in six months they will sign a formal partnership agreement that covers the items in this agreement in more detail, and the additional following items:

    • each partner's work contributions

    • provisions for adding a partner

    • provisions for the departure of a partner, and

    • provisions for selling the business.

7. **Amendments.** This agreement may not be amended without the written consent of all partners.

Christine Wenc

Signature _____

Date _____

SSN # _____

Simon Romero

Signature _____

Date _____

SSN # _____

Brendan Doherty

Signature _____

Date _____

SSN # _____

RESOURCE

For more on partnerships.

Form a Partnership: The Complete Legal Guide, by Denis Clifford and Ralph Warner (Nolo), is an excellent step-by-step guide to putting together a solid, comprehensive partnership agreement. Also, *Business Buyout Agreements: Plan Now for All Types of Business Transitions,* by Bethany Laurence and Anthony Mancuso (Nolo), explains how to draft terms that will enable you to deal with business ownership transitions. If you think you may want more than the simple partnership agreements in this book but don't want to spend a lot of time creating an agreement, there are more detailed partnership agreement forms (as well as many other resources for running your small business) in *Quicken Legal Business Pro* software (Nolo). You can learn more about these resources at www.nolo.com.

Nancy Zastudil, Owner/Director, The Necessarian, LLC:

Growing up in a family of self-starters, I had seen some of the day-to-day operations of small business but what kid ever asks, "Grandpa, what's the legal structure of your antique shop?" Well, not me. I was more interested in playing "Store," as my sister and I called it. We would take turns pretending to be the customer and the shop owner and, as many kids do, we made up the rules as we went along. As a result, our store was wildly successful, we had fabulous uniforms, and we never saved receipts.

Enter the "real" adult world: When I decided I wanted to open an art gallery, I had to be honest with myself and admit that I had no idea what I was doing in terms of actually running a business. But, as silly as it sounds, I knew that somewhere along the way, while playing Store, my intuition was taking notes.

Still, I agonized over how and where to begin, and realized that before I could do anything—ANYTHING—I needed a name and needed to establish the legal structure. I spent weeks thinking of names, listing the possibilities, and trying them out in imaginary conversations and promotional materials. This was an invaluable process because it made the business feel real before I even truly started.

Deciding on an LLC structure came, honestly, from knowing that I didn't want to have a business partner, stakeholders, or employees—at least not right away. I wanted to be solely responsible for my business but also wanted to do what I could to protect my personal assets.

Going into my fourth year of business, I can see that these decisions have served me well. The Necessarian, LLC is not yet as successful as my childhood Store but I can wear whatever I want and I know to save the receipts.

What a Partnership Agreement Can't Do

Although a general partnership agreement is an incredibly flexible tool for defining the ownership interests, work responsibilities, and other rights of partners, there are some things it can't do. These include:

- freeing the partners from personal liability for business debts
- restricting any partner's right to inspect the business books and records
- affecting the rights of third parties in relation to the partnership—for example, a partnership agreement that says a partner has no right to sign contracts won't affect the rights of an outsider who signs a contract with that partner, and
- eliminating or weakening the duty of trust (the fiduciary duty) each partner owes to the other partners.

Limited Liability Companies (LLCs)

Like many business owners just starting out, you might find yourself in this common quandary: On one hand, having to cope with the risk of personal liability for business misfortunes scares you; on the other, you would rather not deal with the red tape of starting and operating a corporation. Fortunately for you and many other entrepreneurs, you can avoid these problems by taking advantage of a form of business called the limited liability company, commonly known as an LLC. LLCs combine the pass-through taxation of a sole proprietorship or partnership (taxes on business income are paid on each owner's individual income tax returns) with the same protection against personal liability that corporations offer.

 CAUTION

Beware of special state rules. For example, California prohibits licensed professionals from organizing as an LLC (but not as a professional corporation or limited partnership). Some other states have extra LLC formalities for licensed professionals, which you can discover by asking your state licensing board.

Limited Personal Liability

Generally speaking, owners of an LLC (called "members") are not personally liable for the LLC's debts. (There are some exceptions to this rule, discussed below.) This protects the members from legal and financial liability in case their business fails or loses a lawsuit and can't pay its debts. In those situations, creditors can take all of the LLC's assets, but they generally can't get at the personal assets of the LLC's members. Losing your business is no picnic, but it's a lot better to lose only what you put into the business than to say good-bye to everything you own.

EXAMPLE: Callie forms her own one-person mail-order business, using most of her $25,000 in savings to establish a professional website and buy mailing lists. Callie realizes that she'll have to buy a significant portion of her sales inventory up front to be able to ship goods to her customers on time, so she plans to buy those items on credit. While she is willing to risk her $25,000 investment to pursue her dream, she is worried that if her mail-order business fails, she will be buried under a pile of debt. Callie decides to form an LLC so that if her business should fail, she'll only lose the $25,000; no one will be able to sue her personally for the business debt that she owes. She feels more secure going into business knowing that even if her business fails, she can walk away without the risk of losing her house or her car.

While some LLCs opt for a structure in which the company is run by specially designated managers, most LLCs are simply managed by the members. This more common setup is called a "member-managed" LLC; one that is run by managers (who are elected by the members) is called a "manager-managed" LLC. A manager-managed LLC might be appropriate if some of the LLC's owners are passive investors (similar to limited partners), while a smaller group intends to actively run the company. If all the LLC owners intend to actively manage the company, you'll generally use the more common member-managed structure.

With this in mind, remember that, like a general partner in a partnership, any member of a member-managed LLC can legally bind the entire LLC to a contract or business transaction. In other words, each member can act as an agent of the LLC. In manager-managed LLCs, any manager can bind the LLC to a business contract or deal.

While LLC owners enjoy limited personal liability for many of their business debts, this protection is not absolute. There are several situations in which an LLC owner may become personally liable for business debts or claims. However, this drawback is not unique to LLCs—the limited liability protection given to LLC members is just as strong as (if not stronger than) that enjoyed by the corporate shareholders of small corporations. Here are the main situations where LLC owners can still be held personally liable for debts:

- **Personal guarantees.** If you give a personal guarantee on a loan to the LLC, then you are personally liable for repaying that loan. Because personal guarantees are often required by banks and other lenders, this is a good reason to be a conservative borrower. Of course, if no personal guarantee is made, then only the LLC—not the members—is liable for the debt.

- **Taxes.** The IRS or the state tax agency may go after the personal assets of LLC owners for overdue federal and state business tax debts, particularly overdue payroll taxes. This is most likely to happen to members of small LLCs who have an active hand in managing the business, rather than to passive members.

- **Negligent or intentional acts.** An LLC owner who intentionally or even carelessly hurts someone will usually face personal liability. For example, if an LLC owner takes a client to lunch, has a few martinis, and injures the client in a car accident on the way home, the LLC owner can be held personally liable for the client's injuries.
- **Breach of fiduciary duty.** LLC owners have a legal duty to act in the best interest of their company and its members. This legal obligation is known as a "fiduciary duty," or is sometimes simply called a "duty of care." An LLC owner who violates this duty can be held personally liable for any damages that result from the owner's actions (or inactions). Fortunately for LLC owners, they normally will not be held personally responsible for any honest mistakes or acts of poor judgment they commit in doing their jobs. Most often, breach of duty is found only for serious indiscretions, such as fraud or other illegal behavior.
- **Blurring the boundaries between the LLC and its owners.** When owners fail to respect the separate legal existence of their LLC, but instead treat it as an extension of their personal affairs, a court may ignore the existence of

the LLC and rule that the owners are personally liable for business debts and liabilities. Generally, this is more likely to occur in one-member LLCs; in reality, it only happens in extreme cases. You can easily avoid it by opening a separate LLC checking account, getting a federal employer identification number, keeping separate accounting books for your LLC, and funding your LLC adequately enough to be able to meet foreseeable expenses.

> **TIP**
> **There's a new flavor of LLC on the scene: the low-profit limited liability company, or L3C.** For details, see the "Benefit Corporations, L3Cs, and Emerging Business Structures for Socially Conscious, Mission-Driven Businesses" section later in this chapter.

LLC Taxation

Like a sole proprietorship or a partnership, an LLC is not a separate tax entity from its owners; instead, it's what the IRS calls a "pass-through entity." This means the LLC itself does not pay any income taxes; instead, income passes through the business to each LLC owner, who pays taxes on the share of profit (or deducts the share of losses) on the owner's individual income tax return (for the feds, Form 1040 with Schedule E attached). But a multiowned LLC, like a partnership, does have to file Form 1065—an "informational return"—to let the government know how much the business earned or lost that year. No tax is paid with this return.

LLCs give members the flexibility to choose to have the company taxed like a corporation rather than as a pass-through entity. In fact, partnerships now have this option as well. (See Chapter 9 for more about taxes.)

You may wonder why LLC owners would choose to be taxed as a corporation. After all, pass-through taxation is one of the most popular features of an LLC. The answer is that, because of the income-splitting strategy of corporations (discussed in "Corporate Taxation," below), LLC members can sometimes come out ahead by having their business taxed as a separate entity at corporate tax rates.

For example, if the owners of an LLC become successful enough to keep some profits in the business at the end of the year (or regularly need to keep significant profits in the business for upcoming expenses), paying tax at corporate tax rates can save them money. That's because federal income tax rates for corporations start at a lower rate than the rates for individuals. For this reason, many LLCs start out being taxed as partnerships, and when they make enough profit to justify keeping some in the business (rather than doling it out as salaries and bonuses), they opt for corporate-style taxation.

LLCs Versus S Corporations

Before LLCs came along, the only way all owners of a business could get limited personal liability was to form a corporation. Problem was, many entrepreneurs didn't want the hassle and expense of incorporating, not to mention the headache of dealing with corporate taxation. One easier option was to form a special type of corporation known as an S corporation, which is like a regular corporation (a C corporation) in most respects, except that business profits pass through to the owner (as in a sole proprietorship or partnership), rather than being taxed to the corporation at corporate tax rates. In other words, S corporations offered the limited liability of a corporation with the pass-through taxation of a sole proprietorship or partnership. For a long time, this was an okay compromise for small-to-medium-sized businesses, though they still had to deal with requirements of running an S corporation (discussed in more detail below).

Now, however, LLCs offer a better option for many entrepreneurs. LLCs are indeed similar to S corporations in that they combine limited personal liability with pass-through tax status. But a significant difference between these two types of businesses is that LLCs are not bound by the many regulations that govern S corporations.

Here's a quick rundown of the major areas of difference between S corporations and LLCs. (Keep in mind that corporations, including S corporations, are explained in more detail in the next section.)

- **Ownership restrictions.** An S corporation may not have more than 75 shareholders, all of whom must be U.S. citizens or residents. This means that some of the C corporation's main benefits—namely, the ability to set up stock option and bonus plans and to bring in public capital—are pretty much out of the question for S corporations. And even if an S corporation initially meets the U.S. citizen or resident requirement, its shareholders can't sell shares to another company (like a corporation or an LLC) or a foreign citizen, on pain of losing S corporation tax status. In an LLC, any type of person or entity can become a member—a U.S. citizen, a citizen of a foreign country, another LLC, a corporation, or a limited partnership.
- **Allocation of profits and losses.** Shareholders of an S corporation must allocate profits according to the percentage of stock each owner has. For example, a 25% owner has to receive 25% of the profits (or losses), even if the owners want a different division. Owners of an LLC, on the other hand, may distribute profits (and the tax burden that goes with them) however they see fit, without

regard to each member's ownership share in the company. For instance, a member of an LLC who owns 25% of the business can receive 50% of the profits if the other members agree (subject to a few IRS rules).

- **Corporate meeting and record-keeping rules.** For S corporation shareholders to keep their limited liability protection, they have to follow the corporate rules: issuing stock, electing officers, holding regular board of directors and shareholders meetings, keeping corporate minutes of all meetings, and following the mandatory rules found in their state's corporation code. By contrast, LLC owners don't need to jump through most of these legal hoops—they just have to make sure their management team is in agreement on major decisions and go about their business.
- **Tax treatment of losses.** S corporation shareholders are at a disadvantage if their company goes into substantial debt—for instance, if it borrows money to open the business or buy real estate. That's because an S corporation's business debt cannot be passed along to its shareholders unless they have personally cosigned and guaranteed the debt. LLC owners, on the other hand, normally can reap the tax benefits of any business debt, cosigned or not. This can translate into a nice tax break for owners of LLCs that carry debt.

Forming an LLC

To form an LLC, you must file Articles of Organization with your Secretary of State or other LLC filing office. You should also execute an operating agreement, which governs the internal workings of your LLC. Also, be aware that an LLC might not be as cheap to start as a partnership or sole proprietorship. A few states charge significant filing fees, plus annual dues (alternately called minimum taxes, annual fees, or renewal fees). These fees can push the costs of starting an LLC into the several-hundred-dollar range. Massachusetts, for instance, charges a $500 fee to file a Certificate of Organization, and California requires that you pay a minimum annual LLC tax of $800 when you start your LLC —on top of its $70 filing fee.

Many brand-new business owners aren't in a position to pay this kind of money right out of the starting gate, so they start out as partnerships until they bring in enough income to cover these costs. And if you're thinking of forming a corporation instead, keep in mind that most states charge at least as much in fees for corporations. This plus the added expenses of running a corporation (legal and accounting fees, for example) will almost always make a corporation more expensive to run than an LLC.

CAUTION

Some LLCs must comply with securities laws. LLCs that have owners who do not actively participate in the business may have to register their membership interests as securities or, more likely, qualify for an exemption to the registration requirements. For information about exemptions to the federal securities laws, visit the Securities and Exchange Commission's website at www.sec.gov and search "Information For: Small Businesses."

RESOURCE

For more on LLCs. Your Secretary of State or other LLC filing office will have lots of information on LLC rules and procedures in your state. To find yours, see the list of LLC offices included in Appendix A. You can also learn more from Nolo's LLC books, including *Form Your Own Limited Liability Company*, by Anthony Mancuso (which has detailed information, step-by-step instructions, and forms for creating an LLC); *Nolo's Quick LLC: All You Need to Know About Limited Liability Companies*, also by Anthony Mancuso; and *Nolo's Guide to Single-Member LLCs*, by David Steingold. Nolo also offers an online 50-state guide to forming an LLC (with the requirements for each state) and a comprehensive LLC package to form your LLC online (see www.nolo.com for details).

Corporations

For many, the term "corporation" conjures up the image of a massive industrial empire more akin to a nation-state than a small business. In fact, a corporation doesn't have to be huge, and most aren't. Stripped to its essentials, a corporation is simply a specific legal structure that imposes certain legal and tax rules on its owners (also called shareholders). A corporation can be as large as IBM or, in many cases, as small as one person.

One fundamental legal characteristic of a corporation is that it's a separate legal entity from its owners. If you've already read this chapter's sections on sole proprietorships and partnerships, you'll recognize that this is a major difference between those unincorporated business types and corporations. Another important corporate feature is that shareholders are normally protected from personal liability for business debts. Finally, the corporation itself—not just the shareholders—is subject to income tax.

SEE AN EXPERT

Publicly traded corporations are a different ball game. This section discusses privately held corporations owned by a small group of people who are actively involved in running the business. These corporations are much easier to manage than public corporations, whose shares are sold to the public at large. Any corporation that sells its stock to the general public is heavily regulated by state and federal securities laws, while corporations that sell shares, without advertising, only to a select group of

people who meet specific state requirements are often exempt from many of these laws. If you plan to sell shares of a corporation to the general public, you should consult a lawyer.

Limited Personal Liability

Generally speaking, owners of a corporation are not personally liable for the corporation's debts. (There are some exceptions to this rule, discussed below.) Limited personal liability is a major reason why owners have traditionally chosen to incorporate their business: to protect themselves from legal and financial liability in case their business flounders or loses an expensive lawsuit and can't pay its debts. In those situations, creditors can take all of the corporation's assets (including the shareholders' investments), but they generally can't get at the personal assets of the shareholders.

EXAMPLE: Tim and Chris publish *Tropics Tripping*, a monthly travel magazine with a focus on Latin America. Because they both have significant personal assets, and because they will have to borrow a lot of capital to start up their magazine, they form their business as a corporation to protect their personal assets in case their magazine fails. They do great for a few years, but suddenly their subscription and advertising revenue starts to suffer when a recession plus political unrest in several Latin American countries reduce interest in travel to that area. Hoping the situation will turn itself around, Tim and Chris forge ahead—and go deeper into debt as it proves impossible to pay printing and other bills on time. Finally, when their printer won't do any more print runs on credit, Tim and Chris are forced to call it quits. *Tropics Tripping*'s debts total $250,000, while business assets are valued at only $90,000— leaving a $160,000 debt to creditors. Thankfully for Tim and Chris, they won't have to use their personal assets to pay the $160,000, because, as owners of a corporation, they're shielded from personal liability.

TIP
Corporations aren't the only option. With the advent of limited liability companies, corporations aren't the only business entities that provide limited liability status for all owners. (See the section on LLCs, above.)

Forming a corporation to shield yourself from personal liability for business obligations provides good, but not complete, protection for your personal assets. Here are the principal areas in which corporation owners still face personal liability:

- **Personal guarantees.** If you give a personal guarantee on a loan to the corporation, then you are personally liable for the repayment of that loan. Because lenders often require a personal guarantee, this is a good reason to be a conservative borrower. Of course, if no personal guarantee is made, then only the corporation—not the shareholders—is liable for the debt.

- **Taxes.** The IRS or the state's tax agency may go after the personal assets of corporate owners for overdue corporate federal and state tax debts, particularly overdue payroll taxes. This is most likely to happen to owners of small corporations who have an active hand in managing the business, rather than to passive shareholders.

- **Negligent or intentional acts.** A corporate owner who negligently (that is, carelessly) or perhaps even intentionally ends up hurting someone, can't hide behind the corporate barrier to escape personal liability. Shareholders are subject to personal liability for wrongs they commit—such as attacking a customer or leaving a floor wet in a store—that result in injury.

- **Breach of fiduciary duty.** Corporate owners have a legal duty to act in the best interest of the company and its shareholders. This legal obligation is known as a "fiduciary duty," sometimes simply called a "duty of care." If an owner violates this duty, the owner can be held personally liable for any damages that result from his or her actions (or inactions). Fortunately for corporate owners, run-of-the-mill mistakes or lapses in judgment aren't usually considered breaches of the duty of care. Most often, breach of duty is found only for serious indiscretions, such as fraud or other illegal behavior. For example, if a corporate officer ignored repeated warnings and written reports that one of its manufacturers was using toxic ingredients in the pet products sold by the corporation, that officer could be held personally liable for any damages that result from that breach of duty to the company.

- **Blurring the boundaries between the corporation and its owners.** When corporate owners ignore corporate formalities and treat the corporation like an unincorporated business, a court may ignore the existence of the corporation (in legal slang, "pierce the corporate veil") and rule that the owners are personally liable for business debts and liabilities. To avoid this, it's important that corporate owners not allow the legal boundary between the corporation and its owners to grow fuzzy. Owners need to scrupulously respect corporate formalities by holding shareholders and directors meetings, keeping attentive minutes, issuing stock certificates, and maintaining corporate accounts strictly separate from personal funds.

Also, bear in mind that while limited personal liability can prevent you from losing your home, car, bank account, and other assets, it won't protect you from losing your investment in your business. A business can quickly get wiped out if a customer, an employee, or a supplier wins a big lawsuit against it and the business has to be liquidated to cover the debt. In short, even if you incorporate to protect your personal assets, you should purchase appropriate insurance to protect your business assets. (Insurance is discussed in Chapter 8.) But remember, insurance won't help if you simply can't pay your normal business debts.

Corporate Taxation

The words "corporate taxes" raise a lot of fear and loathing in the business world. Fortunately, the reality of corporate taxation is usually less depressing than its reputation. Here are the basics—think of it as Corporate Tax Lite. If you decide to incorporate, you'll likely want to consult an accountant or a small business lawyer who can fill you in on the fine print. (See Chapter 17 for information on finding and hiring a lawyer.)

The first thing you need to know is that you'll be treated differently for tax purposes depending on whether you operate as a regular corporation (also called a C corporation) or you elect S corporation status for tax purposes. An S corporation is the same as a C corporation in most respects, but when it comes to taxes, C and S corporations are very different animals.

A regular, or C, corporation must pay taxes, while an S corporation is treated like a partnership for tax purposes and doesn't pay any income taxes itself. Like partnership profits, S corporation profits (and losses) pass through to the shareholders, who report them on their individual returns. (In this respect, S corporations are very similar to LLCs, which also offer limited liability, along with partnership-style tax treatment.) These two types of corporations are explained in more detail just below.

C Corporations

As a separate tax entity, a regular corporation must file and pay income taxes on its own tax return, much like an individual does. After deductions for such things as employee compensation, fringe benefits, and all other reasonable and necessary business expenses have been subtracted from its earnings, a corporation pays tax on whatever profit remains.

In small corporations in which all of the owners of the business are also employees, all of the corporation's profits are often paid out in tax-deductible salaries and fringe benefits—leaving no corporate profit and, thus, no corporate taxes due. (The owner/employees must, of course, pay income tax on their salaries on their individual returns.)

The Tax Cuts and Jobs Act (passed in December 2017) made a major, sweeping simplification to corporate tax rates, replacing eight tiers of rates (ranging from 15% to 39%) with just one: 21% for all corporations. The significantly lower rate, plus the simpler structure, may make C corporations more attractive to even very small businesses starting in 2018 and later.

Fringes and Perks

Like they can for employee salaries, corporations can deduct many fringe benefits as business expenses. If a corporation pays for benefits such as health and disability insurance for its employees and owner/employees, the cost can usually be deducted from the corporate income, reducing a possible tax bill. (There's one main exception: Benefits given to an owner/employee of an S corporation who owns 2% or more of the stock can't be deducted as business expenses.)

As a general rule, owners of sole proprietorships, partnerships, and LLCs can deduct the cost of providing these benefits for employees, but not for themselves. (These owners can, however, deduct a portion of their medical insurance premiums, though it's technically a deduction for the individuals, not a business expense.)

The fact that fringe benefits for owners are deductible for corporations may make incorporating a wise choice. But it's less likely to be a winning strategy for a capital-poor start-up that can't afford to underwrite a benefits package.

Double Taxation

One vexing issue faced by larger corporations with shareholders who aren't active employees is double taxation. Unlike salaries and bonuses, dividends paid to shareholders cannot be deducted as business expenses from corporate earnings. Because they're not deducted, any amounts paid as dividends are included in the total corporate profit and taxed. And when the shareholder receives the dividend, it is taxed at the shareholder's individual tax rate as part of personal income. As you can see, any money paid out as a dividend gets taxed twice: once at the corporate level, and once at the individual level.

You can avoid double taxation simply by not paying dividends. This is usually easy if all shareholders are employees, but probably more difficult if some shareholders are passive investors anxious for a reasonable return on their investments.

S Corporations

Unlike a regular C corporation, an S corporation does not pay taxes itself. Any profits pass through to the owners, who pay taxes on income as if the business were a sole proprietorship, a partnership, or an LLC (though the 2017 Tax Cuts and Jobs Act created a sizeable deduction for owners of pass-through entities: 20% of qualified business income; see Chapter 9 for details). Yet the business is still a corporation giving its owners protection from personal liability for business debts, just like shareholders of C corporations and members (owners) of LLCs.

Until the relatively recent arrival of the LLC (discussed above), the S corporation was the business form of choice for those who wanted limited liability protection without the two-tiered tax structure of a C corporation. Today, relatively few businesses are organized as S corporations, because S corporations are subject to many regulations that do not apply to LLCs. (See "LLCs Versus S Corporations," earlier in this chapter, for more information.)

Forming and Running a Corporation

In addition to tax complexity, major drawbacks to forming a corporation— either a C or an S type—are time and expense. Unlike with sole proprietorships and partnerships, you can't clap your hands twice and conjure up a corporation. To incorporate, you must file articles of incorporation with your Secretary of State or other corporate filing office, along with often hefty filing fees and minimum annual taxes. And if you decide to sell shares of the corporation to the public—as opposed to keeping them in the hands of a relatively small number of owners— you'll have to comply with lots of complex federal and state securities laws.

Finally, to protect your limited personal liability, you need to act like a corporation, which means adopting bylaws, issuing stock to shareholders, maintaining records of various meetings of directors and shareholders, and keeping records and transactions of the business separate from those of the owners.

CAUTION

Corporations must comply with securities laws. Corporations must either register their shares with the Securities and Exchange Commission or qualify for an exemption to securities registration requirements. For information about small business exemptions to the federal securities laws, visit the Securities and Exchange Commission's website, at www.sec.gov/info/smallbus.shtml.

To sum up, the protection afforded by incorporating comes at a price. Figure in the likelihood that you'll have to hire lawyers, accountants, and other professionals to keep your corporation in compliance, and it's easy to see how expensive running a corporation can be.

RESOURCE

Recommended reading on corporations. For more information on the many complexities of running a corporation, read *The Corporate Records Handbook: Meetings, Minutes & Resolutions*, by Anthony Mancuso (Nolo).

Benefit Corporations, L3Cs, and Emerging Business Structures for Socially Conscious, Mission-Driven Businesses

Entrepreneurs who start businesses that want to emphasize sustainability or other goals in the public interest sometimes wonder if they should start a regular for-profit business versus structuring as a nonprofit. The nonprofit structure, however, is fundamentally different from a for-profit business, and business owners may find it too constraining on important issues such as being able to take profits and needing to manage the business with a board of directors.

In recent years, businesses in many states have some new options that are somewhat like for-profit/nonprofit hybrids. Three new structures are benefit corporations, Certified B Corps, and L3Cs. Let's take a look at each one.

RESOURCE

The basics of starting a nonprofit. *Starting & Building a Nonprofit*, by Peri Pakroo (Nolo) provides step-by-step advice on getting a nonprofit up and running, from developing a mission and strategic plan to recruiting and managing board members. Also, check out the "Nonprofits" section of Nolo.com for dozens of articles on the subject.

Benefit Corporations

A benefit corporation is legally required to prioritize a positive social impact in addition to making profits for shareholders. Structuring as a benefit corporation may be appealing for businesses that want to incorporate a social mission into the core of their business.

Specifically, benefit corporations feature the following elements:

- The corporation has a *purpose* to create a material positive impact on society and the environment.
- The corporation is *accountable* through a fiduciary duty not only to corporate shareholders, but also to workers, community and the environment.
- The corporation is run *transparently*, and must publish public annual reports on overall social and environmental performance against an independent and transparent third-party standard.

As of late 2019, legislation has been passed allowing benefit corporations in 36 states and the District of Columbia, with legislation pending in several others. For updates to state adoptions and other details, visit B Lab at www.benefitcorp.net.

Certified B Corps

Benefit corporations are virtually identical to another structure called a Certified B Corp, which is a business that has been assessed and certified to meet sustainability-related criteria by B Lab, a nonprofit. The difference between benefit corporations and Certified B Corps is just that benefit corporations are an actual corporate structure recognized by the state, while the Certified B Corp is a certification conferred by a nonprofit.

If you live in a state that does not recognize benefit corporations, you can still seek to be certified as a Certified B Corp. For more information, check out B Lab's website at www.bcorporation.net.

Low-Profit Limited Liability Companies (L3Cs)

Another hybrid-type business structure available in some states is the low-profit limited liability company, or L3C. An L3C is similar to a nonprofit in that its primary purpose must be to benefit the public. But an L3C is run like a regular profit-making business and is allowed to make a profit as a secondary goal. This type of business structure was born so that charitably oriented LLCs could receive seed money (specifically, "program-related investments," or PRIs) from large nonprofit foundations, taking advantage of IRS rules that allow foundations to invest in businesses principally formed to advance charitable purposes.

Only a small number of states allow L3Cs, including Illinois, Kansas, Louisiana, Maine, Michigan, Missouri, North Dakota, Rhode Island, Utah, Vermont, and Wyoming. It has also been adopted by the tribal governments of the Oglala Sioux Tribe, the Crow Indian Nation of Montana, and the territory of Puerto Rico. As of late 2019, there does not appear to be much momentum behind this structure, so it's unclear what the future holds. In 2016, the IRS issued regulations for examples of investments that qualify as PRIs, and it notably declined to include L3Cs in the examples. This is likely to make foundations even more skittish to invest in L3Cs and puts the future of this structure in doubt. Stay tuned for future developments.

RESOURCE

For more information on L3Cs, check out Americans for Community Development (www.americansforcommunitydevelopment.org), which specifically focuses on L3C developments.

Choosing the Best Structure for Your Business

Although there are many differences among the various types of business organizations, most business owners choose an operating structure based on one legal issue: the personal liability of owners for business debts. It's true that the issue of personal liability can have a huge impact on successful small businesses a few years down the road. But business owners who are just starting out on a shoestring often care most about spending as little money as possible on the legal structure of their business. This is certainly an understandable approach: Far more new businesses die painful deaths because they don't control costs than because they lose costly lawsuits. In short, for many new small businesses, incorporating or organizing as an LLC is as unnecessary an expense as a swank downtown office or a gleaming chrome espresso machine in the lunchroom.

That said, owners of any business that will engage in a high-risk activity, rack up large business debts, or have a significant number of investors should always insist on limited personal liability, either with an LLC or a corporation. This is even more true if the business can't find or afford appropriate insurance.

If you decide that limiting your personal liability is worth the extra cost, you still need to decide whether to form a corporation or an LLC. With the LLC's arrival, many business owners who want

---

Analyzing Your Risks

Starting a business is always risky. In some businesses, however, the risks are particularly extreme. If you're planning to launch an investment firm or start a commercial building construction company, there is little doubt that you'll need all the protection you can get, including limited personal liability as well as adequate insurance. Other businesses are not so obviously risk laden, but still could land you in trouble if fate strikes you a blow. When analyzing your business, note that red flags for riskiness include:

- using hazardous materials, such as dry cleaning solvents or photographic chemicals, or hazardous processes, such as welding or operating heavy machinery
- manufacturing or selling edible goods
- driving as part of the job
- building or repairing structures or vehicles
- caring for children or animals

- providing or allowing access to alcohol
- allowing activities that may result in injury, such as weightlifting or skateboarding, and
- repairing or working on items of value, such as cars or antiques.

If you've identified one or more serious risks your business is likely to face, figure out whether business insurance might give you enough protection. Some risky activities, such as job-related driving, are good candidates for insurance and don't necessarily warrant incorporating. But if insurance can't cover all of the risks involved in your business, it may be time to form an LLC or a corporation.

Keep in mind that insurance will never insulate you from regular business debts. If you foresee your business going into serious debt, an LLC or corporation may be the best business structure for you.

---

limited liability protection realize that incorporation normally only makes sense if a business needs to take advantage of the corporate stock structure to attract key employees and investment capital. No question, corporations may have an easier time attracting capital investment by issuing stock privately or publicly. And some businesses may find it easier to attract and retain key employees by issuing

employee stock options. But for businesses that don't intend to raise capital by issuing stock, choosing to operate as LLCs rather than corporations normally makes the most sense if limited liability is the main concern. If the corporate stock structure isn't something you want or need for your business, the simplicity and flexibility of LLCs offer a clear advantage over corporations.

SEE AN EXPERT

Location matters. Another important consideration in choosing your business structure may be related to the state you choose to locate it in, especially if you are going into business with people who do not live in your state. This is because states differ widely in how they tax different business entities and nonresident business owners. There can be big state tax complications when a business either operates in more than one state or has owners in more than one state. A tax attorney can tell you whether you can reduce your taxes and increase profits by choosing one state over the other as your headquarters. More information on location-related issues is included in Chapter 3.

Chapter 1 Checklist: Choosing a Legal Structure

☐ Identify the number of owners of your business.

☐ Analyze your business's risks and decide how much protection from personal liability you'll need.

☐ Determine how you'd like the business to be taxed (as a pass-through entity or as a corporation).

☐ Decide if your business would benefit from the stock structure of a corporation (by being able to distribute stock options and sell stock).

☐ Choose a business structure.

☐ If you will structure your business as a partnership, draft and sign a partnership agreement.

Picking a Winning Business Name

There's a lot of room for personal and professional creativity when picking a business name, but there are also legal requirements and pitfalls that you absolutely need to understand. In particular, it's important for all business owners to understand the basics of trademark law, which establishes and protects the legal right to use a particular name for businesses, products, or services.

If you choose a business or product name that's too similar to a competitor's name, you could find yourself accused of violating the competitor's trademark (called "infringement" or "unfair competition"), and you could be forced to change your business name and possibly pay money damages. Having to change a business name can be a serious blow to a business that has worked hard to build name recognition among its customers—not to mention the cost of changing signs, stationery, preprinted invoices, and the like.

But suppose you plan to open a local business so small that you don't even expect to compete with businesses in the next county, much less in another state or country. You probably wonder if the arcane world of trademark law really affects you. Until the 1990s, the answer would likely have been no—you didn't really have to worry too much about national or global name conflicts back then. As long as a quick search of your phone book didn't reveal any obvious local conflicts and you

didn't call your business "Ford," "IBM," or some other famous name, you were probably fine. But in today's world of the Internet, mail order, and rapidly growing national chains, "local" obviously isn't what it used to be. Even if you're opening just a tiny bookstore in a small town, if you inadvertently choose the same name as an Internet store that sells books, you may very well be accused of infringing the online store's trademark—even if the online store's headquarters are on a different continent.

One good way to figure out how concerned you need to be about trademark law is to consider the consequences of having to change your business name. If a name change would be cheap and easy and wouldn't seriously confuse your customers, then don't lie awake nights worrying about picking a name that's absolutely bulletproof. However, if changing your name would be messy or expensive (changing signs, ads, your domain name, and business directory listings, to mention a few possibilities), take the time and trouble to be sure the name you plan to use doesn't already belong to someone else.

Are you convinced that paying attention to the law of business names is important? Good. Now you'll learn how to choose a name that won't land you in legal hot water and how to secure the maximum legal protection for it. This chapter will also cover some nonlegal aspects of naming your business, including tips and advice on how to choose the most effective name for your particular business.

CAUTION

Watch out for other legal issues. Besides watching out for trademark conflicts, business owners also need to comply with other legal rules. Many businesses must comply with their county's fictitious business name requirements. (See "Step 3: Register Your Fictitious Business Name (FBN)," in Chapter 7.) Typically, this means you'll need to register a fictitious business name statement (or similar document) with your county clerk and possibly publish it in a local newspaper. And for corporations, LLCs, and limited partnerships, the state filing office (usually the Secretary or Department of State) must approve your business name before it will accept articles of incorporation, articles of organization, or a statement of limited partnership.

An Overview of Trademark Law

In a nutshell, trademark law—which is really a catchall term referring to a large body of statutes, regulations, and court decisions—prevents a business from using a name or logo that is likely to be confused with one that a competing business already uses. This general rule applies both to the name of a business and to the names of any of its products or services.

> ### Trademark Protects More Than Names
>
> This chapter focuses on how trademark applies to business names. But the rules discussed here apply to a lot more—logos, designs, slogans, and packaging features can also be protected by trademark. For example, Nike's slogan, "Just Do It," and American Express's mantra, "Don't leave home without it," are protected by the law of trademark.

Allowing businesses to have exclusive use of certain names helps consumers to identify and recognize goods in the marketplace. When you buy Racafrax brand of wood glue, for instance, you'll know that it will be similar in quality to the Racafrax glue you bought last time. By contrast, if any company were allowed to call its glue "Racafrax Glue," customers would never know what they were getting. And because customers would never know when they were using the Racafrax company's glue, the Racafrax company wouldn't be able to build customer trust or goodwill, even if its glue was the best available. In this way, consumers and businesses alike benefit from trademark protection.

This section will give you a rundown of what's protected by trademark law and how to determine and protect your rights to the names you use. This will help you

Business Names: Getting the Terms Straight

One reason the law of business names often seems confusing is that it is riddled with lots of arcane and often overlapping legal jargon. For example, local, state, and federal agencies often use different terms to describe the same or very similar legal concepts. Here's a brief rundown of the terms you need to know, all of which are discussed in greater detail in the rest of this chapter:

- The term **legal name** means the official name of the entity that owns a business. The legal name of a sole proprietorship is simply the full name of the owner—for example, Jodie Potter. If a general partnership has a written partnership agreement that gives a name to the partnership, then that name is the legal name. Otherwise, the legal name of the general partnership is simply the last names of the owners. (Many sole proprietorships and partnerships present their businesses to the public under names that are different from their legal names—see fictitious business names, below.) And for corporations, LLCs, and limited partnerships, legal names are the names registered with the state filing office (usually the Secretary of State).

- A **trade name** is simply the name that a business uses with the public, which may or may not be the same as the name of the business owner or the business's legal name. Trader Joe's, Amoeba Music, and Nolo are examples of trade names. You see trade names on business signs, in the telephone book, and on invoices. In many transactions,

such as opening a bank account or applying for a loan, you'll need to provide the owners' names, the legal name of the business (if different), and the trade name of the business (if different).

- The term **fictitious business name** is used when the trade name of a business is different from its legal name. For instance, if John O'Toole named his sole proprietorship Turtle's Classic Cars, the name "Turtle's Classic Cars" would be a fictitious business name because it does not contain the owner's last name, "O'Toole." A fictitious business name is sometimes called a **DBA** name. DBA stands for "doing business as," as in "John O'Toole, doing business as Turtle's Classic Cars." Corporations and LLCs may also have to file fictitious name statements if the names they hold out to the public differ from the legal names they registered with the state. For example, if the owners of Corson Mechanics Incorporated decide to operate a repair shop under the fictitious name "Grease Monkeys," they'll have to file a fictitious business name statement.

- The legal name of a business that must register with the state to be legally created is called a **corporate name**, an **LLC name**, or a **limited partnership name**. If a corporation, an LLC, or a limited partnership operates under the same name that's registered with the Secretary of State (or similar state office), then its corporate, LLC, or limited partnership name will be both its legal name and its trade name.

Business Names: Getting the Terms Straight (continued)

- A **trademark** (sometimes simply called a mark) is any word, phrase, design, or symbol used to market a product or service. Technically, a mark that's used to market a service, rather than a product, is called a service mark, though the term "trademark" is commonly used for both types of marks. Owners of trademarks have legal rights under both federal and state law, which give them the power in some cases to prevent others from using their trademarks to market goods or services.

- **Business name** tends to be a catchall term that can refer to any of the names used by a business—the name of a business itself, a corporate name, a fictitious business name, or the name of a business's product or service.

understand what steps you should take as part of forming your business to avoid infringing others' rights (and opening yourself up to lawsuits). And it will also give you the legal basics you'll need to protect your business name and to figure out whether your rights are being infringed by others down the road.

 CAUTION

Pick a name that won't bring legal trouble. The main reason to learn the basics of trademark law is not so you can successfully defend your name in court against another business that tries to use it. Even if you were to win a complex and expensive court fight, you'd be a huge loser when it comes to time, worry, and legal fees. Far better to avoid disputes in the first place by choosing a safe name that has a very low likelihood of leading to customer confusion and, therefore, an infringement lawsuit.

What Is a Trademark?

The definition of "trademark" is simple: Any word, phrase, logo, or other device used to identify products or services in the marketplace is a trademark. This includes the names of products or services themselves and often the name of the business that's selling them. Using a name in public commerce to identify goods or services for sale is enough to make it a trademark; there is no registration requirement. However, registration with the U.S. Patent and Trademark Office will greatly strengthen your power to enforce your rights to the trademark. For example, if you federally register your trademark, you can stop any subsequent user in your field from using the same or a confusingly similar mark anywhere in the United States. (See "Trademark Registration," later in this chapter.)

Business Names and Trademarks Often Overlap

Many trade names double as trademarks and service marks for products and services of the business. For instance, when McDonald's (trade name) advertises McDonald's french fries, the trade name "McDonald's" also becomes a trademark because it is used to identify the maker (or brand) of french fries. And when the company puts up a sign in front of its restaurant, the term "McDonald's" becomes a service mark, identifying who's providing the fast food service of that restaurant. In other words, any time you use your trade name to identify a product, service, or business location, you're using the trade name as a mark—either a trademark or a service mark. As you can see, a name can wear a bunch of different hats: It can be a trade name, a legal name, and a trademark (or service mark) all in one.

Legal Name	Trade Name	Trademarks/Service Marks
McDonald's Corporation	McDonald's	McDonald's french fries Big Mac Mayor McCheese Golden arches symbol
Microsoft Corporation	Microsoft	Microsoft *Word* Bing search engine "Where do you want to go today?" slogan
Trader Joe's Company	Trader Joe's	Trader Joe's Baked Tortilla Chips Trader Giotto's Italian Roast coffee beans Trader Darwin's vitamins
Ronco, Inc.	Ronco	Popeil Pocket Fisherman Dial-O-Matic Food Slicer
Kraft Foods, Inc.	Kraft	JELL-O Gelatin Cheez Whiz Tang Drink Mix "It's the cheesiest" slogan for Kraft Macaroni & Cheese "Good to the last drop" slogan for Kraft Maxwell House Coffee

Keep in mind, however, that a key part of the definition of a trademark is that it must be used in public to identify goods or services for sale. So if you don't use the name of your business or product or service in public in conjunction with something you're trying to sell, it isn't considered a trademark. For example, if a software company called ZZP Web Masters markets bookmarking software for the Internet called "WebWorm," then the name WebWorm is a trademark. If the only marketing done for WebWorm is an ad that reads, "Manage your bookmarks with WebWorm," then the business name ZZP Web Masters will not be a trademark, because it's not used in public to sell WebWorm. But an ad that reads, "WebWorm: The best bookmarking software on Earth, by ZZP Web Masters," includes two trademarks: the product name WebWorm and the trade name ZZP Web Masters.

By the same token, a name that appears only in nonpublic documents—such as an internal memo or a product sample that isn't available to the public—isn't a trademark.

For practical purposes, many if not most business names are also considered trademarks, since most businesses do use their names to promote or sell their product or service.

Trademarks Versus Service Marks

You've probably heard the term "trademark," which applies to names, logos, and slogans that identify products (such as Chia Pet), a whole lot more than the term "service mark," which is used when a name identifies a service (such as H&R Block Tax Preparation Services). Because the legal rules for trademarks and service marks are virtually identical, the term "trademark," or sometimes just "mark," is commonly used for both types of marks. But since the two terms do refer to technically different things, you should be aware of the distinction, especially if your business will primarily provide services.

Trademark Rights

The power of a trademark comes from the fact that you may be entitled to exclude others from using the same mark. If you were the first to use the trademark, then you own certain rights to it and can take legal action against others who use it illegally. In legal terms, if others "infringe your trademark" by using it in a way that's likely to confuse your customers or that has "diluted" your trademark, you can take them to court and force them to stop using it, and maybe even to pay damages.

For example, if ZZP Web Masters had been selling an app called WebWorm for two years and then another company started selling a similar software product called WebWorm, ZZP Web Masters could sue the other company and force it to stop using the product name "WebWorm." If ZZP Web Masters could prove that its business suffered because of the infringement, it might also be entitled to some financial compensation (damages) from the other company.

So far, so good—you're probably even wondering why everyone says trademark issues are such a bear to deal with. Here's why: Just because you own a trademark doesn't mean you can always prevent someone else from using it (and, likewise, another owner of a trademark can't always prevent you from using that mark). Unlike a copyright, which generally gives the same level of protection to all owners, a trademark gives widely varying degrees of protection to the owner, depending on a variety of circumstances. So, as explained below, the key legal point isn't so much whether you own a trademark but whether it qualifies for trademark protection—and, if so, how much.

Strong Versus Weak Marks

The general rule is that distinctive business names, such as Google and Mountain Dew, receive the strongest legal trademark protection. What makes a mark "distinctive" is explained in more detail below, but, for the moment, it's important

that you understand why distinctive names get more protection. The theory is that distinctive names, such as Pepsi or Xerox, make strong connections in the minds of consumers, and play a big role in consumers' buying choices. The opposite is considered to be true for names that aren't very distinctive, such as Quality Vitamins or Brite Paint.

Because distinctive names are thought to play such a big role in helping consumers choose among brands, it follows that the more distinctive a name is, the more likely it is that customers will be confused (in legal theory at least) by more than one business using the name. To avoid this confusion, the law gives more protection to distinctive names, and less or none to names that are merely ordinary and descriptive.

A truly distinctive trademark (also called a "strong trademark") is one that clearly distinguishes the product or service it represents from others. Memorable, unusual names tend to be considered distinctive marks. While there's no magic formula for what makes a trademark distinctive, strong marks are often surprising or fanciful names that have nothing to do with the business, product, or service. In addition to the examples mentioned above, still more examples include Velcro and Comet, the cleanser.

On the flip side, a weak trademark consists of ordinary, descriptive words that merely describe aspects of the product or business, such as durability ("Sturdy Knapsacks"), location ("The Edge of Town Tavern"), or other qualities ("Speedy Dry Cleaners" or "Tasty Vegetables"). Also, trademarks that include personal names are usually considered to be ordinary marks and, therefore, weak. (But, as explained below, weak trademarks can become stronger with use.)

An additional reason why ordinary, descriptive trademarks aren't strongly protected, at least at first, is to make sure that competitors aren't unfairly prevented from using common words to describe their own products. For example, a food delivery service company called "Galloping Gourmet" wouldn't be able to monopolize the word "gourmet" and stop a deli from using the name "Tom's Gourmet Sandwiches."

How Trademarks Can Grow Stronger

A weak trademark can eventually offer good protection if it becomes distinctive and therefore stronger through use. Called "acquiring a secondary meaning" in legalese, this is particularly likely to occur when a product or service with a weak mark becomes a lasting success, making it likely that the public will associate the mark with the product or service being sold. For example, as the designer clothing brand Tommy Hilfiger has become popular nationwide, its previously weak

trademark grows stronger as customers come to associate the ordinary name with a particular company. Other examples of the weak-to-strong phenomenon include Burger King, Tom's Natural Toothpaste, and Ben & Jerry's Ice Cream.

Unfair Competition Laws

What if your weak trademark never becomes strong? Just because you have a weak trademark doesn't mean that others are free to use your business name. Because of a legal doctrine called "unfair competition," you may be able to prevent others from using your descriptive name, so long as you used it first. Although unfair competition law is a separate body of law from trademark law, it can have the same effect. It comes from the same basic idea that it's not fair for another business to rip off your business's good reputation.

For example, if you've been selling dry cleaning services in Bakersfield under the name Jean's Quick Cleaners, and someone else in the same city opens Jeanne's Quick Cleaners, you could claim unfair competition and likely convince a court to prevent the newcomer from using that name. As you can see, unfair competition law can have the same result as trademark law: It can prevent another business from using a name identical or confusingly similar to yours, if you used the name first. Keep in mind, however, that your right to stop trademark infringement is stronger than your right to stop unfair competition, so it will be easier to prevent someone from using your business name if it's a strong trademark.

When Do Trademarks Conflict?

As you surely know, plenty of businesses share the same name, or at least part of the same name, without violating each other's trademark rights. Examples include United Airlines and United Van Lines, Ford Motor Company and Ford Modeling Agency, and Scott Paper Products and Scott Sunglasses. This is perfectly legal, because trademark infringement occurs only when the use of a mark by two different businesses is likely to cause customer confusion. (An exception to this rule is explained in "The Dilution Exception," below.) If customers aren't likely to be confused, then both businesses may legally use the same mark. But if customer confusion is likely, then the rightful owner of the mark can prohibit the other businesses from using it, and can sue for damages (financial compensation) for any unauthorized use.

Dual uses of the same or similar mark can cause customer confusion if it's unclear which company actually makes a product or provides a service, or if customers will be misled as to the source of the product. Customer confusion can happen in a number of different ways. Sometimes dual uses of a mark lead customers to believe that a certain company made a product when it actually did not. Or a customer may see trademarks being used in two different places and think that the companies are jointly owned or somehow affiliated, which may not be true.

Determining whether two marks legally conflict (in other words, whether customer confusion is likely) is one of the trickiest bits of trademark law. In making this determination, courts deem the following factors to be particularly important:

- how strong (distinctive or well-known) the original trademark is
- how much the products or services really compete against one another, and
- how similar the trademarks are in appearance, sound, or meaning.

We'll look at each of these in more depth in the next few sections. As you read on, keep in mind that trademark conflict is a legal question—which means that legal rules, as opposed to common sense, will dictate the outcome.

How "Strong" Is the Mark?

As discussed above, distinctive ("strong") marks receive the most protection, because, in legal theory, they are more likely to stick in consumers' minds and play a role in their buying choices.

Because strong trademarks tend to stick in customers' minds, so the theory goes, customer confusion is likely if more than one company uses a strong trademark. To protect consumers from such confusion, courts will typically prohibit more than one company from using a strong trademark. Besides protecting consumers, prohibiting multiple uses of a strong trademark prevents businesses from stealing customers or getting a free ride off another business's good reputation by using an established business's trademark.

For example, the very strong and well-known trademark Microsoft is firmly implanted in millions of people's minds. If a company called itself Microsoft Consulting, plenty of people would be confused about whether Bill Gates had anything to do with that consulting company. If Bill Gates sued Microsoft Consulting for trademark infringement, he would have a very good chance of winning.

Trademark law doesn't give much, if any, protection to weak trademarks, because they don't trigger a strong association in customers' minds between the mark and a particular product or service (or so the legal thinking goes). For that reason, courts are less inclined to find that customer confusion is likely when more than one business uses a weak trademark. Note that this is true even if customer confusion does in fact exist.

For example, if Smith Jewelry and Smith Hardware exist in the same town, customers may wonder if they're owned by the same family. Nevertheless, trademark law won't protect the name of either business, since the name Smith is so common. (However, unfair competition law may protect the hardware store Smiths if the jewelry store Smiths started getting into the hardware business, making the businesses direct competitors.)

Do the Products or Services Actually Compete?

If the products or services that share the same trademarks are in completely unrelated fields or industries, or if they're sold in different geographical regions (and not on the Internet), there's obviously far less chance that customers will be confused. In other words, the less products or services actually compete, the less likely it is that there will be a trademark violation.

For example, a pizza joint named Rocket Pizza probably won't be confused with a record store named Rocket Records, even if they exist in the same city. And an auto shop named Armadillo Repairs in Portland, Maine, most likely won't run into any trademark conflicts with Armadillo Auto Repairs in San Diego. Because they are so far apart and serve purely local customers, chances are slim that customers would confuse the two companies.

EXAMPLE: You open a coffee shop in Austin, Texas, and name it Pam's Coffee Stop. A year later, you're driving through Albuquerque, New Mexico, and notice a small café also named Pam's Coffee Stop. After thinking about it, you decide that there's little chance of a trademark violation by either business. The trademark is ordinary and descriptive and therefore weak, plus the shops are so far away from each other that they're not competitors. But this gets you wondering what you'd do if a big national chain started using the name and moved into your area. The answer is, you would retain the right to use the name because you were the first to use it in your area (as long as the national chain hadn't registered the name with the U.S. Patent and Trademark Office before you first used it). But the chain could prevent you from expanding into other areas of the country if this ever became your goal.

> ⚠ CAUTION
>
> **New marketing techniques, new competitors.** As mentioned at the beginning of this chapter, with the prevalence of online marketing, mail-order catalog businesses, and ever more frequent travel, the old rule that small, local businesses don't have to worry about trademarks from other geographical regions has largely gone out the window. Today, even small, local businesses commonly establish websites; hundreds of thousands of businesses send out catalogs; and some local restaurants and hotels seek to reach a national (or even worldwide) pool of tourists. The upshot is that many formerly local businesses that just a few years ago never

would have been confused with each other are now competitors, which of course increases the likelihood of customer confusion and trademark infringement if their names are the same. (Be sure to read "Trademark Issues Online," below, to learn about trademark considerations in today's ever-shrinking world.)

Of course, there are plenty of gray areas in which two businesses aren't in head-to-head competition but use the same marks for products that are similar enough to make a customer stop and think, for example, "Is a Parker calendar made by the same company as Parker pens?" Even though a company with the same name may not be stealing business from a competitor, it may be unintentionally taking advantage of that company's goodwill and getting a free ride from its advertising.

Whether infringement exists in these gray areas often depends on how strong the original trademark is (as discussed above). If the original trademark is weak, there's probably not much goodwill or reputation to rip off (few customers would be confused by the similar name), so a court wouldn't be likely to find there was infringement. But if the original trademark is strong, there's a greater likelihood that the newer trademark will benefit from the older one's reputation, making it likely for the court to agree that there's been an infringement.

EXAMPLE: Your pet products company begins selling a chew toy that looks like a weasel, which you name the Garden Weasel. Soon after your toy hits the market, the makers of the nationally marketed Garden Weasel five-way garden tool contact you, claiming that you are infringing their trademark. Because you feel that the products are unrelated enough to minimize the chance of customer confusion (the products don't compete with one another), your first thought is to stick with the Garden Weasel name.

Think again. The Garden Weasel trademark is distinctive (memorable and unusual) and, therefore, strong. If you are sued—and you may well be—defending the lawsuit is likely to cost you tens or possibly even hundreds of thousands of dollars that you almost surely can't afford. And if the Garden Weasel mark is strong enough, you may lose the suit, even though the products don't compete. A better approach would probably be to tweak your name a bit, to something like the Chewy Weasel or the Garden Ferret, for instance.

Christopher Johnson, publisher of the *Weekly Alibi* **(formerly** *NuCity***), a free weekly newspaper in Albuquerque, New Mexico (www.alibi.com):**

When you are starting a small business, there are so many things to think about— important things like financing, initial marketing, etc. For many people (myself included), the last thing to cross your mind is whether the use of your business name is legal. About three years after I started my weekly newspaper, NuCity, right when the company was finally stable, a weekly newspaper with a similar name (New City) in a different state took note of us and threatened litigation for trademark infringement. So, just at the time that my newspaper was really taking off, I had to decide between fighting a weak lawsuit or changing the name of the paper altogether.

Of course, we came up with a much better name, and though it was an expensive process to change all our printed and marketing materials, in the end it was well worth it. Rest assured that the first thing that we did prior to making a final decision on our new name was to verify that no one else had a trademark on that name. I now own the national and international trademark rights to Weekly Alibi *and can't wait to act like a moron and threaten other newspapers with lawsuits.*

In the future, I will check to see if a name is available before I start any business. If you are starting a business where your name has significant marketing value, it is well worth your time to check to see if your chosen name is available to use and then to complete the process to secure your trademark rights to it.

Sight, Sound, and Meaning Test

Obviously, dual use of identical trademarks can cause customer confusion, as discussed above. But what about merely similar trademarks? If two marks look alike, sound alike, or have the same meaning, a court could decide that they conflict with each other, just as if they were identical. Small or superficial differences between two trademarks may not be enough to prevent customer confusion. The difference in spelling, for example, does not make the name "Ekzon" sufficiently different from "Exxon" to avoid trademark problems. And even though they're expressed in two different languages, the names "La Petite Fleur" and "The Little Flower" have the same meaning, which increases the likelihood that some customers could confuse the two.

EXAMPLE: You open an auto lubrication business and name it Jiffy Oil. A few weeks later, you receive a stern letter from the attorneys of Jiffy Lube, a national chain of auto lubrication businesses. The letter informs you that the name "Jiffy Oil" infringes on their rights to the trademark "Jiffy Lube," because customer confusion is likely because the names are very similar, are used to describe an almost identical service, and mean pretty much the same thing. They demand that you change your business's name or be taken to court. You'd be wise to comply with their demand. Their "Jiffy Lube" trademark, though a descriptive term (for fast lubrication), has become a very strong mark over time—customers have come to recognize it as a specific brand of service. And because your shop is a direct competitor of Jiffy Lube, the chance of customer confusion is high.

The Dilution Exception

As mentioned several times, there is a big exception to the rule that one trademark infringes another only where there is the likelihood of customer confusion: Even when customer confusion is improbable, courts will stop a business from using a trademark that's the same as or similar to someone else's if the use serves to diminish—or "dilute"—its distinctiveness. This legal protection kicks in only when a mark is so well known that even if you were to use it in a different context from the original trademark, lots of people would think of the original trademark. For example, a court might stop an athletic shoe manufacturer from using the trademark Exxon or a gas station from calling itself Nike. Even though customers would not be likely to confuse an oil company with a shoe maker, this sort of copying is a legal no-no, since allowing others to use the very famous trademark can chip away at its distinctiveness and slowly reduce its legal strength.

Trademark Issues Online

As in many other legal areas, the traditional principles of trademark law are scrambling to keep up with the fast clip of technological change. The Internet has changed many of the rules regarding trademark issues, just as it has created some entirely new ones. This section outlines a number of Internet-related concerns regarding trademarks and business names.

The Internet Has Changed the Rules

As described in the previous section, one of the touchstones of trademark infringement is whether or not the two trademarks in question are likely to cause customer confusion. In the pre-Internet world, small, local businesses didn't have to worry too much about name conflicts as long as no one in their area had a similar name. But geographic distance is irrelevant online.

Particularly if you plan to put your business online, you'll have to consider not only the trademarks of businesses already on the Internet, but also those of businesses located anywhere the Internet reaches—which, of course, is just about everywhere. If you create a webpage for a small home-based business, your business is no longer local in character. You're essentially launching a national or worldwide business that can compete with businesses everywhere, whether or not those businesses are online.

For example, if you create a website for your antique restoration business, Dalliance Designs, you could be competing with every antique restoration business in the country. If one of these owns the trademark "Dalliance Designs," your effort to share the market with that business opens a potentially ugly can of legal worms.

The Internet has changed trademark rules for everybody—even businesses that don't go digital. Every time a small, local business launches a website introducing itself in a keystroke to consumers all over the globe, the chances go up that the business might find itself in competition with other businesses several time zones— or even continents—away. Although courts are still chewing over many trademark issues raised by online commerce, it is already clear that, in some circumstances at least, an Internet business with the same name as yours poses just as great a threat of a trademark lawsuit as does a bricks-and-steel business across the street.

EXAMPLE: Jarrod is a mechanic who opens a small machine shop in a rural area of California. He's lived in the area for 30 years, and knows every business for miles around. Nevertheless, as part of choosing a name for his business, Jarrod carefully checks the phone book and the county register for fictitious business names. He ultimately settles on his first choice, Checkers Tool and Die.

All goes smoothly for a few months, until a customer compliments Jarrod on his slick-looking website. This leaves Jarrod totally confused, since he doesn't have a website for his business. But in talking with his customer about this mysterious website, Jarrod realizes that a machine shop in Florida is also using the name "Checkers Tool and Die," and it sells a number of specialized parts via an online catalog. This doesn't particularly worry Jarrod until his customer (a lawyer, naturally) goes on to explain that if the distant business can prove it owns the trademark to "Checkers Tool and Die" and convince a court that it shares the same market as Jarrod, it might be able to force Jarrod to stop using the name.

Although at least one customer has been confused, Jarrod doesn't really expect the Florida outfit to go after him—after all, his business is small and local, provides primarily repair services (with parts as a sideline), and doesn't sell on the Web. Nevertheless, even the possibility of legal trouble worries him—especially because he'd like to open a retail machine parts shop next to his repair shop. After learning that the Florida outfit has been using the name Checkers Tool and Die for years and seems to be putting lots of energy into expanding its website, Jarrod decides to be safe and spend the time and money necessary to change the name of his business to White Mountain Tool & Die before he expands.

Domain Name Conflicts and Cybersquatting

Besides making sure that your business name won't create trademark trouble, if you plan to create a website for your business, you'll also need to choose a domain name that's legally safe. A domain name (such as Nolo.com) functions as its Internet "address" online. Later sections of this chapter discuss the process of choosing and registering a domain name; for now, the focus is on the trademark issues that can arise regarding domain names.

The first thing you should understand is that, generally speaking, your domain name will function as a trademark if you conduct business at your site—that is, if you offer products or services for sale. This is true whether or not you register it with the U.S. Patent and Trademark Office (PTO). As discussed in "Trademark Registration," below, registering your domain name with the PTO will strengthen your power to enforce your trademark rights to it, but using it for a commercial purpose is all that's technically necessary to establish your trademark rights. For instance, amazon.com is the domain name for the online mega-retailer—and the name amazon.com also serves as a trademark. This means that trademark law prohibits anyone else from using the name "amazon.com" for their business.

Keep in mind, however, that if your domain name is generic, such as software.com or books.com, it won't qualify for much trademark protection. This rule applies to generic business or product names such as a lawyer, building supplies, or pet food—the law will generally not allow you to establish any trademark rights to these generic terms. But as discussed earlier (in talking about weak trademarks), even generic domain names can grow stronger with use. Consider etrade.com, which has become almost synonymous with online stock trading. Originally, the name wouldn't have deserved much trademark protection since it wasn't distinctive at all—anyone can slap an "e" on the beginning of a word. Now, however, the mark has acquired "secondary meaning" and is entitled to trademark protection.

For most business owners, the best way to make sure their customers will find them online is simply to tack ".com" onto their regular business names. However, while trademark law will allow two or more companies to use the same name as long as it won't confuse customers, the technical limitations of the Web won't allow for two identical domain names. In other words, Ford Trucks and the Ford Modeling Agency won't both be able to use "ford.com" as a domain name. Because each website must have its own unique address, you may be out of luck if someone is already using your business name plus ".com" as a domain name. As you can imagine, this is where things can get sticky.

Dealing With Domain Name Conflicts

If you're starting a brand-new business that you haven't named yet, choose a name that also can be used as a domain name. That way, you can register it as a domain name right away and sidestep the whole issue of what to do if your domain name is already taken. You'll need to decide for yourself how important it is to you to have a domain name that's the same as your business name. If it's really important, then you may have to work hard to come up with a business name that's good for business, available as a domain name, and available as a trademark. If it's not that important, then your naming process will be somewhat easier—but you may regret it down the road when your business name can't be registered as a domain name.

A few possible scenarios may arise when someone is using your business name as a domain name. One is that you may simply have missed your chance to get that domain name yourself—even though you have trademark rights to it—and will either have to choose a different name or buy it from whoever registered it first. These are likely to be your only options if your mark isn't nationally famous and if customers aren't likely to be confused by another business using your name.

EXAMPLE: Gene and Beth run a combination bookstore-café in New Orleans called BooksPlus. After about a year of planning, they decide to launch a website—but are disappointed to find out that the domain name "booksplus.com" is already taken. By doing a search on the Web, and by going to the booksplus.com website, Gene and Beth discover that the owner of booksplus.com is a freelance editor in Chicago. Since Gene and Beth's bookstore doesn't have any national exposure, they probably won't be able to force the editor in Chicago to give up the name, because the editor's site probably would not confuse customers into thinking there was some association with their bookstore.

On the other hand, you may be able to assert your trademark rights against someone using your trademark as a domain name if either applies:

- His or her use of the trademark is likely to cause customer confusion.
- Your trademark is distinctive and nationally known—even if the other party's use of it is not likely to cause customer confusion. (As discussed above, laws against trademark dilution protect famous marks from use by others, even if customer confusion is not likely.)

EXAMPLE: Assume that Gene and Beth's bookstore, BooksPlus, already had a well-established national mail-order catalog business and the name BooksPlus was familiar to a national audience. In this situation, they might be able to assert their trademark rights in court and force the Chicago editor to give up the "booksplus.com" domain name.

You will have to weigh carefully the pros and cons of attempting to force someone to give up a domain name based on a potential trademark infringement. On the one hand, the possibility of prevailing and getting the domain name you want may make this course worth it, depending on your business model. On the other hand, remember that lawsuits cost time and money; they can easily exceed $10,000 in legal and court fees (and can sometimes cost ten times that amount). If your case is a marginal one, you may be better off simply choosing a different domain name or even buying the name from the other party, who might prefer to sell rather than to fight a losing battle.

 CAUTION

Don't neglect your trademark rights. Your trademark rights can become weakened if you fail to defend your trademark when you know or should know that it's being infringed. For this reason, it's probably a good idea to go after a website or any other business or individual that infringes your trademark.

Dealing With Cybersquatters

You may find that the domain name you want has already been registered by someone who wants to sell it back to you at a profit. For instance, say you own a well-known car racing magazine called *Auto Racing Today*. When you are ready to launch a website, you discover that the domain name "autoracingtoday.com" is already registered by another business, which offers to sell the name back to you for $10,000. This practice, known as "cybersquatting," became a real problem in the late 1990s before businesses realized the importance of reserving domain names as early as possible.

A 1999 federal law known as the Anti-Cybersquatting Consumer Protection Act makes cybersquatting illegal and provides remedies for those injured, including getting the domain name back and possibly receiving money damages. To win a cybersquatting lawsuit, you'll have to sue the cybersquatter in federal court and prove all of the following:

- The domain name registrant (the cybersquatter) acted in bad faith by registering the name solely to make a profit by selling it back to you.
- Your mark was distinctive at the time the domain name was registered.
- The domain name is identical or confusingly similar to your trademark.
- You were the first to use the trademark in commerce.

An alternative to a lawsuit is to use a procedure set forth by ICANN (short for Internet Corporation for Assigned Names and Numbers), the international group now in charge of Internet domain name policy. ICANN's process for resolving cybersquatting disputes is known as the Uniform Domain Name Dispute Resolution Policy (UDRP), and typically will cost far less and take less time than a lawsuit. The case you'll have to prove is similar to what would be involved in a federal lawsuit. You will have to show that all of the following are true:

- The domain name is identical or confusingly similar to your trademark.
- The registrant has no legitimate interests in or rights to the domain name.
- The domain name was registered or is being used in bad faith.

Another advantage of the ICANN procedure is that it can be used in international domain name disputes, while a lawsuit based on the Anti-Cybersquatting Act can only be brought against domain name registrants in the United States. For more information, visit ICANN's website at www.icann.org.

Name Searches

By now you get the picture that a dispute over business names can be thorny. To avoid potential trademark hassles later on, you need to do some early digging before you finally settle on a name for your business. The main way to accomplish this is to conduct a name search to find out whether another business is already using a name that's identical or similar to the one you want to use. The information in this section will help you figure out how to go about researching your chosen name, and what to do once you've found one that you'll be able to use—and protect—as a trademark.

The scope of your search will depend largely on the size and geographical scope of your business and your plans for its future. If you plan from Day One to sell a product nationally—whether via catalog, through retailers, or online—you'll obviously need to worry about trademarks across the country. If, on the other hand, you're starting a small home-based service business, don't plan to advertise, and are relatively certain you won't expand geographically, a search of names in your county, and perhaps state, may be all you need—though it's always wise to search widely so that you at least know what's out there.

Keep in mind that the extent of your search encompasses not only how widely you search geographically, but also how deeply you search—in terms of looking not only for identical names, but also for those that are merely similar or have a slight resemblance to yours. Searching for the exact name (also called a "direct hit" search) is quick and cheap, but risks missing look- and sound-alikes. A more in-depth search, such as one that looks for names with slight variations in spelling, is safer, but can get quite complicated and expensive.

Sources of Name Information

Domain name research can be difficult because there is no one place to look. In large part, this is because a business can—and millions do—establish a trademark simply by using it. Since millions of marks aren't registered with the government, in addition to checking federal and state trademark databases you'll want to check many other sources of information, such as business directories and phone books, for unregistered trademarks. You should check some or preferably all of the following resources for name conflicts, depending on how extensive a search you need.

The Internet

It is probably best to start with the Internet because this resource is huge, fast, and free. Just Google the name to quickly see whether someone else on the Web is using it and how.

Another easy way to check trademarks online is to go to a domain name registrar and put in variations of the name you want to use. (Go to www.internic.net for a list of registrars.) If another company has reserved a domain name that contains your trademark, chances are you won't be able to use it. If the domain name qualifies as a trademark—which essentially means that the other company is using it to sell a product or service online—then, as described earlier in this chapter, you won't be able to use it as a trademark if your use would be likely to confuse customers.

Phone Directories

Don't overlook the phone book—the online version at www.yellowpages.com—as a valuable source of local name information. If you find someone who's using the name you want in your local area and your businesses are similar, there's no reason to waste money further searching the federal trademark register or other databases. However, if your businesses are different enough, you might still be able to use the name.

Industry Sources

Trade publications and business directories can be great sources of business name information (and they can also give you good ideas for names). You can also call trade associations and chambers of commerce to ask if they can provide lists or directories of businesses in the area.

Federal Trademark Database

All those starting a business, no matter how tiny and local, should search the federal trademark database to determine whether the name they want to use has already been registered by a similar business in the United States. The most important reason to do this is to avoid being sued for "willful infringement." If you use a trademark already registered at the federal level (even if yours is a tiny, local business), you can be sued for knowingly violating someone else's trademark—even if you didn't actually check the federal database and had no idea it was there. Searching the federal database can be complicated, and there are a few different ways to go about it—including hiring a trademark search firm to do the work for you. (See "Searching the Federal Trademark Database," below.)

State Databases

Many state corporation and LLC filing offices (usually the Secretary of State) maintain databases of registered names of corporations, limited partnerships, and LLCs. To find out whether a name appears in your state's corporate, LLC, or limited partnership database, contact your state corporate filing office or look on its website to determine its process for name searches. You may be able to search for names by phone, by mail, or online.

In addition, check your state's trademark registry. This registry is often part of the Secretary of State's department, though sometimes it has its own department. Find out the trademark office's rules for searching, or you can hire a trademark search firm to do the work for you.

County Fictitious Business Name Databases

Many counties maintain databases of fictitious business names (FBNs) that have been registered in that county. Even if you won't be using a fictitious business name—because you'll use your own name or your corporate, limited partnership, or LLC name—it's a good idea to check the FBNs used by other businesses in your county or state. Depending on how widely you're planning to search, you may want to search nearby counties or every county in the state.

Keep in mind that the free or relatively cheap searches offered by state and county agencies usually check only for exact matches—and won't tell you whether a similar name is included in that database. If, for example, the county clerk's office tells you that "The Dog House" does not appear in its fictitious name database, you might be surprised later to find that "The Dawg Haus" has been in business for years. In short, you may have to do a more extensive search than the one provided by the state or county office.

 CAUTION

County and state databases have limits. Just because a name doesn't appear in any county or state name databases, that doesn't mean another business doesn't already own that trademark. Use of the name, not registration, is what creates trademark ownership. Plenty of businesses own trademarks that they have never registered, so it's important to check for unregistered trademarks using the resources discussed above. Also, many businesses won't bother registering at the state level, but will register a federal trademark. If you plan to invest time and money in establishing your trademark, it's essential that you do a federal trademark search, too.

EXAMPLE: Tom and Jen, both veterinarians in California, search their county's fictitious business name database for the name "Critter Care," which they want to use for the animal hospital they're planning to open. They don't find anyone else using the name in their area, so they believe they can use it. But just to be safe, Jen decides to check the California state trademark directory for the name. She finds out that a California corporation has already obtained state trademark protection for the name "Critter Care." Because that corporation was doing business under its own name and not a fictitious one, it didn't have to register with any county fictitious name databases—so even if Tom and Jen had checked fictitious names statewide they wouldn't have found it. (Tom and Jen also would have found the name by checking the Secretary of State's corporate name database.)

Searching the Federal Trademark Database

As discussed above, to avoid a charge of willful infringement, it's a very good idea to check the federal trademark registry, maintained by the U.S. Patent and Trademark Office (PTO). Although tiny microbusinesses might get away without a federal search, most businesses should accept the fact that the Internet and other communication technologies have simply created too many potential trademark conflicts, even for small businesses. They need to search the PTO's database of federally registered trademarks.

If possible, begin your search with the free trademark database on the PTO's website. The PTO's database consists of all federally registered marks and all marks for which registration is pending. To start, go to the Trademark section of the PTO's website at www.uspto.gov/trademark and choose "Search Trademark Database." Then follow the instructions you see on the screen.

If using the Internet isn't feasible for you, visit your local Patent and Trademark Resource Center (PTRC)—there's at least one in every state—and use its research materials. (The PTO maintains a list of PTRCs nationwide; you'll find the list at the PTO website, at www.uspto.gov.) If a PTRC isn't convenient, a large public library or special business and government library near you should carry the federal trademark register, which contains all federal trademarks and service marks arranged by categories of goods and services.

Another option is to hire a professional search firm to do the work for you. You can order a complete search of registered and unregistered marks through TradeMark Express, CompuMark, Corsearch, or one of the PTRCs that offer electronic search services for very reasonable fees.

If you decide to hire a search firm, the cheapest and easiest type of national search is a direct-hit search, which will reveal whether another business has registered an identical name with the PTO. You can often hire one of the companies mentioned above to do a direct-hit search for a few hundred dollars or less. But while direct-hit searches are quick and cheap, they usually won't turn up trademarks that are similar, but not identical, to the name you're considering. For example, if you want to name your softball training center "The Strike Zone," a direct-hit search may not turn up a trademark for "The Stryke Zone." And, as discussed above, any mark that looks like, sounds like, or means the same as your name could present a trademark conflict.

More extensive national searches take a lot more time and money but may be necessary if you plan for your business to reach a wide audience and want to eliminate any risk of infringing someone else's existing trademark. For an in-depth search, it may make the most sense to hire a search firm; expect a fee of several hundred dollars for a professional, comprehensive search. If you do decide to hire search services, you're likely to save money if you do some quick, preliminary searches on the Internet yourself—to rule out some of your choices.

Analyzing Your Search Results

If, after your search, you determine that the name you've chosen does not already belong to someone else (or that someone else isn't using a similar name), you can go ahead and use it. Assuming you really are the first user of the name, you'll own the trademark, which will give you the right to stop others from using it in certain situations. But since registering a trademark conveys important additional rights and protections, you may want to register your name with the federal and state governments. See "Trademark Registration," below, to learn more.

But what if your search (or a search done by a professional firm) turns up an identical or similar name to the one you want to use? If the name is a famous trademark, it's probably time to pick a new name. Remember that if using your business name diminishes a famous trademark's distinctiveness or disparages

its reputation for quality, the owner of the famous trademark may stop you from using your name even if its customers aren't likely to be confused between its products and yours.

 TIP

Be sure to check domain names. If your Internet business will be important to you, pick a name that can also be used as a domain name. You can check whether a domain name is available at any domain name registrar, listed at www.internic.net.

If the name has been registered for official trademark protection, especially at the federal level, consider that a huge "No Trespassing" sign that should be taken seriously. Owners of federally registered trademarks have the right to use their trademarks anywhere in the country, and it is easy for them to sue and recover damages. If your search shows that the name is being used but isn't registered at the federal or state level, then you might have a bit more leeway—but not much more. Because use, not registration, conveys trademark rights, you still need to be very careful not to infringe that owner's rights.

That said, there are a few instances when taking a name that is already being used by someone else is okay. As mentioned, if the name is being used for a company that provides a very different product or service from the one you plan to sell, then you may have good reason to move forward with your plans to use the name. This is especially true if the two businesses serve only local markets and are hundreds of miles apart.

For example, just because a tiny clothing store in Boston calls itself Nature's Calling doesn't mean that you, in Aspen, Colorado, can't use Nature's Calling for your plumbing business. But if you wanted to start a clothing store in your town called Nature's Calling, and one already exists in Boston, then you should at the very least do more research before using it. If a federal trademark register search indicates that the Boston store has registered the mark "Nature's Calling," your subsequent use is a clear legal no-no. But even if the name is not registered and the Boston store seems like a local outfit, it could have plans to expand its territory or—even more likely—to create a website. Neither of these actions would necessarily prohibit your use of the name on your original store, but they could prevent you from using it more widely. The bottom line is that even if you feel certain that your business is different enough from that of the trademark owner to allow you to use the name, you should proceed only with lots and lots of caution.

TIP

How would you feel? If you are uncertain as to whether your proposed trademark would infringe an existing trademark, use a variant of the Golden Rule: How would you feel if you owned the existing trademark and someone else started to use it? Ask a few friends the same question. If any of the answers is "Pissed off," consider choosing a different name, or at least invest a few hundred dollars in a consultation with an experienced trademark lawyer.

RESOURCE

Comprehensive information on trademark issues. For more help understanding the nuances of different types of trademarks, picking a bulletproof name, searching and registering trademarks, defending your trademark and dealing with infringers, and using trademarks in other aspects of your business, see *Trademark: Legal Care for Your Business & Product Name*, by Stephen Fishman (Nolo). And you'll find lots of free information on trademarks and business names in the Patent, Copyright & Trademark area of Nolo's website.

Choosing a Domain Name

Assuming that your business will create a website—usually recommended—you'll need to choose a domain name and register it. (See Chapter 14 for more on doing business online.)

A great domain name should be memorable, clever, and easily spelled. But keep in mind that names that are ordinary and descriptive won't qualify for much trademark protection. Many good domain names—for instance, coffee.com, drugs.com, and business.com—are not eligible for trademark protection because they are the names of whole categories of products or services. Besides, virtually every such generic domain name is undoubtedly already registered by someone else. Likewise, domain names that use surnames or geographic names are unlikely to get trademark protection. (Of course, it's possible for a generic name, such as etrade, to become famous and develop "secondary meaning.")

TIP

You may want to register several domain names. In addition to your business name, you may want to register the names of your products or services, or other related names. Remember, names of your products or services may be as important as your business name, from a marketing perspective. It's also a good idea to register common misspellings of your primary domain name and names that reflect the nature of your products or services. For example, if you design and sell gourmet aprons, and your primary domain name is kitchenstuff.com, you might also want to register aprons.com so that customers who are looking for aprons and enter "aprons.com" into their browser will land at your site. It will, of course, cost more for multiple registrations, but the increased traffic may be worth it.

One potential problem in picking a domain name is that millions of names are already taken. For example, if your business name is Flaky Cakes, you may find that FlakyCakes.com already belongs to someone else, so you'll have to use a different domain name or change your business name if it's important to you that your business name and domain name are the same.

If you do find a domain name that's available, make sure the domain name you pick doesn't conflict with someone else's trademark. Even if you come up with a domain name that is brilliant from a marketing standpoint, be aware that your domain name is at risk if it legally conflicts with any of the millions of commercial trademarks that already exist. Remember, your domain name will probably function as a trademark just as your regular business name will—assuming you conduct business at your site. (This is true whether or not you register it with the U.S. Patent and Trademark Office—registering your domain name with the PTO will strengthen your enforcement rights, but using it for a commercial purpose is all that's technically necessary to establish your rights to it.) It follows that you are not allowed to use a domain name that's likely to cause customer confusion between your company and another, whether that company is online or off. (See Chapter 14 for detailed information on registering domain names.)

 RESOURCE

Apply for federal trademark registration. In addition to applying for protection for your business name, you should also try to register your domain name with the U.S. Patent and Trademark Office (www.uspto.gov). While you don't need to register to establish your rights to your domain name, registering it will strengthen your power to enforce your rights to it against infringers. It will also prevent someone else from registering the same name—which could save a lot of headaches in the future.

Trademark Registration

By now you understand that registering your trademark will strengthen your rights to it and make it easier to protect the name in case of a dispute. Registration is simply the process of notifying the state or, more commonly, the U.S. government that you're using a particular trademark.

When registration is complete, the trademark gets placed on an official list of registered names commonly called a trademark register. The U.S. Patent and Trademark Office (PTO) maintains two registers, the Principal Register and the Supplemental Register. State trademark offices have their own systems.

When people refer to a federally registered trademark, they're generally talking about marks on the Principal Register. Trademarks that appear on the Principal Register get the most protection, and the penalties can be harsh for those who improperly use a name that appears on it. The Supplemental Register, on the other hand, is reserved for weaker, less distinctive trademarks that don't qualify for the Principal Register. The main function of the Supplemental Register is to provide notice of a mark's current use to anyone who does a trademark search. After five years on the Supplemental Register, a mark may qualify to be moved to the Principal Register if it's been in continuous use during that period. Most states maintain just one register for all trademarks.

The PTO provides registration forms and instructions, which are available from a number of sources, including the PTO's website at www.uspto.gov. For simple trademarks such as business names (as opposed to trademarks for special packaging or product design—called "trade dress" in the biz), the instructions will probably be easy enough to follow.

You can also fill in and submit the form online at the PTO's Trademarks section.

State registration processes are generally similar to the federal system's procedure. Contact your state's trademark office for more information.

State Versus Federal Trademark Registration

State registration doesn't give as many benefits as federal registration, so it generally makes the most sense to register federally for the widest scope of protection. Some trademarks, however, don't qualify for federal registration, because they aren't used in national, international, or territorial commerce—in other words, they're only used within the state. These marks can only be registered at the state level. Although use of a trademark on the Internet almost guarantees the right to apply for federal registration, state registration may be the only option if you truly are only using the mark within your state.

Winning Names for Your Business, Products, and Services

Now that you have a general idea of the legal hurdles you need to clear and the snags and traps to watch out for, let the naming begin! Despite the trademark hassles involved, choosing names for your business and its products or services remains one of the fun parts of starting your business. It gives you a chance to use your creative juices to come up with a name that is both marketable and infused with your individual personality (or the collective personalities of all the business partners). A business name can help you establish the overall vibe of your business, from strictly professional to downright funky to a dozen things in between.

In addition to legal restrictions and personal preferences, the traditions and realities of your particular industry or business will probably have a lot to do with what kind of business name you choose. Good, memorable business and product names range from the clever (Super Elastic Bubble Plastic, Garden Weasel, Liquid Paper) to the straightforward (24 Hour Fitness, Fruit Roll-Ups, Jenny Craig Weight Loss Centers) to sometimes even the cryptic (Chia Pet, Floam, Yahoo!). In part because there really are so many different kinds of businesses and so many approaches to choosing a distinctive name, it's impossible to give any kind of specific advice on choosing a great name. There are, however, a few things that are helpful to keep in mind when choosing your business names:

- **Especially for small local businesses that don't plan to expand geographically, straightforward, informative names often work better than evocative ones.** For example, if you plan to open a shop selling aquarium supplies and tropical fish in Seattle, "Seattle Aquariums & Fish" may be a far more effective name than "The Lure of the Ocean." Also, since humble, descriptive names qualify for less trademark protection (unless they are already famous), choosing an ordinary name—especially one with a geographic identifier—will make you less likely to infringe on someone else's trademark.

- **Think about how your customers will locate your business and your products.** If you don't expect customers to seek out or remember your company as a whole, but only its products, it's silly to focus much attention on the business name (which you may never use as a trademark). For instance, while millions of people know the product The Clapper and its commercial jingle ("Clap on! Clap off! The Clapper!"), few know or care who its makers are.

- **Before you finally commit to a name, get some feedback from potential customers, suppliers, and others in your support network.** They may come up with a downside to a potential name or suggest an improvement you haven't considered. Doing this type of homework is especially important if you will market your goods or services to customers who are members of several different ethnic groups. You obviously don't want to choose a name or symbol and learn later that it offends or turns off a key group of customers. For example, one organization we know couldn't figure out why it got such a cold shoulder from Mexican Americans. The answer turned out to be that the shape, size, and typeface used on its signs was similar to a "No Trespassers—Keep Out" sign widely used in Mexico. A quick Google search yields plenty of other examples—such as Kentucky Fried Chicken's "finger lickin' good" slogan, translated in China as "eat your fingers off."

- **Niche businesses are often identified by their trade names, even when the focus is on the products.** This means that it is wise to pay particular attention to picking a memorable name if you will try to capture a particular, small field. The publisher of this book, Nolo, is a good example. Even though book buyers in other fields usually identify books they want by title or author, Nolo customers have come to recognize its name, often going into a bookstore and asking where the Nolo books are. In other words, Nolo has come to mean "self-help law" to many customers familiar with it, in contrast to the name HarperCollins—a large publisher of books on many topics— that might not evoke anything particular in most book customers' minds.

- **In certain service businesses in which an owner's personal attention and savvy is important (for example, architecture or accounting), it is common to use the owner's name, as in Charles Schwab.** In other service and retail businesses, it is more common to use creative names—Kinko's and Fuddrucker's come to mind—not only for the business itself, but sometimes for its products, too.

> **EXAMPLE:** Jerri and Orlando operate a car wash named Storm, which develops a good deal of name recognition in the city. Besides relying on the reputation of their trade name, they come up with clever names for various service packages (such as Sunday Shower, Typhoon Tuesday, and the Everyday Squall Special) in hopes that those names will catch on as well.

- **Be sure your trade or business name will still be appropriate if and when your business grows.** For example, if you open Miami Surf Shop, will it be a problem (or an advantage) if you want to open a second store in Orlando? Especially if you plan to sell products on the Internet, you should think twice about giving your business a geographical identifier. Similarly, if you start a business selling and installing canvas awnings using the name Creative Canvas Awnings, your name might be a burden if you decide to also start making other products such as canvas signs. On the other hand, the name Creative Canvas would let you move into all sorts of canvas products, such as duffel bags, canvas signs, and drop cloths.

TIP

Think nationally even if you act locally. As discussed throughout this chapter, even though you may plan to open just one local office or store, it's a good idea to be sure your name is safe from trademark conflicts on a statewide or even national basis (and, if appropriate, from domain name conflicts). Then, if your business takes off, you won't bump into someone else who already uses the name online or in another area.

Chapter 2 Checklist:
Picking a Winning Business Name

☐ Become familiar with the basics of trademark law, including what types of trademarks qualify for maximum legal protection.

☐ Draft lists of business, product, and domain names that could work.

☐ If you plan to do business online, check to see whether your proposed business names are available as domain names. (Ideally, your domain name(s) will be the same as your business or product names.)

☐ If the online aspect of your business will be important to you, narrow your list to those names that are available as domain names.

☐ Do a trademark search of the names on your list.

☐ If any names are already being used as trademarks, eliminate the ones that either are already famous trademarks or would lead to customer confusion if you also used them.

☐ Choose among the names that are still on your list.

☐ Register your business and product names as domain names whenever possible.

☐ Register your business and product names as trademarks.

Choosing a Business Location

Choosing a Business Location

For many types of businesses, location can mean the difference between feast or famine. Other enterprises will do more or less the same whether they're located in downtown Manhattan or in a deep crevasse on Mars. Not only does the importance of location vary greatly from business to business, but what makes a location desirable for one business might not work for another. Since there's no universal definition of what makes a location good for business, it's important for every business owner to figure out how location will (or will not) contribute to the success of the business—and to choose a spot accordingly.

That said, there are some basic issues to consider when choosing a business location. For starters, make sure the location makes economic sense. You won't want to spend a fortune for a spot on an exclusive commercial strip unless it's really going to pay off. It's obviously important that the rent for your business space fits into your overall budget. But don't be too frugal in this area—even the best-run business will fail if its customers can't find it or don't want to go to an unsafe neighborhood. And, of course, the location that you choose needs to be legally acceptable for whatever you plan to do there. Especially if you are planning to work from home or in a nonbusiness area, you'll need to check zoning laws to see if they prohibit your type of business. This chapter will help you figure out how to find a suitable place that meets all the needs of your business and complies with your local laws.

SKIP AHEAD

Planning to work from home? If you've already decided that you want to run your business from home, you can skip most—but not all—of this chapter. Read "Complying With Zoning Laws" for a good introduction to zoning rules, and see "Zoning Rules for Home Businesses" for more detailed information. After you read this material, turn to Chapter 10 for a more in-depth treatment. That chapter is devoted to the special issues facing home business owners—including zoning, the home business tax deduction, and risk management.

Picking the Right Spot

Your first task is to figure out how important location is to your business. For some businesses, the classic "location, location, location" advice definitely applies. But for others, location may be a lot less important than getting affordable rental space. And location is practically irrelevant for plenty of businesses, such as wholesalers, service businesses that do all their work at the customer's location (like roofers or plumbers), mail-order companies, and Internet-based businesses.

Especially if you can pass on your rent savings to your customers, picking a spot in an out-of-the-way area might be to your advantage. In other words, if location isn't that crucial to your business, don't blow all your start-up money on an expensive space in a thriving location.

If, on the other hand, you determine that location will be important to your business success, you'll need to figure out the best place to locate so that lots of customers can find you. It's one thing to know that you need a good location, but it can be harder to figure out what makes a location good. Ask yourself these questions:

- Will customers come on foot?
- Will customers drive, and, if so, where will they park?
- Will more customers come if you locate near other similar businesses?
- Will the reputation of the neighborhood or even of a particular building help draw customers?

As you ponder these and similar questions, here are a few things you'll want to consider.

Planting Yourself in Rich Soil

The key to picking a profitable location is to figure out what factors will increase customer volume for your unique business, and then to concentrate on finding a location that achieves as many of them as possible. For example, if you're opening a coffee shop, you may assume your customer volume will be highest if there's lots of pedestrian traffic nearby during the hours you plan to be open. Furthermore, if you envision your café to be a mellow place to sit and read, you'd probably prefer a university area or shopping district full of people with time to kill, rather than an area buzzing with busy businesspeople. If, on the other hand, you plan to open a small coffee shop with no tables—just fast, high-volume service—a busy downtown office district might be the right spot.

Audrey Wackerley, owner of Retro Fit, a vintage clothing store in San Francisco, California (www.retrofityourworld.com): *When we first opened, we got a space in the perfect neighborhood, with lots of thrift stores, coffee shops, and other walk-in type businesses on a strip with lots of foot traffic (plus, it was only a few blocks from my apartment). But we were on a cross street a few doors around the corner from Valencia Street, the main strip. We did okay, but nothing like the shops on Valencia itself. Finally, we got a good deal on a storefront on Valencia Street, and we moved. Our business practically tripled! We paid a bit more for the better space, but our boost in sales more than made up for it.*

Keep in mind that different types of businesses attract customers in different ways. One key distinction is foot traffic versus automobile traffic. An auto repair shop, for example, will obviously draw customers in radically different ways from the coffee shop. For the auto shop, the choicest locale is a well-traveled street, where it will be seen by many drivers who will easily be able to pull into the lot. For an urban coffee shop, on the other hand, a popular location might be in an area where there are lots of people passing on foot. But of course no rule is absolute—for example, some coffee shops thrive on busy thoroughfares because commuters stop for "to go" coffee and baked goods every morning.

Also think about whether it would benefit your business to be around similar businesses that are already drawing the type of customers that you want. A women's clothing store, for example, would no doubt profit from being near other clothing shops, because many women shopping for clothes tend to spend at least a few hours in a particular area. The point is, the perfect location for any business is a very individual matter. Spend some time figuring out the habits of the customers you want to attract, then choose a location that fits.

Keeping Rent Within Your Budget

One obvious and important factor in finding a business space is how much you can afford. Chances are that you have found or will find a fabulous spot that you can only dream about because the monthly rent is so high. While it's okay to dream, don't be foolish enough to overpay for a space that you can't afford. As part of your business planning (discussed in detail in Chapter 4), determine how much rent you can afford each month, and stick to it.

One good way to find out how much rent is reasonable for an area is to call a commercial broker or agent in your area and have a chat about how much space generally goes for in the areas you're considering. Brokers and agents will usually give you an average figure for what commercial space costs per square foot per year in a given area; once you have this figure, you can compare it to the costs of any potential spaces you're considering. But keep in mind that agents and brokers are self-interested professionals who may benefit from higher rents. In other words, don't necessarily accept the figures they give you at face value.

Square footage rates are generally given in cost per year, so once you multiply the rate by the square footage of a space, you'll need to divide it by 12 to determine the monthly rent.

Pamela Slim, author, *Escape from Cubicle Nation* **and** *Body of Work.*
(www.pamelaslim.com):

When choosing a location for my downtown Mesa, Arizona, small business incubator, I looked for both great physical qualities in the space (nice light, ample room, good parking) as well as trusting my instincts about the feeling of the area. I visited a whole number of spaces that were beautiful and very functional. But it was not until I saw my space that I knew instinctively it was in the exact right spot. Not just because it was located between a cookie store and a toy store (that helped!), but because it was exactly in the center of town. I love being in the middle of the action on Main Street, and am so happy with my choice!

EXAMPLE: Jennifer and Oliver are planning to open a theater in a certain neighborhood of their city. They call a few real estate brokers out of the phone book whose ads indicate they handle commercial space leasing. All the brokers say that commercial space in the area they like usually goes for $10 per square foot. (Jennifer and Oliver know that this is an annual figure, which works out to about $0.83 per square foot per month.) A few weeks later, Jennifer and Oliver notice a building for rent, and they call the agent for more information. The agent tells them that the monthly rent is $1,800, and that the space is 2,400 square feet. Jennifer and Oliver do the math and see that the rent is slightly less than the going rate for the area:

	Monthly rent		$ 1,800	per mo.
x	12 months	=	$ 21,600	per year
÷	2,400 sq. feet	=	$ 9	per year/sq. ft.

For comparison's sake, they do the math to determine what the rent would be if the space rented out for the going rate, $10 per square foot:

	Cost per sq. ft./mo.		$ 10	
x	2,400 sq. feet	=	$ 24,000	per year
÷	12 months	=	$ 2,000	per mo.

They're not quite ready to enter a lease, but the fact that this space is somewhat of a bargain puts it near the top of their list.

Though being realistic about your rent is important, don't sabotage your business by picking a cheap, but bad, location. This may seem obvious, but sometimes new business owners become blind to common wisdom when presented with an opportunity to rent a super-cheap space. Even if they've already determined that location will play a key role in their success, they either believe that the savings in rent will make up for slow sales or convince themselves that they'll be the pioneers in a new area that is sure to swell into a hot business district by the middle of next week. While this does occasionally happen (bless those brave pioneers), it's generally a poor idea to move into a dead section of town, since it almost certainly won't bloom fast enough to support your business in its financially vulnerable start-up days.

Unless you have a sound reason to believe that you'll get enough customers in your oddball location, don't let the lure of low rent tempt you into a bad business decision. At least in popular urban areas, rent can be the highest overhead expense for many new businesses.

Getting the Right Physical Features

When picking your space, your biggest consideration might not be where it is but what it is. Ask yourself whether the building facilities are appropriate or adaptable for your business. For example, if you're planning to open a coffeehouse, you might fall in love with a beautiful brick warehouse space in a funky shopping district. But if the place doesn't have at least minimal kitchen facilities, you should probably forget it. Unless you can convince your landlord to put in the needed equipment—plumbing, electrical work, and the rest (discussed below)—it's highly unlikely that laying out the cash to do it yourself will be worth it.

Sure, some improvements might be relatively cheap, such as putting up a wall or two or adding new light fixtures. But if the building lacks something major that is essential to your business operation, take it as a sign that the place isn't right for you—even if it has loads of other great qualities.

You'll have to decide for yourself which features your business absolutely can't live with or without.

EXAMPLE: Charlotte and Sandra plan to open an alternative health store that will offer products such as medicinal herbs, aromatherapy products, and yoga supplies. They also plan to offer services such as aromatherapy sessions and consultations with nutritionists and herbalists. Charlotte and Sandra have high hopes for the service side of their business, so their physical space needs to be comfortable and appealing to customers. After looking at a number of storefront spaces in their chosen neighborhood, they find one that seems just perfect—until they notice the lack of windows. Except for the glass front door, the place has almost no natural light. Even though not having windows doesn't absolutely prevent them from doing business, Charlotte and Sandra decide that, given their expected customer base and their own feelings, they need a brighter space.

Another consideration that's important for most businesses these days is having modern phone lines and broadband Internet access. Anything less than a reliable high-bandwidth Internet connection can seriously impact your productivity (and drive you crazy to boot). Some buildings may have outdated phone lines that can result in dropped telephone connections— not exactly a good thing for business. When you're considering a specific space, ask the agent or the landlord for any information on the phone and data lines into the space.

In addition to dealing with concerns about high-tech communications wiring, don't overlook plain old electrical power as an important consideration in choosing a business space. Make sure that any space you're looking at has enough power for your needs, both in terms of the number of outlets and the capacity of the circuits. If you'll mostly be running computer equipment, a copier, a coffee machine, and the like, chances are that any reasonably equipped commercial space will have enough power for you. But if you'll be running machinery or other electricity-hungry equipment, make sure to find out from the landlord how much juice the circuits can handle and whether a generator is available during power outages. Also, if you'll keep sensitive computer equipment at your office, ask the landlord how many hours of air conditioning are included in the terms of your lease, and negotiate longer hours if necessary.

Another common need for many businesses is adequate parking. If a significant percentage of your customers will come by car and there isn't enough parking at your chosen spot, it's probably best to look elsewhere. In fact, the city might not allow you to operate there if parking isn't adequate.

TIP

Check local planning and health department requirements. If you're starting a small food manufacturing business to produce energy bars, you may need to rent a space with a certain number of vents, a fire-resistant roof, and walls of proper material and adequate thickness. You may also need a safe place to park refrigerated delivery trucks. And your business may be subject to special waste disposal requirements, so you may need extra space for waste storage or equipment. Contact your city or county departments of planning, health, or fire, or another appropriate agency to find out. You should also check out state and federal laws that apply to your business. (See Chapter 7 for a discussion of licenses and permits.)

Complying With Zoning Laws

A certain spot may be good for your business, but if it's not properly zoned for what you plan to do, forget it. Local zoning laws (often called "ordinances" or "land use regulations") prohibit certain activities from being conducted in particular areas. To use an obvious example, a nightclub wouldn't be allowed to operate in a district zoned for residential use. Sure, only a fool would try to open a disco on a quiet residential street—but there are less obvious zoning restrictions that you must observe.

Expect Zoning Laws on Parking Spaces and Business Signs

Local zoning laws commonly require a business to provide parking, and they also may regulate the size and type of business signs. Be prepared for your city or county to look into both these issues. If there's already a parking problem in your proposed area, you may have to come up with a plan for how to deal with the increased traffic your business will attract.

Also, be ready for zoning officials to get really nitpicky about your business sign. Many local laws limit the size of business signs (no signs over five feet by three feet, for instance), their appearance (such as whether they're illuminated, flashing, colorful, or made of neon), and their placement (flat against the building, hanging over the sidewalk, or mounted on a pole). There are even some regulations attempting to limit the use of foreign language on signs. Be sure to find out what your local regulations are before spending money on having signs made.

Zoning ordinances typically allow certain categories of businesses to occupy different districts of a city or county. For example, mixed commercial and residential uses might be allowed in one district while another district allows heavy industry and warehouses. So if you open your small jewelry-making business in a space zoned for commercial use, you could be in for a real headache if zoning officials decide you're a light-industrial business that's not allowed to operate in a commercial district. Similarly, you may not be allowed to run a commercial business—particularly one that's open to the public—in an industrial zone.

In addition to regulating the types of businesses allowed in certain areas, zoning laws also regulate specific activities. Depending on your area, you might be subject to laws regulating parking, signs, water and air quality, waste management, noise, and the visual appearance of the business (especially in historic districts). In addition to these regulations, some cities restrict the number of a particular type of business in a certain area, such as allowing only three bookstores or one pet shop in a certain neighborhood. Finally, some zoning laws specifically regulate home businesses.

TIP

Know your neighbors. More often than not, zoning laws are enforced for the sake of the other people and companies in the neighborhood (this is particularly true of home-based businesses). While some areas are strict about their zoning laws, most of the time you won't have a zoning official knocking unannounced on your door unless neighbors have complained or you're in flagrant violation of the laws. Enforcement is often triggered by complaints, so it's a good idea to get to know your neighbors and develop good relationships with them. And, if you plan to run your business from home, be sure to read Chapter 10, which covers special zoning issues for home businesses.

RELATED TOPIC

If you have a home business. Zoning rules for home businesses are explained in detail in Chapter 10, which also has a full discussion of several other special issues facing home business owners—including the home business tax deduction and risk management.

Never sign a lease for a business space without first knowing that you'll legally be able to do business there. However, it's okay to sign a contingent lease, with a clause stating that the lease won't be binding if you don't get zoning approval. Being forced to move your business is a headache enough, but not nearly as catastrophic as having to pay rent on a lease for a space that you can't use.

When determining whether you'll be able to do business at a potential location, never assume that you'll be allowed to do a certain activity simply because the previous tenants of the space did it. For all kinds of reasons, some businesses get away with zoning violations, even for long periods of time. But new occupants are sometimes scrutinized more carefully than already existing businesses. It may not be fair, but a new business may be told it can't do what an old one had long been doing.

It's also possible that the previous tenants had an official okay to operate outside the zoning restrictions. For example, the previous occupants might have had a zoning variance (an exception to zoning laws) for their particular business—one that won't necessarily be extended to you. And lots of times when zoning laws change, businesses that are already in place are allowed to keep doing what they were doing, even if the activity violates the new zoning law (a system referred to as "grandfathering"). When a tenant with a grandfathered exception leaves and new occupants come in, however, the new business usually has to abide by the new, more restrictive zoning law.

Finding Out What Laws Apply

How do you find out whether a given location is properly zoned for your business and whether you need to get any approvals? The answer varies from area to area. In some cities and counties, zoning approval is part of the tax registration process (discussed in Chapter 7). In San Diego, for instance, when you apply for your business tax certificate, you must also pay a Zoning Use Clearance fee to have your business approved for the location listed on your application. The city of Albuquerque also requires businesses to get zoning approval before allowing them to obtain a tax registration certificate, though there is no fee for the zoning clearance. Other cities don't require proof of zoning approval before issuing a tax registration certificate—but that doesn't mean you should take the zoning laws any less seriously. Whether or not you're required to deal with your local zoning department before starting your business, you'll still be subject to its monitoring and enforcement.

If your city doesn't include zoning approval as part of its start-up requirements for new businesses, you'll need to do some detective work. Generally this involves talking with your local zoning officials. Most zoning agencies are part of city or county planning departments; check your city or county website. If your business will be located in a city, you probably only need to worry about city zoning ordinances. Businesses in rural areas should contact the county zoning or planning offices.

Getting zoning approval typically begins with filling out a form issued by the city planning department in which you provide information about your proposed location and what you plan to do there. In some cities, you may be required to submit detailed building plans to show exactly how you intend to use the space in question. Your application may be evaluated simply on the information you provide in the form, or the zoning department may send out an inspector to more closely examine the potential business space. Once the zoning department has all the information it requires to make a decision, it will either approve your application without limitations, approve it with certain conditions, or deny it altogether.

How Vigilant Are Zoning Officials?

There's a world of difference from area to area in how strict zoning officials are. Many zoning departments aren't terribly rigid about enforcement, mostly responding to complaints from neighbors or other citizens about businesses that create a nuisance or other trouble. In a few areas, however, zoning agents relish sniffing out minor infractions and enforcing their zoning ordinances to the letter.

If you're considering going ahead with your business despite what you consider to be a minor zoning problem, you should do your best to find out how strict the zoning police are in your area. Start by asking other local businesspeople about their experiences. If they tell you that there's little enforcement other than responding to complaints, you can breathe a little easier about what might be a minor infraction, such as including tennis racket stringing (which officials might consider a light-industrial activity) at your sports shop in an area zoned only for commercial use. Even so, it never pays to engage in a prohibited activity that is fundamental to your business. While tennis rackets could be strung elsewhere, a health club wouldn't want to have to locate its juice bar two blocks away.

But no matter how mellow your zoning department, at the very least you need to know what the rules are for your proposed location. Ignoring the rules while counting on lax enforcement is just plain dumb.

Dealing With Zoning Snags

If your zoning board has a problem with any of the activities you plan to conduct at your chosen location, you have a few options, usually ranging from making appropriate changes to your business to giving up on that location and finding a new one. Obviously, some zoning conflicts are simply not fixable—for example, you'll never be allowed to open a nightclub on a quiet residential cul-de-sac. But a creative (and, when necessary, assertive) business owner can often persuade zoning officials or the zoning appeals board to work out an acceptable accommodation that will allow the business to use the desired location.

For borderline situations, one approach is simply to advocate an interpretation of the zoning law that's favorable to you before you get an official "No." Communicate with zoning officials, and try to persuade them to give you their seal of approval.

If the zoning officials have already denied your application, it's often possible to appeal their decision, usually to a higher authority such as a board of appeals within the zoning agency or the city council. If you're successful, the zoning board may grant you a "variance," which is basically a one-time exception to the local zoning laws. Or the board may give you a "conditional use permit," which essentially gives you approval to operate your business as long as certain conditions are met, such as restricting the maximum occupancy to a certain number or providing additional parking spaces.

When lobbying for an exemption from a zoning requirement, be aware that you're asking for special treatment, so make your case as persuasive as possible. If your business will be valuable to the community, present evidence of that fact. Proof can include demographic data about the area, testimony from community leaders, or statements from other local businesspeople. Your goal is to show that the value of allowing your business in the area is greater than the trivial zoning conflicts that may exist. If you can compromise in some other area, offer to do so.

EXAMPLE: Carolyn wants to open a small printing shop, Nelson's Press, on a commercial strip where storefront space is cheap and plentiful. Before signing a lease, she applies for zoning approval. The local zoning board rejects her application because Carolyn's proposed location is zoned commercial, but her print shop would technically be a light-industrial business. Carolyn decides to try to get an exception, because her printing operation will be small (only one small offset printing press) and would be an asset to the neighborhood, which has been struggling economically.

She submits detailed plans of her business to the zoning board, showing the business's small scope and including specific protocols for dealing with toxics such as ink. She also submits letters from other business owners in the neighborhood documenting how commerce in the area has languished for years and arguing that new businesses would help revitalize the strip. Many of the business owners also note that a local printer would be convenient for the existing area businesses, which currently have to go across town for their print jobs. A few weeks later, Carolyn gets a conditional use permit allowing her to proceed with her printing business, as long as she doesn't expand her business with additional presses and follows a number of standard rules governing the chemicals she'll use in printing.

Zoning Rules for Home Businesses

Similar to business owners who operate from commercial office spaces, those who run home businesses need to make sure they don't violate their local zoning rules. As home businesses have exploded in popularity, more local governments have adopted specific provisions in zoning laws controlling them. Mercifully, most of the rules are straightforward and fair—with some exceptions. If you're unlucky and find that you're subject to prohibitive municipal ordinances or private land use restrictions, take a hard look at whether you should set up shop in your home after all. But more often, you'll find that you'll need to jump through a simple hoop or two and pay a modest fee to run your business from home.

Dwellings in residential or mixed-use zones are often allowed to run businesses that have little likelihood of causing noise or pollution, creating traffic, or otherwise disturbing the neighbors. Examples include freelance writers, artists, attorneys, accountants, architects, insurance brokers, and piano teachers.

To find out local rules, contact your city's planning or zoning department and ask for information on its rules for home businesses. Often, home businesses are allowed with some restrictions—such as limiting employees to residents, curbing the number of customers allowed, and prohibiting business signs posted outside. Also ask the local zoning authority whether any special rules exist for the specific type of business or activities you plan to conduct.

As to whether or not you need a permit to run a home business, local rules vary. If a permit is required, getting one is usually a simple matter of filling out a form provided by the planning department and paying a fee. You may also need to deal with other departments in addition to the zoning office. For example, depending on your business activities, you may need to get approvals from your county health or fire department.

RELATED TOPIC

For more on home office zoning. For more detail on permits for specific business activities, see Chapter 7 on start-up requirements. And see Chapter 10 for a full discussion of special issues facing home business owners—including zoning, the home business tax deduction, and risk management.

Commercial Leases

Chances are that you'll rent rather than buy a space for your business. After all, most small start-ups don't have the funds to purchase real estate, and it's usually not a good idea to saddle your business with high interest payments, anyway. But just because you've rented plenty of apartments or flats over the years, don't assume that you know the score when it comes to leasing business space.

Practically and legally speaking, there are significant differences between commercial leases and residential leases. Commercial leases are not subject to most consumer protection laws that govern residential leases—for example, there are no caps on deposits or rules protecting a tenant's privacy. Also, commercial leases are generally subject to much more negotiation between the business and the landlord, because businesses often

need special features in their spaces, and landlords are often eager for tenants and willing to extend special offers. While a residential tenant will usually just take an apartment or flat more or less as is, a business owner will often need to modify the existing space—for example, by adding cubicles, raising a loading dock, or rewiring for telephones, Internet access, and computers.

Because company owners must negotiate modifications suitable for their own operations, commercial leases are relatively flexible creatures. Of course, your bargaining power will vary a great deal from situation to situation. For example, getting a landlord to accept your demands would probably be a lot easier for a long-term lease in a largely vacant office building than for a six-month lease in a hot commercial area. Likewise, local independent landlords are often more willing to make concessions than huge property management companies or real estate investment trusts.

When negotiating a commercial lease, keep in mind that the success or failure of your business may ride on certain terms of the lease. The amount of the rent is an obvious concern, as is the length of the lease. (You probably don't want to tie yourself to a five- or ten-year lease if you can help it, in case your business grows faster or more slowly than you expect or the location doesn't work out for you.) But other, less conspicuous items spelled out in the lease may be just as crucial to your business's success. For instance, if you expect your shoe repair business to depend largely on walk-in customers, be sure that your lease establishes your right to put up a sign that's visible from the street. Or, if you are counting on being the only sandwich shop inside a new commercial complex, make sure your lease prevents the landlord from leasing space to a competitor. If you are starting a new service company that you expect to grow quickly, make sure there's room for expansion.

The following checklist includes many items that are often addressed in commercial leases. Pay attention to terms regarding:

- rent, including allowable increases and method of computation
- whether the rent includes insurance, property taxes, and maintenance costs (called a gross lease), or whether you will be charged for these items separately (called a net lease)
- whether the rent includes heat, air conditioning, phone, garbage collection, water, and other utilities
- the security deposit and conditions for its return

- who is responsible for code compliance, security, and fire safety
- the length of the lease (also called the lease term) and when it begins
- whether there's an option to renew the lease or expand the space
- how the lease may be terminated, including notice requirements, and whether there are penalties for early termination
- exactly what space is being rented, including common areas such as hallways, restrooms, and elevators, and how the space is measured (some measurement practices include the thickness of the walls)
- specifications for signs, including where they may be placed
- whether there will be improvements, modifications (called buildouts when new space is being finished to your specifications), or fixtures added to the space; who will pay for them; and who will own them after the lease ends (generally, the landlord)
- who will maintain the premises and provide janitorial services
- whether the lease may be assigned or subleased to another party, and
- whether disputes must be mediated or arbitrated as an alternative to court.

RESOURCE

For more on leasing office spaces.
For detailed information on finding a space and
negotiating a lease, see *Negotiate the Best Lease
for Your Business*, by Janet Portman (Nolo).

CAUTION

**Beware the Americans with
Disabilities Act.** The Americans with Disabilities
Act (ADA) requires all businesses that are open to
the public or that employ more than 15 people to
have premises that are accessible to people with
disabilities. Make sure that you and your landlord
are in agreement about who will pay for any
needed modifications, such as adding a ramp or
widening doorways to accommodate wheelchairs.

Chapter 3 Checklist: Choosing a Business Location

- ☐ Determine how much rent you can afford.

- ☐ Decide what neighborhood best suits your business.

- ☐ Find out what the average rents are in the neighborhoods you're considering for your business.

- ☐ Identify the features and fixtures your business space will need.

- ☐ Make sure spaces that you're considering are or can be properly zoned for your business.

- ☐ Examine all commercial leases carefully —and negotiate the best deal you can.

- ☐ If working from home, make sure your business activities will not violate any zoning restrictions on home offices.

Drafting an Effective Business Plan

f you think only Type A personalities compose business plans, think again. Talk to a random sample of successful business owners—even the most laid back —and you'll be amazed at how many took the time to put their business plans into writing. If you're truly determined to succeed, you'll follow their example. Why? Because without a plan, you're leaving far too many things to chance. Just as a blueprint is used to ensure that a building will be structurally sound, a business plan will help you make sure that your business will be able to stay afloat.

The purpose of a business plan is simple: to bring together in one document the key elements of your business. These include the products or services you'll sell, what they'll cost to produce, and how much sales revenue you expect during your first months and years of operation. Most important, your plan will help you see how all the disparate elements of your business relate to one another, which will allow you to make any necessary alterations in order to maximize your business's potential to turn a profit.

Business plans are often written by business owners who want to borrow money or attract investment. This is good as far as it goes: Lenders and investors do want to understand as much as possible about how a business will work before deciding whether to back it financially. Unless you're prepared to show them a well-thought-out plan for making your business profitable, you won't have much chance of convincing them to finance your project.

But creating a business plan is a good idea even if you don't need to raise start-up money. The process of creating one often brings up issues and potential problems that you hadn't thought of before. And the discipline involved in developing financial projections, such as a break-even analysis and a profit and loss forecast, will help you decide whether your business is really worth starting, or whether you need to rethink some of your key assumptions. As any experienced businessperson will tell you, the business you decide not to start (often because its business plan doesn't pencil out) can play a greater role in your long-term success than the one on which you bet your economic future.

This chapter explains how to create a thorough business plan. It simply and straight-forwardly outlines a number of descriptive sections and financial reports that will help guide you in running your business—and that will help attract funding if you need it.

 SKIP AHEAD

For those who already have a plan. If you've already written a business plan, you may want to skip ahead to Chapter 5, "Raising Start-Up Money." However, you might also want to review this chapter as a way of evaluating the work you've already done.

RESOURCE

For more help on the business of business plans. *How to Write a Business Plan*, by Mike McKeever (Nolo), is a comprehensive guide on how to write a business plan—including how to evaluate the profitability of your business idea; estimate operating expenses; determine assets, liabilities, and net worth; and find potential sources of financing. *Business Plan Pro* (Palo Alto Software) offers a fast, easy way to generate the plan you need to launch or expand your business; for details and a sample business plan, see www.businessplanpro.com.

Also, the U.S. Small Business Administration (SBA) website (www.sba.gov) includes several resources to help you write a business plan, including a step-by-step online Business Plan Tool.

Different Purposes Require Different Plans

All good business plans have two basic goals: to describe the fundamentals of the business idea, and to provide financial calculations to show that it will make good money. But, depending on how you intend to use it, a business plan can take somewhat different forms:

- **If you will use your plan to borrow money or interest investors,** write it with an eye toward selling your vision to skeptical people. Generally, you should include a persuasive introduction and a request for funds, in-depth market research information, an evaluation of your main competitors,

your key marketing strategies, and a management plan. In addition, your plan should contain detailed financial information—including your best estimates of start-up costs, revenues, and expenses. Finally, since your plan will be submitted to people who don't know you well, the writing should be polished and the format clean and professional. (See Chapter 5 for a discussion of business financing basics.)

- **If your plan will primarily be for your own use**—that is, if you don't need to raise money— don't worry so much about making a sales pitch or slick presentation (although you'll probably want to do a quick market and competitive analysis). But don't skimp when it comes to doing your numbers. You'll need to include estimates of start-up costs, revenues, and expenses. The last thing you want is to experience the very real misery of realizing too late that your business never had a chance to make a solid profit.

TIP

Plan to get the help you need. Not all businesspeople are great writers. But excellent writing skills can be a big help in creating a compelling business plan. Consider paying a freelance writer with business savvy to help you polish your plan. Similarly, if you are challenged by numbers, find a bookkeeper or an accountant to provide some help with the math.

Describing Your Business and Yourself

The first several sections of your plan should describe the beauty of your business idea. If you will show your plan to potential lenders, investors, or colleagues, you'll want to show them right up front that you've hit on a product or service that customers really want. In addition, you'll want to show that you are exactly the right person to make this fine idea a roaring success. Your goal is to have them say, "Wow! What a great business idea! And yes, I see exactly why Carlos Burns is the ideal person to make it a big success."

To accomplish these goals, you should include the following in your plan:

- a statement of the purpose of your business
- a detailed description of how the business will work
- an analysis of your market
- an analysis of your competitors
- a description of your marketing strategy, and
- a résumé setting out your business accomplishments.

Again, depending on how you intend to use your business plan, you may be able to skip some of these elements. For example, if you don't need to raise start-up money and are writing a plan mostly for your own use, you may decide to skip the résumé of your own business accomplishments. But think twice before you leave out too much. Any new business will need to be introduced to loads of people—suppliers, contractors, employees, and key customers, to name a few—and showing them part or all of your business plan can be a great way to do it.

State Your Business's Purpose

What will your product or service be? And why does the great big world—or your small town or narrow niche market—need the product or service you want to offer? The first paragraph of your plan should address this question as directly and compellingly as possible. For example, if you're planning to open a pet-grooming salon, you might start with the proposition that in today's busy world, pet owners need and want to keep their pets clean and groomed, but often don't have time to do it themselves. Similarly, if you want to start a sea kayaking guide service, you might start with the proposition that more and more people are participating in this exciting sport but need equipment, planning, training, and logistical help to do it in other parts of the world.

A statement of business purpose doesn't need to be complicated or lengthy. In fact, some of the best simply state the obvious. If the need for your business will be clear to lenders or investors (for example, a sandwich shop in a fast-growing office area), one paragraph may be all you need. But if the value of your business idea isn't so readily apparent (for example, an innovative software company), you will want to say more. Show how your business will solve a real problem or fill an actual need. And explain why customers will pay you to accomplish the task.

Describe Your Business

Once you've stated the need that your business will fill, describe exactly how you'll go about filling it. In this section, don't write a bunch of fluffy text about the brilliance of your entrepreneurial idea. Instead, outline in detail exactly how your business will operate. While the degree of detail may vary depending on what kind of business you're starting and who will be reading your business plan, your description should include specifics such as:

- how you will provide the product or service
- where you will buy key supplies
- who your customers will be and how they will pay you
- how many employees you will have, and what they will do
- your hours of operation, and
- your business location (if possible, include details about how your customers will find you).

 CAUTION

Be sure to include the costs of creating a website and doing business online. You can end up spending a bundle, especially if you're running a full e-commerce operation. When budgeting for online business activities, remember to include not only the costs to develop a website, but also the ongoing costs of maintaining and promoting it. Put careful thought into your online operations early on in your business planning efforts, to make sure they don't become an unexpected drain on your business later on. See Chapter 14 for advice on developing an online presence, including selling and marketing online.

Keep in mind that even the smallest, simplest business involves a swarm of pesky details. While you're writing your business description, don't assume there's anything obvious about your business, even if it's a tiny one-person operation. For example, if you plan to start a pet-grooming business, how many different types of services will you offer: Shampooing? Flea bathing? Nail cutting? Hair trimming? Teeth cleaning? Will you charge separately for each individual service, sell them in packages, or both? How will you attract customers and regularly stay in touch with the best ones? How will you accommodate animals with special needs such as allergies or behavioral problems such as aggressiveness? How will people drop off and pick up their pets? Will your business need insurance in case an animal is injured or dies while in your care?

> **TIP**
>
> **A little repetition is okay.** The description of how your business will operate is likely to be the longest section of your plan and will probably discuss topics that are also covered elsewhere. No problem. For example, you should discuss the key issue of how you will establish and keep a competitive edge in your big-picture business description as well as in the marketing strategy section. (See "Describe Your Marketing Strategy," later in this chapter.)

Use the process of writing your business description as an opportunity to change or refine your business idea. When you write and rewrite this section, you'll probably come up with ideas and questions you haven't yet thought through. If so, great—this gives you an opportunity to fill in the gaps before you actually open for business. And even if you discover a flaw so big that you decide not to start the business after all, your business plan has done its job. While undoubtedly disappointing, it's far better for your business to fail on paper than in real life.

Define Your Market

Who will buy your product or service? Even the most innovative business will fail if it doesn't quickly find enough customers to make a profit. In this section, your task is to demonstrate to a potential investor or lender (or convince yourself) that there are indeed customers out there, ready and willing to buy your product or service. Describe your anticipated customer base, and show that there is a demand for your product or service by referring to news reports, trade journal articles, or other reports. Use whatever data you can get your hands on. And don't neglect your imagination—unconventional arguments are fine, as long as they are convincing. Here is a brief list of points you may wish to make:

- **Similar businesses have been successful.** For example, if fitness clubs with meditation rooms and mindfulness coaches are all the rage in Los Angeles, you might explain why this is a good indication that your similar business would succeed in Chicago, where the market is currently dominated by more old-school gyms.
- **Marketing surveys or demographic reports point to a growing need for your product or service.** For instance, to buttress your contention that there will be a need for your new line of paralegal training materials, point to U.S. government reports listing paralegal as one of the fastest-growing occupations.
- **Media reports confirm the popularity of and demand for your business.** For example, include newspaper clips or transcripts of television news reports on the surge of demand for antibacterial air fresheners as evidence that your germ-killing Sani-Scent™ will sell.

- **Your conversations with potential customers show a need for your business.** It's often a good idea to carry out an informal survey of your most likely customers and include the results. For example, if you will run a business repairing and reconditioning acoustic guitars and similar stringed instruments, you might include results of a survey of guitarists and other musicians on what kind of repair services they need, as well as quotes from them saying that they'd use your services.

In addition to establishing that there is a solid demand for your business, do your best to define and describe exactly who your customers will be. If you're opening a bar with live entertainment, for instance, you might identify your market as primarily childless, urban 21- to 35-year-olds, who tend to have more disposable income and leisure time than others. Similarly, if you're planning an antique restoration service, you might identify your target market as professionals and others in the 40- to 70-year-old age range with household incomes of $150,000 or more. The better you can show that you know exactly who your target customer is, the more confident lenders and investors will be that you can actually find these people and sell to them.

 TIP

Include a profile of your target customer. Explain why and how a fictional person would need and use your product or service. Do your best to flesh out a believable person. Creating a typical customer gives a face to an otherwise abstract market definition and gives your market analysis more impact. For more information on defining your target customer, see Chapter 13.

Analyze Your Competition

Just because you have a great business idea doesn't mean you'll be successful. Other businesses may have already cornered the market or be poised to do so. For example, lots of small business owners who ran successful video rental businesses were wiped out when Netflix hit the market. It's often all too easy for a bigger, better-capitalized outfit to copy your best features and pull the rug out from under your business. Use this section to explain why your business really will have few direct competitors—or, if competitors will abound (as is far more likely), to show how your business will develop and keep an edge. Don't be shy about detailing competitors' strengths as well as weaknesses as part of showing why your business will better meet customers' needs.

Businesses With Specialized Knowledge Are Hard to Copy

The business owner who knows the most about how to beat out competitors usually wins. But what is business knowledge, and how can you exploit it? In the broad sense, it's anything a business knows how to do that can give it a meaningful edge over competitors. Common examples include:

- the ability to buy products for resale cheaper than competitors
- a great location
- a unique, hard-to-duplicate product
- excellent customer service, and
- superior customer accessibility—longer hours or better parking, for example.

Consider the example of Laura and Brad's import business. They were importing clothing from Guatemala, but with competition from hundreds of other small importers, it was hard to make a dime. Leaving Brad to manage the business for a few weeks, Laura spent some time working with a dozen weavers in a small Guatemalan town. They focused on creating specially woven and dyed fabric suitable for luxury window coverings. Realizing that the high end of the import business was an underexploited niche, Laura quickly created a product with a hard-to-copy look and a solid profit margin. In short, she transformed a not particularly savvy, barely profitable import business into a highly intelligent, highly profitable one.

In discussing the competition, it's important to put yourself in the shoes of a customer who is comparing your business to a competitor's. From the customer's perspective, what factors are most important in choosing which business to patronize? Some obvious considerations are quality of products or services, convenience (access), reliability, and price. Your competitors will probably excel in some of these areas and be weaker in others. The same will probably be true of your business. The trick is for you to find a spot, or niche, among the competition, and offer a combination of elements—such as price and convenience—that no one else offers.

 CAUTION

Think twice before competing on price. No matter how efficient your business is and how little you charge, someone will always charge less. Given the purchasing power and other efficiencies of big business, few small operators can successfully compete on pricing alone. Far better to look for another edge—quality, uniqueness, or customer convenience, to mention a few.

EXAMPLE: John wants to open a business to sell and service classic cars. In developing his business idea, he discovers that there are about a dozen existing companies within a 20-mile radius of his proposed location that already provide some or all of the services he envisions. Before finally committing to opening the business, he needs to identify and create a convincing competitive edge. One day, talking to a friend, he realizes that his edge could be a better system for finding parts. If he could locate new and used classic car parts nationwide, rather than just in his region, he would have a huge advantage over other shops. John begins by developing a database of websites that specialize in classic and reproduction car parts, organized by make and model. By using these online dealers—plus other dealers nationwide who aren't online, but whom John will get to know as he attends regional trade shows and does more national business—John will be able to get parts faster than any of his competitors. Putting some extra energy into the parts aspect of his business gives John a key marketing hook to convince his knowledgeable (and often finicky) customers that his business really is a step ahead.

Describe Your Marketing Strategy

By now you've shown that there are people out there who will buy your product or service from you instead of from your competitors. Great, but your job isn't done. Investors and others interested in supporting your business will want to know how you'll reach your customers in a cost-effective way. The answer to this question is, in a nutshell: marketing strategy.

RELATED TOPIC

Learn about marketing in Chapter 13: Small Business Marketing 101. Refer to that chapter for a detailed explanation of crafting a marketing strategy and using cost-effective tools. For the purposes of your business plan, you'll need at least a cursory description of your marketing approach. Some businesses may want to go a step further and draft a separate marketing plan.

Any marketing strategy worthy of the name should be based on the particular characteristics of the market you're trying to reach, with the goal of reaching as many customers as possible for the least expense. For instance, if you're trying to reach a very tiny group of people, such as left-handed ophthalmologists, or even a slightly larger audience, such as digital video editors, it makes no sense to spend the big bucks required for television advertising. On the other hand, if your market consists of all children between the ages of six and ten, TV advertising at the right times and on the right channels might be an efficient way to reach them.

In describing your plan for reaching your customers, explain what methods you will use, such as radio or newspaper advertising, online marketing, or directory listings, such as trade directories or the yellow pages. If you plan to use nontraditional guerrilla marketing tactics, such as putting up posters all around town or staging publicity stunts, explain exactly what you plan to do. And no matter what kind of marketing strategy you outline, be sure to explain why you think it will work.

Small businesses that don't have much of a marketing budget shouldn't be shy about their smaller-scale plans. Even if you don't plan to spend much (if any) money on marketing or advertising, you should have a plan for how you'll reach your first customers. In your business plan, simply explain what this strategy is. The following example shows how a small business with a minimal advertising and marketing budget might explain it's strategy.

EXAMPLE: Rather than spending money on traditional advertising, Turtlevision, a video postproduction firm, plans to keep its marketing costs very low, at least for the first year or two. The company plans to list its services in local video-related directories and use various online communities to promote the business. In addition, the company will offer services at a discount to various nonprofit organizations to develop a strong portfolio and to generate good word of mouth. (For example, it plans to offer discounted services to a nonprofit organization to stream educational videos online.) Turtlevision hopes that it will receive recommendations from satisfied customers that will give it a start in the right direction.

CAUTION

Spam is bad. No matter how delectable you find the potted meat product, do not fool yourself into believing that sending out masses of unsolicited emails (a practice known as "spamming") will be good for your business. Most Web-savvy entrepreneurs already know what nutritionists have told us for years: Spam is bad for you. At the very least, it's bad for any goodwill that may exist for your business. No one likes getting junk email, no matter what fabulous deal it may offer. Be a good Internet citizen and use more savory marketing tactics than spam.

TIP

Marketing without advertising can be successful. Especially in niche or local markets, people often make purchasing decisions based on the recommendations of people they respect, not on ads. If you doubt this, think about how you chose your dentist or plumber or the company that recently fixed your roof. Chances are good that you got a recommendation from someone you trusted. To be the beneficiary of positive word of mouth, you need to run an excellent business. Assuming you do, there are loads of cost-effective ways to let potential customers know about your great service. See Chapters 13 and 14 for more on the subject of marketing.

Describe Your Business Accomplishments

Above and beyond demonstrating the beauty of your business, you'll want to show that you're the right person to run it. Do this by creating a résumé showing your business accomplishments. Here you have the chance to highlight all of your relevant experience and training, as well as any other personal information likely to inspire confidence in you as a businessperson.

Prospective lenders and investors will want to know a number of things about you:

- **Do you understand the business?** Emphasize that you understand the basic tasks of the business inside and out. Surprisingly, lots of people start small businesses in areas where they are amateurs. For example, a person who isn't mechanically inclined but who loves German cars may want to open a VW repair shop. Lack of hands-on experience will likely be a red flag to investors, who know a nonexpert boss can't roll up his or her sleeves and help out in emergencies. Do your best to show them otherwise.

- **Can you manage people?** All sorts of organizations, including small businesses, fail because their leaders—no matter how technically competent—can't work well with others. Bad people management is one of the surest ways to create a poor workplace atmosphere, one with low morale, mediocre productivity, and high turnover. If you have successfully worked with, and preferably led, people, you should emphasize this experience.

- **Do you understand money?** A surprising number of people who open small businesses don't know how to manage—or make—money. Even though their business idea is a good, competitive one and their employees are energetic, they make such poor financial decisions that their businesses don't prosper. Knowing this, people who will consider funding your business will want to see if you or another key person in your business has money management skills. If you do—even if your experience was in a very different business—emphasize it.

Making Financial Projections

In addition to describing how your business will work, including how it will reach plenty of customers and fend off competitors, you'll also need to do some number crunching to show that your business will in fact turn a profit. All the rosy descriptions in the world won't make your business a success if the numbers turn up red.

Elissa Breitbard, founder of Betty's Bath & Day Spa in Albuquerque, New Mexico (www.bettysbath.com):

As time-consuming as it is to write a business plan, it is a critical factor to success—a symbolic security blanket. Our pre–start-up business plan bridged the chasm between the dream phase and a reality-based vision. In particular, churning out our first break-even analysis and cash flow statements was momentous, for the statements revealed the feasibility of our spa business. Even though the numbers weren't totally accurate (we have a lot more massage clients and fewer hot tub clients than projected), the important thing was to play with different scenarios and numbers and see that the business was, in fact, viable. The business plan helped us secure funding (not only from the bank, but also from family and friends) and provided me with a base of confidence—a concrete way to address some of the fears and issues that arise with taking a risk.

There's always talk about how many businesses fail; less discussed is the fact that the owners who have taken time to methodically set their business intentions in writing have a high rate of "making it."

Projecting the finances of your business may seem intimidating or difficult, but in reality, it's not terribly complex. Basically, it consists of making educated guesses about how much money you'll need to spend and how much you'll take in, then using these estimates to calculate whether your business will be sufficiently profitable.

Predicting and planning the finances of your business are critically important if you plan to seek start-up funding, either through lenders or investors. But even if you don't have plans to raise start-up money, you'll want to demonstrate to yourself that your business idea will fly. If your first projections show your business losing money, you'll have an opportunity while still in the planning stage to make sensible adjustments, such as raising your prices or cutting costs. If your projections show your customer base growing gradually, you can plan for how you will get through the initial lean months. If you neglect to make financial projections, you won't realize your plan is a money loser until you actually start losing money. At that point, it may be too late to turn things around.

Nonetheless, many new entrepreneurs avoid crunching their numbers, often due to fear that their estimates will be wildly off base and yield useless results. This is a poor reason to avoid forecasting your finances. If you do your best to make realistic predictions of expenses and revenues and accept that your guesstimates will not be absolutely correct, you can learn a great deal about what the financial side of your business is likely to look like in its early months and even years of operation. Even a somewhat inaccurate picture of your business's likely finances will be much more helpful than no picture at all.

For a basic understanding of your business's projected financial situation, you'll need to make the following estimates and calculations, all of which are discussed in detail in the rest of this chapter:

- **A break-even analysis.** Here you use income and expense estimates for a year or more to see whether, in theory at least, your business will be able to turn a profit. If you have trouble projecting a solid profit, you might need to consider abandoning your idea altogether.

- **A profit/loss forecast.** Here you'll refine the sales and expense estimates that you used for your break-even analysis into a formal, month-by-month projection of your business's net profit for at least the first year of operations.

- **A start-up cost estimate.** As the name suggests, this is simply the total of all the expenses you'll incur before your business opens. These costs should be included in your business plan to give a true picture of how much money you'll need to get your business off the ground.

- **A cash flow projection.** Even if your profit/loss forecast tells you that your business will have higher revenues than expenses, that doesn't mean that you'll always have enough cash available on key dates, such as when rent is due or when you need to buy more inventory. A cash flow projection lays out how much cash you'll have— or how much you'll be short—month by month. This lets you know if you'll need to get a credit line or set up other arrangements to make sure funds are available.

Clare Zurawski, Albuquerque regional manager of WESST, a New Mexico nonprofit dedicated to helping people start or grow their own businesses (www.wesst.org):

I consider a cash flow projection to be the heart of any business plan. It's a fantastic planning tool because it reflects so many facets of the enterprise, from market research to product pricing and production cost management. For a start-up business, two sets of projections can be really useful: one conservative set assuming a slow ramp-up phase, and another set reflecting either moderate or aggressive growth. If the lower end of the range is unacceptable, some fine-tuning of your margins is probably necessary.

Get to Know Your Numbers

The calculations involved in accounting aren't terribly complex. The main reason people get confused is not that they're bad at math—it's that they don't understand what the numbers mean. It's important that you take a little time early on to learn what your key financial numbers are, and how they relate to one another. To help you keep the numbers straight, keep in mind this formula:

	Sales revenue
−	Costs of sale (variable costs)
=	Gross profit
−	Overhead (fixed costs)
=	Net profit
−	Taxes
=	After-tax profit

You'll have a much easier time understanding all the various financial calculations involved in accounting—including break-even, profit/loss, and cash flow analysis—once you're familiar and comfortable with this basic formula.

The best way to do your financial projections is to use spreadsheet software such as Microsoft *Excel*. If you have never used spreadsheet software, take heart: It is quite easy to learn. Ask a friend to show you how it works or even tackle it yourself, and in a couple of hours you'll likely be able to start your number crunching in earnest.

It usually makes sense to develop your initial financial projections with spreadsheet software and not the fuller featured accounting software that you should use to track your actual income and expenses once your business launches. Accounting programs such as *QuickBooks* or *Sage Accounting* work great for ongoing bookkeeping and financial management, but are not nearly as flexible for the task of developing estimates and projections.

Also, it's generally wise to steer clear of business planning software, which is usually nothing more than a word processing function and some empty spreadsheets to fill in. Most readers of this book probably already have word processing and spreadsheet software, which will offer better and fuller features than whatever is offered with a business plan program.

The rest of this chapter will walk you through each of these financial forecasts. When you're done, you should be able to tell whether your business will actually make enough money to pay the bills and turn a profit. Assuming the answer is yes, you'll also see whether you need to obtain start-up money from investors or lenders and, if so, how much. Finally, once your business is up and running, you can refer back to your forecasts to see how your performance is measuring up.

Break-Even Analysis

Your break-even point is the point at which the income you'll bring in just covers your expenses. Expenses include the costs of providing your product or service (also known as variable costs, because they change depending on how many products or services you provide), plus your overhead, like rent, salaries, and utility bills (commonly called fixed costs).

 FORM

Break-Even Analysis Worksheet. The Nolo website includes a downloadable interactive worksheet to help you calculate your break-even point. See Appendix B for the link to this worksheet and other forms in this book.

Because break-even analysis offers a glimpse of your ultimate profitability, it's a great tool for weeding out losing business ideas. For example, if you see that you'll need to achieve a highly optimistic sales number just to cover your costs, you should rethink your entire business plan. Maybe you'll figure out a way to adjust parts of your business so that you can realize a profit from lower sales. If not, it might be best to ditch your less-than-brilliant business idea.

To find your break-even point, first make a best-guess estimate of your sales revenue for the products or services you plan to sell. Then predict how much profit you'll make on each sale (by subtracting the costs of the sale from the revenue it generates) and figure out a "gross profit percentage," which tells you how much of each sales dollar exceeds the cost of the product or service itself. Finally, estimate what your fixed costs, such as rent and insurance, will be. After a few calculations, you'll see whether the profit you'll make on each individual sale (also called gross profit) will cover your fixed costs.

Before examining the details of calculating your break-even point, let's look at a simple example to illustrate the overall process. All the calculations are explained in more detail below; for now, just focus on the process as a whole.

EXAMPLE: Michele is starting a side business selling her own handmade jewelry. To calculate her break-even point, she makes her very best estimate of how much jewelry she thinks she could sell in a year. She figures she could sell an average of 20 pieces a month at $20 apiece, making her yearly income $4,800. Then she figures out how much she'd make on each sale, above the cost of materials. (For this super-simplified example, let's leave the cost of her time out of the equation.) Since the materials for each piece cost Michele $5, she'd be making $15 on each sale. In other words, her gross profit would be $15 per piece. Next she calculates her gross profit percentage, which is her gross profit ($15) divided by her selling price ($20). This puts her gross profit percentage at 75%, which means that $0.75 of each sales dollar exceeds the cost of the piece of jewelry itself. Next Michele would figure out what her fixed costs would be—say, the cost of her tools and the monthly fee for her booth at a local arts and crafts mall. She figures that these fixed costs total $50 per month, or $600 per year.

To calculate her break-even point, Michele will *divide* her annual fixed costs ($600) by her gross profit percentage ($0.75) to arrive at a break-even point of $800. This means that just to cover the costs of the materials and her tools and booth, Michele must bring in $800 per year. Anything above that amount will be her pretax profit. Since she earlier estimated that she could sell $4,800 worth of jewelry per year, Michele figures that she'll easily reach her break-even point—and make a $4,000 profit, as well.

How to Use the Break-Even Analysis Worksheet

To use the break-even analysis worksheet on the Nolo website, follow the steps outlined below. Each step is also explained in greater detail later in this section. You should read the detailed information before using the worksheet. Enter figures into only white cells; do not enter anything in blue cells.

Step 1: Enter your estimated total annual revenues. This figure will not be used in the worksheet calculations but will help you in the next step, in which you will break down your estimated revenues into categories.

Step 2: This step will result in an average gross profit percentage for your business as a whole, based on calculations for up to three categories of products or services your business will provide. First, enter the name for the category, then enter an average sales price, variable cost, and estimated revenues for each category. The total of your estimated revenues for all categories should equal your estimated total annual revenues from

Step 1. If they do not, the worksheet will still calculate an average gross profit percentage based on the total of your category revenue estimates. However, you may want to evaluate why your category revenue estimates do not match the estimate for your business as a whole. Once you have entered numbers for all categories you plan to use (you do not need to use all three categories), your average gross profit percentage for your business as a whole will be displayed at the bottom of the section.

Step 3: Enter the type and amount of all fixed costs you anticipate for your business. Enter monthly figures; the worksheet will automatically calculate an annual amount.

Result: The worksheet will show you your break-even point, which is the amount of revenue you'll need to bring in before your business starts making any profits.

Before explaining exactly how to do the calculations, this chapter quickly discusses two items that you need to understand before actually crunching your numbers: making financial estimates and categorizing your expenses.

Making Estimates

When you estimate your income and expenses, your estimates should extend over enough time to catch up with seasonal fluctuations. Depending on your type of business, your revenue and expenses may vary wildly from month to month. For example, if you plan to manufacture custom snowboards, most of your sales will be in the late fall and early winter months, while the opposite would be true if you made surfboards. A good way to account for this is to make estimates for each month of the year, then add them up to get a yearly figure. In making these estimates, it is wise to cover at least a one-year period, which is enough time to account for normal ups and downs, but not so long as to be overly speculative.

Categorizing Your Expenses

Your business expenses break down into two categories: fixed expenses (fixed costs) and variable expenses (variable costs). This division is not only important for your break-even analysis, it's also a standard method of categorizing expenses

for accounting and tax reporting. The difference is explained here:

- **Fixed costs.** Commonly referred to as "overhead," these include all regular expenses not directly tied to the product or service you provide. Rent, utility bills, phone bills, payments for outside help, such as bookkeeping services, postage, and most salaries (except in service businesses) are common fixed costs.

- **Variable costs.** These costs—sometimes also called product costs, costs of goods sold (or COGs), or costs of sale—are directly related to the products or services you provide and include inventory, packaging, supplies, materials, and sometimes labor used in providing your product or service. They're called "variable" precisely because they go up or down depending on the volume of products or services you produce or sell. In the case of services, one of the biggest variable expenses is almost always the wages or salary of the service provider. (See "Salaries and Labor Costs— Fixed or Variable?" below, for a more complete explanation.)

Estimate Your Sales Revenue

Start your break-even analysis by making your best estimate of annual sales revenues. Your estimate will obviously depend on several different variables, such as your type of business, what you plan to charge for each product or service you'll offer, and how successful you'll be at selling products and services.

Though at first it may seem overwhelming to project revenues based on so many untested variables, it is essential that you take the plunge and try out some numbers. Even though your estimates won't be anywhere near 100% accurate, they'll force you to focus and refine key elements of your business idea and may even help you spot big potholes in your plan. And besides, you need these estimates before you can move ahead with your break-even calculations, so get over it and start estimating.

RELATED TOPIC

Pricing help still to come. There are many issues to consider and various methods to use when figuring out how much to charge for your goods and services. Pricing issues are addressed separately, in Chapter 6, where you'll also find info on service billing options and how to put together solid bids and proposals.

One good way to estimate how much money you'll be bringing in is to compare your business to similar ones. Retail businesses, for example, often measure annual sales revenue per square foot of retail space. Thus, if you plan to open a pet supply store, you'll want to find out the annual sales revenue per square foot of other pet supply shops. Direct competitors probably won't share this information with you, but industry trade publications almost always provide it. Attending industry trade shows where you can meet and talk with people who own similar businesses in other parts of the country is another good way to gather valuable information.

EXAMPLE: Inga is planning to open a used bookstore in Milwaukee called Inga's Book Haus. She plans to sell mostly used books, which generally have a high profit margin, but she'll also stock a limited selection of new books at the front of the store to attract more customers. She'll sell some miscellaneous trinkets, such as postcards and magnets, as well.

To figure out how much sales revenue she can realistically expect for Inga's Book Haus, Inga calls up a couple of friends who are in the book business. One who works at a nearby used bookstore confides to Inga that the store sells approximately $450 worth of books per square foot per year. Another friend owns a new-and-used bookstore in Madison; she tells Inga that they bring in about $400 annually per square foot. Neither of these stores is exactly like the one Inga envisions; the one in Milwaukee doesn't sell any new books, and the one in Madison does a healthy trade in textbooks, which Inga doesn't expect at her store. To round out her information, Inga also looks into some trade publications and does a bit of sleuthing at local new-and-used bookstores, examining their prices and how busy they seem to be. Ultimately she decides that an annual income of $350 per square foot is realistic. She has her eye on a few storefronts, all around 1,200 square feet, so she estimates her annual revenues to be $420,000.

Basing your projected revenue on the numbers of similar companies also works for nonretail businesses such as wholesaling or manufacturing companies—but it can be somewhat tricky to find a solid basis for comparison. Unlike retail businesses, sales per square foot doesn't really apply. If you're not already well-acquainted with your field, you'll have to do some research. Study similar businesses to find out how many employees they have, how wide their distribution is, and how much annual income they earn. Base your income projections on similarly sized businesses with a comparable range of distribution.

If yours is a service business, your estimate of sales revenue will depend on how many billable sales you'll be able to make each month. A big part of this calculation is how many hours you and any employees will work and how much you'll be paid per hour by your clients. But don't overlook the fact that all of your time won't be billable—you won't be providing

Salaries and Labor Costs—Fixed or Variable?

Whether you'll categorize labor expenses as fixed or variable costs often depends on the type of workers you pay and the kinds of products or services you're selling. Salaries or wages of the managers and employees who are necessary to keep your business going (you or your bookkeeper, for example) are usually best seen as fixed costs. But salaries or wages for employees who create the products or provide the services you sell may be more appropriately treated as variable costs. For example, an ad agency that pays six freelance copywriters to service clients' accounts should treat their paychecks as variable costs.

To figure out whether a labor cost should be designated as fixed or variable, ask yourself: If I sell one, ten, or 100 more products or services this week, will my labor costs go up? If not, you're probably looking at a fixed cost. For instance, suppose you're trying to decide whether your receptionist's salary should be categorized as a variable cost or a fixed cost. If you produce and sell 100 more Snuggie blankets, will your reception costs go up? Probably not. So your receptionist's salary should be part of your overhead. But if you have to hire five temporary employees to answer the phones at Christmas time to handle the spiking demand for Snuggies, their wages should be classified as variable costs. (Hint: Money paid to workers who are temps or independent contractors is usually categorized as variable costs, because those payments are usually tied to providing a product or service.) Of course, if you sell more products or services regularly, you'll probably decide to expand your business and increase your overhead, because you'll have to hire more support staff, managers, and other necessary employees just to get along. At that point, you might revisit your allocation of fixed and variable costs.

services every hour you're at work. For example, if you run a landscaping business, a sizable portion of your time will be spent not performing landscaping work but managing your accounts, maintaining your equipment, and soliciting new clients. You'll need to make a realistic assessment of how much of your time will be taken up by these nonbillable activities and how much time you'll spend providing actual services to clients to get an accurate picture of how much money will be flowing in.

Calculate Your Average Gross Profit Percentage

Your next task is to figure your average gross profit percentage. It may sound complex, but basically it's just a figure that represents how much of each sales dollar will be left over after paying for the costs of the products or services themselves. There are a number of steps involved in calculating this figure, but none involves anything more than simple math: addition, subtraction, multiplication, and division. Once you know your average gross profit percentage, you'll easily be able to figure out how much money you'll need to bring in to cover all the costs of your business.

In a nutshell, to figure your average gross profit percentage you'll need to:

1. Figure out your gross profit for each major category of your products or services.

2. Determine an average gross profit for your business overall, including all your products and services.

3. Divide your average gross profit by your average selling price.

In case you're wondering what the difference is between "gross profit" and "average gross profit," here's a quick explanation. (The details will be covered while going through the calculations, below.) When you sell an individual product, the money that you earn above the cost of the item itself (called your variable cost, or sometimes cost of goods) is called gross profit. For instance, if your pet store sells a doghouse for $200, and you bought the doghouse for $110, then what's left over for you after the sale is $90: your gross profit. If your business sells more than one kind of product, you'll need to calculate an *average* gross profit for your total product line to get a realistic figure. The average gross profit for your pet store would include all of your products in the calculation—cat scratching posts, pet food, play toys, and so on—including their sales prices and what they cost you.

The next few subsections take you through the process of calculating your business's average gross profit.

Figure Your Gross Profit by Category

As described above, your gross profit is the amount of money you make on each sale, above what it costs you for the product or service itself—that is, the variable cost or cost of sale. Gross profit is determined simply by subtracting the variable cost of your product or service from its sales price.

Variable costs are generally fairly easy to estimate. If you're selling products bought from a wholesaler, your variable costs may be as simple as what you pay for the products themselves. If you'll assemble the products, then include your costs for the parts and labor needed to put them together. Also remember to include items such as packaging or freebies in your variable costs.

If you sell only services, variable costs basically include what you pay to whomever provides the services (you or perhaps an employee), not including time spent on administrative tasks and managing accounts, which is generally considered to be a fixed, not variable, cost. It can sometimes be tricky to figure out the variable costs of a service business. Do your best to separate out the costs that are not associated with individual projects—those are your fixed costs.

EXAMPLE: Turtlevision, a digital video editing service, pays its staff editor $50 per hour for 80 hours per month of editing work. In addition, Turtlevision pays an office assistant $15 per hour for 100 hours per month of administrative work. Turtlevision's monthly variable costs would include the editor's salary of $4,000, but not the salary paid to the office assistant, which is not tied to any particular client or project.

One kink in figuring out your business's gross profit is that your selling prices and variable costs may vary a great deal from product to product (or service to service). For instance, say you buy cat collars for an average of $4, and sell them for an average price of $10 (your gross profit per cat collar would be $6). Doghouses, on the other hand, cost you an average of $110, and you sell them for an average price of $200 (your gross profit per doghouse would be $90).

To account for these differences, you should categorize your products or services and figure an average gross profit for each category. There are a few steps to follow, but hang in there—each one is pretty simple.

First, estimate the average selling price and average variable cost for products or services with roughly similar selling prices and variable costs. For instance, you might group all your animal collars together— for cats, dogs, and ferrets—since their selling prices ($9 to $13) and variable costs ($3 to $5) aren't too different. Don't lump together products or services with considerably different selling prices or variable costs. As a general rule, the more tightly you define your categories, the more accurate your estimates will be.

After you've estimated the average selling price and average variable cost for each category, subtract the average variable cost from the average selling price for each category, and you'll have an average gross profit dollar figure for each category.

	Animal collars	Bird-houses	Dog-houses
Average selling price	$ 11	$ 60	$ 200
– Average variable cost	4	30	110
= Average gross profit	$ 7	$ 30	$ 90

The next step is to figure out a gross profit percentage for each category. A gross profit percentage tells you how much of each dollar of sales income is gross profit. To calculate each category's gross profit percentage, divide the average gross profit figure by the average selling price.

Animal collars category:

Average gross profit	$ 7
÷ Average selling price	$ 11
= Gross profit percentage	63.6%

Using the above example, it follows that if you sold $1,500 in cat collars, 63.6% of that—$954—would be gross profit, or the amount left over after paying costs of sale. As you can see, converting your gross profit into a percentage allows you to quickly figure out how much of your income will be left over after variable costs have been covered.

Calculate Your Average Gross Profit

After you've found the gross profit percentage for each category, you'll be able to determine your average gross profit for your business as a whole.

First, estimate your annual sales revenue per category. Earlier you estimated your total annual sales revenues; now divide that figure as best you can into your estimates for each category. For example, if you estimated total annual revenues of $100,000 for your pet supply business, divide that among your categories, such as collars, birdhouses, and doghouses— say $25,000 in collar sales, $40,000 in birdhouses, and $35,000 in doghouses. Base your division on your best sense of which categories and products will make up a big part of your business, and which will have a smaller share. Then, for each product category, multiply the estimated sales revenue by the category's gross profit percentage (arrived at above) to figure out your total gross profit dollars per category.

Animal collars category:

Estimated sales revenue	$ 25,000
× Gross profit percentage	63.6%
= Total gross profit	$ 15,900

Finally, add together the gross profit dollar amounts for each category to arrive at a total annual gross profit for your business. Divide the total annual gross profit figure by the total annual sales that you estimated for all products or services. The result will be an average gross profit percentage for your business.

Let's look at how this process works with Inga's Book Haus.

EXAMPLE: As you may recall, Inga plans to sell new and used books, plus some peripheral items, such as postcards and refrigerator magnets. Because the profit margins for new books, used books, and trinkets are different, Inga figures a gross profit percentage for each of these categories. (Inga might want to establish separate categories for hardback, paperback, and coffee table books, but we'll keep things simple.)

To accomplish this, first Inga estimates an average variable cost for each category. In addition to the cost of the merchandise, she includes the cost of free bags, bookmarks, and wrapping paper for gifts. For instance, used books cost her an average of $3, and she figures the bookmarks and bags that go with each sale will cost her an average of $0.10. So her total average variable cost in the used book category is $3.10. She doesn't include fixed costs, such as rent or salaries, here.

Next, Inga fills in an average selling price for each product category. Her average selling price for used books, for example, is $7. She then subtracts the average variable cost (arrived at above) from the average selling price to get an average gross profit figure for each product category. Subtracting her average variable cost for used books ($3.10) from her average selling price for used books ($7) leaves her with an average gross profit for used books of $3.90.

Used book category:

	Average sales price	$ 7.00
−	Average variable cost	3.10
=	Average gross profit	$ 3.90

Inga does the same calculation for new books, which also shows an average gross profit at $3.90, and trinkets, which has an average gross profit of $1.40.

To determine the gross profit percentage, she'll simply divide the gross profit by the selling price in each category to get a gross profit percentage for each category. Dividing her average gross profit for used books ($3.90) by her average selling price ($7) gives Inga a gross profit percentage of 56% for used books. That means that for every dollar she'll bring in from used books, $.044 will be eaten up on Inga's costs, leaving $0.56 to cover fixed costs and go towards a net profit. Her gross profit percentage is 33% for new books and 70% for trinkets.

New book category:

	Average gross profit	$ 3.90
÷	Average selling price	12.00
=	Gross profit percentage	33%

Trinkets category:

	Average gross profit	$ 1.40
÷	Average selling price	2.00
=	Gross profit percentage	70%

Using the gross profit percentages and estimated sales revenues for each category, Inga can calculate the gross profit dollar figure for each category. For example, her estimated annual sales of used books is $300,000. (Remember that Inga estimated her total annual sales revenue to be $420,000. She thinks used books will account for a little over two-thirds of her sales.) By multiplying $300,000 by the used book category's gross profit percentage (56%), she estimates an annual gross profit of $168,000. Adding up the gross profit figures for each category, Inga figures that her total gross profit will be $215,000. Finally, by dividing this amount by her annual estimated revenues of $420,000, she easily determines her overall average gross profit percentage, which is 51.2%.

	New books	Used books	Trinkets
Average variable cost per product	$ 8.00	$ 3.00	$ 0.50
+ Bookmarks, bags	0.10	0.10	0.10
= Average total cost	$ 8.10	$ 3.10	$ 0.60
Average selling price	$ 12.00	$ 7.00	$ 2.00
− Average total variable cost	8.10	3.10	0.60
= Average gross profit	$ 3.90	$ 3.90	$ 1.40
Average gross profit	$ 3.90	$ 3.90	$ 1.40
÷ Average selling price	12.00	7.00	2.00
= Gross profit percentage	33%	56%	70%
Average sales	$ 100,000	$ 300,000	$ 20,000
x Gross profit percentage	33%	56%	70%
= Annual gross profit	$ 33,000	$ 168,000	$ 14,000

Annual gross profit	
New books	$ 33,000
+ Used books	168,000
+ Trinkets	14,000
= Total annual gross profit	$ 215,000
÷ Total annual sales	$ 420,000
= Average gross profit percentage	51.2%

Estimate Your Fixed Costs

You're done with the hard part. Compared to calculating your gross profit percentage, fixed costs are a breeze. Simply estimate your monthly fixed expenses, including items such as rent, utility bills, office supplies—basically, any anticipated costs that don't depend on the product or service you sell. Because many of these costs recur monthly, it's usually easiest to estimate them per month and total them for one year. It's also a good idea to throw in a little extra (10% or so) to cover unpredictable miscellaneous expenses. Once you've arrived at a total, you'll know you'll need to make at least this much gross profit (and probably more) to keep your business afloat.

EXAMPLE: Here is a list of Inga's monthly estimates for fixed costs.

Rent	$ 3,500
Wages for part-time clerks	2,500
Utilities	800
Telephone	700
Office equipment	700
Insurance	500
Advertising	700
Accounting	300
Electronic payment system fees	300
Misc.	1,000
Total fixed expenses per month	$ 11,000
Total fixed expenses per month	$ 11,000
x Number of months in a year	12
Annual total fixed expenses	$ 132,000

CAUTION

Don't forget you have to eat.
Notice that Inga has chosen not to list a salary here as an expense. She, like many solo operators, figures that her savings, help from friends and family, and some extra crumbs the business may produce should be enough to live on for the short term. Once she figures out how much profit the business will bring in regularly, she'll decide how much profit she can expect to take out of the business and add that number to her fixed costs. Leaving out payments for your own living expenses in your break-even analysis, however, can be dangerous, at least if you're planning to live off your business's profits from the get-go. If this is your plan, you should add to your fixed costs the minimum amount you'll need to take out of the business to cover your living expenses. Then, if you can't project your income to be higher than your fixed costs when the amount you'll need for living expenses is included, you'll know you can't plan on living off the company. This may be a clue that your business is not a good bet.

TIP

Keep fixed costs as low as reasonably possible. If your business is slow to get started—and lots of businesses take months or even years to become solidly profitable—high fixed costs can quickly eat up your savings. Rather than committing yourself to high overhead, it's usually better to keep expenses low, allowing increases only when your income justifies spending more. For example, few businesses really depend on a pricey physical location for their success. If your business won't depend on a big casual walk-in trade, don't overpay for a trendy zip code. Operating from a low-cost warehouse district, an older office building, or even your garage may work just fine, at least at the beginning.

Calculate Your Break-Even Point

Once you have estimated your average gross profit percentage and your fixed costs, it's easy to figure out how much revenue you'll need to break even. Remember, your gross profit percentage represents how much of each dollar of revenue is actual profit, left over after paying for the product or service itself. To figure out your break-even point, you'll divide your estimated annual fixed costs by your gross profit percentage. The result will be the amount of sales revenue you'll need to bring in just to cover your costs.

EXAMPLE: The break-even point for Inga's Book Haus will equal her annual fixed expenses divided by her average gross profit percentage.

	Annual fixed expenses	$ 132,000
÷	Average gross profit percentage	51.2%
=	Break-even point	$ 257,813

If you're having trouble understanding how this equation works, you're not alone. Conceptually, it's a little tricky to see how dividing your fixed costs by your gross profit percentage yields your break-even point. Think of it this way: However much money your business brings in, some of it will be eaten up by the cost of the product or service itself (your variable costs), leaving you a reduced amount left over to pay your bills. How much is left over is determined by your gross profit percentage—this number tells you just how much will be left over, on average, from each dollar, after paying for your product or service itself (your variable costs). When you divide your estimated annual fixed costs by your gross profit percentage, the resulting number (the break-even point) is the exact amount that's enough to cover your fixed costs.

EXAMPLE: Another extra-simplified example should help illustrate this concept. Michele (from my earlier example) plans to go into business selling jewelry. Her gross profit percentage was 75%, meaning that for every dollar she brought in, $0.25 would be eaten up by the cost of the jewelry materials, leaving Michele $0.75 to cover her fixed costs. Michele's fixed costs were $600 per year. So, you're wondering, why isn't Michele's break-even point $600? Because if Michele earned exactly $600 in a year, only 75% of that would be available to cover her fixed costs—the other 25% would have already been eaten up by the costs of her jewelry, leaving her unable to pay all of the $600 in fixed costs. To account for this, Michele needs to divide her fixed costs ($600) by her gross profit percentage (0.75) to arrive at the higher amount that she'll need to bring in to cover her fixed costs and her variable costs. Dividing $600 by 0.75 results in $800, her break-even point; if Michele brings in $800, 25% of it will go toward the cost of the product, and the rest ($600) is just enough to cover her fixed costs.

Analyze Your Result

If your estimated revenue exceeds your break-even point, great—but that's not the same thing as saying you are free to put the excess money in your pocket. Again, remember that every dollar you bring in doesn't come for free; you had to pay something for the cost of your product or service (variable costs). The portion of excess sales revenue that's really yours (ignoring taxes for the moment) is equivalent to your gross profit percentage of that excess revenue. To determine how much of the excess revenue is pretax profit, multiply the excess by your gross profit percentage. The result is your estimated net profit.

EXAMPLE: Earlier, Inga (the used bookstore owner) estimated her annual sales revenue to be $420,000—over $160,000 more than she needs to break even.

	Estimated revenue	$	420,000
−	Break-even point		257,813
=	Excess revenues	$	162,187

To figure out how much of her excess revenue will be actual pretax profit, Inga multiplies it by her gross profit percentage.

	Excess revenues	$	162,187
×	Gross profit percentage		51.2%
=	Net profit	$	83,040

Inga is happy to see her projections show a profit. But she needs to remember that none of her estimates included any payments to herself, meaning she'll probably need to take some of that net profit just to meet her living expenses.

If, on the other hand, your break-even point is higher than your expected revenues, you'll have some decisions to make. For example, you'll have to decide whether certain aspects of your plan can be amended to come up with an achievable break-even point. For instance, perhaps you could find a less expensive source of supplies, do without an employee, or save rent by working out of your home.

But don't change your numbers without a very good reason. When confronted by a break-even point that exceeds your estimated revenues, you may be tempted to tweak and squish your numbers into a profitable forecast, even if those numbers aren't realistic. Unless you really do have a good reason to think you can break even at a lower point, you'd be wise to guard against this temptation. For example, to have your plan pencil out in the black, you might boost your sales estimates in hopes that you'll somehow be able to pull it off. But can you really sell 50,000 Sausage Shooters™, 3,000 books on medieval dentistry, or 2,000 Grumpy Cat mini-tees per month?

Generally speaking, when trying to pencil out a more profitable break-even point, it's best to focus on your costs. The most reliable way to tilt a business from the red to the black is to reduce what you will pay out, not to make a more optimistic projection of what you'll take in.

Profit/Loss Forecast

If your break-even analysis shows that, based on realistic estimates of revenue and expenses, your business will turn a profit, your next job is to use these figures to create the profit/loss forecast component of your business plan. Similar to a break-even analysis, a profit/loss forecast (sometimes called a P & L forecast) uses your estimates for sales revenue and variable costs to calculate your gross profit, then subtracts your fixed expenses from gross profit to arrive at net profit.

If you use accounting software, it will generate a P & L statement automatically once you enter monthly sales and expense estimates. You can also use the worksheet on this book's companion page on Nolo. com, as described below.

 FORM

Profit/Loss Forecast Worksheet. The Nolo website includes a downloadable interactive worksheet to help you do a profit/ loss forecast. See Appendix B for the link to this worksheet and other forms in this book.

Inga's Book Haus Profit/Loss Forecast: Year One Total

	Jan	Feb	Mar	April	May
Sales Revenues	$ 30,000	$ 35,000	$ 35,000	$ 35,000	$ 35,000
Gross Profit (51.2%)	15,360	17,920	17,920	17,920	17,920
Fixed Expenses					
Rent	4,500	4,500	4,500	4,500	4,500
Salaries	2,500	2,500	2,500	2,500	2,500
Utilities	250	250	250	250	250
Telephone	250	250	250	250	250
Office Equipment	700	700	700	700	700
Insurance	500	500	500	500	500
Advertising	700	700	700	700	700
Accounting	300	300	300	300	300
Fees for Electronic Payment System	300	300	300	300	300
Miscellaneous	1,000	1,000	1,000	1,000	1,000
Total Fixed Expenses	11,000	11,000	11,000	11,000	11,000
Net Profit (Loss)	$ 4,360	$ 6,920	$ 6,920	$ 6,920	$ 6,920

	June	July	Aug	Sept	Oct	Nov	Dec	Year Total
	$ 35,000	$ 35,000	$ 35,000	$ 35,000	$ 35,000	$ 35,000	$ 40,000	$ 420,000
	17,920	17,920	17,920	17,920	17,920	17,920	20,480	215,040
	4,500	4,500	4,500	4,500	4,500	4,500	4,500	54,000
	2,500	2,500	2,500	2,500	2,500	2,500	2,500	30,000
	250	250	250	250	250	250	250	3,000
	250	250	250	250	250	250	250	3,000
	700	700	700	700	700	700	700	8,400
	500	500	500	500	500	500	500	6,000
	700	700	700	700	700	700	700	8,400
	300	300	300	300	300	300	300	3,600
	300	300	300	300	300	300	300	3,600
	1,000	1,000	1,000	1,000	1,000	1,000	1,000	12,000
	11,000	11,000	11,000	11,000	11,000	11,000	11,000	132,000
	$ 6,920	$ 6,920	$ 6,920	$ 6,920	$ 6,920	$ 6,920	$ 9,480	$ 83,040

The main difference between a P & L and a break-even analysis has to do with timing. A break-even analysis looks at profit and loss on a yearly basis, while your P & L forecast calculates monthly net profit. A P & L forecast also differs from a cash flow projection (discussed below) in the kinds of income and expenses that it includes. A cash flow projection looks at all sources of income and expenses, including loans, transfers of personal money into the business, start-up costs, and all other types of cash inflows and outflows. A P & L forecast, on the other hand, is only concerned with money earned from normal business operations. For this reason, a P & L forecast will tell you whether your business operations are generating enough income to cover your expenses, which is something you can't glean from a cash flow projection.

Here's how to translate your break-even figures into a profit/loss forecast: Start by breaking down your annual sales estimate into monthly amounts. If you expect significant seasonal fluctuations in sales, account for them here.

Next, figure your gross profit for each month. The easiest way to do this is to multiply each month's sales revenue by the

---

How to Use the Profit/Loss Worksheet

To use the profit/loss worksheet on the Nolo website, follow the steps outlined below. Each step is explained in greater detail elsewhere in this section. You should read the detailed information before using the worksheet. Enter figures into only white cells; do not enter anything in blue cells.

Step 1: Enter your estimated sales revenues for each month. If you will be starting a business in a month other than January, you may change the months to begin with your starting month.

Step 2: Enter the average gross profit percentage for your business as a whole. You need to enter this figure just once, in the first column under "January." The worksheet will automatically enter it for every other month.

Step 3: Enter your anticipated fixed expenses for each month. The worksheet uses common categories, and contains some rows you may customize for expenses specific to your business. If you do not anticipate a certain type of expense, you may leave cells blank.

Result: When you have entered estimated sales revenues, a gross profit percentage, and fixed costs for all months, the worksheet will display your estimated net profit or loss for each month.

gross profit percentage for your business as a whole, which you calculated earlier. (If you rounded off your gross profit percentage, you'll get a slightly different gross profit figure here than you did in your break-even analysis.)

Enter your monthly fixed expenses by category, and add them together to get monthly totals. Then, for each month, subtract your total fixed expenses from your gross profit and enter the result in the net profit row. If the result is a negative number, it means your expenses are more than your gross profit. Put parentheses around the result; in accounting symbols, a number in parentheses is a negative number.

EXAMPLE: Inga's one-year profit/loss forecast for her bookstore is shown earlier in this chapter.

CAUTION

Your profit/loss forecast doesn't include the whole picture. Other income and costs such as loans and start-up expenses aren't included in your P & L forecast, which reflects only money earned and spent as part of providing your products or services. For the full picture of all money that comes into and goes out from your business—including start-up costs, loans, taxes, and other money that isn't earned or spent as part of your core business operation—you'll need to do a cash flow analysis. (See "Cash Flow Projection," below, for a complete explanation.)

A completed P & L forecast will outline your business's profitability month by month. If your expenses are higher than revenues for a month or two, don't panic—most start-up businesses lose money for at least a few months—but you will need to figure out how to make it through these lean months (for example, by getting a start-up loan). More important in the big picture is whether you can see a trend toward stable profitability. If not, you may need to revisit parts of your plan (or possibly scrap your idea altogether). But, as mentioned earlier, resist the temptation to inflate your sales estimates; a more realistic approach is to lower your costs. Once you have a P & L forecast that shows consistent profits each month, based on realistic estimates, you're ready to move forward.

Start-Up Cost Estimate

If your profit/loss forecast shows your projected income will be higher than expenses each month, that's a positive sign. But beware that you haven't yet accounted for an important category of expenses: business start-up costs. The worst part about start-up costs is that you need to pay them before your business is actually making any money. That's why you should have a firm grasp on what you really need to spend to successfully start your business, along with a plan for where that money will come from. Of course, potential lenders or investors will want to see that you've accounted for these costs in your planning. But it's also important that you understand for yourself how high this initial financial hurdle will be so that you can figure out how to clear it. Obviously, you don't want to start a business with high start-up costs but low projected profits, since it will take you far too long to recover your initial investment.

CAUTION

Buy only what your business really needs. Too many new small business owners weigh down their new enterprises with unneeded start-up costs. Unless a particular item is absolutely necessary to generate revenue, don't buy it—or, if you do, spend as little as possible on it. Sure, you need a desk, but unless customers will see it (and sometimes even if they will), buying a secondhand desk for $80 makes a lot more sense than paying $800 for a new one.

Compared to the projections explained earlier, estimating your start-up costs is a breeze—just list them and add them up. Include items like business registration fees and tax deposits you need to pay up front; rent and security deposits you'll have to pay before business starts; and costs of any initial inventory, office supplies, equipment, and anything else you'll have to cover before your business starts bringing in money.

EXAMPLE: Inga makes a list of the start-up expenses she expects to pay before she'll start selling books.

Initial inventory	$	15,000
Shelving and furniture		5,000
Rent deposit (security deposit and last month's rent)		7,000
Office supplies, stationery		500
Point-of-sale tablet		500
Business registration fees		200
TOTAL START-UP EXPENSES	$	28,200

If you don't have enough cash to pay all of your start-up costs out of pocket, you'll either need to come up with the money or figure out a way to spread the costs over the first few months of business, when you'll have at least some cash flowing in. For instance, maybe you could lease, rather than buy, needed equipment.

The next and final financial projection you'll need to do as part of your business plan—a cash flow projection—will help you plan and manage your incoming and outgoing cash so that you can cover needed expenses when they come due.

Cash Flow Projection

To round out the collection of financial information in your business plan, you should include a cash flow projection. Though your profit/loss forecast may show that your business should make enough sales at a high enough price to cover your estimated expenses, a cash flow projection analyzes whether the cash from those sales, as well as from other sources, such as loans or investments, will come in fast enough to pay your bills on time. Cash flow management is important once your business is up and running, especially if you plan to stock a good-sized inventory or extend credit to customers. A high sales volume won't be enough to cover your expenses if your customers are slow to pay you and your checking account is empty.

 FORM

Cash Flow Projection Worksheet. The Nolo website includes a downloadable interactive worksheet to help you do a cash flow forecast. See Appendix B for the link to this worksheet and other forms in this book.

How to Use the Cash Flow Projection Worksheet

To use the cash flow projection worksheet on the Nolo website, follow the steps outlined below. Each step is explained in greater detail later in this section. You should read the detailed information before using the worksheet. Enter figures into only white cells; do not enter anything in blue cells.

Step 1: Enter any cash you expect to have in the bank at the beginning of the period for which you are doing a cash flow projection. You may change the months to begin with a month other than January. For most start-up businesses, the amount you enter here will be zero. Do not enter any amounts beyond the first month. The worksheet will automatically add any estimated cash available at the end of each month to your cash available for the next month.

Step 2: In the "Cash-Ins" section, enter any estimated paid sales (not credit sales) you expect, plus any loans or other money you intend to put into the business.

Step 3: In the "Cash-Outs" section, enter the amounts you expect to pay out from your business, in the month you expect to make the payments. The worksheet uses common categories and contains some rows you may customize for expenses specific to your business. If you do not anticipate a certain type of expense, you may leave cells blank.

Result: When you have entered all anticipated cash-ins and cash-outs, the worksheet will display your projected cash flow.

Inga's Book Haus Cash Flow Projection: Year One

	Dec	Jan	Feb	Mar	April	May
Cash at Beginning of Month	$ 0	$ (17,200)	$(16,540)	$ (8,920)	$ (3,400)	$ 4,220
Cash-Ins						
Sales Paid	0	30,000	35,000	35,000	35,000	35,000
Loans and Transfers	15,000	0	0	0	0	0
Total Cash-Ins	15,000	12,800	18,460	26,080	31,600	39,220
Cash-Outs						
Start-up Costs	28,200	0	0	0	0	0
Books & Other Products	0	14,640	17,080	17,080	17,080	17,080
Rent	3,500	4,500	4,500	4,500	4,500	4,500
Salaries	0	2,500	2,500	2,500	2,500	2,500
Utilities	0	250	250	250	250	250
Telephone	0	250	250	250	250	250
Office Equipment	0	1,400	0	2,100	0	0
Insurance	0	3,000	0	0	0	0
Advertising	0	700	700	700	700	700
Accounting	0	300	300	300	300	300
Electronic Payment System Fees	0	300	300	300	300	300
Loan Payments	0	500	500	500	500	500
Miscellaneous	500	1,000	1,000	1,000	1,000	1,000
Total Cash-Outs	32,200	29,340	27,380	29,480	27,380	27,380
Cash at End of Month	$ (17,200)	$ (16,540)	$ (8,920)	$ (3,400)	$ 4,220	$ 11,840

	June	July	Aug	Sept	Oct	Nov	Dec
$	11,840 $	17,360 $	21,980 $	29,600 $	34,420 $	42,040 $	49,660
	35,000	35,000	35,000	35,000	35,000	35,000	40,000
	0	0	0	0	0	0	0
	46,840	52,360	56,980	64,600	69,420	77,040	89,660
	0	0	0	0	0	0	0
	17,080	17,080	17,080	17,080	17,080	17,080	19,520
	4,500	4,500	4,500	4,500	4,500	4,500	4,500
	2,500	2,500	2,500	2,500	2,500	2,500	2,500
	250	250	250	250	250	250	250
	250	250	250	250	250	250	250
	2,100	0	0	2,800	0	0	0
	0	3,000	0	0	0	0	0
	700	700	700	700	700	700	700
	300	300	300	300	300	300	300
	300	300	300	300	300	300	300
	500	500	500	500	500	500	500
	1,000	1,000	1,000	1,000	1,000	1,000	1,000
	29,480	30,380	27,380	30,180	27,380	27,380	29,820
$	17,360 $	21,980 $	29,600 $	34,420 $	42,040 $	49,660 $	59,840

Cash flow projection is also important in your planning stages to show how you intend to survive the first few lean months of business—particularly after you figure in your start-up expenses. If you'll have more than enough cash to cover your expenses for the first months of business, then you're one of the lucky few. More likely, you'll be pressed to figure out how to cover a cash deficit for at least the first few months, and maybe longer. One way to do this is to put off or cut some expenses. Another is to hit up your family or friends for a loan, find a bank or another lender willing to provide a start-up loan (which is much easier said than done), or sell part of your business to investors. The important thing is to do your best to predict your cash needs in advance, both to give yourself ample time to come up with a plan for getting the cash and to inspire more confidence in lenders or investors.

Your cash flow projection will use many of the same figures you developed for your profit/loss forecast. The main difference is that you'll include all cash inflows and outflows, not just sales revenues and business expenses. Also, you'll record costs in the month that you expect to incur them, rather than simply spreading annual amounts equally over 12 months. Inflows and outflows of cash that belong in your cash flow analysis include loans, loan payments, and start-up costs. Once you're turning a profit, you'll also include income tax payments in your cash flow analysis, but, for now, assume that you'll be free from income taxes for your first year.

For each month, simply start your projection with the actual amount of cash your business will have on hand. Next, fill in your projected cash-ins for the month, which should include sales revenues, loans, transfers of personal money—basically, any money that goes into your business checking account. Add these together along with the cash you have at the beginning of the month to get your total cash-ins for the month.

Next, enter all your projected cash-outs for the month, such as your fixed expenses and any loan payments. Remember also to include costs of products and materials you use in your products or services— your variable costs. Add together all your cash-outs to obtain a total for the month. Subtract total monthly cash-outs from total monthly cash-ins, and the result will be your cash left at the end of the month. That figure is also your beginning cash balance at the start of the next month; transfer it to the top of the next month's column, and do the whole process over again.

EXAMPLE: Inga completes her cash flow projection for her first year in business, as shown above. She starts her projection one month early to account for the money she must spend before she opens her bookstore. In her cash-in section, she figures in $15,000 that she will put into the business: $10,000 of her own savings and an interest-free loan from her sister of $5,000. In her cash-out section, she includes what she'll pay for the initial set-up of the business, as well as that month's rent and a $500 allowance for unexpected expenses. Inga also includes in her cash-out section a $500 payment each month to her sister for the loan.

Notice that Inga's cash-outs look a bit different from her expenses in her profit/loss forecast, even though they add up to the same totals. There are a few reasons for this. One is that Inga includes her inventory costs in the cash-outs section, instead of accounting for those costs in the gross profit calculation, as in her profit/loss forecast. Also, Inga's cash-outs section of the cash flow projection reflects that some expenses are not paid equally every month. For instance, her insurance is paid twice a year, and she plans to buy office equipment in a few chunks.

Also notice that Inga's estimated paid sales (as opposed to sales on credit) for the year come to the same total as her estimated annual sales revenue. That's because, for her first year, at least, Inga doesn't plan to take credit cards or checks, only cash and ATM purchases. That way all her sales will be paid immediately.

Inga's happy to see that by the end of April she should have cash left in the bank after all her expenses are paid (though she hasn't yet provided for money for her living expenses). Still, she needs to close the cash deficits that she predicts for her first three months in business. Based on her

cash flow projection, an extra $17,200 up front would keep her cash flow (barely) in the black. She decides to apply for a loan of $15,000 and try to juggle expenses to cover the remaining $2,200 shortfall.

Once you've completed a year's worth (or more, if you want) of a cash flow projection, you'll have a blueprint for your business's financial situation from month to month. If any months are projected to have a cash deficit, you'll need to tweak your plan to make sure you can cover all of your important expenses. As usual, this means you'll have to juggle, reduce, or cut costs. A cash flow projection that shows difficulty in paying all your bills won't only scare investors away; it may mean that your plan needs serious revision. On the other hand, if your cash flow projection shows that you'll be in the black every month, then you'll be in a good position to show your numbers to potential sources of money —and to get your business under way.

 CAUTION

Credit transactions complicate the picture. Cash flow analysis is concerned with when your business receives or spends money, not when sales or purchases are made. This means that you'll need to account for delayed payments if you do any sales or purchases on credit.

Putting It All Together

Congratulations! You've finished the descriptive and financial aspects of your business plan. While you kick back and enjoy a cold one, think about how you want to put all the information together. If you put the plan together for your own information, then you might want to simply review it, edit anything that needs fixing, print it out, and put it into a binder for your reference. If you plan to present the information as part of a loan request or as a package for investors to review, you might want to do some extra polishing. As mentioned earlier, consider hiring a writer to help develop the information into a well-written, persuasive document. The bottom line is to package the information as needed for your specific purposes. One of those purposes may be to raise start-up money.

Chapter 4 Checklist: Drafting an Effective Business Plan

☐ Decide how you will use your business plan: to attract investors or for your own use as a blueprint for your business.

☐ Draft narrative sections of your business plan that describe your business in detail.

☐ Put together financial projections for your business, including a break-even analysis, a profit/loss forecast, and a cash flow projection.

☐ Have a friend or business associate look over your plan—both the descriptive elements and the financial analysis—and make edits or suggestions.

☐ Edit your plan and prepare a final draft. Assemble the various sections of the plan into a final document, and package it as necessary for however you intend to use the plan.

Raising Start-Up Money

There are plenty of businesses that cost practically nothing to start, especially if you already have a computer or whatever tools you use in the activity that will be the focus of the business you're starting. Consultants, freelancers, and creatives of all types typically already have the minimum equipment they need to get started—say, a laptop, a camera, a sewing machine, jewelry-making tools, or whatever else used in the core business activity. Other businesses like restaurants, retail stores, or manufacturers will need a moderate to significant amount of cash to get operations rolling.

If yours is a business that will require some capital to launch, your first order of business is to do the financial analysis and business planning discussed in the previous chapter. Having a solid business plan in place is a must if you plan to seek start-up funds.

Before you start your quest for cash, however, you'll also need to understand the types and sources of financing generally available to start-up businesses. Further, it's important to be realistic about your business's prospects for raising funds and the impact that a loan or an equity investment can have on the business—and on your life. (Spoiler: Money from lenders or investors can seriously spike the pressure on a start-up's owners.)

This chapter provides an overview of key concepts you need to know about small business financing, common sources of start-up funds to consider, and how to develop a realistic plan to obtain the start-up funding you'll need.

Realities of Funding a Start-Up

Let me start by saying I have a huge beef with how business media, incubators, schools, and others relentlessly emphasize "getting your business funded" as the presumed goal for start-up businesses. It bugs me to no end that even the term "start-up" has come to mean not just any business starting from scratch, but only those seeking aggressive growth via major capital investments from venture firms.

This worldview is a dramatic distortion of reality. Statistics consistently show that approximately 1–3% of new businesses obtain funding from venture capital firms. But you'd never know this if you Googled "business start-up" or "how to launch a business." The vast majority of the articles you'd find would focus on things like "How to Pitch to Angel Investors," "Perfecting Your Pitch Deck," or about a million other puff pieces about the urgent need to raise millions and become the next hot IPO.

When I use the term "start-up," I'm talking about any new business, not just the 1% that launch with venture financing. I'll give the basics on how venture financing works in this chapter, but my focus will be on the best funding strategies for the other 99% of us.

With that in mind let's look at some other hard realities regarding funding for a start-up:

- **First:** It's much harder for start-up businesses to secure *any* kind of financing—whether debt or equity financing (details on each below)—than for existing businesses. The simple reason is that start-ups lack any history of success or credit-worthiness. If you have a history of making money with one or more previous ventures, that can help a lot. On the other hand, if you have no experience in starting or running a small business, your plea for funds will be an especially hard sell.

- **Second:** If you do have plans to court investors in your business, in exchange for a share of equity in your company (this is called "equity financing"), you need to know that professional investors (i.e., those outside your circle of family or friends) are laser-focused on whether they are likely to increase their investment several-fold in a relatively short amount of time (the shorter, the better, in their view). Because investors know that not every business succeeds, they need their "winner" businesses to yield high profits. Unless you have a

personal relationship with an investor, you should expect them to make a purely money-motivated decision about funding your start-up. No amount of passion or personal story or creativity or charisma will convince a professional investor to just "give you a chance." It's all about the numbers.

- **Third:** Think hard about what your day-to-day vision of your business is, and how much you are comfortable with starting a business that needs start-up capital at a level that requires lenders or investors. If you really believe in your business idea, and have done detailed planning and analysis that show a high potential for success, you might feel eager to take on a higher level of risk and higher capital needs. Going this route requires that you be at peace with the very real possibility you will lose your entire investment or default on a loan. It also means you must be accountable, either through your obligations to repay the loan, or to any management obligations you make to an equity investor. Many of us choose self-employment for the freedom to make our own decisions, so the pressure of needing to achieve ambitious financial milestones can be very stressful. Only go that route if you really feel able to go "all in" on your business.

Ruth E. Dove, co-founder, Coffee + Creatives: *Sometimes starting a business feels like such a slow process, and the beginning so informal, that lining up the business and money-related processes can feel like a task that can wait until the business is more established. However, the sooner an entrepreneur formalizes these necessary systems, the less likely one is to run into complicated and time-consuming tax, banking, and other financial issues. The fulcrum of wanting to run a business is to have control over a revenue stream. Treat money with the respect it deserves as an integral part of the business, and it will work for you, instead of you working for it and having to spend more of it on making up for not starting on the right foot.*

The bottom line is that starting a business with financing from loans or investors requires careful planning and a high level of commitment to the business. Losing your own money to a failed start-up is one thing (and can be catastrophic if you risked your life savings), but the consequences of defaulting on a loan or needing to declare bankruptcy due to being in over your head to creditors can be even more dire. If you're not sure whether you are ready for that level of commitment, start-up loans or equity financing might not be the right path for you. Instead,

consider starting small, bootstrapping, and growing your business slowly.

If, on the other hand, you are gung-ho about putting in the hard work to develop a winning business plan and find someone willing to give you money to get your business off the ground, it is possible. Your chances of successfully raising start-up money will be improved by understanding some basics about how financing works and by knowing where to look, beyond the traditional funding sources like major commercial banks.

Debt Versus Equity Financing

An initial, fundamental distinction you should understand is the difference between debt financing and equity financing. It's simple and straightforward: With debt financing, you borrow money that needs to be repaid; equity financing involves receiving money in exchange for an ownership share (a.k.a. equity) in your business. We'll dig in a bit more later in this chapter, but for now just recognize this fundamental difference.

Note that lenders and equity investors can be people you know, such as family, friends, or business associates, or they could be banks, incubators, or venture capital firms (though as noted above, venture-funded start-ups are *far* rarer than is generally understood).

Start-Up Funding Stats

A fact that surprises many entrepreneurs is that the most popular source of start-up funding is the source closest to home: personal savings. Surveys of business owners consistently show that most of them use their own money to start their ventures. According to a 2014 survey conducted by Gallup and Wells Fargo, 82% of entrepreneurs reported their ventures were self-funded, while just 1% reported using venture capital. Only 3% reported using crowdfunding.

Self-Funded	82%
Loans	41%
Lines of Credit	41%
Friends & Family	24%
Crowdfunding	3%
Venture Capital	1%

Source: Wells Fargo/Gallup Small Business Index, Q2 2014.

Unless you originally planned to get money by acquiring equity investors, chances are that a business loan is a more practical option for your business. Besides the fact that only the smallest percentage of businesses meet equity investors' criteria, equity financing also presents potentially complicated legal and structural issues. Plus, it will dilute the shares that you and any other original founders of the company own. This means your share of

business profits will be reduced. Potentially even more troubling, it also means you may have to share management control and decision-making authority with your investors, raising the distinct possibility of conflict.

One way to avoid this is to bring on investors as limited partners who will have no authority over business decisions. (See "Partnerships," in Chapter 1, for more on this arrangement.) Still, equity financing involves more structural complexities than raising money via a loan.

Business Loans

Business loans traditionally have come from banks, but since the early 1990s there are alternatives to commercial banks, called Community Development Financial Institutions, that are far friendlier to small start-ups. (More on CDFIs below.) Loans can also come from family and friends; for the purposes of this section, let's focus on loans from actual financial institutions. The basics of commercial loans are as follows.

Loans can be secured or unsecured. When you obtain a secured loan, you give the creditor an interest in some kind of asset—such as business equipment, real estate, inventory, or receivables—in case you default on the loan. An asset used to secure a loan is called collateral. Lenders tend to be conservative when appraising the value of the collateral, and they will

What Happens If I Default on a Loan?

A few things can happen when a business defaults on a loan. If the loan was secured by collateral, the creditor/lender can take possession of that property, often without even having to go to court. In this case it's important that the secured property and the lender's security interest are clearly stated in the loan document.

If the loan was unsecured, the creditor can sue the business to collect. If the creditor wins in court, they can garnish the business's bank accounts or place liens on property owned by the business. If you didn't create an LLC or a corporation as your business structure, then your personal assets are at risk here as well. (More on this below.)

Regardless of what property can be taken to satisfy your debt, you can pretty much count on some harsh effects on your credit rating, which typically results in getting socked with higher interest rates for everything from credit cards to mortgages, since you'll be deemed a higher-risk borrower. Sometimes only your business's credit rating will be affected, but your personal credit rating can suffer as well.

In any case, the possible outcomes of defaulting on a loan should demonstrate not only how important it is to proceed cautiously, with a solid business plan in place, but also to structure your business to protect your personal assets. Forming an LLC or corporation serves to separate the business from your personal assets; failing to create this kind of entity makes you a sole proprietor or partnership by default, which means all your personal assets like real estate or vehicles are at risk of loss to satisfy any claims against your business. Note that for new entrepreneurs, it's not uncommon for a lender to require collateral of personal property such as a house, even if the business is set up as a separate entity like an LLC.

only lend a percentage of that value. The loan amount compared to the value of the collateral is called a loan-to-value ratio. An unsecured loan is a loan that is not backed by any collateral.

Because a strong credit history or established cash flow is essential in obtaining an unsecured loan, most start-ups aren't in a good position to obtain one. Also, banks usually require start-up business owners to personally guarantee the loan, which puts your personal assets at risk—even if you are incorporated or have formed an LLC. A personal guarantee can sometimes be avoided if you put up sufficient collateral, but personal guarantees are a necessity for most loans to start-up businesses.

Certain details regarding your loan are obviously crucial, such as the length of time over which you'll pay it off (the term), the interest rate, and any fees you'll need to pay. Most small business loans are short-term, from one to three years. As with most other loans, the longer the loan, the higher the interest rate. Interest rates can be variable or fixed, usually a little higher for a fixed rate. In addition, you may have to pay points or other fees for various aspects of the application process, such as document reviews or credit checks. Find out if there will be any fees for prepayment of the loan.

Community Development Financial Institutions

As mentioned above, since the early 1990s an alternative to big commercial banks has provided small start-ups with a user-friendly alternative for business financing. Community Development Financial Institutions, or CDFIs, are a fast-growing segment of the business financing market specializing in loans to underserved communities and populations. CDFIs are certified by the U.S. Treasury and may be known in your community as microlenders or small business incubators. These funding organizations can be especially helpful for start-ups, businesses with poor credit, and businesses seeking relatively small loans, generally up to $100,000.

CDFIs usually, but not always, have a specific focus, such as improving economic opportunities in blighted communities or supporting businesses owned by women or minorities. But many of these organizations offer assistance broadly, not just to specific populations or communities. Even better, CDFIs often offer guidance and expertise to your business in addition to financing, which will help your chances of success.

Lines of Credit

A very helpful resource to manage a small business' cash flow is a revolving line of credit from the bank. A line of credit works on the same principle as a credit card, but generally offers better cash terms than credit card cash advance terms. The business can borrow funds up to the credit line limit on an as-needed basis and has to pay interest only on the outstanding balance (not the entire credit line). The business can choose to pay funds back and reborrow them as necessary during the time the credit line is open. Credit lines can be open for a specified period, such as five or ten years, or can be open-ended (like a credit card).

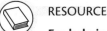 **RESOURCE**

For help in finding a CDFI. To find a certified CDFI in your area, go to the CDFI Fund website at www. cdfifund.gov.

Equity Investments

As described above, any person or business that gives your business money in exchange for an ownership share could be called an "equity investor," including people you bring on as partners. For the purposes of this section, what I mean by an "equity investor" is someone outside your company, not an original founder, whom you approach in your search for funds. I'm also not talking about family or friends here, but they certainly can be equity investors; I talk about raising money from family and friends later in this chapter.

Equity investments can come from investors who work in venture capital firms, or individuals often known as "angel investors." What all types of professional investors have in common is that they will be motivated by making a hefty return on their investment in as short a time frame as possible. While typical rates of return that investors want or expect varies by industry and economic conditions, the National Venture Capital Association says the average early-stage (i.e. start-up phase) equity investor seeks a 10-fold return on their investment within eight years.

Professional investors tend to have specific interests such as biotech, sports, manufacturing or other niche specialties.

If you plan to seek equity financing you'll need to research which firms or angel investors are active in your field.

Venture capital firms and angel investors typically have strict formulas for what they will invest in. In all fairness, being strict this way is usually critical to their overall success in making money as an investor. If professional investors gave money to every enterprise that piqued their curiosity, even in the absence of a compelling business plan predicting rapid growth and profits, they would burn through an awful lot of money—which could easily cut short their careers as investors. There's no quicker way to ending a career as an investor than running out of funds.

According to conventional wisdom (and all the grains of salt that go with that), investors expect 30–40% of start-ups to fail to return any of their investment, 30–40% to return the original investment, and 10–20% to produce substantial returns. Because of this, investors are always biased towards growth-oriented companies that can scale quickly and efficiently. These are the firms that carry the load for all the losers—and there are always losers.

Have I mentioned that venture-backed firms represent only 1% of startups overall? I keep mentioning it because there's such a disproportionate amount of information and resources on this topic, leading to a radically skewed image of venture capital being an important part of entrepreneurship. For 99% of new businesses, it is no factor at all.

What Happens If My Business Fails and I Have Equity Investors?

Equity investors balance the risk of the business failing with the possible reward of being a part-owner of a successful, profitable company. Unlike a business loan situation, you don't typically have any obligation to pay an equity investor back if the business fails. If the business fails, everyone's shares are worthless, including the investor's.

Note, however, that the legal documents between the company and the investor will determine the terms, and some investors try to include provisions that protect them in case the business fails. It's not uncommon for investors to insist on having rights to claim money left in bank accounts, accounts receivable, proceeds of assets sold, or intellectual property of a company that fails.

As you can see, the details of your agreement with an equity investor can be extremely important. While this book advises a DIY approach for many business start-up tasks, executing an agreement with an equity investor is a transaction that calls for professional guidance.

What Lenders and Investors Look For

In addition to making sure you have a solid business plan that shows your business idea to be a winning one, any bank or institution considering funding your business (whether through debt or equity financing) will want to know other specific details of your current and prospective financial situation. The more you can present a convincing picture of your venture's sunny financial prospects, the higher your chances of success. Part of the trick is understanding specifically what lenders and investors are looking for and getting into their mind frame.

In the most general terms, lenders are focused on whether or not you can repay the loan within the time frame specified in the loan terms. If the loan is secured with collateral, the lender is generally more willing to approve the loan, since they have more of a guarantee of being repaid. With unsecured loans, the lender will be more interested in whether your business plan looks solid and likely to succeed. If your plan is sketchy or reads like a pipe dream, you won't be likely to be approved for a loan (which might be a blessing if your business idea wasn't solid after all).

Equity investors are concerned less with whether you have the resources to repay a loan, and more with whether your business plan looks likely to yield rapid growth and profits in a short amount of time.

Once your business is underway, you may want additional funding for growth or expansion. Lenders are particularly interested in certain measures of existing businesses to determine whether an expansion loan is a worthy credit risk. One such measure is your business's balance between debt and equity—a relationship that is called a debt-to-equity ratio. Your debt-to-equity ratio is the extent to which your business is in debt to lenders, versus how much you and any other owners have invested in the business. The ratio is calculated simply by dividing outstanding debt by the owners' equity in the business.

EXAMPLE: Sara is considering financing options for her sole proprietorship, which has been in operation for about two years. So far, she has invested $50,000 of her own money into the business and obtained one loan for $15,000, of which she has paid back $5,000. Her debt-to-equity ratio is calculated as follows:

Outstanding debt:	$10,000
÷ Owner's equity:	$50,000
= Debt-to-equity ratio:	20%

In the most basic terms, lenders want to see a low ratio of debt to equity to make sure your business is not overextended and has sufficient assets to repay the loan. Commercially acceptable debt-to-equity ratios generally range from 50% to

150%—but since any ratios over 100% reflect more debt than equity, they should be viewed with caution. Conversely, if you have nearly no debt, lenders may take it as an indication that your business is not leveraging its assets to make the most of business opportunities.

Of course, when you're seeking a loan for the first time, your debt-to-equity ratio will be zero. The point is to understand the ratio and how lenders view it so that you can keep it in the right range as your business grows.

 TIP

Establish a relationship with a bank. It's smart to establish a relationship with a bank early in the life of your business, even if you don't need start-up funding. Open an account and use the services it offers to small businesses to establish your business as a trustworthy and reputable customer. With a solid relationship in place, you'll be in a better position to apply for funding down the road—say, via a loan or a line of credit—when your business is growing and needs money to expand.

Alternatives to Institutional Funders

If a bank, a CDFI or an equity investor isn't your speed, you do have a few more options. Here's an overview.

Family and Friends

Since start-ups are so commonly turned down by banks and other traditional funders, entrepreneurs often turn to friends and family for an injection of cash. But as you surely know, you must be careful when mixing money, blood, and friendship.

The best way to proceed is to be as businesslike as possible when getting money from family or friends. Draft a promissory note outlining the amount of the loan, the interest rate, and its repayment terms. Make it clear to the person who is lending you the money that you will treat the loan just like a commercial loan from a bank. And follow through with that promise by generating financial reports at least quarterly—and paying back the loan according to the agreed-upon terms.

Credit Cards and Personal Financing

If all other options have failed, many tenacious entrepreneurs turn to credit cards and home equity loans to get their ventures off the ground. This route may work, but you must watch for serious potential pitfalls. Credit cards often charge much higher interest rates than business loans, and they require minimum payments set at such a level that it could take decades to pay off your debt. If you keep high balances on the credit cards and pay just the minimum, your debt can quickly spiral out of control.

Another issue is that a business owner who resorts to credit cards to finance the business may not be as disciplined in managing the debt and spending. While bank lenders typically require financial reports and other proof of solid financial management, credit cards do not—potentially allowing you to get sloppy with your finances. Don't make this mistake. If you use credit cards as start-up funding, be just as serious about your bookkeeping and financial management as if you had a big bank looking over your shoulder.

Home equity loans will usually offer better interest rates than credit cards, but of course, they require you to put your home at risk. If your business fails and you are unable to pay your home loan, you may face foreclosure. Be sure you evaluate this sobering possibility before taking out a loan against your home to finance your new business.

Crowdfunding and Social Media

Crowdfunding refers to a specific method of raising money online that harnesses the power of social media to spread the word about your business or project. Crowdfunding sites are essentially social media sites that are geared towards enabling users to raise money for various types of projects (more on that in a moment) from other folks online.

To raise money through crowdfunding, you typically choose a crowdfunding platform (such as one of those mentioned below), create a campaign with information about your project and why it needs funding, set a dollar amount goal and a deadline, and promote your campaign using social media, such as Facebook, Twitter or Instagram. You can also spread the word about your campaign using good old email. The crowdfunding platform will typically keep a percentage of the funding raised, generally 5% to 10%.

Many crowdfunding campaigns offer rewards, which might include the actual products (or sometimes services) you're aiming to sell. When you offer the products themselves as a reward, the crowdfunding campaign essentially becomes a pre-order system and can be really effective. Of course no matter what the reward, it's essential you follow through and provide the reward in a timely manner.

The most prominent crowdfunding platform is Kickstarter (www.kickstarter. com). Other sites like Indiegogo (www. indiegogo.com) and Crowdrise (www. crowdrise.com) are more geared toward nonprofits.

When choosing which crowdfunding platform to use, besides knowing which types of projects are allowed, be sure you understand whether the site is an "all-or-nothing" model or a "keep what you raise" model. For example, Kickstarter uses an all-or-nothing model, so if you don't meet your fundraising goal by the deadline, then your backers don't pay and you don't get anything. Indiegogo, on the other hand, offers a "flexible funding" option that allows you to keep what you raise, even if you fall short of your fundraising goal. Whether or not you meet your goal, you'll be charged a 5% fee of the total raised.

Crowdfunding typically works best for businesses and people who already have a strong social media presence, or at a minimum the skills and resources to tackle online marketing effectively. If your business (or an embryonic version of it) has hundreds or thousands of followers on Facebook and interacts with them daily, you'll be likely to get a lot of mileage from a crowdfunding campaign that you promote appropriately on Facebook. If, on the other hand, your business rarely uses social media, it will be harder to get traction with a crowdfunding campaign, even one that's well-crafted and compelling.

Here are some general tips for using social media to raise money for your start-up:

- **Use social media in combination with other traditional outreach tools.** Social media is great for spreading the word about offline events or sharing links to press coverage or other information

(for details, see Chapter 14). When used as a component of a multichannel promotional push (which may or may not include a crowdfunding campaign), social media can dramatically expand the reach and exposure of your message.

- **What's hot might not be effective, and what's effective one day may be old news the next.** Kickstarter and Indiegogo are hot crowdfunding options today, but in a year or two they may have fallen out of favor. The bottom line is that you have to constantly stay on the lookout for what's new, innovative, and effective in social media crowdfunding, and be ready to switch courses if your methods become outdated.

- **Crowdfunding fatigue is real.** While crowdfunding can absolutely be an effective way to raise funds from your supporters, it is also a bit of a victim of its own success. Social media is so full of appeals for money—many of them extremely worthy—that there is a bit of a "tune-out" factor happening. People who may have jumped on board just a couple years ago, with their credit cards ready, now are weary of being asked for funds every time they check Facebook. What this means is that your appeal will need to be particularly well presented. Don't be discouraged if you fail to meet your goal.

• **As with networking in the real world, the payoff from networking online isn't usually immediate or direct.** Keep a broader, longer-term perspective when engaging in social media. Networking isn't the same as direct solicitation, and you shouldn't expect every "friend" to rain funds on your project. But over time, the exposure, relationships, and goodwill you generate through your social media efforts will undoubtedly pay off in some measure.

Chapter 5 Checklist: Raising Start-Up Money

☐ Learn about debt and equity financing so you can develop a realistic vision of how each works and how that kind of funding might affect your business.

☐ Consider the realities of taking on debt or equity investors, and whether they are compatible with your vision of running your business at a scale you are comfortable with.

☐ If you decide to pursue either debt or equity financing from banks, CDFIs, venture firms or angel investors, make sure your business plan is thorough and polished.

☐ If you decide to ask family or friends for money to start your business, make sure to treat the transaction professionally and put your terms in writing.

☐ If you are savvy at marketing or communications online, consider crowdfunding, which can be structured as pre-sales of your product or service.

Pricing, Bidding, and Billing Projects

Pricing is a crucial factor in any business strategy, yet many fledgling business owners have little idea how to go about setting prices that are both competitive and profitable. This chapter explains how to develop your pricing strategy and introduces you to some standard methods for setting prices, whether your business sells services or products.

In addition, this chapter offers guidance for business owners who need to make bids to get work. Service businesses typically fall into this category, though sometimes product-based businesses also need to bid for jobs. This chapter also includes some general tips for the process and an outline for what typical proposals include.

On a cautionary note, be aware that antitrust laws forbid business competitors to fix, or even merely discuss, prices. For this reason, you won't find newsgroups or bulletin boards online where other businesses in a certain industry offer specific info on their pricing. Both online and off, pricing discussions among businesses in the same industry are not just taboo, they're illegal.

 SKIP AHEAD
Product sellers can skip ahead. Business owners who plan to sell only products don't need to deal with service-pricing or service-billing issues. If you don't plan to offer services, skip ahead to "Pricing for Businesses Selling Products."

Directly sharing pricing info with competitors is illegal, but publishing general information about pricing guidelines is not. Good thing, since pricing is discussed first in this chapter.

Pricing and Billing for Service Businesses

Two major components of running a service-based business are setting prices and figuring out how to bill clients. Having rates that are well-thought-out is a key factor in soliciting clients confidently. And if you know the best way to bill them, you can manage your projects for maximum profitability and establish yourself as a true professional. This section explains these two essential tasks for service businesses. Once you understand what drives the pricing and billing processes, you'll find them much easier.

Setting Hourly Rates

Those who work as freelancers or own service-based businesses often find it difficult to figure out what rates to use. Many people struggle with assigning value to their time. Remember that your service rates are not just a measure of the value of your time—they also need to cover your overhead and yield your profits.

There's no single formula to put a price on your services, but there are a couple of common approaches. One formula is based on adjusting the number of billable hours so that revenue equals salary, overhead, and profit. And some businesses base their rates on what the market will bear. Each of these approaches is described in more detail below.

Billable Hours Formula

Many service businesses use a fairly simple formula to calculate their hourly rate. To keep it simple, look at this formula as if you're a solo freelancer without any employees:

	Desired annual salary
+	Annual fixed costs (or overhead)
+	Desired annual profit
÷	Annual billable hours
=	Hourly rate

The gist of the formula is that it adds together all the money you want to bring in each year and divides that total by the number of hours you plan to work each year. The result is the hourly rate. This simple formula can be adjusted depending on the specifics of your business.

But first, it's a good idea to get a solid grasp on the concepts behind the formula:

- **Desired salary.** This is straightforward. How much would you like to earn annually? Include only salary here; desired profit comes later.

- **Fixed costs.** This is also a simple concept. How much will you spend each year on rent, utilities, office equipment, computers, and other items of overhead? As discussed in Chapter 4, fixed costs are independent of individual projects or services. You pay them regardless of how much business you're doing.

- **Desired profit.** You're in business to make a profit, not just to bring home a paycheck. A typical profit goal is 20% above salary and overhead (fixed costs).

- **Billable hours.** There's no single way to estimate this. Basically, the fewer billable hours you estimate, the higher your hourly rate will be; the more billable hours, the lower your hourly rate. A common way to approach this estimate is by calculating the number of potential billable hours in a year. With 52 weeks in the year and a 40-hour workweek, there are 2,080 potentially billable hours each year. Reduce that total by the number of nonbillable hours you expect to have—vacation, administrative work, or selling, for example. Just use your best estimate here. Very generally, the percentage of your time that is billable will probably be 50% to 80%. Much below that won't be very profitable, and higher than that usually isn't realistic. Use this percentage to determine how many billable hours you'll likely have each year. For instance, if 70% of your time will be billable, you will have 1,456 billable hours (2,080 hours x 70%).

Now add together your desired salary, fixed costs, and desired profit. Then divide that total by your billable hours. The result will be the hourly rate you'll need to charge to cover your fixed costs and bring in your desired salary and profit.

EXAMPLE: Samantha is starting a translation service and wants to figure out her hourly rate. She sets a first-year salary for herself of $30,000 per year and estimates her annual fixed costs to be approximately $25,000. This totals $55,000 for salary and overhead. A 20% profit brings the total to $66,000. Samantha thinks she'll have to spend a good amount of time doing sales and getting her business off the ground, so she figures only about 60% of her time will be billable, resulting in 1,248 available billable hours. By dividing her salary, fixed expenses, and profit ($66,000) by 1,248 billable hours, Samantha sees that her hourly rate should be $52.88. She rounds that up to $55 per hour.

	Salary	$	30,000.00
+	Fixed costs		25,000.00
	Total salary & fixed costs		55,000.00
+	20% profit		11,000.00
	Total salary, fixed costs, & profit	$	66,000.00
÷	Billable hours		1,248.00
=	Hourly rate	$	52.88

Setting Market-Based Rates

Another way to set your hourly rate is to throw the formula out the window and simply set your rate for what the market will bear. Beware that this might not yield a profitable hourly rate, because you're not basing your rate on the actual numbers you'll need to achieve. On the other hand, it may be more likely to deliver a rate that customers will accept.

If you base your rates on the market, use any market information you can get to guide you—including what competitors charge, industry standards, and your own experience of using various rates. If you constantly fail to snag clients once you provide a quote, that's a sign your rates may be too high. On the flip side, if you get every job you bid on, you could probably get away with nudging, or even shoving, your rates upward.

It's not a bad idea to use a combination of the formula-based and market-based approaches. Using the formula will help ensure that you set a rate that is profitable, and using the market to adjust the rate up or down will help you stay competitive. For example, if the formula yielded an hourly rate of $45, but other similar businesses charged $65 to $75 per hour, you could feel comfortable increasing your rate to $55 per hour, making your business a bargain while still turning a profit.

 FORM

Billable Rate Worksheet. The Nolo website includes a downloadable interactive worksheet to help you calculate an hourly rate for your service business. See Appendix B for the link to this worksheet and other forms in this book.

TIP

It is legal to research and use competitors' rates. The antitrust laws mentioned earlier are intended to protect consumers by maintaining competition in the marketplace. The laws are supposed to prevent anticompetitive agreements among competitors to set prices at a certain level. On the other hand, setting your rates to position your business among similar businesses is perfectly legal, so long as you obtained your competitors' pricing information from another source, not directly from them. After all, researching the market and setting prices accordingly is the essence of competition.

Billing Options

Service businesses and freelancers typically use a variety of billing options to accommodate different types of projects and clients. Common billing options include flat fees, hourly billing, and retainer arrangements. Each of these options is discussed below.

Flat Fees

With flat fee billing, you and your client agree to a total fee for a specific project. In the right situations, it is efficient and professional to charge your client a flat fee for your services. The fee should roughly reflect the number of hours you'll work multiplied by your hourly rate. Contractors typically discount their hourly rates for larger projects.

Billing a flat rate per project usually makes clients happy because they know up front what their costs will be. Project-based billing can also benefit you. A flat fee encourages efficient project management and reduces the hassle of tracking and billing for your hours (though you should always keep track for your own records).

However, flat fees aren't the best idea for every project. You will feel underpaid if it takes much more work to finish a project than you expected, and the customer will feel overcharged if the project takes much less time than you estimated. If you want to bill flat rate, it's crucial that you and the client both understand and agree on the project's exact scope. In fact, this agreement should be reached even before you quote a fee. Once the client accepts your fee, the project details should be outlined in a contract. Payment terms can vary, but contractors typically require a deposit up to one-half of the total fee on signing the project contract.

Sometimes it's not possible to pin down a project with specificity at the outset. Some clients simply don't want to hammer out all the details. Other times, a short deadline makes it difficult or impossible to carefully consider all aspects of the project before you start work. In these cases, you're asking for trouble if you set a flat fee.

How to Use the Billable Rate Worksheet

To use the billable rate worksheet on the Nolo website, follow the steps outlined below. Each step is explained in greater detail later in this section. Enter figures into only white cells; do not enter anything in blue cells.

Step 1: Enter your desired annual salary. This is your take-home pay, not your overall business profit.

Step 2: Enter your estimated annual fixed costs. (For more on estimating fixed costs, see Chapter 4.)

Step 3: Enter a profit goal for your business as a percentage by which you want to exceed salary and fixed costs. A 20% profit goal is typical.

Step 4: If you know how many billable hours you plan to perform in a year, enter that amount. Or, if you're not sure how many billable hours you plan to work in a year, you can work backward by estimating the number of *nonbillable* hours you plan to spend—such as on vacation or doing administrative work—and subtracting those hours from the total number of possible billable hours in one year (2,080). The worksheet asks for your estimated nonbillable hours of various types for time periods that are easiest to estimate (for instance, vacation is estimated in weeks, while administrative work is estimated in hours per day), then converts those figures into annual hourly amounts. If you enter figures both for your estimated billable hours and estimated nonbillable hours, the calculator will use the first figure, estimated billable hours.

Result: The worksheet will show you what hourly rate you should charge in order to make your desired salary, cover your fixed costs, and make your desired profit, assuming you work the number of billable hours you estimated.

Suppose, for instance, that a client calls and needs a new section developed for a website ASAP. The owners of the site desperately want you to start immediately, but you have only a vague idea of the work involved. A flat fee here would be a really bad idea—the project could take much longer than you expect, leaving you to do the work for an unfairly low flat rate.

If the project isn't carefully outlined before you start, forget the flat fee—hourly billing is the safest way to go.

Hourly Billing

Billing clients by the hour is pretty straight-forward. You keep track of how many hours you work, and bill the client accordingly. As explained above, you should use this type of billing—also called "time and materials billing"—in situations in which the project isn't well defined.

While billing by the hour will protect you from being underpaid for a poorly defined project that takes more time than you thought it would, the client will never be happy if you present a huge, unexpected bill. Even when you choose hourly billing for a project without a clear scope, do your best to work efficiently, communicate with the client, and avoid handing over a surprising bill.

Keep in mind that it is up to you to demonstrate your value to the client, explaining why your hourly rate is justified and how you spent your hours. Even if you can't define the project specifically enough to set a flat rate, do your best to estimate how long the project will take, and try to keep your hours within your estimates.

TIP

Set reasonable hourly increments when billing. For instance, will you bill the client a full hour for work that takes you 20 minutes to finish, or for a five-minute phone conversation?

Be careful or your client may see it as unfair. Many people use increments of 15 or 30 minutes for billing purposes. It can be good client relations to show some short phone calls on the bill with no charge attached. That makes the client feel better about the times you round up to the nearest 15 minutes for other tasks.

Jennifer F. Mahoney, owner of an illustration service in Northern California (www.candraw.net):
It's helpful to learn about the accounts payable process for each client and to understand who in the company releases checks. It's often an entirely different person or department from the one who calls you to offer work. You don't necessarily want to strain your relationship with the person who calls offering you work just because a different department of the business doesn't pay on time. Pave the way for timely payments as much as possible by getting to know the correct procedure, and when it's time to press for payment, you'll know the right person to call.

Retainer Arrangements

In a traditional retainer arrangement, the client pays an ongoing fee, usually monthly, to keep the contractor "on call" for certain services. Retainer arrangements

Charging for Outsourced Services

Sometimes a service business needs to hire another contractor (typically called a subcontractor) to get a job done for a client. You can charge your client for the subcontractor's work in different ways. You can simply charge your standard hourly rate for all work completed, whether your company did the work or a subcontractor did. This approach can work for or against you, depending on what you pay the subcontractor. Under a common second approach, businesses mark up the cost of the subcontractors and bill the client accordingly. Businesses vary a lot in how much they mark up subcontractors' rates. I've seen 10% markup and 100% markup. You'll have to decide what seems fair to your client and profitable to you.

Sometimes the client will hire and pay the sub directly, without a markup. This can work if that piece of the work is discrete, or distinct from the rest, and the client is responsible for supervising the sub's work and has appropriate liability insurance. However, many contractors prefer to choose and supervise all workers on the same project, for many reasons: They like to have total control over the project, they like to choose subcontractors whose work they trust, they usually make a fair profit on the subcontractor, and it simplifies the project as well as the contractor's potential liability to the subcontractor and the client.

In any case, let your client know in advance whether you plan to use subcontractors on a project, especially if the subcontractor is a highly skilled specialist and the rate you bill for the subcontractor will be higher than your standard rate. Clients never like to be surprised with bills higher than they expected.

EXAMPLE: Glenn is a construction contractor with a standard hourly rate of $85 per hour. When hired for a remodeling project, Glenn tells his client he will need to hire a few subcontractors over the course of the project who may have rates higher or lower than his. Glenn and the client come to the understanding that they'll agree to all subcontractors and their rates before Glenn hires them. When it's nearly time to bring in a plumber, Glenn tells his client he'd like to hire Khalsa, whose rate to the client will be $103 per hour. Khalsa's own rate is $90 per hour, but Glenn marks up the rate by 15% to $103 so that he can make a reasonable profit for managing Khalsa on the project.

are usually best for clients with regular and predictable needs—for example, maintaining a law firm's website, providing maintenance services for an apartment building, sewing and tailoring costumes for a theater, or doing public relations for a ski resort. As with flat-rate billing, you should always define the amount and scope of services expected of you under a retainer arrangement.

In some professional businesses, especially law offices, a "retainer" is requested at the outset that is really a deposit, or a prepayment of fees and costs, usually under a written fee agreement. Lawyers also sometimes use the traditional monthly-fee retainer described above.

Bidding and Creating Proposals

Sometimes it's not possible to sell a service or product just by offering it to the public for a certain price. Many service businesses (and some businesses selling products) must submit a bid or a proposal on a project to be considered for the job. (The terms "bid" and "proposal" are often used interchangeably.) If the client accepts the bid, then a contract is typically executed to confirm the sale.

Because bids can make or break a sale, you should take care when putting one together, both with the contents of the bid

and its production. Often, the hardest part of bidding is breaking down the project into smaller parts so that you can make good estimates of how much work, time, and materials it will require. Once that's done, it is usually quite easy to write the proposal. This section outlines how to put together a bid to help ensure your chances of success.

 SKIP AHEAD

When you don't need to get it in writing. Businesses selling products usually don't need to worry about bids or proposals. If you don't need to learn about the bidding process, skip ahead to "Pricing for Businesses Selling Products."

 TIP

When a proposal becomes a contract. A proposal usually converts to a contract when a client accepts your terms. In practice, however, you should suggest that you sign a separate contract to finalize the agreement with the client. This is partly because it's an opportunity to make sure the client truly understands what you said in your proposal. It's also a good idea because there are things you should cover in a contract that you wouldn't necessarily put in a proposal, such as who provides the insurance, how you will handle extras or change orders, specifics of each side's remedies for breach of contract, which state's laws apply, and whether you will mediate or arbitrate any disagreements. (See Chapter 11 for an in-depth look at how to use contracts in your business.)

Get All the Information You Need

You won't be able to make an effective bid on a project until you thoroughly understand all the details involved. Ask the prospective client as many questions as necessary to flesh out the full scope of the project. A prospective client who's putting a project out to bid typically issues a Request for Proposals (RFP) detailing the information the proposal must include and sometimes very detailed format requirements. If you have questions, ask them.

Often, the client will want to be involved in certain aspects of the project, so it's important you both agree who will take a primary role in various tasks or duties. You should hash out the breakdown of duties and workflow right at the beginning.

Break Down the Project and Make Estimates

Next, break down the project into manageable components and estimate how much time, labor, and materials you'll need for each one. This is generally the best way to make accurate estimates.

For instance, your head will spin if you try to estimate how long it will take you to complete an entire landscape design project. But once you break the project into parts—grading, spreading gravel, paving, planting trees, and so on—making estimates for the individual bits won't seem nearly as overwhelming.

Multiply the number of hours you expect the project to require by your hourly rate. This will be the total fee for the project. It's common for freelancers to round down a bit if the project is a large one. This is reasonable, because it's usually more profitable for a freelancer to work consistently on one project than to work piecemeal on several smaller projects.

Sometimes however, freelancers are tempted to lower their estimates out of fear. After adding up all the hours needed for a large project and multiplying this by their normal hourly rate, they think the fee looks too high and start slashing it to make it more acceptable to the client. Guard against this temptation. It's fine to reduce your fee slightly when you anticipate efficiencies on a large-scale project, but don't sell yourself short just to get the job. Not only will you regret it after you've worked long hours on the project for an unreasonably low fee, but you'll fail to earn respect from clients if you don't ask for the compensation you are worth.

Consider Expenses

Who will be responsible for expenses incurred during the project? The answer varies from project to project; there are no hard and fast rules. Typically, contractors are responsible for covering their own normal expenses of doing business. (However, this is not always true. Attorneys, for example, commonly bill clients for copies and printing costs.) Clients usually bear any costs that aren't typical to the contractor's business, such as travel, international phone calls, or equipment rental fees.

In any case, you and the client should agree in advance who will cover which expenses. In addition, make sure to address whether there are any limits on reimbursable expenses or whether the client must approve expenses in advance. Also nail down how you will bill the client for expenses.

For example, travel expenses are quite often billed to clients. It's wise to make a specific breakdown of the expenses that will be covered, such as airfare, rental car, lodging, taxi, train, parking, and food.

 TIP

Proposing reasonable limits on client expenses. Even if your client has deep pockets and seems willing to cover whatever expenses you incur, you should offer some limits on reimbursable expenses. This will help to head off any potential conflicts or unpleasant surprises over reimbursement bills. It also shows the client that you care about giving a good deal.

You can handle payments for expenses a number of different ways. A few possibilities are discussed below:

- **Set an amount that the client will pay, regardless of the amount actually incurred.** For instance, you and the client can agree that the client will pay $1,000 to cover all travel costs. If your actual costs are lower, the extra money will be yours; if higher, you'll eat the difference.

- **Bill the client for actual expenses incurred.** You can do this with or without a cap. For instance, you could agree that the client will reimburse you for all actual travel costs. Or, you could agree the client will reimburse you for actual travel costs up to $500.

- **Set a per diem rate for certain expenses.** "Per diem" simply means "per day." Food is typically billed at a set per diem rate—say, $50 or $75 per day.

EXAMPLE: Samantha is working on a bid for a translation project that will require her to travel to Brazil. Her client, Bahia Travel Company, says it will cover travel expenses and asks Samantha to draft a proposal specifying the terms. Samantha drafts the following terms regarding travel expenses, which she will include in her proposal:

"Samantha will be responsible for all expenses involved in the project, except for travel-related expenses, which Samantha will bill to Bahia Travel Company monthly, as follows:

Airfare. Billed as actually accrued, including all taxes, not to exceed $1,500 per round-trip ticket. Tickets will be economy class.

Rental car. Billed as actually accrued, including insurance and taxes, not to exceed $50 per day for no more than five days.

Lodging. Billed as actually accrued, including all taxes, not to exceed $175 per night for no more than five days.

Food. Billed at $75 per day for no more than five days.

Taxi. Billed as actually accrued for no more than five days.

Parking. Billed as actually accrued for no more than five days."

Write Your Proposal

Once you've finalized the important details of the project, it's time to put together your proposal. Your goal is to present all important information clearly and to demonstrate you have a solid plan for getting the job done right. Proposals should always be professional and somewhat formal in tone, but don't be afraid to let your personality show. If you feel stiff, you won't usually have a better bid, just a more stilted one.

> **Clare Zurawski, Albuquerque regional manager of WESST, a New Mexico nonprofit dedicated to helping people start or grow their own businesses (www.wesst.org):** *A thorough, fair, and clearly presented proposal is a sure way to impress your would-be clients with professionalism, and paves the way for effective communication going forward.*

Some project proposals are two to three pages long; some exceed 20 pages. There's no hard and fast rule here. You should use as much space as it takes to outline the project details with adequate—but not

excruciating—detail. An outline for a project proposal might go something like this:

- **Project overview.** Describe the big picture, including relevant details about the client and an overview of the project.
- **Project objectives and scope.** Offer detailed information about the project, including all the different components of the project and how they fit together.
- **Proposed approach.** Describe how you would approach the project and how you would achieve the client's goals. Be specific, and don't assume that the client knows anything about how you do your work.
- **Specific responsibilities.** Outline what you understand your specific responsibilities would be.
- **Deliverables.** This is a term for the specific products that your work will yield. For instance, deliverables might include a 20-page written report, a set of tax documents, or a 100-page travel guide.
- **Timetable.** Scheduling is always an important part of project management, so you should always outline when you expect certain parts of the project will be completed.
- **Fee and payment terms.** In stating your fee, you don't have to explicitly state your hourly rate or how you

arrived at your amount. Simply make it clear that your fee is based on your understanding of the project requirements as outlined in the rest of the proposal. It's also a good idea to mention that work beyond the scope described in the proposal will be quoted and billed separately.

- **Expenses.** Outline whatever agreement you and the potential client have regarding who will cover which expenses.

- **Conclusion.** Wrap up the proposal. Strive for a professional tone that expresses your enthusiasm for the project. Though some proposals serve as the project contract once the client has accepted them, you will usually say here that you expect to sign a separate formal contract.

Pricing for Businesses Selling Products

As with pricing services, there are different ways to figure out what to charge for the products that your business sells. Of course, your cost of acquiring or making the products will play a big part in your pricing decisions. But you may have difficulty deciding on an appropriate markup. This section will walk you through a few issues to consider when pricing goods.

CAUTION

Don't discuss your product pricing strategy with competitors. Antitrust laws forbid you to fix prices with your competitors and even to share price information or discuss prices with them. Steer clear of this potentially serious legal trouble by simply avoiding pricing discussions altogether.

Establish an Overall Pricing Strategy

Before deciding how much you'll charge for your widgets, you should think about and adopt an overall pricing strategy for your business. Keep in mind that the very same widget might be sold for $0.99 at your local 99¢ store, $5 at a chain retailer, and $25 at a swank boutique. The price can vary so much because each of these stores has its own pricing strategy—and you should, too.

The concept is simple: Will your business use a high-end, middle-end, or low-end strategy? Each strategy can be profitable if you work within its logic. Here's a quick description of how each strategy typically works:

- **High-end** shops can charge high prices so long as they offer something in return, such as a great selection of hard-to-find or highly specialized products, extraordinary customer service, an exclusive atmosphere, or simply top-notch quality.

- **Middle-end** shops charge average prices and succeed on the basis of other factors, such as selection, customer service, and convenient hours and locations. None of these factors are exceptional enough to justify high-end prices, but they're attractive enough to draw customers who aren't necessarily looking for the very lowest price.
- **Low-end** shops succeed by forgoing some amenities, such as a reliable selection or a convenient location. They attract customers by offering the lowest prices. Customers might have to paw through bins of merchandise or drive across town to a cold, cheerless warehouse store, but they'll do it because they know they'll get a bargain.

Whichever strategy you choose, it's important that you stick with it and use it consistently. You will confuse customers and push them to your competitors if you offer a confounding mix of high- and low-end items in the same store.

Research Markup Data

Once you've got your pricing strategy in place, you must decide how much you'll mark up your products for sale. You can set your prices appropriately after you do some research to figure out how much other similar businesses mark up their goods.

One easy source of markup information is simply the manufacturer's suggested retail price or MSRP, also called the suggested list price. If you buy a line of floor lamps that cost you $30 per unit and the MSRP is $90, then you know the manufacturer is recommending a markup of 200% of cost. You don't have to follow the recommendation (the days of adherence to MSRPs are over), but you'll get a good idea of what may be typical in the marketplace for that item.

In addition to using MSRPs, ask your manufacturers and suppliers for information they may have on average markup rates. Your suppliers can be a valuable source of this kind of information, beyond setting MSRPs for each product.

You can find good information about industry standard markup rates in many sources. Trade associations and journals may give you valuable data. Directories and guidebooks are also available on many industries. These books tend to be expensive ($100 and up) but are often treasure troves of valuable industry info. Hoover's Inc. is a company that specializes in providing comprehensive market data; its website (www.hoovers.com) offers a wealth of information and publications for sale. Many of the titles offered at Hoover's are from Plunkett Research, another firm specializing in market data. Plunkett has its own website at www.plunkettresearch.com.

What's Up With Markup?

Markup is the amount that's tacked on to the cost of an item to arrive at its selling price. For instance, a wristwatch that cost $25 to the retailer may be marked up by $37.50, for a selling price of $62.50. What can be confusing is that markup rates are sometimes expressed as a percentage of cost, and other times as a percentage of selling price.

For example, the markup percentage for the wristwatch is 150% of cost or 60% of selling price. What does this mean? The percentage of cost calculation works like this: The cost of the watch ($25) is multiplied by 150%, resulting in a $37.50 markup, which is added to its original cost ($25) to arrive at the selling price of $62.50.

Here is the percentage of selling price calculation: The selling price ($62.50) is multiplied by 60%, resulting in the same $37.50 markup arrived at with the percentage of cost calculation. As you can see, these two different ways of expressing a markup percentage yield the same result.

When you search markup rates, be sure you know which type of percentage you're dealing with: percentage of cost or percentage of selling price. If you apply a percentage of selling price markup rate to the item cost, or use the percentage of cost markup with the item's selling price, you'll end up with the wrong result. For instance, if you mistakenly calculate the wristwatch markup by multiplying the item cost ($25) by the percentage of selling price markup rate (60%), you'll end up with a markup of $15, and a selling price of just $40.

Don't stop there. Do your own research, and look specifically for info pertaining to your type of business. Search online, visit the library of a local business school, ask local trade associations, and generally do some sleuthing to turn up the data you need.

Chapter 6 Checklist: Pricing, Bidding, and Billing Projects

☐ Never discuss the topic of pricing with competitors—basically, anyone in the same industry as you.

☐ If you're in a service business, set hourly rates carefully, by using a formula, basing the rates on market conditions, or a combination of these approaches. However you set your rates, remember that you'll need not only to earn a salary but also to pay for your overhead and make a profit.

☐ If you're in a service business, become familiar with various ways to bill clients and understand which methods are best for specific situations.

☐ If you will have to bid for work, learn how to put together a professional proposal.

☐ If you plan to sell products, develop an overall pricing strategy to guide pricing decisions.

☐ If you sell products, research the market to understand what typical markup rates are used by others in your industry.

Federal, State, and Local Start-Up Requirements

By now you've finished hammering out the details of how you plan to operate your business. In a perfect world, you could hang up your "open" sign and start selling your products or services at a nice profit. Sorry! In the real world of small business, things are not quite that easy. Before you can legally begin your business, you need to take care of a number of pesky requirements with government agencies from the city to the federal level. Although none of these requirements are difficult or even terribly time-consuming, lots of entrepreneurs get stymied at this point because it's so hard to find one centralized source of information that explains what to do. They're left to ferret out each bureaucratic requirement one by one and hope they've found all of them by the time they start doing business.

For example, your city tax office can tell you what forms you must file there but won't tell you how to obtain a permit in order to sell retail goods. And while your state sales tax agency may be able to tell you everything you need to know about getting a seller's permit, it won't explain how to obtain a federal employer identification number, which is required for most businesses. The process of finding out what you need to do and how to go about doing it can feel like putting together a jigsaw puzzle without knowing how many pieces it should have or how it should look when completed.

To help you figure out what you need to do and where you need to do it, all the basic start-up requirements are discussed here in one chapter. It guides you through the bureaucratic maze and explains the typical registration requirements that apply to most businesses. (Businesses with employees have to meet a few extra requirements, explained in Chapter 16.) There are far more specific regulations for certain small businesses, such as those relating to toxic waste disposal, than we could cover here—particularly at the state and city level. But this chapter explains the basic regulatory structure that every businessperson will have to deal with and points out which agencies typically deal with certain types of requirements. By the time you finish reading this chapter, you'll know a number of registration requirements that you will have to meet, plus you'll have a good idea of where to check for other requirements that may apply to you, depending on what type of business you're starting and where you'll be conducting it.

Sure, dealing with city and state bureaucrats can be a mind-numbing endurance contest. But once the mystery is taken out of the registration process and you have a clear idea of which requirements may apply to you, you'll be able to tackle the bureaucracy with a minimum of time and stress.

CAUTION

It may take more time to start a corporation, an LLC, or a limited partnership. Although starting up a company that offers limited liability—a corporation, an LLC, or a limited partnership—isn't rocket science, the process is more complex than starting a sole proprietorship or general partnership. While this chapter outlines the basic start-up requirements for businesses that offer limited liability, you will also need to understand some additional formalities and requirements. For example, if you plan to create one of these types of businesses, you may need to comply with federal and state securities laws. Step 1, below, gives you a brief overview of the extra formation step you'll have to take to set up a business with limited liability. Once you have formed your corporation, LLC, or limited partnership, you'll be ready to use the information in this chapter on permits, licenses, and tax-filing requirements.

"Why Am I Filling Out All These Forms?"

Why do you have to sort your way through a tangled bureaucracy to start a small business? At the most basic level, there are three purposes to the various business permit and license requirements:

- **To identify you.** No matter what kind of business you run, society has an interest in making sure that you are accountable for your actions. That's why businesses that don't use their owners' names as part of their business names must often register a fictitious business name statement with the state or county. That way, a member of the public who has a problem with Racafrax Designs or Acme Sandblasting can easily find out who the owners are, complain to them, and, if necessary, sue them.
- **To protect the public.** Government agencies issue permits and licenses to ensure that your business offers safe products or services that won't harm people or the environment. For example, if you open a food service business, your city's department of health understandably wants to make sure that your kitchen is sanitary and will likely require that you obtain a permit, license, or other official approval before you can start serving snacks.
- **To keep track of your finances for tax purposes.** Several of the registration requirements are based on the government's nasty habit of taxing everything that moves (and lots of things that don't). To be sure that they collect every possible tax and fee, local, state, and federal governments use various registration requirements to keep tabs on your business.

Jennifer F. Mahoney, owner of an illustration service in Northern California, (www.candraw.net):

I'm lucky enough to have a technical skill to combine with a regular drawing skill that puts me in a market niche among illustrators. Lacking any entrepreneurial "uncles," it took me a while to get a clue about the business world, like finding untapped markets, understanding agreements, getting paid, handling copyright issues, and finding out how many regulatory bodies need a portion of my modest income. It all felt like groping in the dark: Where are all the rules written down? I'm doing well for myself now, supporting my family, but I wish it hadn't taken me so long to figure out.

Here are the general start-up steps discussed in this chapter:

Step 1: File organizational documents with the Secretary of State or similar filing office (corporations, LLCs, and limited partnerships only).

Step 2: Obtain a federal employer identification number (FEIN).

Step 3: Register your fictitious business name with your county or state.

Step 4: Obtain a local tax registration certificate (also known as a business license).

Step 5: Obtain a permit to sell retail goods and collect state sales tax.

Step 6: Obtain specialized vocation-related licenses or environmental permits if necessary.

Step 1: File Organizational Documents With Your State (Corporations, LLCs, and Limited Partnerships Only)

 SKIP AHEAD

Sole proprietors and partnerships can skip this step. Only corporations, LLCs, and limited partnerships need to file organizational documents with the state. If you're starting a sole proprietorship or partnership, skip ahead to Step 2.

Unlike sole proprietorships or partnerships, businesses that offer limited liability don't just pop into existence as soon as their owners start selling products or services. If you want to create one of these types of businesses, you'll need to take the first step of filing registration papers with your state filing office, which typically is the Secretary or Department of State.

 RESOURCE

Where to find your state filing office. State filing offices, such as the Secretary of State, other state agency websites are listed in Appendix A and on the Nolo website; see Appendix A for the link.

Because these business structures are regulated at the state level, each state has different rules for creating and managing them. For the most part, however, these laws are fairly similar. For corporations, the organizational document is usually called the articles of incorporation; for LLCs, it's generally called the articles of organization (although some states call it a certificate of organization or formation). Limited partnerships also have to file registration documents with the state. To create any of these business structures, you'll need to do additional reading or consult other resources. (See "Additional resources from Nolo," below.)

When you file your organizational documents with your state, you will usually be registering your corporate, LLC, or limited partnership name at the same time. Typically, the agency in charge (most often the Secretary of State) must approve all names before they can be registered, otherwise your organizational papers will be rejected. Your name won't be approved if another business of the same legal structure (corporation, LLC, or limited partnership) in your state has already taken the business name you want to use. In other words, a California corporation may not use a name that's used by an existing California corporation, a New Mexico LLC may not use a name that is used by another New Mexico LLC, and so on. Some states check all of their name

databases—LLC, corporate, and limited partnership—regardless of what form of business you're creating. To save time and headaches, do some research before you file your papers to make sure your proposed name is available. You can usually call or write to the state filing office to confirm availability. Quite a few states now also allow you to check for name availability online. Ask your state's filing office for its procedure.

 TIP

Reserve your name. Many states allow you to reserve a corporate, LLC, or limited partnership name once you've learned it's available. Doing so is a good idea, as it can't then be taken by someone else before you have a chance to file your papers.

It's also very important to remember that just because your name is accepted by your state filing office doesn't mean it's free and clear for you to use. As discussed in detail in Chapter 2, trademark and unfair competition laws may prevent you from using a name used by another business, including businesses that aren't included in your state's corporate, LLC, or limited partnership name databases. For instance, the name of a local general partnership wouldn't be registered in your state's corporate name database but may have been in use for years. Or the name you've chosen may have been taken by a corporation in another state, so it would not appear in your state's database. To avoid running afoul of trademark and unfair competition laws, it's wise to do a trademark search before choosing any name for your business, or for its products or services. (See Chapter 2 for a full discussion of the legal issues surrounding business names.)

 RESOURCE

Additional resources from Nolo. Nolo publishes a wide range of information on corporations, LLCs, and limited partnerships. Books on LLCs include:

- *Nolo's Quick LLC: All You Need to Know About Limited Liability Companies*, by Anthony Mancuso. Explains the basics of LLCs.
- *Form Your Own Limited Liability Company*, by Anthony Mancuso. Offers guidance and forms on creating an LLC, as well as legal and tax information about this form of business.
- *Your Limited Liability Company: An Operating Manual*, by Anthony Mancuso. Offers detailed information and forms for managing LLCs in compliance with various state and federal laws.
- *Nolo's Guide to Single-Member LLCs*, by David M. Steingold. Gives an overview on how to form and run an LLC with one member, including the unique tax and liability issues.

Nolo also offers an online LLC formation service.

On the corporate side, *The Corporate Records Handbook: Meetings, Minutes & Resolutions*, by Anthony Mancuso, provides forms and instructions for running a corporation and handling corporate meetings and documentation. Nolo also publishes *Incorporate Your Business: A Step-by-Step Guide to Forming a Corporation in Any State*, by Anthony Mancuso.

For more information on limited partnerships, see *Form a Partnership: The Complete Legal Guide*, by Denis Clifford and Ralph Warner.

Step 2: Obtain a Federal Employer Identification Number (FEIN)

Sole proprietors and partners don't need to explicitly "create" their business by registering with any state office; once they're engaged in business activity, their business more or less exists by default. (See Chapter 1 for more information about creating all types of businesses, including sole proprietorships and partnerships.) If you're starting a sole proprietorship or a partnership, getting a federal employer identification number (FEIN) from the Internal Revenue Service should be your first registration task, mainly because you can get one before you've registered with any other agency or filled out any other forms.

Corporations and LLCs must also apply for an FEIN, but they have to file their organizational documents with the state first. (See Step 1, above.)

What an FEIN Is and Who Needs One

A business's federal employer identification number (alternately called an FEIN, an EIN, or an employer ID) is roughly equivalent to a Social Security number for an individual. It's a number used by the government to identify your business, which you'll use over and over again on most of your important business documents. To mention just a few places you'll use it, you'll typically need to enter it on your business's local tax registration forms, your federal tax return, and any applications for business licenses.

Some of you are probably saying, "But I don't plan to have employees, why do I need an employer ID number?" Blame the IRS for the confusing terminology. Although it's called an "employer" ID number, FEINs are required for most businesses, even those that don't have employees. The one exception is sole proprietors with no employees, who can use their own Social Security number instead of an FEIN. Partnerships, LLCs, and corporations need FEINs whether they have employees or not.

Applying for an FEIN

Getting an EIN is easy and free. To apply online, you'll need to do it during the hours of operation from Monday through Friday from 7 a.m. to 10 p.m. Eastern Time. Simply go to www.irs. gov/businesses, click on "Employer ID Numbers," and follow the prompts. Note that you must complete the application in one session, as you will not be able to save it and return to finish it later. Your session will expire after 15 minutes of inactivity, and you will need to start over. Upon completion you will get your EIN right away, and you'll be able to download and print your EIN confirmation notice.

If for some reason you can't apply online, you can apply by fax or by mail. Note that the IRS no longer issues EINs by telephone for U.S.-based taxpayers; only international applicants can receive an EIN by phone. Obtain Form SS-4 from the IRS website at www.irs.gov, or by phone by calling 800-TAX-FORM (800-829-3676) Monday through Friday, 7 a.m. to 7 p.m. local time. You can also get tax forms from local tax offices, and often your local library or community center. Complete and fax the form to the IRS using the fax number listed in the instructions under "Where To File or Fax;" these numbers are subject to change so make sure you're using the latest instructions. If you apply by fax, you'll typically receive your EIN by fax within four business days.

To apply by mail, complete and mail Form SS-4 to the address listed in the instructions under "Where To File or Fax." Make sure you submit it at least four to five weeks before you will need the EIN; you will typically receive your EIN within approximately four weeks.

Form **SS-4** (Rev. December 2017) Department of the Treasury Internal Revenue Service	**Application for Employer Identification Number** (For use by employers, corporations, partnerships, trusts, estates, churches, government agencies, Indian tribal entities, certain individuals, and others.) ▶ Go to *www.irs.gov/FormSS4* for instructions and the latest information. ▶ See separate instructions for each line. ▶ Keep a copy for your records.	OMB No. 1545-0003 EIN

Type or print clearly.

1	Legal name of entity (or individual) for whom the EIN is being requested		
2	Trade name of business (if different from name on line 1)	3	Executor, administrator, trustee, "care of" name
4a	Mailing address (room, apt., suite no. and street, or P.O. box)	5a	Street address (if different) (Do not enter a P.O. box.)
4b	City, state, and ZIP code (if foreign, see instructions)	5b	City, state, and ZIP code (if foreign, see instructions)
6	County and state where principal business is located		
7a	Name of responsible party	7b	SSN, ITIN, or EIN

8a	Is this application for a limited liability company (LLC) (or a foreign equivalent)? . . . . ☐ Yes ☐ No	8b	If 8a is "Yes," enter the number of LLC members . . . . . . ▶
8c	If 8a is "Yes," was the LLC organized in the United States? . . . . ☐ Yes ☐ No		

9a	**Type of entity** (check only one box). **Caution.** If 8a is "Yes," see the instructions for the correct box to check.

☐ Sole proprietor (SSN) _____ ☐ Estate (SSN of decedent) _____
☐ Partnership ☐ Plan administrator (TIN) _____
☐ Corporation (enter form number to be filed) ▶ _____ ☐ Trust (TIN of grantor) _____
☐ Personal service corporation ☐ Military/National Guard ☐ State/local government
☐ Church or church-controlled organization ☐ Farmers' cooperative ☐ Federal government
☐ Other nonprofit organization (specify) ▶ _____ ☐ REMIC ☐ Indian tribal governments/enterprises
☐ Other (specify) ▶ Group Exemption Number (GEN) if any ▶

9b	If a corporation, name the state or foreign country (if applicable) where incorporated	State	Foreign country

10	**Reason for applying** (check only one box)	☐ Banking purpose (specify purpose) ▶ _____
	☐ Started new business (specify type) ▶ _____	☐ Changed type of organization (specify new type) ▶ _____
		☐ Purchased going business
	☐ Hired employees (Check the box and see line 13.)	☐ Created a trust (specify type) ▶ _____
	☐ Compliance with IRS withholding regulations	☐ Created a pension plan (specify type) ▶ _____
	☐ Other (specify) ▶	

11	Date business started or acquired (month, day, year). See instructions.	12	Closing month of accounting year
		14	If you expect your employment tax liability to be $1,000 or less in a full calendar year **and** want to file Form 944 annually instead of Forms 941 quarterly, check here. (Your employment tax liability generally will be $1,000 or less if you expect to pay $4,000 or less in total wages.) If you do not check this box, you must file Form 941 for every quarter. ☐
13	Highest number of employees expected in the next 12 months (enter -0- if none). If no employees expected, skip line 14.		

Agricultural	Household	Other

15	First date wages or annuities were paid (month, day, year). **Note**: If applicant is a withholding agent, enter date income will first be paid to nonresident alien (month, day, year) . . . . ▶

16	Check **one** box that best describes the principal activity of your business.	☐ Health care & social assistance	☐ Wholesale-agent/broker
	☐ Construction ☐ Rental & leasing ☐ Transportation & warehousing	☐ Accommodation & food service	☐ Wholesale-other ☐ Retail
	☐ Real estate ☐ Manufacturing ☐ Finance & insurance	☐ Other (specify) ▶	
17	Indicate principal line of merchandise sold, specific construction work done, products produced, or services provided.		
18	Has the applicant entity shown on line 1 ever applied for and received an EIN? ☐ Yes ☐ No If "Yes," write previous EIN here ▶		

	Complete this section **only** if you want to authorize the named individual to receive the entity's EIN and answer questions about the completion of this form.	
Third Party Designee	Designee's name	Designee's telephone number (include area code)
	Address and ZIP code	Designee's fax number (include area code)

Under penalties of perjury, I declare that I have examined this application, and to the best of my knowledge and belief, it is true, correct, and complete. | Applicant's telephone number (include area code)

Name and title (type or print clearly) ▶

Signature ▶ Date ▶ | Applicant's fax number (include area code)

For Privacy Act and Paperwork Reduction Act Notice, see separate instructions. Cat. No. 16055N Form **SS-4** (Rev. 12-2017)

FORM

Where to find the FEIN application form. In addition to the IRS website, a copy of Form SS-4 is available on the Nolo website (see the link to this book's companion page in Appendix B).

A sample Form SS-4 appears above. Although much of the information you'll have to put on the form is pretty basic, the following tips will help you get the job done.

Line 1 asks for the legal name of the entity that is applying for the FEIN. Sounds simple enough, but, depending on your business, it can get a little tricky.

Sole proprietors should enter a full individual name—first, last, and middle initial. Do not enter any fictitious business name (FBN) you use or plan to use. (A fictitious business name is a name you use for your business that doesn't contain your legal name. FBNs are explained in more detail in the next section.)

A partnership should use the legal name of the partnership as it appears in the partnership agreement. For example, say Gene Cook and Beth Lynch own a partnership that they refer to as "Cook and Lynch, Partners" in their partnership agreement. This is the name they should write on Item 1. If you own a partnership but don't have a written partnership agreement, insert the name you plan to use for all official business and on all government forms—either a business name that contains each partner's last name or the trade name that you will present to the public (also known as your "fictitious business name," or your "DBA name," discussed below). (See Chapter 2 for the full spiel on the various types of business names.)

An LLC should enter the official company name as it appears in its articles of organization (or certificate of organization or formation).

A corporation should use its legal name as it appears in its articles of incorporation (or certificate of organization).

Line 2 asks for the trade name of the business. This is the same as asking for your fictitious business name or your "doing business as" (DBA) name. You can leave this line blank if you plan to do business under the same name you entered on Line 1. For example, if Gene Cook and Beth Lynch plan to do business under the name Cook and Lynch, Partners, and they entered that name on Line 1, they can leave Line 2 blank. Similarly, if a sole proprietor named Stacey Stickler will use just her name to identify her landscape design services, she too can leave Line 2 blank.

But when your company's legal name doesn't match its trade name, you should enter the trade name on Line 2. For example, if Stacey Stickler decides to do business as Stickler's Landscape Design, she should enter "Stickler's Landscape

Design" on Line 2. A partnership that wants to do business under any name other than its legal name would do the same thing. For example, if "Cook and Lynch, Partners" want to do business under the trade name "CooLyn Enterprises," they will enter "Cook and Lynch, Partners" on Line 1 and "CooLyn Enterprises" on Line 2. (You'll find more on trade names and fictitious business names just below.)

While it may seem like splitting hairs, this is actually quite important. Think about it: The FEIN form introduces you and your business to the IRS and identifies you in an official way. Using the correct name will help you avoid snafus with the IRS and other government agencies. For example, if Cook and Lynch alternate between calling their business "Cook and Lynch" and "CooLyn Enterprises" on government documents, they will almost surely experience a raft of bureaucratic headaches.

Line 3 to end of form asks for fairly straightforward information. For advice, see the Instructions for Form SS-4, included with the form on the Nolo website; see the link in Appendix B.

Step 3: Register Your Fictitious Business Name (FBN)

As discussed in Chapter 2, any trade name that doesn't contain the legal names of the owners (for sole proprietorships or general partnerships) or that doesn't match the company's corporate, limited partnership, or LLC name on file with the state, is called a fictitious business name (FBN). Fictitious business names are sometimes called assumed names, or "DBAs," for "doing business as"—as in, "Spikey Andrews, doing business as Coffee Corner," or "Alibi Corporation, doing business as Ferryville Bait and Tackle." Some states simply use the term "trade name," though this can be confusing because it doesn't indicate whether the name is the same as or different from the legal name. In this chapter and the rest of the book, the term fictitious business name will be used for any business name that doesn't contain the legal name of the business owner.

Most states require a business that uses a fictitious business name to register that name, usually with the county clerk in the county where its primary business site is located. Depending on your state, this requirement goes by different names: fictitious name certification, DBA filing, trade name registration, or something similar. FBN registrations are typically done at the county level, although, in some states, you register your FBN with the Secretary of State or another state agency. The registration process is covered in more detail below.

States like to keep track of business names for a couple of reasons: One is to prevent customer confusion between two local businesses that use the same name. (Before a business can register its fictitious business name, many states either search their business name registries or require that the business do so to make sure the name isn't already being used.) Another reason is to give customers a quick way to find out who the owner of a company is without having to hire a private investigator. This allows customers to easily contact the owners to make a complaint or to take legal action against them. Requiring owners to register their business names makes it harder for fly-by-night businesses to operate anonymously and defraud customers.

The Importance of Filing an FBN Statement

Do not neglect or put off registering your fictitious business name. Without proof of registration, many banks will not open an account under your business name. Also, if you don't register your name, it won't appear in any fictitious name databases in your state. This means that another business will be less likely to find out you're using it and may start using the name itself. Even though you have other legal avenues to stop another business from using a name that you used first (see Chapter 2), you don't want to create customer confusion between the two businesses and get into a name dispute

with another business. If you lose a dispute over a name, at the very least you'll have to redo stationery, signs, and anything else that contains the name, such as T-shirts or maybe even your company logo.

Who Needs to Register

The rules for registering fictitious business names depend on which business structure you use.

Sole Proprietorships

Generally speaking, a sole proprietor who includes his or her last name in the business name—such as O'Toole's Classic Cars—does not need to file an FBN statement. But it is not enough to include only initials and a nickname or part of a name. For example, a business called J.R.'s Classic Cars would likely have to file a fictitious name statement indicating that it really is John O'Toole's business.

In addition, in many states, if your business name falsely implies that more than one owner is involved, you must file a fictitious business name statement. If Jason Todd were a sole proprietor, for example, and named his business Jason Todd and Sons or Jason Todd & Associates, he would probably have to file an FBN statement, even though he included his last name in his business name. Check with your county clerk for your state's rules.

Partnerships

If a partnership includes the last names of all the partners—for example, Lawrence Anderson and Nancy Fawcett name their business "Anderson and Fawcett Metal Designs"—they don't have to file a statement. Otherwise, an FBN statement will be required. For example, if three partners, Lynch, Cook, and Briggs, did business only under the name "Lynch & Cook," they would have to file an FBN statement. Check with your county clerk for your state's specific rules.

Corporations, LLCs, and Limited Partnerships

A corporation, an LLC, or a limited partnership does not need to file an FBN statement unless it operates under a name that's different from its official name as stated in its articles of incorporation, articles of organization, or certificate of limited partnership. For example, an LLC that registered with the Secretary of State under the name "Landmark Lanes, LLC" wouldn't have to file an FBN statement as long as it conducted business under that name. Any other trade name, "Landmark Bowl," for instance— or even "Landmark Lanes" without the "LLC" tacked onto the end—might be considered to be "fictitious" and would have to be registered. The same is often true for corporations: If "Inc." is included in the corporations's name in the articles of incorporation, but not in the company's trade name, an FBN statement usually must be filed. Check with your county clerk or Secretary of State or other state filing office to determine your state's specific rules.

Filing With Your County

In some states, FBN registration is accomplished through the Secretary of State or another state agency; however, in most states, you'll register your FBN at the county level. (This is generally true despite the fact that most laws governing fictitious business names are state laws.) The result is that each county in your state may have different forms and fees for registering an FBN. Your first step should be to call your county clerk's office to find out its requirements and fees. Some counties allow you to order the FBN registration form by phone or download it from their website; others require you to request it in writing with a self-addressed, stamped envelope. Unless you live a good distance from the nearest county clerk, it may be easiest just to go to the office and complete the form in person.

Searching the County (or State) Database

In many areas, you'll be instructed to search the county or state database of registered fictitious business names before submitting your statement to make sure no one else has already registered the name you want to use. Typically, you can search a county's database (often an easy-to-search computerized system) for free if you go to the office in person. Sometimes you can pay a fee for a staff person to do the search for you. If you want the clerk's office to do the search, you must usually submit the request and fee by mail.

CAUTION

County databases won't tell you if a name is trademarked. Oftentimes, fictitious business names are registered at the county level, and you may be required to search your county database before registering your fictitious name to make sure it isn't already registered. Ironically, this requirement may well do more harm than good. The reason is that lots of people who find that no one in the county has registered a certain name are misled into believing that the name is available to use. The truth of the matter is that someone in a different county, state, or even country might own trademark rights to that name.

Only owners of the tiniest of businesses can feel safe by doing merely a county-wide search of a name they want to use. If someone else has trademarked that name, you may well run into legal trouble, depending on your geographical scope and the products or services you sell. Particularly with the explosion of e-business, geographical distance is becoming irrelevant as the Internet makes neighbors out of businesses on opposite sides of the globe.

To avoid being accused of unfair competition or trademark infringement, it is wise to check neighboring counties' FBN databases, look into state registries of corporate and LLC names, or even do a full international trademark search. Failing to do an appropriate search puts you at risk not only of lawsuits, but also of having to change your name down the line when you already have stationery, business signs, and invoices printed. (See Chapter 2 on trademark and business name issues for more information on choosing and researching a name that won't get you into legal trouble.)

Completing and Submitting an FBN Statement

If the name you've chosen is available (both at the county level and with regard to trademark issues), simply fill out the FBN statement and submit it to your county clerk (or other agency, depending on your state) along with the appropriate fees. You typically can submit the form in person or by mail. Depending on the county, fees range from $10 to $50 for registering one business name and one business owner. Sometimes you may be charged an additional fee, around $5 to $15, to register additional business names to be used at the same business location or to register additional owners.

Publishing Notice of Your FBN Statement

Once you've filed your name and paid the necessary fees, you may have one more task to complete before you start doing business under that name. Many states require you to have your FBN statement published in an approved newspaper in the county where you filed it. The county clerk or state agency will provide a list of acceptable publications for posting your FBN statement, though usually any newspaper of general circulation in the county will suffice. Publishing your statement is typically simple: Just submit your statement to your publication of choice, which will have a standard format to present the required information.

send in the affidavit for you after your ad has completed its run. Make sure to find out whether the publication you use will do this (and double-check afterward to make sure it has actually done it). If not, you'll have to get the affidavit from the publication yourself and submit it to the county clerk or state agency within the prescribed deadline. If the affidavit isn't filed in time, you may have to start the process all over again.

Check with your county clerk for the details and requirements of publishing the FBN notice.

TIP

Obscure publications are cheapest. As long as a newspaper is on the approved list or doesn't otherwise violate your county's rules (for instance, in some counties you can't publish an FBN statement in a free newspaper), there's nothing wrong with picking the cheapest one.

The published notice must run for a certain frequency and duration, usually once a week for a month or so. After the FBN has been published for the required period, you'll usually need to submit an affidavit (sometimes called proof of publication) with the county clerk or state agency to show that publication has been completed. Many newspapers that provide publication services will automatically

TIP

Save your ad receipt. For practical reasons, you may need to prove that you completed your fictitious business name filing requirements—including publication—before your ad has actually completed its publication run. Banks, for instance, want to see that you have met fictitious name rules before they allow you to open an account in that name. Fortunately, a receipt from the newspaper showing that you have paid for publication, along with a copy of the FBN statement certified by the county clerk or state agency, is generally sufficient to prove that you've met all the registration requirements, even though the ad hasn't yet run for four weeks. So be sure to get a certified copy of your FBN statement from the county clerk or state agency when you submit it, as well as a receipt from the newspaper when you pay for publishing it.

After You File

Your FBN registration will be good for a certain period of time, usually for five years or so, before it must be renewed. You (or someone at your business) should keep track of your expiration date, as your county clerk or state agency may not notify you when your renewal date approaches. Also, if certain facts in your statement change, such as the number of owners or your business address, you may have to renew your FBN statement. Check with your county clerk or state agency to find out which types of changes trigger a renewal requirement. If you no longer want your FBN registered, you may file a form (often called a statement of abandonment) to cause the registration to expire.

Step 4: Obtain a Local Tax Registration Certificate

Most cities require all businesses (including home businesses) to register with that city's tax collector, regardless of business type, structure, size, or name. Businesses located in rural, unincorporated areas must usually register with the county clerk rather than a city tax collector. (While this section often refers to city tax collectors and city requirements for businesses, just keep in mind that if you're operating outside of a city, the same types of requirements generally apply but are administered by county government.)

Depending on where you register, the locality may use different names for the process: tax registration, business tax application, business license application, or tax certification, for example. In this book, the terms "tax registration" and "tax registration certificate" are used—and it's best if you don't use the term "business license" when you really mean "tax registration certificate" (or whatever term is used in your locality for tax registration). True licenses, which are discussed in Step 6, below, are typically administered at the state level. Certain businesses must obtain them if they engage in regulated activities, such as selling alcohol or cutting people's hair. Getting such a license often involves taking a test or otherwise proving you're qualified to do a certain activity.

TIP

Some businesses need to satisfy more requirements. Your tax registration certificate is not the same as a specialized license your business might need—such as a permit from the local health department for handling food, from the Federal Communications Commission for broadcasting over the radio waves, or from a regional air management district for emitting particles into the air. (Step 6, below, discusses these specialized licenses and permits.) Whether or not you need one of these licenses or permits, you'll still need to get a tax registration certificate.

The reason you need to register with your local tax collector is that, just like the federal and state governments, your local government wants a cut of your business income. The tax registration requirement is basically your local government's way of keeping track of your business so that it will be able to collect any taxes due.

Cities and counties have been known to tax businesses with even more flair and creativity than the feds or the states. Localities tax businesses based on criteria such as net profit, gross income, number of employees, total payroll, number of vehicles, number of machines, and sometimes even seating capacity.

In addition, most cities categorize businesses and use different tax structures for each category. In Charlottesville, Virginia, for instance, when a business's gross receipts are greater than $100,000, the following tax rates apply: Bakeries are charged a 0.2% tax on gross receipts; landscapers pay a rate of 0.36%; and architects and other professionals pay a rate of 0.58%. Other types of businesses in Charlottesville pay flat fees in addition to the gross receipts tax, such as wineries ($500 per year), coin machine operators ($150), and fortune-tellers ($1,000).

In addition to being assigned a category and a tax rate, businesses may be subject to special taxes for particular activities. In Chicago, for instance, businesses that sell soft drink syrup or fountain soft drinks must pay an extra "Fountain Soft Drink" tax of 9% of the syrup price, and businesses that offer sightseeing boat rides must pay an extra "Amusement Tax" of 9% of the ticket price.

For the privilege of registering to pay local taxes, you'll usually have to pay an annual fee, which varies from city to city but is generally in the $25 to $100 range. Sometimes the annual fee depends partly on how much tax your business is expected to owe the following year, based on city (or county) tax rates. If the fee is based on estimated taxes, at least part of the registration fee may be a nonrefundable administrative fee. In that case, the other part of the fee will go toward paying your estimated taxes or will be returned to you if your taxes turn out to be lower than expected. In San Francisco, California, for instance, the registration fee is based on your gross receipts for the previous year.

 CAUTION

Local rules can change without notice. Be sure to check with your local office for the most current rules and rates. The information here is relatively current, but these rules often change. The point is to give you a taste of the various ways local governments handle business taxes. As you can see, there's a lot of variation.

For your city's requirements, call your city tax collector or check your city's website. The tax collector's office will be able to provide you with the forms necessary to register in your city, as well as any breakdown of business categories and tax tables. If you're doing business outside city limits, call your county clerk, usually listed under "County Clerk" in the county government section of the phone book, or check your county's website.

Step 5: Obtain a State Seller's Permit

In most states, any business—whether it's a sole proprietorship, an LLC, a corporation, or any other type—must have a seller's permit if it sells any tangible goods to the public. Tangible goods are things you can touch, such as furniture or food. Businesses that sell only services are often exempt from the seller's permit requirement. In the five states that do not impose general sales taxes (Alaska, Delaware, Montana, New Hampshire, and Oregon), you may not be required to get a permit for most sales transactions. However, local governments, such as cities and counties in those states, may charge sales taxes (as in Alaska), and certain transactions in those states may be subject to something similar to a sales tax, though it may have a different name. If you live in one of the nontaxing states, be sure to check with the sales tax agency to find out if your specific transactions will be subject to tax and if you'll need a seller's permit.

RESOURCE

Where to find your state tax agency. State sales tax agencies' websites are listed in Appendix A and on this book's companion page on Nolo.com.

CAUTION

States are getting much more aggressive about taxing sales conducted online. If you plan to conduct sales online, make sure you understand whether those sales will be taxable. In a nutshell, online sales that used to be considered nontaxable because they were made to out-of-state buyers are the subject of a flurry of state legislation, as states are attempting to define many of these sales as taxable. See Chapter 9 for a more detailed discussion of sales taxes online.

In states that do charge sales taxes, a seller's permit will allow your business to collect sales taxes from customers to cover any sales tax that you'll owe to the state. You'll typically pay any taxes you owe at year end, semiannually, or quarterly. Some you may have to pay monthly. The general rule is that the higher your sales volume, the more often you'll owe your payment.

It's important to understand that if you plan to sell tangible goods, you'll often need a seller's permit whether or not those sales will be taxable. For instance, most states exempt certain sales from state sales tax, such as sales of food or sales to an out-of-state customer. But, in most states, you'll need a seller's permit even to conduct these types of nontaxable sales. This means you need to get a sales permit before you begin to sell tangible goods; when the sales are made, you'll distinguish the taxable ones from the nontaxable ones. When it comes time to report and pay sales taxes to the state, you'll owe tax only on the taxable sales. (See Chapter 9 for a detailed discussion of reporting and paying sales taxes.)

TIP

Keep track of your service and product sales separately. Many businesses both perform services and sell products. A metalsmith, for instance, both repairs jewelry and sells raw materials, such as precious metals and gemstones. If a business sells both labor and goods, it will need a seller's permit (assuming it's in a state that requires one). Plus, to assure proper tax reporting, that business will need to keep its labor sales separate from sales of goods, since sales of services aren't taxed in most locales. (Chapter 12 explains simple bookkeeping and how to account for taxable sales separately from tax-exempt sales.)

To obtain a seller's permit, contact the agency in your state that governs sales taxes.

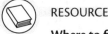

RESOURCE

Where to find your state agency. Appendix A lists websites for sales tax and seller's permit agencies by state. This list also is included on this book's companion page on Nolo.com (the link is also in Appendix A).

The process of obtaining a seller's permit typically consists of submitting a simple application form and, sometimes, paying a fee. Some states require a deposit from businesses that have a blemished history of not paying their sales taxes on time.

Step 6: Obtain Specialized Licenses or Permits

Depending on the nature of your business, you might be finished with your list of bureaucratic tasks. But before you run off to rev up your cash register, cool your jets—you may be surprised to find out that even your simple little business is subject to an extra regulation or two. Some business activities are prohibited until you obtain a license or permit to engage in them, and some business locations require special approval from the local planning department. These extra requirements are especially likely to apply to your business if it has any potential for harming the environment or hurting the public, but they also apply in lots of seemingly risk-free situations.

Figuring out what additional permits or licenses you might need can be confusing, because there are literally hundreds of independent agencies from the local to the federal level that regulate various businesses. Obviously, you don't want to waste your time calling each and every one of them to find out whether your business is subject to its rules. This section will help streamline the process by first outlining the basics on what types of activities are generally regulated and by whom. This should help you figure out when your business is likely to face a special regulation. Then you'll find here a few resources that help to make sense of the crazy patchwork of local, state, and federal regulations that might apply to your business.

TIP

Regulations have different focuses. Very generally speaking, local regulations tend to focus on the location of your business and whether it poses a nuisance or a threat to public safety. State and federal regulations typically focus more on the type of work you do and your qualifications to do it.

Zoning and Local Permits

Local business regulations usually deal with the physical location of the business and the safety of the premises and equipment. City zoning laws regulate which activities are allowed in particular locations. For example, your zoning board might not approve your business location if it's in an area zoned exclusively for residential use, there isn't enough parking to support your business, or there are too many similar businesses nearby. Even if your business activities are acceptable for the time being, you might not be allowed to put up the sign you want or put in additional seating once your business takes off.

If your business doesn't comply with zoning laws, you'll either need to get a permit known as a conditional use permit or be granted an exception to the law, sometimes called a variance. Your city or county planning department is generally in charge of zoning laws. Contact them to find out whether your business complies with local rules and, if not, how to request a conditional use permit or a zoning variance. (Chapter 3 discusses zoning laws and picking a business location. Chapter 10 discusses zoning specifically for home businesses.)

Assuming your business has met zoning requirements, it still might need to be approved by other city agencies, such as the fire or police departments, the building inspector, or the department of public health. To ensure compliance with local laws, such as health and fire codes, noise laws, and environmental regulations, you may need one or more permits from these agencies. When you register with your local tax collector, you may receive information on these agencies and which types of businesses need to contact them. Your county clerk might also be able to direct you to information about regulatory agencies in your area.

Audrey Wackerley, owner of Retro Fit, a vintage clothing store in San Francisco (www.retrofityourworld.com):
Getting the right permits turned into a total hassle for our clothing store. After we'd been in business for a year and a half, a cop walked in our store and said we needed a "second-hand" permit. We had never even heard of one! It's not like we hadn't really made an effort to get all the permits we needed. Before we opened we spent hours in all these different buildings downtown, waiting in endless lines (it's a lot like going to the DMV), asking a million questions to find out what permits we needed to open our store. We had a business license, a seller's permit, a sign permit ... we thought we had everything we needed. But all of a sudden this cop said he'd shut us down if we didn't get the second-hand permit within five days. Five days! The permit cost $700, which was a real stretch for us right then. But what could we do? We had to scramble to get the money together and buy that stupid permit. The cop also let us know that we needed a separate jewelry permit in order to sell jewelry, but getting the second-hand permit was enough of an ordeal. We just decided to stop selling jewelry.

State and Federal Regulations

State regulations often focus on how you conduct your business. For instance, your state wants to make sure that your cosmetologists are competent and that your carpenters do safe work. Your state regulates these business activities through licensing. Businesses are more likely to need a state license or permit if they are highly specialized or if they affect the public welfare. In other words, if there's a risk that poor handling of your business activities might harm the public, chances are good that a state license is required. Common examples of state-licensed businesses are bars, auto shops, health care services, and waste management companies.

John Tilles, cofounder of Portland Kayak Company, a river rafting outfit in Portland, Oregon (www.portlandkayak.com):
I was impressed by Oregon's straightforward and simple process for starting a business. On the other hand, the absolute toughest and most frustrating aspect of our business is staying on top of the permit regulations in order to use state and federal land and rivers. This is a constantly changing scenario, and the politics involved is often nonsensical.

Don't assume that your business is so simple or straightforward that you don't need a special license. You'd be amazed at how many activities states regulate. To name a few, locksmiths may need a license from the Bureau of Security and Investigative Services; people who train guide dogs may need one from the State Board of Guide Dogs; and furniture makers may be subject to licensing from the Bureau of Home Furnishings. If you think some of these regulations sound far-fetched, take a look at a list of your state's regulatory agencies.

The federal government doesn't regulate small businesses as heavily as local and state offices do, but you may need a federal permit or license to engage in certain activities, including:

- operating a common carrier for hire, such as a trucking company (Interstate Commerce Commission)
- constructing or operating a radio or television station (Federal Communications Commission)
- manufacturing drugs or meat products (Food and Drug Administration)
- manufacturing alcohol or tobacco products, or making or selling firearms (Bureau of Alcohol, Tobacco, Firearms, and Explosives), and
- providing investment advice or counseling (Securities and Exchange Commission).

License and Permit Information Resources

Fortunately, many states have special agencies that act as clearinghouses for information on permits and issuing agencies, and several of them have very helpful websites. If you aren't sure what regulations might apply to your business, contact one or all of them to help figure out what you need to do to keep your business in full compliance.

 RESOURCE

Where to find information on permits. Appendix A includes lists of state agency websites, including agencies in charge of license and permit requirements. The lists are also on this book's companion page on Nolo.com (see the link in Appendix A); they are in PDF format, allowing you to click directly through to the websites.

Keep in mind that while the Web is a potentially awesome resource for navigating the permit requirements in your area, many state and local governments are still lagging in posting this kind of practical information. Don't waste your precious time searching endlessly through a state website trying to find the information you need. If it's not readily available at the site, chances are it's either not there or is so hopelessly buried that it's not worth your time to ferret it out. In these situations, it may well be better to just get on the phone or even go to the state office in person.

Chapter 7 Checklist:
Federal, State, and Local
Start-Up Requirements

☐ File organizational documents with the Secretary of State or similar filing office (corporations, LLCs, and limited partnerships only).

☐ Obtain a federal employer identification number (FEIN).

☐ Register your fictitious business name with your county or state.

☐ Obtain a local tax registration certificate.

☐ Obtain a permit to sell retail goods and collect state sales tax.

☐ Obtain specialized vocation-related licenses or environmental permits, if necessary.

Risk Management

Chapter 1 explained the different business structures that exist and how they relate to liability issues. As discussed, creating a corporation or an LLC generally protects business owners from personal liability. If the corporation or LLC loses a lawsuit or otherwise finds itself in debt, only the business will be liable for the debt, not the owners. But in a partnership, each partner is 100% personally liable for all the business's debts and obligations. True, these debts should normally be shared among the partners, and one partner can sue the others to force them to pay up. But this not a very satisfying option if the other partners are broke or have disappeared.

Shielding owners (or employees, as discussed below) from personal liability is a totally different issue from shielding the business itself. In fact, when an individual owner or employee avoids personal liability, you can usually assume that the business will be stuck with it. The owners and employees might be happy they are not personally liable, but there's not much to cheer about when the business assets are wiped out to satisfy a judgment.

The bottom line is that a successful lawsuit against a business can be devastating, whether or not the owners are personally liable for the damages. No matter who ultimately faces liability, every business should consider where risks lurk and how to avoid them. In our litigious society, you must take liability issues seriously and take active steps to protect your business and yourself.

Though the world of possible lawsuits is limited only by lawyers' imaginations, most claims arise from predictable—and often preventable—situations. If you analyze the true risks that face your business and employees, you can learn to recognize where your business is truly vulnerable and reduce the likelihood of ending up in court.

This chapter outlines the typical risks your business might face, and offers guidance on how to reduce them. It also discusses who and what may be at risk—including the owners, the staff, and the business itself. Then it offers risk management strategies and techniques to reduce your exposure to liability.

The encouraging news is that there are things you can do to protect yourself and your business. Hiring carefully, training thoroughly, having solid personnel policies in place, maintaining a safe working environment, and purchasing insurance are important risk management techniques that all businesses should use. It's crucial to do as much as you can *before* any legal issues arise.

SEE AN EXPERT

Get advice on possible liability claims. Liability issues typically involve gray areas, so the only way to determine absolutely whether someone will be held responsible for a particular act is to find out in court—an expensive way to get an answer. Use the information in this chapter as a foundation for understanding what can go wrong, and do your best to reduce your risks, but consult an attorney if you fear possible legal trouble. And run, don't walk, to an attorney if you receive an official document such as a court order, a subpoena, or a written complaint that signals the start of a lawsuit. (See Chapter 17 for advice on finding and working with an attorney.)

Who Might Sue or Be Sued

Pretty much anyone you deal with in your business can sue you or the business, and vice versa. What you want to do is ward off claims by understanding your risks and taking steps to avoid problems. This section lists what could possibly go wrong for a business, divided according to which people are involved. You can read it as a checklist now, or come back later to make sure you've covered the most likely risks for your business.

The most likely kind of claim or lawsuit that could be brought by or against your business will be over a contract or agreement of some sort. That's because businesses routinely buy, rent, make, sell, or provide products or services—and all of those transactions involve contracts, whether written or oral. Most small businesses find their main problems are money related, whether it's getting paid by reluctant customers or insurers or meeting their own financial obligations by paying their suppliers, landlord, or employees. Problems like these are called "contract" claims, because they stem from contractual agreements.

A less likely but extremely serious risk can also arise when someone in or around your business gets injured—financially or personally—by some act not related to a contract. For example, if one of your employees injures someone by being negligent, typically the business will be liable. A lot of your risk management efforts will be directed at preventing these kinds of claims—called "torts" in legalese—because they can be very costly to you and your business.

Co-Owners

If you are a co-owner of your business, you and the other co-owners have many obligations to each other. That's because mismanaging the business, whether on purpose or unintentionally, can damage the owners' investment and may expose all owners to liability.

Claims between and among owners can arise from one owner's:

- lying—for instance, about cash flow or customer complaints
- self-dealing—working for personal interests instead of the business's
- stealing the business's money or taking business assets for personal use
- handing out profits incorrectly
- selling property for less than it's worth
- conspiring—for example, to defraud or push out one of the co-owners
- failing to live up to the business agreement—for instance, by not contributing the amount of time and money agreed
- mishandling company funds
- mistreating the employees
- making bad deals
- producing bad products or providing poor service
- defrauding lenders, customers, landlords, or suppliers
- failing to pay payroll and/or income taxes
- violating laws and regulations of various kinds: safety or securities regulations, local ordinances, employment laws, or antitrust laws
- failing to properly hire, train, and supervise employees, or
- failing to observe formalities, such as recording corporate minutes or keeping personal money separate from business money.

There are many possible claims involving those who venture into business together. For example, even if you've done nothing wrong personally, a partner could sue you for your share of partnership debts, which may result in an expensive verdict or settlement. If your co-owner is your spouse and you get divorced, the business could get mired in the tussle over marital assets. Or if you and your co-owners decide to stop being in business together, you could sue each other over mismanagement, unfair competition, wrongfully expelling a partner, or other irregularities in splitting up.

Landlords, Customers, and Other Parties to Business Contracts

As mentioned above, business contracts are a common source of claims and problems. Lenders, suppliers, landlords, and customers could sue you—just as you could sue them—over contracts. For instance, your landlord could claim rent was in arrears or that you damaged the premises. Or you could sue your landlord for failing to make promised repairs or improvements. You could take over a lease or a contract and find that you are obligated for more than you agreed to take on. Customers could claim that your goods are shoddy and your return policy inadequate. Or you could have a supplier who gives you substandard goods.

Injuries outside of contractual agreements are the other main risk. Claims can be based on acts that were either intentionally bad or just unintentionally unfortunate. Customers could be accidentally injured on your premises or by your products. You or another partner could physically assault, harass, or make racially derogatory remarks about a supplier or customer. Your customers could claim that you were not careful enough in hiring, training, and supervising the employees—who subsequently hurt someone or something. You could have a claim if a business contact assaults your employee or steals your property. The people who hire your former employee could claim you gave a falsely positive recommendation.

Employees

Many businesses simply can't operate without employees to help. These extra minds and bodies may be essential to the business, but they can also be the targets and sources of liabilities and lawsuits.

Owner's Claims Against Employees

A business owner may sometimes be compelled to sue an employee. Theft and property damages are common impetuses—although it may not be cost-effective to take a pilfering employee to court for small reimbursements or money owed for small repairs.

In almost every case, someone who is injured by your employee will choose to sue you—not the employee. An injured person nearly always looks for a way to sue the employer, who usually has assets, including insurance. An employer who has to pay an injured person for harm caused by an employee could theoretically sue the employee for reimbursement, but it's not worth the trouble if the employee has no money.

A rare but important problem is that employees sometimes steal customer lists or a secret process or invention, then go into business in competition with their former bosses. An employee with a head full of business information and years of experience in the field can be a formidable competitor, even without stealing trade secrets or a customer list.

RESOURCE

For more information on restricting business information. State laws vary considerably on how much and how long you can effectively restrict a former employee or associate from going into competition with you. For guidance, see the article on nondisclosure agreements in the free Legal Articles section on Patent, Copyright & Trademark on www.nolo.com, and the website www.ndasforfree.com.

Damian Taggart, chief business development officer, Meow Wolf (www.meowwolf.com): *Don't shy away from having a big vision. The steps to success are: vision, funding, capacity, execution, in that order. Many times we stop ourselves from thinking big enough to attract investment and inspire others because we get those steps out of order. We talk ourselves out our real vision because we are worried about where the funding will come from or who we'll hire to execute it. Initially, focus on crafting a vision with value that you sincerely believe in and share that enthusiasm with others. If you have a good idea and allow space for others to contribute to it and be a part of it, you will almost certainly succeed.*

At Meow Wolf we practice a "yes, and" improvisational ethos where instead of saying no to an idea we say yes, and add to it. Another key aspect of how we do business is to completely dispense with manipulative or strategic communication. When negotiating a business deal we come to the table in as frank, open and straightforward a way possible. This kind of authenticity in business keeps you honest and builds trust.

A final thought is that you should learn to relish risk and failure. I wish I had taken many more risks earlier on in my career as an entrepreneur. Many moments in the life of a small business owner can be stressful. Should I hire nationally and move an untested employee from across the country? Should I take a chance and get a sizable business loan? Should I add new shareholders or partners? In general, taking chances that have considerable upside is the way to go. Allow yourself and your employees plenty of opportunity to fail and you will begin forging a path toward long-term success.

Owner's Responsibility for Claims Against Employees

A business owner's responsibility for harm done by an employee is an area of potentially very serious liability. There are two different ways an employer may be held responsible for the harmful acts of an employee: when the employer is at fault in some way, and when the employer isn't at fault at all. This is surprising, but unfortunately true.

In general, an employer is liable for everything an employee does "within the course and scope of employment," because the employee acts as the employer's agent. This means that for legal purposes, it is as if the employer directed an employee's every move, simply by authorizing the employee to act. For instance, the U.S. Supreme Court held that a real estate corporation was "vicariously liable" for its salesman's illegal discrimination when he refused to accept a biracial couple's offer to buy a house. (*Meyer v. Holley*, 537 U.S. 280 (2003).) The ruling expressly held that the corporation's sole owner was not personally liable. This effectively protected the corporation owner's other assets by limiting liability to the corporation itself—exactly why some business owners choose to incorporate.

An employer obviously should be held responsible when the employer tells the employee to do something and the employer knows that act will probably cause harm. An employer who knows or should know that the employee is harming someone or something will also be held culpable.

Risks Facing Employees

Employees may have to pay an injured person for damages for injuries they cause at work by:

- failing to act reasonably and carefully—for example, working without enough sleep when they need to stay alert
- acting with reckless disregard for the safety or interests of others—for example, removing safety equipment from a machine or ignoring warnings, or
- hurting someone deliberately or breaking the law.

If the person injured is a coworker, the legal relief is usually limited to workers' compensation benefits.

Liability for Independent Contractors

An independent contractor is someone who works for you but is not a regular employee. (For a discussion of the differences between an independent contractor and an employee, see Chapter 16.)

Employer liability for an independent contractor's acts is a complex area. Because a typical independent contractor works offsite, using his or her own equipment, without direct supervision, a business owner usually has little control over how the work is done. Nonetheless, the employer may still be liable to anyone who is hurt by the finished product that the independent contractor produces—for instance, if the employer uses the product at the business site or sells it to the public.

Fortunately, independent contractors often have insurance, so an employer who is sued can in turn sue the independent contractor for mistakes. For more information, see *Consultant & Independent Contractor Agreements*, by Stephen Fishman, and *The Employer's Legal Handbook*, by Fred S. Steingold (both published by Nolo).

In addition, an employer is often legally responsible for an employee's acts—even when the employer did not direct the employee to do the act that caused the trouble and didn't know that the employee was doing it—if the employer *should have* done something to prevent the situation from arising. For example, an employer may be liable for carelessness in hiring, training, or supervising an employee who causes some harm on the job. This can be true even when the harm happens after work hours or away from the work premises, as long as there is some connection to the job.

Claims by Employees Against Owners

Employment-related claims may pose a major liability risk to businesses with employees. Lawsuits alleging wrongful termination, sexual harassment, or other types of illegal discrimination are a serious risk to all businesses—and possibly to individual owners, managers, and employees. Here's an extremely brief and simplified outline of the types of workplace-related suits commonly faced by businesses.

Wrongful termination

In every state but Montana, every employee without a written employment contract has a job only as long as both the employer and the employee agree to continue the employment. An employee can quit at any time, for any reason or no reason, and the employer can fire the employee any time, for any or no reason. This is a legal doctrine called "employment at will."

There are major qualifications to that general rule, however, that may open an employer to a lawsuit for firing a worker. For instance, an employer can't fire someone for an illegal reason, such as wrongful discrimination (discussed below), in retaliation for union organizing, or whistleblowing—reporting the employer's wrongdoing to a government agency. In these cases, the employees could sue their former employers for wrongful termination.

And employees who have written contracts setting out conditions of termination—an increasingly rare breed —can sue a business on a claim that the company did not have "good cause" to terminate the employment. This is a "breach of contract" claim. Most businesses avoid these claims by making it clear in writing that all their employees are at will.

Defamation

A business that gives out false and damaging information about a former employee may be sued for harming that individual's reputation—also called defamation.

Defamation may rear its head for business owners and managers who are asked to give references for former employees. In most states, there is a legal defense called a "privilege" that protects people who give job references in good faith or when negative information is true. However, if sued for defaming a former employee, it would still cost time and money to prove that defense in court and win the case.

Another problem is that, while you may believe something to be true, it is always possible to argue about the truth of subjective evaluations and personal experiences. To combat this, some managers refuse to comment at all about any former employee, except to confirm that the employee worked for the business and when. Though this may be a wise policy for problem former employees, it also limits the opportunity to pass along good information about good workers. It's best to use discretion.

Another time for business owners and managers to beware of the possibility of defaming a worker is during the firing process, when emotions often run high. It's always wise to keep termination discussions brief—and tied to specifics about an individual's work performance.

Sexual harassment

Sexual harassment is any unwelcome sexual conduct on the job that creates an intimidating, hostile, or offensive work environment—and by now you're surely aware that it can expose a business to liability. Some courts categorize harassing behavior as either "quid pro quo" or "hostile environment." In quid pro quo harassment—literally, "do this for that"—a worker is confronted with demands for sexual favors to keep a job or get a promotion. Hostile environment harassment is found when sexual jokes,

pictures, innuendoes, or comments are allowed to persist in the workplace.

A business can help avoid these types of claims by putting a strong sexual harassment policy in place and strictly enforcing it—along with offering periodic training for all employees on how to recognize and report sexual harassment on the job.

Illegal discrimination

Federal law prohibits discrimination in employment based on race, skin color, gender, religious beliefs, national origin, disability, or age. And state and local ordinances sometimes protect additional characteristics, such as marital status, obesity, or sexual orientation. That makes it illegal to use any of these factors in decisions about hiring, promoting, making job assignments, firing, or paying workers. It is even a bad idea to ask questions about those parts of an applicant's background before the business gives the offer to hire. Savvy businesses use clear job descriptions, review standards, and termination guidelines to avoid claims of discrimination. And, of course, epithets or hostility on the job based on these protected characteristics should not be tolerated.

But discrimination law can get more complicated, making it necessary to pay attention to reality rather than blindly enforce workplace policies. An apparently neutral job requirement may disproportionately harm members of a protected group. For instance, in several states, black male employees have successfully challenged grooming codes requiring all workers to be clean-shaven, based on medical evidence that black men are disproportionately likely to suffer from a skin disorder giving them painful ingrown hairs after shaving.

A growing number of discrimination complaints these days are filed by employees who have disabilities. A federal law, the Americans with Disabilities Act, requires an employer to make "reasonable accommodations" for an employee who has a disability but is otherwise able to do the job—as long as the employee requests an accommodation and the business can provide it without suffering hardship. The accommodation may be buying a special chair, computer, or other equipment, or installing a safety bar in the restroom. It may be allowing the employee to reduce work hours to undergo chemotherapy, or reassigning an employee to a job that requires less lifting or standing.

How far you must go to accommodate an employee varies depending on the facts of each situation. You need not always provide the most expensive accommodation or the exact one an employee requests. At a minimum, you and your employee should discuss and negotiate what accommodations are possible and reasonable.

The Americans with Disabilities Act also requires many businesses and buildings to be made accessible to people with disabilities. Not complying with that law is another form of illegal discrimination.

Another growing area of discrimination claims arises from bringing religion into the workplace. Employees may complain that they are being harassed by evangelical coworkers of a different religion or upset by required prayers at business meetings. But if the business forbids all religious practice, employees may claim that they have a right to practice their religion at work, including praying and proselytizing. Employers often handle this by restricting religious and personal postings to a designated bulletin board and prayer groups to nonwork times. However, a business should generally accommodate employees' religious practices, including religious garb and religious holidays.

Privacy

The flip side of bringing an employee's personal beliefs into the workplace is that many employees do not want an employer to know about their lives outside the office. Be sure to check the laws in your state before you start monitoring employees' off-duty pursuits, social media activity, or drug use. A manager who inquires about whether an employee went to church on

Sunday may be both invading privacy and appearing to discriminate based on religious beliefs.

Recent years have seen a great deal of legislative activity regarding what employers may or may not do in terms of monitoring employees' activity on social media. Federal laws prohibit employers from discriminating against an employee or applicant based on information they glean from social media related to the individual's race, color, national origin, gender, age, disability, or immigration status. More specific laws regarding employers' access to or use of social media information about employees or applicants exist at the state level. Several states have passed laws prohibiting employers from requiring passwords or login information from employees for their social media accounts.

Laws vary a great deal from state to state, so if you have any plans to track your employees' or applicants' social media activity and use that information in hiring or termination decisions, be sure to learn your state's laws. One good source of updated information is the National Conference of State Legislatures website at www.ncsl.org.

In some states, a business may legitimately require a drug test prior to offering a job. The employer may also require drug testing on the job if there are specific and significant reasons why drug testing is necessary, such as when employees handle dangerous machinery or drive on the job. However, many potential legal hazards can be addressed simply by having a rule that forbids being "under the influence" of any substance at work. An employee can be held responsible for truly dangerous or inappropriate behavior without requiring an invasive or humiliating test. Keep in mind that some prescription and over-the-counter drugs also may temporarily affect an employee's mood or concentration.

Personal injuries

An employee who is injured on the job cannot usually sue the employer or another employee for damages, because state workers' compensation laws provide insurance benefits to cover those injuries. State or private disability insurance may also help compensate an injured employee, although only a handful of states have disability insurance programs.

Outsiders

People you never expect to come into contact with your product or service could be injured by it. In some states, even trespassers who get injured on your property can sue you. And you or your employee might get into an auto accident in a company car, or on company business, and sue or be sued. You might also commit a crime that, as a side effect, harms someone.

Risk Management Strategies

"Risk management" refers to actively addressing, managing, and reducing risks for any business. It is a rapidly growing field, partly because of the widespread and realistic fear of lawsuits. Your first goal is not to win a lawsuit, but to avoid a claim altogether. Your second goal is to resolve a claim without a lawsuit. Only as a last resort should you venture to court, because it's usually very expensive, and the outcome is always a gamble.

Insurance is part of a risk management program, but beware that it does not in itself constitute risk management. Sometimes the protection of insurance is adequate, but in some cases insurance may be either too expensive or simply unavailable for particular activities. (See "Insurance and Warranties," below, for more specifics on insurance.)

Here's one example of risk management: Many commercial and industrial sites have residual contamination from solvents, metals, and chemicals. If you buy the property, you may legally have to pay for environmental cleanup, even though the mess wasn't your fault. So, before you purchase, you should consider some ways to manage your risk.

Here are some possibilities:

- You could evaluate the likelihood and extent of contamination with scientific sampling by an engineering firm that also provides an estimate of the probable cost of cleanup. Then you would weigh whether the purchase is worth the additional costs.

- You could try to get protection through contracts—for instance, you could try to purchase insurance directly, or to negotiate a reimbursement agreement or an agreement to purchase environmental insurance from the seller.

- You could ask the relevant government agencies for a "comfort letter," in which they promise—or at least come close to promising—that their lawyers will not go after innocent landowners. Your bank may require this letter as a condition of a loan.

- You could look into a federal "brownfields" program, which gives you certain immunities from future surprise liability if you clean up urban industrial land.

As you can see, many options are available to manage that one potentially expensive risk.

Find Out What Can Go Wrong

A good place to start your risk management program is to outline what the business is trying to protect—for example your people, physical and financial assets, and reputation. Then you can move ahead to anticipating potential threats.

Liability Lurks All Around You

There is a sea of laws and regulations controlling safety, land use, business, employment, and other matters that business owners must abide by—and ignorance of them is no excuse. You never know when you will be hauled up short for parking too many cars on the street, having an unsafe workplace, or causing an environmental disaster. You should have a pretty good idea, though, of the kinds of laws that apply to you, especially if you are in a heavily regulated industry, such as manufacturing, food preparation, or professional services. There can be harsh penalties (including prison time) if, for example, you fail to report a workplace death to the appropriate agency.

Finally, it should be no surprise that you can also get in trouble by breaking various criminal laws. Businesses traditionally have special problems with failing to pay taxes; with property crimes such as theft, fraud, and arson; and with antitrust laws that prohibit forming monopolies.

In addition to general risks, find out what can go wrong in your field. Talking with an insurance agent who is familiar with your type of business is one of the best ways to assess the possible risks you face. Talking with people who own or work in similar businesses is also useful, especially outside your local area; if they don't compete with you, it's more likely

you can trust what they tell you. Reading trade magazines and websites will keep you abreast of the kinds of lawsuits being brought. And, finally, ask your employees what risks they see and what problems are waiting to happen. They may be one of your best sources for ideas to prevent problems.

Focus on Prevention

Once you've identified the main ways that your business is vulnerable, you should brainstorm ways to protect against these risks.

Setting a Solid Foundation

Most obviously, you should choose your partners, lenders, landlords, business sites, vendors, agents, and employees carefully. In particular, investigate in depth any deal that seems too good to be true—including the sales pitches of people who encourage you to set up in a franchise or buy expensive equipment.

Next, if you will be a joint owner of the business, get a clear understanding with your co-owners about all aspects of your business: what you want to accomplish, what you expect from one another, and how or when you might split up or buy out a co-owner. Agreements known as buy-sell agreements outline how the business will handle transfers of ownership. (Buy-sell agreements are discussed in Chapter 15.)

Money is usually the first big issue; control is next. You would be wise to have your business formation agreement in writing, whether it's a simple one-page partnership agreement or a detailed operating agreement for an LLC. If possible, co-owners should agree to mediate disputes. Mediation is generally quicker, simpler, and cheaper than a lawsuit, which is why the business community has adopted it enthusiastically.

It goes without saying that you should operate your business on the up-and-up. That includes:

- filing all the required papers and getting the right permits
- telling the truth on all documents and to everyone with whom you deal
- keeping track of company funds, inventory, and important documents
- paying your debts
- delivering what you promise
- observing business formalities, such as keeping your personal money separate from business accounts
- putting important agreements into written contracts
- maintaining safety standards, and
- complying with all applicable laws, especially by paying your income and payroll taxes quarterly.

Owners must make sure their businesses comply with bureaucratic requirements. Applying for permits and licenses, filing reports, paying taxes, and so on are necessary evils for all businesses, and failing to do these things may, in some cases, expose the owners to personal liability. (Permits, licenses, and other bureaucratic hurdles are covered in detail in Chapter 7.) Even if a manager or another employee is in charge of filling out and filing the paperwork, ultimately it's your responsibility as an owner to make sure your business is in compliance. Check in regularly to make sure that paperwork is getting done.

Risk management can affect your decisions about what your business actually does. You may need to change or eliminate certain activities that are uninsurable or too risky. What is too risky may depend on the law and the availability of insurance in your state—especially for construction, manufacturing, and professional services.

Implementing Procedures and Checklists

Particularly if you can identify one or more risks in your business, it is essential to have procedures in place in case one of those foreseeable incidents occurs. If there's a likely risk of customer injuries on your premises (as would be the case of an ice rink with lots of new skaters, including young children), or employee injuries (for example, if you run a photo lab where injuries might result from chemical exposure), you should have clear procedures on how to handle any injuries that occur. Failing to have a plan in place for foreseeable accidents isn't just irresponsible: It raises the likelihood that any such accidents might be worsened by your poor response. And it increases the chances that your business could face a lawsuit for damages.

Put procedures in writing, and don't make them overcomplicated. Simple checklists can be extremely effective. For example, the ice rink in the example above should consider preparing a checklist of "Yes/No" questions for employees to use when a skater is injured. Your checklist should help ice rink employees answer an initial question about what constitutes a true injury and not just a painful fall. If the checklist helps determine that a fall does qualify as a true injury, the ice rink should have another procedure or flowchart of actions to be taken, such as 1) determining if the skater is conscious, and if not, calling 911, or 2) if the skater is conscious, asking the skater if he or she can recite his or her name and address. The flowchart should identify further steps to minimize the injury (such as putting ice on a swollen foot) and streamline the process of getting medical attention promptly.

Besides having procedures in place, it's of obvious importance to make sure the appropriate staff are trained in how to implement them. Depending on lots of different factors, you might decide to train all staff, or just train department managers and give them the responsibility to train staff on the procedures.

A few simple checklists, step-by-step procedures, and/or flowcharts kept in a slim binder with enough copies for key staff and managers, and with appropriate training, can make a huge difference in protecting your business from a lawsuit. Injured customers or employees who perceive a system is in place to take care of them will be less likely to feel your business is to blame for their injury and therefore less likely to sue in the first place. And if they do sue, being able to show that you swiftly executed your well-thought-out procedures will go a long way in lowering your liability for injuries or damages.

Covering Employee Issues

Employees make businesses vulnerable. Every business owner who hires employees should be very concerned about workplace-related liability issues and take steps to decrease the risks from possible claims and lawsuits. Lay the groundwork to hire carefully, train thoroughly, supervise adequately, have solid personnel policies in place, and maintain a safe working environment.

If you are unsure what your employment policies should be and what laws you must follow, search "Employment Law Assistance" on the U.S. Department of Labor website (www.dol.gov) and your own state's department of labor. (Websites for state labor agencies are listed in

Appendix A under "State Unemployment Compensation Agencies," and on this book's companion page on Nolo.com.) You can also consult a personnel specialist or HR manager, or review other employers' personnel manuals to see what's covered. Nolo (www.nolo.com) also provides good free information online.

With many workplace issues, the most effective risk management technique is to implement effective policies and training programs. For instance, straightforward hiring and firing policies, including a written policy that employment is "at will," help protect you against claims of discrimination and wrongful termination. A solid orientation and annual training program for employees on sexual harassment and discrimination issues will significantly reduce your liability exposure in those areas. Every business with employees should have written, posted policies to clarify what behavior is expected and what will not be tolerated.

Similarly, workplace safety issues can be addressed through training programs and posted materials. You can ask consultants who know your type of business to evaluate your workplace for compliance with the Occupational Safety and Health Administration (OSHA)—the agency that establishes and oversees workplace safety standards. Workplace safety will be an ongoing consideration and expense.

Nolo Resources on Employment Law Matters

See the "Employment Law" section of Nolo. com (under "Free Legal Information") for lots of useful articles on subjects covered in this chapter, including discrimination and drug testing. In addition to the articles, Nolo publishes comprehensive employment law books for small businesses on the following subjects:

- **In-depth information about employment matters, including employers' potential liabilities and employee lawsuits:** *The Employer's Legal Handbook,* by Fred S. Steingold; *The Manager's Legal Handbook,* by Lisa Guerin and Sachi Barreiro; *Dealing With Problem Employees: A Legal Guide,* by Lisa Guerin and Amy DelPo; *The Essential Guide to Federal Employment Laws,* by Lisa Guerin and Sachi Barreiro; and *Create Your Own Employee Handbook: A Legal & Practical Guide for Employers,* by Lisa Guerin and Amy DelPo.
- **Sexual harassment and illegal discrimination in the workplace:** *The Essential Guide to Handling Workplace Harassment & Discrimination,* by Deborah C. England.
- **Drug testing and privacy issues:** *The Manager's Legal Handbook,* by Lisa Guerin and Sachi Barreiro.
- **Workers' compensation laws and disability insurance:** *The Employer's Legal Handbook,* by Fred S. Steingold.

Beyond establishing and communicating personnel and other policies, your business needs to have enforcement mechanisms in place. The toughest written sexual harassment or safety policy won't protect a business from a major lawsuit if there's no one to complain to who has power to change the situation, or if complaints go uninvestigated and policies unenforced.

An "open door" policy and a safe channel to launch complaints are very helpful. Employees who understand that their employer is taking care of their concerns are less likely to become frustrated and sue.

In many states, you can ask the employee to agree to refer serious issues to a mediator and then, if they can't be resolved within a reasonable time, to an arbitrator. A mediator is someone who helps people come to an agreement, while an arbitrator makes a binding decision. Some states automatically refer civil lawsuits to a mediator to see if the parties can settle before a judge will hear the case. Many employers have such an agreement in their personnel manuals that every new employee reads and signs.

It helps morale if the employer pays the costs of mediation and arbitration. After all, the employee probably has very little spare money, and a one-day mediation can commonly cost anywhere from $500 to $3,000. Some community mediation groups will take on small business claims for free or a nominal cost.

CAUTION

A lawsuit may still be possible. Agreements between employers and employees that make arbitration the employee's exclusive remedy are not always binding. Judges do not like to see employees give up their rights to complain to government agencies or to bring lawsuits, especially if the employee has to agree to arbitrate future disputes as a nonnegotiable condition of employment, such as in a written employment contract. The law in this area is changing rapidly, so you should find out what is legal in your own state. For a good short discussion of mandatory arbitration, see *The Employer's Legal Handbook*, by Fred S. Steingold (Nolo).

Deal With Problems

When a problem does arise, stay as calm as possible while you get as much information as you need to decide what to do. You won't do yourself or your business any good with an unconsidered response.

If a problem comes up in an area that is addressed in a written contract, a calm meeting or phone call is a good idea, followed up by a letter summarizing the meeting or conversation. Any meeting with a problem employee should be witnessed by at least one person who is neutral. If you are out of your depth, contact an expert such as an accountant, a lawyer, a doctor, an employment law specialist, or a mediator. Keep employment matters confidential.

Finally, realize that you might end up paying something to settle a claim or to defend yourself, whether or not you feel responsible for what went wrong. As discussed in Chapter 1, owners of sole proprietorships and partnerships are personally liable for all business debts, including damages stemming from a lawsuit against the business. It doesn't matter much whether these owners are personally named or found liable in a lawsuit, or whether only the business itself is—either way, they'll be personally responsible for paying the damages. This fundamental rule regarding sole proprietorships and partnerships is a major reason why many business owners choose to create an LLC or a corporation.

If your small business is an LLC or a corporation (or if you are a limited partner in the business), then you, and owners like you, will ordinarily not be personally responsible for any damage awards against the business. Only business assets can be used to satisfy those debts. Of course, that could wipe out your business.

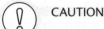 CAUTION

Personal guarantees may bind you. As a practical matter, most suppliers and banks require a personal guarantee from small business owners on contracts and loans. This means that there will be personal, individual liability on claims arising from those contracts. Similarly, business owners will personally sign the document that creates their business, so the co-owners can sue one another personally on claims that arise out of starting, running, or winding up the business.

Paying for What Goes Wrong

If you have been prudent, and if the business is reasonably successful, there will be some extra money in the bank for emergencies. There may be business assets, such as machinery or a building or inventory, that you can sell or pledge to raise money—subject, of course, to agreement by your co-owners. You may also have some insurance that applies. An insurance company has to pay for an attorney to defend you against a claim your policy covers. It will likely also pay some, maybe most, of any eventual settlement or judgment against you if the claim is covered by your policy. (Insurance is discussed in more detail below.)

All business owners—even owners of corporations and LLCs—may face personal liability in certain situations. Those who recklessly or intentionally cause harm may be found personally liable for injuries caused by their actions. The same is true for business owners who don't carefully investigate a deal before making a business decision.

Insurance and Warranties

Insurance coverage is a powerful tool in risk management. However, there's no requirement that you obtain property or liability insurance for your business, unless:

- your state requires liability insurance for a company vehicle
- state and federal law requires it because you have employees
- a contract job (usually with a government agency) requires the contractor (your company) to have a certain amount of insurance, or
- your lender requires it as a condition for getting a loan.

But just because you don't have to get insurance doesn't mean you shouldn't. Even if you form a corporation or an LLC, which shields your personal assets from business liabilities (see Chapter 1), it won't protect you from losing your business if disaster strikes. Careful as you may be, fate sometimes deals an unforeseen blow. If you face unexpected trouble, you'll be thankful you've taken steps to protect yourself.

CAUTION

Employers are subject to special insurance requirements. Employers must typically pay for workers' compensation insurance and unemployment insurance. A handful of states also require employers to pay into a state disability insurance fund. All of these insurance programs are specifically set up for employers

and are largely regulated by state agencies. (See Chapter 16 for some of the special rules governing employers' and employees' contributions to these insurance programs.)

There is an art to insuring your business: You want to get the maximum protection from insurance without blowing your whole bankroll on policies for every conceivable risk. Once you start to look, you'll find every imaginable type of insurance policy out there, although your business will probably need only a few of them at most. The two most common and generally useful types of policies are property insurance and liability insurance. This section will explain the basics of these and introduce you to many other kinds of policies that cover specific risks involved in your business. It will also shine some light on the process of shopping for and buying the policies you need.

TIP

Caring for your policy. Treat your insurance policy just as the precious, and possibly irreplaceable, document that it is. Store it carefully. Keep an old policy even after you change insurance providers. A claim could come up that arises from a long-ago event, and that document may be your only way to track down an insurer that you had in the past. Believe it or not, if the insurance company or its successor is still in business and you have a copy of the old policy to prove it covered that event, the insurance company should provide the protection you paid for at the time.

Property Insurance

This chapter concentrates mostly on liability issues, but other types of losses can also be devastating to a business. Property insurance can cover your business for damages or loss to your business property due to theft, fire, or other causes. There is a good deal of variation among policies on what property and what risks are covered and what the coverage is. Be sure you're absolutely clear on these terms when you choose a policy.

You'll want to make sure that your property insurance covers the premises themselves as well as the business's assets that are kept there, including:

- fixtures to the property, such as lighting systems or carpeting
- equipment and machinery
- office furniture
- computers, telephones, and other office machines, and
- inventory and supplies.

Most basic property insurance policies will cover these items.

 TIP

If you rent your business space. Your lease may require you to get a specific amount or type of property coverage. Be sure to check your lease for any insurance requirements before you purchase a policy.

If you purchased your business property. You almost certainly paid for title insurance, which protects you from challenges to your ownership of the property. You may also want to purchase a life insurance policy that is dedicated to paying the mortgage if anything happens to you. You usually get the best deal if you buy this on your own, not from your mortgage lender or broker.

You'll need to understand not only which property is covered by your policy but what types of losses will be covered. Read it carefully to determine what causes of damage are insurable. Most general business property insurance policies will provide *basic, broad,* or *special* coverage—with special offering the broadest coverage and basic the narrowest.

A basic form policy will normally cover fire, explosions, storms, smoke, riots, vandalism, and sprinkler leaks. A broad form policy typically covers damage from broken windows and other structural glass, falling objects, and water damage. With both basic and broad form policies, certain risks may be listed as excluded—that is, not covered. Note that theft isn't typically covered under either a basic or broad form policy, a fact that surprises many business owners. (See "Theft Insurance," below.)

Special form coverage offers the widest range of protection, as it typically covers all risks—including theft—except for those risks that are specifically excluded. While premiums for special form policies are more expensive, it may be worth the added expense if your business faces unusual risks—or simply to make sure you're covered against theft.

A basic policy may not cover the other property that you have at your business premises—for instance, if you rent a laptop or other equipment, or if customers leave their goods with you as happens at a jeweler, dry cleaner, or repair shop. If you expect to regularly have property that belongs to others at your business, get a policy that covers it.

If the policy you are considering excludes one or more items that you want covered, find out whether it can be included and at what cost. You may have to purchase what's commonly called a "rider" or an "endorsement" to add special coverage to the policy. For example, accounting records, cash, and deeds are often excluded from standard property insurance policies but can usually be covered with some extra paperwork—and an additional premium.

You may find other ways to bring the property you want covered under the scope of the policy. For example, if you want the policy to cover your personal stereo that you keep at the office, but the policy only covers business property, one option is to transfer title of the stereo to the business.

Be sure that you clearly understand the dollar limits on your policy and any deductibles or copayments you'll have to make. Also, make sure the policy covers the replacement cost of the property, not merely its depreciated value. Computer equipment, for example, loses value incredibly fast. If you lose your two-year-old computer to theft, you'll definitely want your insurance to pay for a new computer rather than the value of the stolen one, which might be barely enough to cover the shipping costs of a new machine.

 CAUTION

Possible policy adjustments for home-based businesses. Owners of home-based businesses should figure out whether their homeowners' or renters' policies forbid business use of the home or exclude coverage of business-related claims. Make sure that your policy won't be limited or voided entirely by running a business out of your home. It's better to come clean with your insurance company about your home business and maybe spend some extra premium dollars than to find out after a catastrophe that you had no insurance after all.

Liability Insurance

Find out what an available "commercial general liability" (CGL) insurance policy will cover. Ask, for instance, whether it covers negligence—that is, carelessness or recklessness. Most CGL policies do not cover certain employment law claims such as harassment, discrimination, and wrongful termination. And all insurance companies will refuse to insure you against bad business decisions, criminal acts, or intentional acts of harm.

Personal Injury Liability Insurance

Say, for instance, that someone—a customer or supplier—puts a foot through a floorboard weakened by dry rot, trips on an electric cord, or is hit by a shelving unit that falls over. One accident like that could result in a verdict against your business for tens of thousands or even millions of dollars, even if you were only marginally at fault. For this reason, liability insurance is probably a wise investment for any business that has even minimal contact with the public.

Liability coverage insures you against the notorious slip-and-fall situation, when someone gets injured on your premises and sues you for the ranch. A general liability policy (versus a product liability or vehicle liability policy, discussed below) will cover damages that your business is ordered to pay to an individual, such as a customer, supplier, or business associate who was injured on your property.

Product Liability Insurance

A related, though technically different, type of insurance is product liability insurance, which protects you from lawsuits by customers claiming to be hurt by a product you made, sold, or provided. If your business has a product that has a risk of harming anyone, no matter how far-fetched, you might consider this type of insurance. Plaintiffs have won product liability lawsuits even when they were ignoring warnings or misusing products. An insurance premium will be less expensive than a big award to a tragically injured plaintiff.

Auto Insurance

Auto liability coverage will not be provided by a general business liability policy, but it is legally required in most states. Even if it's not required in your state, it's foolish not to protect yourself against this potentially devastating risk. Insurance coverage for employees' personal cars that are used for business is known as "nonowned auto" liability insurance. This protects your business if an employee hurts someone or damages property while driving his or her car on the job. If your employees will use their own cars for business activities, it's important that you get this type of coverage even if your state doesn't require it. Many nonowned auto liability insurance policies do not protect employees themselves, just the business; employees usually need to get their own coverage.

In addition, some states require drivers to be covered by other types of auto insurance, including personal injury protection (PIP) coverage and uninsured/underinsured motorist (UM/UIM) coverage. If your state mandates certain types of coverage, it will generally also require that you purchase a minimum level of the insurance. Check with your state's department of motor vehicles to find out insurance requirements for drivers in your state.

Specialized Insurance

Property and liability insurance are the two most important types of coverage for small businesses, but there are many other kinds of policies. Some of the more common ones are listed below. Keep in mind that a broad property or liability policy might already cover one or more risks listed here. For instance, if you have special form property insurance (discussed above), you'll probably be insured against theft.

Employment Practices Liability Insurance

This is a relatively new kind of insurance. It can protect you against a number of employee claims including harassment, discrimination, and wrongful termination. It can be a very useful supplement to commercial general liability insurance.

Business Interruption Insurance

This type of insurance will cover you if your business is forced to close for a period of time for a reason covered under the policy, such as damage from a fire or an earthquake. In that case, your policy will pay approximately what you would have earned if you had been open as normal.

"Key Man" Insurance

This is a life insurance policy that the business owns, pays for, and collects on. It protects the business when a crucial person dies unexpectedly and the business grinds to a halt. The "key" person whose life is insured can be the founder, the owner, or an employee—the person who knows everything and holds things together, especially in a small business. This insurance gives the business some extra cash that buys time to decide what to do: whether to hire a replacement, sell the business as a going concern, or wind down gracefully. It is similar in effect to business interruption insurance.

Malpractice Insurance

Often expensive, this type of insurance protects you from lawsuits arising from professional mistakes. Doctors, lawyers, real estate agents, accountants, and a number of other professionals typically need malpractice insurance. It is also known as "errors and omissions" (E & O) insurance.

Theft Insurance

Because many basic policies do not cover losses due to theft, you may want to purchase specific insurance to cover you in case office equipment is stolen. Be sure to find out whether the policy covers employee theft as well as ordinary burglary and robbery. If not, you can usually purchase that type of coverage separately.

Special Coverage

Other types of insurance include credit insurance for accounts receivable, insurance for intellectual property, such as trade secrets or patents, and disability insurance for owners of the business. (This is not the same as state-mandated disability insurance for employees, discussed in Chapter 16.) Some businesses need insurance for issues that arise out of advertising, while others might need to guard against a big bill for environmental cleanup of purchased real estate. If you are an importer and travel frequently to dangerous foreign locations, you might want kidnap and ransom insurance. Talk with an insurance agent or broker about whether your specific business activities might warrant one or more of these special types of coverage.

Many corporations have special liability insurance called "directors' and officers'" (D & O) insurance, because there are occasions when directors and officers are sued individually for making employment and other decisions. This comes up, for example, in sexual harassment cases. An insurance agent can tell you when a small corporation needs this type of coverage.

Investigating and Purchasing a Policy

You have to do your homework to make an intelligent and cost-effective insurance purchase. You must understand both the large and fine print so you can compare policies and purchase the best one for your business. For example, when comparison shopping among different insurance companies, it's useless to compare two policies unless they cover the same types of property, the same risks, and the same payouts and deductibles. You can't make an informed decision until you understand all these details.

Insurance brokers, who gather information from different insurance companies, can help you decipher policies and figure out your best deal. Make sure any broker you consult understands all the nooks and crannies of your specific business activities and the risks that may be involved. Try to find one who specializes in policies for your type of business. You may be surprised to learn that specially tailored policies already exist that cover your particular needs. For instance, a "producer's package policy" for filmmakers covers several risks unique to the film business, such as the costs of production—often in the tens or hundreds of thousands of dollars—in case of lost or destroyed film or digital media. An insurance broker who knows your type of business will be able to direct you to these specialized policies, while a run-of-the-mill broker may not. Check trade magazines and websites for the ads of specialized brokers, and ask other business owners whom they use and what they buy.

You'll probably encounter insurance companies that offer package deals that are cheaper than buying several individual policies separately. As long as all your needs are met—and not exceeded—these deals can be a good way to go. As always, be sure you understand the extent of coverage in each area rather than relying on any general promises that the package covers "all your business needs."

 RESOURCE

Finding help with business insurance on the Internet. A couple of websites that may be helpful are www.irmi.com, the website of the International Risk Management Institute, and the Insurance Information Institute's website at www.iii.org.

Manufacturer's and Extended Warranties

While insurance can protect you when property is damaged or stolen, product warranties can protect you in case equipment malfunctions for various reasons. Don't overlook the value of warranties when considering ways to reduce risks and potential losses related to your equipment.

Most products come with a standard manufacturer's warranty against defects for a certain period of time. Warranties generally range from 90 days to one year of coverage. It's not uncommon for the warranty to cover parts and labor for different time periods—for example, parts might be covered for one year, and labor for 90 days.

In addition, you can purchase extended warranties for most equipment that offer coverage for longer periods, generally from two to five years. Though some manufacturers offer extended warranties to supplement the standard manufacturer's warranty, many extended warranties are sold by companies other than the manufacturer. These companies make big profit margins on extended warranties, leading many consumer advocates, including *Consumer Reports* magazine (in an April 2018 online article), to generally advise people against purchasing extended warranties.

The truth is there may be some situations in which purchasing an extended warranty makes sense for your business. Generally speaking, the more expensive and important a piece of equipment is to your business, the more an extended warranty might be a smart idea. For example, if your business cannot live without a certain piece of equipment such as a computer, and would be financially hard-pressed to replace it if it went south, an extended warranty might be a godsend—but always account for the repair time during which you won't be able to use the equipment.

When considering whether to buy an extended warranty, be sure to consider the following factors.

Be clear about when the extended warranty coverage begins and how long it lasts. In particular, don't pay for extended coverage that overlaps with the original manufacturer's warranty. If coverage begins as of the date of purchase of the extended warranty, as opposed to the date of purchase of the equipment, then wait until the original warranty is about to expire before purchasing the extended warranty. Most warranty companies allow this—but be aware that you will usually not be able to purchase an extended warranty if the original warranty has expired. Find out in advance what deadlines apply to the extended warranty purchase.

Make sure you trust the warranty company. Particularly if the warranty is being sold by a third-party warranty company, evaluate the reputation and reliability of that company. If the extended warranty is being sold through a major national retailer, chances are it is not a fly-by-night scam—though it still may not be worthwhile. But be aware that scam warranty companies do exist.

Evaluate the value of the extended coverage. Weigh the cost of the extended warranty and what it will cover against the cost of the equipment and the likelihood it will need repair. Just as with insurance, warranties generally exclude certain types of damage from coverage. The more limitations on coverage, the lower the value of the warranty.

When you do have warranty protection, whether from an original manufacturer's warranty or an extended warranty, it's crucial to keep track of important warranty details—especially the expiration dates, so that you can purchase extended coverage if you so choose. As mentioned above, you will usually not be allowed to purchase an extended warranty if the original or previous extended warranty has expired—so be careful not to let those important dates slip by if you intend to purchase extended coverage.

FORM

Warranty Track Worksheet. The Nolo website includes a downloadable interactive worksheet to help you track your warranty information. See Appendix B for the link to this worksheet and other forms in this book.

Simply enter all relevant information into the worksheet about warranty coverage for every piece of business equipment you buy. If you don't have information for every column, it's okay, but be sure to include the warranty expiration date. Keep the list sorted by "Warranty Expiration Date" (Column C) in ascending order, so that the warranties about to expire will be at the top of the list. Make it a habit to enter this information as soon as you purchase any equipment, and to review and update the worksheet periodically so that you don't miss any expiration dates and the chance to purchase extended coverage.

Chapter 8 Checklist: Risk Management

☐ Have active risk management strategies. Start by evaluating your risks and identifying specific ways to reduce them.

☐ If your business has employees, establish personnel policies, including hiring and firing guidelines, policies prohibiting sexual harassment and discrimination, and effective enforcement mechanisms.

☐ Research and purchase appropriate insurance for your business. Contact an insurance agent or broker familiar with your business to answer your questions and to price out various policies.

☐ Get a property insurance policy that covers against all the types of losses that your business may face, such as theft, fire, and water damage.

☐ Get a liability insurance policy if your business will have any contact with the general public, or if you determine there's a significant risk that someone could sue your business for injuries or other damages.

☐ Get auto liability coverage for any vehicles used for business, including the personal cars of employees that are used for business.

☐ Consider other, specialized insurance coverage.

Paying Your Taxes

t's no fun for any profitable business to share its hard-won earnings with the government. But, like it or not, as soon as your business is in the black, everyone—from your city and county to your state and, of course, the IRS—will demand a piece of the action. Although it's not necessary to become a tax expert before going into business, you do need to know what taxes you'll have to pay and how to pay them. Understanding your tax liability will help you be better able to:

- plan your finances, including whether you'll have enough cash to stay in business

- avoid tax-reporting and deposit errors, which can result in hefty penalties, and

- make good business decisions that will reduce your tax burden.

Even if your business won't make a fast profit, you may owe taxes. Lots of new businesspeople believe that if there is no profit, there is no tax. Sadly, this is not the case. Local taxes on gross receipts and taxes on sales of retail goods (sales taxes) are but two examples of taxes that may need to be paid regardless of whether a business is turning a profit. So, even if your business may not be profitable for a year or two, you need to prepare for the possibility of owing some taxes.

This chapter gives you simple, straight-forward information on the taxes that owners of sole proprietorships, partnerships, and LLCs will face. It provides basic instructions for filing returns and paying taxes correctly and on time. After covering the basics, it offers three sections that discuss the specific tax rules that apply to each business type—sole proprietorships, partnerships, and LLCs. Simply read the section that's appropriate for your business form and skip the others. The last three sections cover paying estimated taxes, local taxes, and sales taxes—all of which apply more or less evenly to all business types. If your business is home based, see the section on home business tax deductions in Chapter 10, "Laws, Taxes, and Other Issues for Home Businesses." If your business has employees, refer to Chapter 16, "Building Your Business and Hiring Workers," for information on the special taxes employers face.

 RESOURCE

Help with corporate taxation.
This chapter offers only some broad outlines of corporate taxation. The full maze of corporate tax rules is far too complicated to cover in detail here. If you're thinking about incorporating, keep in mind that doing so will subject you to more complicated (and occasionally unpleasant) tax rules. See the "Corporations" section, in Chapter 1, for an overview of the potential tax advantages and disadvantages of corporations. If you need more detailed information, take a look at *Tax Savvy for Small Business*, by Frederick W. Daily, or *Incorporate Your Business: A Step-by-Step Guide to Forming a Corporation in Any State*, by Anthony Mancuso (both published by Nolo).

SEE AN EXPERT

Having an accountant handle your federal and state taxes is almost always well worth the expense—especially after 2017's major tax law changes. The Tax Cuts and Jobs Act includes many changes to allowable deductions, how business losses can be claimed, and more. It's especially important to use a tax preparer who understands the new law. While it's wise to learn the basics as outlined in this chapter, it's almost always a good idea to turn over the task of preparing federal and state income tax returns to a professional accountant. If you have well-organized records (see Chapter 12, on bookkeeping), annual tax prep for a small to medium-sized business will probably cost less than $1,000. For really small operations it might be even less than $500. Considering the importance of competent tax preparation, you should accept early on that this is an unavoidable cost of running any business. (See Chapter 17 for advice on finding and working with professionals like accountants.)

Tax Basics

One of the first things you should understand is that there's little rhyme or reason to the world of taxes. Don't drive yourself nuts by trying to figure out the logic of a system that has virtually none. The bottom line is that the federal, state, and local governments tend to tax everything that they legally can. And this includes virtually every aspect of a business that can be quantified. For example, depending on the type of business and its location, a business might have to pay taxes based on its gross income, net profit, or gross retail sales; how many employees it has; how much employees are paid; how much property it owns or leases; its seating capacity; or how many vehicles the business owns—and the list goes on and on.

To complicate matters further, the many different taxes are administered by different government agencies, each with its own rules, forms, and filing procedures. It's little wonder that the mere mention of taxes often induces anxiety and sometimes even panic in otherwise well-adjusted businesspeople.

The Agencies Behind the Taxes

The first step in understanding small business taxes is to recognize who levies which taxes. Here's a quick breakdown:

- **Federal taxes.** The United States Internal Revenue Service, the top dog of tax agencies, collects the following taxes from small businesses and their owners: taxes on individual or corporate income, self-employment taxes (which go to the Social Security and Medicare systems), and payroll taxes. (See "Special Hurdles for Employers," in Chapter 16, for information on payroll taxes.)

Talking About Income—Key Terms Defined

A lot of different jargon is used to describe the money that comes into and flows out of your business. These financial terms are discussed in more detail elsewhere in the book, where we discuss financial projections and accounting. (See Chapters 4 and 12.) Because these concepts are also important in understanding your taxes, here are some brief definitions:

- **Gross versus net.** It's crucial to understand this distinction. "Gross" generally refers to total revenue, before deducting expenses such as salaries, rent, product costs, or office supplies. "Net" means what's left over after subtracting costs and expenses. (As you can see, a gross figure will be higher than a net figure, because deductions come out of the gross and result in the net.) Thus gross income (sometimes called gross receipts or gross sales) refers to the total money your business brings in, before you've begun to cover any of your costs. Net profit refers to your income after deducting costs and expenses. In some contexts, "net" may refer to your after-tax profit. In other words, it may reflect not only your costs and expenses, but also any taxes you owe on your income. Be aware that the terms gross and net are often bandied about loosely. It's important to understand which deductions are included when using these terms.
- **Fixed versus variable expenses.** Fixed expenses are the ones that will be more or less the same regardless of how well your

business is doing. They include rent, utility bills, insurance premiums, and loan payments Variable expenses are the costs of the products or services themselves and anything that goes along with your product, including packaging or shipping. Variable expenses increase or decrease depending on how much business you're doing.
- **Gross profit.** Gross profit refers to how much money you make on each sale above the cost of the item itself (its variable cost). Unlike the term "gross income," which refers to all the money your business brings in before expenses are accounted for, the term "gross profit" does take into account the cost of the product or service you're selling. For example, if a widget costs you $3 and you sell it for $5, your gross profit is $2. The terms "profit margin" or "gross margin" are sometimes used to mean the same thing. The key thing to remember about gross profit is that fixed expenses such as rent or utility bills are not deducted—only the cost of the product or service itself.
- **Net profit.** This is what's left over after subtracting fixed expenses from gross profit. Put another way, net profit means the amount of money you have left over after subtracting all expenses—fixed and variable—from your gross income. Sometimes the term "net income" is used to mean the same thing as net profit.

Talking About Income—Key Terms Defined (continued)

- **Current versus capital expenses.** Current expenses include ordinary, day-to-day business expenses, such as office supplies or salaries. For tax purposes, you can deduct them from your business income in the year that you pay for them. Capital expenses, on the other hand, include payments for business assets (also called "capital," "fixed," or "depreciable" assets) that have a useful life of one year or more, such as computers or office furniture. Capital expenses generally can't be fully deducted in the year they are incurred but must be deducted over a number of years—a process known as depreciation, capitalization, or amortization.

- **State taxes.** States typically collect the following taxes from businesses and their owners: taxes on individual or corporate income, sales taxes on sales of retail goods or sometimes services (usually called "sales taxes" but sometimes "gross receipts taxes"), and payroll taxes. States also often collect special taxes (called "excise taxes") on certain types of business activities such as distributing alcohol, cigarettes, or gasoline. In addition, some states collect taxes on LLCs and limited partnerships.

- **County and city taxes.** Cities, counties, or sometimes both typically impose taxes on businesses based on several factors. Most cities assign businesses to categories (for example, retail businesses, wholesalers, and services) and then tax each category based on certain criteria, such as gross receipts, gross payroll, or number of employees. In addition, counties often assess and collect property taxes on real and personal property owned by businesses within the county. Cities and counties also may impose a sales tax. This tax may be collected by the state along with the state sales tax.

 CAUTION

A tax by any other name is ... a fee. In addition to the taxes listed above, your business may have to pay additional fees for business licenses or tax registration. For instance, many cities and counties require all businesses in the area to register with the local tax collector and pay a registration fee. And, if your business needs to obtain a special license, such as a permit to handle food or a cosmetology license, you'll usually have to pay for it. While these fees arguably could be called taxes, this chapter does not deal with them as such. The various registration, permit, and license requirements—including their associated fees— are covered in Chapter 7.

Forms and Schedules and Returns, Oh My!

This chapter makes many mentions of tax forms, tax schedules, and tax returns. Basically, these are simply different names for the forms you have to fill out and submit to your federal, state, and local tax agencies.

Technically, a "tax form" is the principal document that businesses and their owners must use to report all the basic information about the business's or individual's income. For instance, every individual who earns income must fill out Form 1040, *U.S. Individual Income Tax Return*, and all partnerships and LLCs must file Form 1065, *U.S. Return of Partnership Income*.

A "schedule" is an additional sheet of information the IRS requires businesses and business owners to attach to their tax forms. For instance, sole proprietors must submit Schedule C with their Form 1040 to report their income from their business, and partners and LLC owners usually need to report their business income on Schedule E. Partnerships and LLCs also must include various schedules with their Form 1065s.

Finally, a "tax return" is simply a general term for the whole package you send off to the IRS: your tax form, any schedules, and any attached documents.

Understanding Deductions

Increasing profits while keeping taxes as low as possible is the name of the game in any business. The main way to do this is by claiming business deductions. When you deduct an expense, you subtract it from your taxable income—which means you'll have less income to report and pay taxes on. Of course, you can't deduct just any old expense you want. To stay out of tax trouble, you need to understand which deductions are allowed and which are not. (Note that deductions are often irrelevant for local and sales taxes, which tend to be based on gross income—also called "gross receipts"—without taking any deductions into account.)

What Expenses Are Deductible?

Allowable deductions are outlined in great length (to put it mildly) in the Internal Revenue Code—although the basic guidelines are summarized here below. You'll need to follow these rules when filling out your federal tax return, which you use to report your business income and deductions. When you file your state income tax return, you'll generally fill out a form that uses the information from your federal return, with a few adjustments to reflect your state's rules on deducting business expenses. As far as local taxes go, they may simply be based on gross income (also called "gross receipts") without taking any deductions into account. Your main concern should be the federal rules.

The Section 179 Deduction

The IRS allows every business to treat a certain amount of capital expenditures as current expenses and fully deduct them in the year they were made. This major exception is known as a "179 deduction," because it's established in Internal Revenue Code § 179.

Tax law changes since 2003 dramatically increased the limit from $25,000 in 2003 to $250,000 in 2009—and federal stimulus legislation doubled the limit to $500,000 for tax year 2010. Between 2010 and 2015, the limit bounced up and down as legislation expired and was renewed; then the Tax Cuts and Jobs Act of 2017 set the limit at $1 million for tax years 2018 and beyond. After 2018, the limit will be indexed to inflation. This allows businesses to write off, up to the current year limit, expenditures that normally would have qualified as capital expenditures.

Whether and to what extent you should take advantage of a 179 deduction depends on your circumstances. Generally, you should take a 179 deduction only when your taxable income is high enough that you'll get a decent tax benefit right away. Businesses with low incomes might want to depreciate assets instead (take their deductions slowly) so that they'll have more deductions available in future years when their income might be higher.

The Internal Revenue Code (IRC) states that any "ordinary and necessary" business expenses can be subtracted from your business income for federal tax purposes. (IRC § 162.) Figuring out whether most expenses qualify is a no-brainer. Product costs, office rent, equipment and machinery, office supplies, your business computer system, business insurance, salaries, payroll taxes, and office utility bills are just a few examples of costs that easily count as deductible expenses. As long as an expenditure is, in fact, made for business—not personal—purposes, the general rule is that you can deduct it from your business's gross income.

It gets a little more complicated when expenditures aren't clearly made for business reasons. The IRS has special rules for expenses that border on the personal, such as travel, and vehicle expenses. These costs are deductible, but only according to special IRS rules (for details, see IRS Publication 535, *Business Expenses,* available online at www.irs.gov).

How Are Expenses Deducted?

In addition to figuring out whether an expense is deductible, you need to understand how particular expenses may be deducted. First, you need to know that there's a major distinction between current and capital expenses. Current expenses can best be described as your everyday costs of doing business, such as rent, supplies, utility bills, and the like. These expenses are fully deductible in the year they occur. Capital expenses, on the other hand, are not fully deductible in the year you incur them. You incur a capital expense when you purchase an item with a useful life of at least one year—called a "business asset." Business assets include items such as vehicles, furniture, heavy equipment (like a forklift or printing press), and real estate.

Rather than fully deducting a capital expense in the year it was made, you must spread out the deduction over a number of years. (A major exception to this, the 179 deduction, is discussed below.) This process is variously called "depreciation," "amortization," or "capitalization." Different types of assets have different depreciation rules, and the number of years over which the cost of an item must be depreciated varies. Depreciation rules are explained in IRS Publication 946, *How to Depreciate Property*, available online at www.irs.gov, as well as in other IRS publications that cover specific types of assets.

Note also that start-up expenses—those incurred before you actually launched your business—are subject to special tax rules. The general rule is that businesses may write off up to $5,000 of their start-up costs in the first year of business, as long as start-up costs do not exceed $50,000. The $5,000 deduction is reduced by the amount of your start-up costs that exceed $50,000. Whatever you are unable to deduct, you can amortize—a process in which you stretch out the deduction over

time. Start-up costs that can't be deducted outright are amortized over the next 15 years.

Where to Get Tax Forms and Schedules

Besides the flood of tax forms that are available at libraries as April 15 comes near, you can obtain the most current tax forms, schedules, and publications by ordering them over the phone or downloading them off the Web:

- Download federal tax forms and other publications from the IRS website, including IRS Publication 535, *Business Expenses*, at www.irs.gov. If you'd prefer to have them mailed to you, call the IRS at 800-829-3676.
- For state tax forms, contact your state tax agency. You'll find a list of websites in Appendix A for tax agencies in each state, and on this book's companion page on Nolo.com (see the link in Appendix A).
- Local tax forms and instructions are often automatically sent to businesses once they've registered with their city or county. Otherwise, contact the agency in charge of business taxes in your city or county (depending on where your business is located) for more information on how to obtain local tax forms. To find your local tax agency, look in the city and county government sections of your telephone book under "Tax Collector," "Business Tax Division," or "City Clerk," or check your city or county website.

RESOURCE

Learn more about tax deductions.
This introduction to tax deductions only begins
to scratch the surface of a huge and complex
body of information. *Deduct It! Lower Your Small
Business Taxes*, by Stephen Fishman (Nolo), does
an excellent job of leading you through the maze
and includes detailed advice on how to write off
your start-up costs.

SEE AN EXPERT

Consider working with a tax expert.
Especially as your business grows and its finances
become more complicated, you may well want to
hire a tax adviser to help you use the tax rules to
your best advantage. (See Chapter 17 on hiring
and working with tax professionals.)

Hobby Businesses

For many small business owners, their
"business" is more a labor of love than a
reliable source of income. This is most often
the case when an owner has other means of
financial support—such as a regular job or
a spouse who brings home wages or other
income—that allows a microbusiness to
continue even though it makes little or no
money. These types of tiny businesses are
usually operated from the home (renting
an office would be too expensive) and are
often based on activities near and dear
to the owner, which has earned them the
nickname "hobby businesses."

There is no one type of hobby business.
Examples might include a basement
jewelry studio, a jazz band for hire, or an
antique refinishing business. The owners
would probably keep on making jewelry,
playing jazz, or restoring antiques even if
they never made a penny, but are trying
to turn their hobbies into profitable
businesses.

Often, profits fail to materialize. For
most regular businesses, spending more
than a year or so of losing money is a cue
to close up shop. But if you love what
you're doing, it might make sense for you
to stick with your losing business rather
than fold it up. This is true because if you
have another source of income (as many
owners of hobby businesses do), the losses
from your hobby business can be used to
offset that income. Deducting business
losses—including everyday expenses and
depreciation on assets such as computer
equipment—not only lowers the amount of
income on which taxes are calculated, but
also may drop you into a lower tax bracket.
This is what is commonly referred to as a
tax shelter: an unprofitable business whose
losses offset the owner's taxable income
from other sources.

Of course, most entrepreneurs would
much rather earn a healthy profit than
lose money. And the savings made
possible by a tax shelter do not always
justify continuing a marginal or losing

business. But they definitely can make a difference in deciding whether it's worth it to keep your unprofitable—but enjoyable—business going.

EXAMPLE: Kay and Reza are married and file joint tax returns. Reza earns a salary as a chef in a local restaurant, and Kay is a magazine editor. Kay has a passion for plants and decides to try to make a business of selling some of the hundreds of plants she grows in her backyard greenhouse. After she's spent thousands of dollars on exotic plants and better lighting, the greenhouse heater goes on the fritz and more than 300 of Kay's expensive, exotic plants die. Her expenses for the year total nearly $10,000, and she has not yet sold any plants. The silver lining for Kay and Reza comes at tax time, when they deduct the $10,000 loss from their joint taxable income of $105,000. This not only reduces their taxable income, but—depending on their income level and any other deductions they take—might drop them into a lower tax bracket as well.

On the down side, if you consistently use your unprofitable business as a tax shelter, deducting your losses from your other income year after year, you'll probably attract the attention of the IRS. An issue that often arises with hobby businesses is whether the venture is really a business at all. To deduct expenses from your taxable income, those expenses must have been incurred by a legitimate profit-motivated business—not merely a personal hobby. As you might expect, not every hobby counts as a business. If you claim a loss from your hobby business and you're audited, you'll have to prove to the IRS that your hobby is in fact a legitimate business.

Proving Your Hobby Is a Business

Before you start claiming deductions for the costs of your favorite art projects or toy car collections, make sure your venture will pass IRS scrutiny and qualify as a real business. Thankfully, the IRS's definition is broad. Basically, any activity that you undertake to make a profit counts as a business. You need only prove to the IRS that you're trying—not necessarily succeeding—to make a profit with your venture. The IRS uses a few different criteria to decide whether your business truly has a profit motive.

The main test for profit motive is called the "3-of-5" test. If your business makes a profit in three out of five consecutive years, it is legally presumed to have a profit motive.

While the IRS gives a lot of weight to the 3-of-5 test, it is not conclusive. In other words, if you flunk the 3-of-5 test, you still may be able to prove that your business is motivated by profit. You can use virtually any kind of evidence to prove this. Business cards, a well-maintained set of books, a separate business bank account, current business licenses and permits, and proof of advertising will all help to persuade an IRS auditor that your activity really is a business.

Watch Out for Local Tax Rules

When planning out your hobby business, don't forget that local requirements and taxes will increase your costs of doing business, both in time and money. Lots of small business owners are surprised to find out that state and local tax regulations for small businesses can be more of a bear than IRS rules. For example, if you sell tangible products, you may be subject to state sales taxes. Plus, many cities impose taxes or fees on small businesses and require them to go through some sort of registration process, and counties often have similar requirements for businesses in rural areas. Generally speaking, these rules apply to any money-making activity within the locality—even if the hobby business doesn't intend to claim any federal or state tax deductions.

> **John Tilles, cofounder of Portland Kayak Company, a river rafting outfit in Portland, Oregon (www.portlandkayak.com):**
> *The real can of worms for us was in dealing with taxes. As a new and under-capitalized business, a professional accountant was out of the question. This left me to figure it out as I went, which was pretty straightforward in the early days, but, as the years went on and things became more complicated, I finally had to use a professional C.P.A.*

In practice, many tiny hobby businesses—so tiny that the word "business" even seems excessive—might be able to get away unnoticed, assuming you don't deduct business losses on your tax return. Even so, you should be aware that, depending on your local rules, you may be penalized if you're caught doing business without the permits or licenses required by your state or local government. These penalties may include fines and back taxes.

Income Taxes for Sole Proprietors

As mentioned throughout this book, a sole proprietorship is one and the same as its owner (the sole proprietor) for most legal and tax purposes. It follows that the sole proprietor must report and pay federal and state income taxes on all business profits, including any profits the sole proprietor leaves in the business for expansion. In other words, the business itself does not file tax returns or pay income taxes. (Note that the Tax Cuts and Jobs Act of 2017 created a tax deduction for owners of pass-through entities. See the sidebar, "Tax Deduction for Pass-Through Entities," below.)

Federal Income Taxes

You're probably already familiar with the process of filing IRS Form 1040, based on income you earned at a job. Good—this means much of the process of filing federal income taxes as a sole proprietor will already be familiar to you. That's because income from your business will be treated as personal income, which you report on Form 1040 much as you report wages or returns on investments. But there are two additional steps you'll have to take: You'll have to use a separate sheet (called Schedule C) to report your business profit, and you'll also have to pay self-employment taxes based on your income, reported on Schedule SE.

Income Tax

You report business profits or losses on Schedule C, *Profit or Loss From Business (Sole Proprietorship)*, which is submitted once a year with your 1040 return, usually by April 15. A sole proprietor who owns more than one business must file a separate Schedule C for each business.

You're not required to file Schedule C if your sole proprietorship doesn't make at least $400 profit in the business year, though it's a good idea to file one anyway. If your business loses money in any year, filing Schedule C allows the loss to be deducted from any other income you make for that year, reducing your total taxable income. Or, you can carry over the loss into a future profitable year to offset those profits and thereby reduce your taxes. Another reason to report losses or profits under $400 on Schedule C is that doing so triggers the beginning of the time window during which

the IRS can audit you. Otherwise, the IRS can audit you anytime, virtually forever.

Simplified Tax Schedule for Super-Small Sole Proprietorships

Extra-small sole proprietorships may be able to use a simplified schedule to report their income, Schedule C-EZ *Net Profit from Business*. To use this simplified form, which works just like Schedule C, you must have:

- less than $5,000 in business expenses
- no inventory during the year
- no employees during the year
- used the cash method of accounting; see Chapter 12 for an explanation of the difference between the cash and accrual methods of accounting
- owned and operated only one sole proprietorship during the year
- no expenses deducted for business use of your home, and
- not reported a net business loss.

If you depreciate assets or have unallowed passive activity losses from previous years, you may not be able to use this schedule. See the IRS instructions for details on who may use Schedule C-EZ.

Though Schedule C-EZ is easier to fill out than Schedule C, you won't save enough time or trouble to warrant trying to squeeze a too-large business into it. Don't, for example, neglect to claim more than $5,000 in business expenses or to claim depreciation expenses just so you qualify to use the schedule. The marginal convenience of the simplified schedule just isn't worth it.

Tax Deduction for Pass-Through Entities

Under the Tax Cuts and Jobs Act, effective in the 2018 tax year, taxpayers with a qualified trade or business (more on this below), including sole proprietorships, partnerships, LLCs, and S corporations, will be able to deduct 20% of their qualified business income. This deduction was added to achieve parity between pass-through entities and corporations, which were given major tax breaks in the new tax law (corporate taxes are discussed below). This provision is set to expire December 31, 2025.

So, for example, if your solo freelance business generates $100,000 in profit, you'll be able to deduct $20,000 before income tax is calculated, based on your personal tax bracket.

What is a "qualified pass-through business," you ask? It includes any trade or business *other than* a "specified service trade or business" which includes a wide range of service businesses from health, law and accounting to performing arts, consulting and financial services. The good news for these types of businesses is that they also get the 20% deduction as long as their business income is not higher than $157,500 for single filers, or $315,000 those who file a joint return. The deduction phases out for owners of specified service businesses with incomes above this limit.

The Tax Cuts and Jobs Act made the biggest changes in U.S. tax law in decades, so it's an especially smart idea to talk with a knowledgeable accountant about your specific situation.

There's an important procedural difference between reporting and paying taxes on income from a job and income from a sole proprietorship: Regular employees are subject to tax withholding by their employers, but sole proprietors usually have to estimate their taxes for the year and pay them in quarterly installments. The IRS is a stickler when it comes to making these quarterly payments and won't hesitate to fine you for doing it incorrectly or late, and especially for not doing it at all. Even if you pay your taxes in full by April 15 (or whenever your business year ends), failure to make quarterly payments means you'll be charged a penalty, typically about 9%. (See "Estimating and Paying Your Taxes Quarterly," below.)

Self-Employment Taxes

Sole proprietors must also make contributions to the Social Security and Medicare systems, called "self-employment taxes." Regular employees contribute to these two programs through deductions from their paychecks. Sole proprietors must make their contributions when paying their other income taxes. And they have to pay more than employees do—employees only have to pay half as much into these programs, because their contributions are matched by their employers. Sole proprietors must pay the entire amount themselves.

The self-employment tax rate is 15.3%, of which 12.4% goes towards Social Security and 2.9% goes toward Medicare. While the Medicare portion is calculated based upon a sole proprietor's total profits, the Social Security portion is capped at a certain amount that changes each year ($132,900 for 2019).

In other words, profits of $132,900 and less will be taxed at 15.3% (Social Security and Medicare combined), and profits above that will be taxed at 2.9% (Medicare only). In comparison, regular employees only pay a 7.65% tax on wages of $132,900 or less, and a 1.45% tax on wages above that. Note also that there is a Medicare surtax of 0.9% on income above $200,000 for individuals and $250,000 for couples filing jointly.

Fortunately, there is a small silver lining to this dark tax cloud: Half of the total self-employment tax you'll pay can be deducted from your taxable income at year end. And if your sole proprietorship makes less than $400 profit in the business year, you don't have to pay self-employment taxes.

Self-employment taxes are reported on Schedule SE, which, like Schedule C, *Profit or Loss From Business (Sole Proprietorship),* is submitted yearly with your 1040 income tax return. Once you determine the amount of self-employment taxes you owe on Schedule SE, you enter the result on your 1040 form in the "Other Taxes" section and add it to your personal income tax obligation. Remember, however, that most sole proprietors must estimate their total taxes for the year and pay them in quarterly installments. (See "Estimating and Paying Your Taxes Quarterly," below, for more information.)

State Income Taxes

You must report and pay state income taxes in much the same way as federal income tax. Any profit generated by a sole proprietorship is generally treated as personal income of the sole proprietor and reported on an individual state tax return. In most states the sole proprietor will need to attach a separate schedule, similar to the federal Schedule C, to report business income. Unlike the federal rule, some states require this schedule to be filed even if a business loses money or makes less than $400 profit. In these states, you won't owe any taxes unless you've made a profit, but you must file the form in any case.

Like federal taxes, many states require businesses to estimate and pay their income taxes in quarterly installments.

Tax rules vary considerably from state to state, so it's important that you check with your state tax agency for its requirements.

RESOURCE

Where to find your state tax agency. Appendix A includes website addresses for state tax agencies, which are also included on this book's companion page on Nolo.com.

Income Taxes for Partnerships

Although a partnership itself does not pay taxes (its owners do), it does need to submit an annual informational return to the IRS—and usually the state—to report its income. As is true for sole proprietorships, taxes are paid only by the partners (business owners), not the business itself, and the partners have to pay taxes on all business profits, whether or not

they take any money out of the business (though the 2017 Tax Cuts and Jobs Act provides a 20% deduction on qualified business income for pass-through entities; see the sidebar, "Tax Deduction for Pass-Through Entities," above). This section explains what partnerships need to do to comply with the IRS and state rules.

Federal Income Taxes

Partnerships are called "pass-through tax entities," which means that profits pass right through the business to the owners, who report them on their individual income tax returns. The partnership itself is not taxed, but it must report its income and losses each year. (Although few do, a partnership can also elect to be taxed as a corporation, by submitting Form 8832, *Entity Classification Election,* and electing corporate tax status.) Besides income taxes, partners must also file and pay self-employment taxes.

FORM

Where to find the *Entity Classification Election* form. The Nolo website includes a copy of the IRS Form 8832. See Appendix B for the link to this form and the other forms in this book. You can also find IRS forms on www.irs.gov.

Income Tax

Even though the partnership itself does not pay taxes on profits, it must report profits and losses on an informational return, Form 1065, *U.S. Return of Partnership Income.* No tax is due with this return, which is generally due by April 15.

Along with Form 1065, the partnership must also submit a Schedule K-1, *Partner's Share of Income, Deductions, Credits, etc.,* for each partner, reporting each partner's share of profits or losses. The K-1 schedule is used to inform the IRS of the partners' chosen profit division. Often, partners own equal shares of the business, which normally means they will choose to share profits and pay taxes equally—such as four partners each getting 25% of a business's profits and paying 25% of its taxes. But if they so choose, partners can divide profits and losses unequally. (See Chapter 1 for more on partnerships.) A copy of the completed K-1 must also be given to each partner on or before the date that the partnership return is due to the IRS.

As mentioned, profits earned by a partnership are taxed as personal income of the individual partners. Each partner reports an allocated share of business income or losses on an individual federal income tax return (Form 1040) using Schedule E, *Supplemental Income and Loss.* Schedule E repeats the income information reported on Schedule K-1 (which each partner

should have received from the partnership). Since the partnership already filed Schedule K-1 with the IRS, partners do not need to submit this schedule with their individual tax returns.

Partners who earn income from a profitable partnership often must estimate their taxes and pay the total in quarterly installments.

 SEE AN EXPERT

When partners don't share and share alike. Remember that each partner is taxed on his or her allocated share of the partnership profits, not on the amount actually distributed. However, it is possible in some circumstances for partners to legally divide items on a less-than-even basis. For instance, they could agree that one partner may deduct, on his or her personal tax return, all the interest paid on a partnership property mortgage. But a partner's share of partnership losses that can be deducted is limited to the partner's basis (investment) in the partnership. You should see a tax attorney if you want to get into this kind of tax planning.

Self-Employment Taxes

Partners and other self-employed individuals who earn more than $400 profit during the business year must contribute to Social Security and Medicare through federal self-employment taxes. The self-employment tax rate is 15.3%, of which 12.4% goes towards Social Security and 2.9% goes towards Medicare. While the Medicare portion is calculated based upon the partner's total share of profits, the Social Security portion is capped at a certain amount that changes each year ($132,900 for 2019).

Put another way, profits of $132,900 and less will be taxed at 15.3% (Social Security and Medicare combined), and profits above that will be taxed at 2.9% (Medicare only). Note also there is a Medicare surtax of 0.9% on income above $200,000 for individuals and $250,000 for couples filing jointly.

On a brighter note, a partner can deduct half of the total self-employment tax from his or her taxable income at year-end. And if the partner makes less than $400 in profit, no self-employment taxes need be filed or paid.

Self-employment taxes are reported on Schedule SE, which, like Schedule E, *Supplemental Income and Loss*, is submitted yearly with a partner's 1040 return. Once you determine your self-employment tax with Schedule SE, enter the result on your 1040 form in the "Other Taxes" section, which you must add to your personal income tax obligation. But don't forget about estimating and paying taxes quarterly—most partners of profitable businesses must do so, or face the IRS's penalties. (See "Estimating and Paying Your Taxes Quarterly," below, for more on

quarterly taxes.) A husband and wife who operate a business as partners must each report their share of the business profits as net earnings on separate Schedule SEs, even if they file a joint 1040 return.

State Income Taxes

Like the federal government, most states require partnerships to file informational returns reporting business income and losses. Fortunately, many of these state forms are almost identical to the federal Form 1065. Partnerships may also be required to file a schedule analogous to the federal Schedule K-1 for each partner, indicating the partner's share of the business profit or loss. The partnership must give each partner a copy. Typically, the state schedules are similar to the federal version but account for differences between state and federal tax laws. Generally, no tax is due with the partnership return or schedules.

Any partnership profit is taxed as personal income of the partners, who report their shares on their individual state income tax returns. Partnership income is usually recorded on a schedule similar to the federal Schedule E and included with the state tax form. Keep in mind that some states require partners to file this schedule even if the partnership loses money and no taxes are due.

Finally, like federal taxes, state income taxes must often be paid in quarterly installments.

Income Taxes for LLCs

The limited liability company or LLC (explained in greater detail in Chapter 1) is a relatively new business ownership structure. LLCs combine several key attributes that distinguish the traditional partnership and corporation, allowing LLC owners (usually called "members") to enjoy the protection from personal liability that a corporation offers, while avoiding the complicated and often expensive corporate tax system. LLC profits are taxed to the owners as individuals (like a sole proprietor or owners of a partnership). (Note that the 2017 Tax Cuts and Jobs Act provides a 20% deduction on qualified business income for pass-through entities; see the sidebar, "Tax Deduction for Pass-Through Entities," earlier in this chapter.) Although members (owners) can instead choose to have the LLC taxed like a corporation, this choice is somewhat unusual. (But see Chapter 1 for reasons why some LLCs may want to be taxed like corporations.) In this section, assume your LLC will stick with pass-through tax status.

Federal Income Taxes

Like owners of partnerships, most LLC owners will report business profits on their individual federal income tax returns. Although this means the LLC itself is not taxed, it must still report its income and losses to the IRS each year if it has two or more members. In addition to regular income taxes, members may be obligated to pay self-employment taxes, which are also based on business income.

Income Tax

LLCs with only one member are treated as sole proprietorships for tax purposes, so that business profits and losses are reported on Schedule C, to be submitted with the member's regular individual income tax return. If the LLC has two or more members, it must file an annual informational return with the IRS, similar to the requirement faced by partnerships. Since the IRS hasn't yet come up with tax forms specifically for LLCs, LLC profits and losses are reported on Form 1065, *U.S. Return of Partnership Income.* No tax is paid with this return, which is generally due by April 15.

Along with Form 1065, an LLC must also submit a Schedule K-1 (again, the same schedule used by partnerships) to the IRS for each member, reporting each member's share of profits or losses. The K-1 schedule is used to inform the IRS of the members' chosen profit division. A copy of the completed K-1 must also be given to each member on or before the date that the LLC return is due to the IRS.

Often, members own equal shares of the business, which normally means they will choose to share profits and pay taxes equally—such as four members each getting 25% of a business's profits and paying 25% of its taxes. But if they so choose, LLC members can divide profits and losses unequally. (See Chapter 1 for more on LLCs and profit allocations.)

Profits earned by an LLC are taxed as personal income of the individual members. Members use the information from Schedule K-1 to report business income or losses on their individual federal income tax returns (Form 1040) using Schedule E, *Supplemental Income and Loss*. Since the LLC will already have filed Schedule K-1s with the IRS, members do not need to submit this form with their returns.

Like sole proprietors and partners, LLC members will have to estimate their taxes for the year and pay them in quarterly installments.

Self-Employment Taxes

LLC members who earn more than $400 profit during the business year must contribute to Social Security and Medicare through federal self-employment taxes. The self-employment tax rate is 15.3%, of which 12.4% goes toward Social Security and 2.9% goes towards Medicare. While the Medicare portion is calculated based upon the member's total share of profits, the Social Security portion is capped at a certain amount that changes each year ($132,900 for 2019).

This translates into a 15.3% tax on profits up to $132,900 (Social Security and Medicare combined), and a 2.9% tax on profits above that amount (Medicare only). In comparison, regular employees pay only a 7.65% tax on wages of $132,900 or less, and a 1.45% tax on wages above that. Note also there is a Medicare surtax of 0.9% on income above $200,000 for individuals and $250,000 for couples filing jointly.

CAUTION

There are some gray areas in the rules on self-employment taxes for LLC members. Since LLCs are partnership-like in some respects and corporate-like in others, the rules on whether LLC members are subject to self-employment tax are not fully settled. Generally speaking, an LLC member who is actively involved in the business must pay self-employment taxes, while an LLC member who is inactive and merely invests in the company may be exempt from the self-employment tax obligation. If you're not sure whether this tax would apply to you, it may be wise to consult an accountant to get a definitive answer for your situation. (Chapter 17 gives information on finding professionals to advise you.)

Fortunately, if self-employment taxes are due, you can deduct half of the total self-employment taxes you pay from your taxable income at year-end. And an LLC member who earns less than $400 profit in the business year, will be totally exempt from having to pay self-employment taxes.

Self-employment taxes are reported on Schedule SE, which, like Schedule E, *Supplemental Income and Loss*, is submitted yearly with an LLC member's 1040 return. Once you determine the self-employment taxes you owe on Schedule SE, the result is entered on your 1040 form in the "Other Taxes" section, which is added to your individual income tax obligation. If the LLC member is required to pay advance quarterly tax installments, however, any self-employment taxes will be included in those payments.

State Taxes

Though the federal government treats LLCs with pass-through tax status almost exactly like partnerships, the tax treatment LLCs receive in their states of formation may vary somewhat. Most states follow the IRS's lead and treat LLCs as pass-through entities unless the members have elected corporate tax treatment for the LLC. Some states, however, also impose special taxes on LLCs themselves, despite treating them as pass-through tax entities in most other respects.

Most states collect income tax from LLC members on their share of business profits, following the IRS classification scheme for LLCs, which treats LLCs as either partnerships or sole proprietorships. An LLC with a single owner is usually treated as a sole proprietorship, and business profits will be taxed on the sole member's individual state income tax return. LLCs with two or more owners are typically treated as partnerships and must file the same tax returns as owners of partnerships in that state.

Unlike the IRS, which imposes no taxes on LLCs themselves, several states levy taxes on LLCs in addition to taxing LLC members on their share of LLC income. These taxes are alternately called "franchise taxes," "annual fees," "surcharge taxes," or other similar names. Depending on the state, these additional costs can range from $10 to thousands of dollars, so be sure to understand your state's rules well in advance of tax time. (Appendix A includes website addresses for state tax agencies, which can tell you how your state treats LLCs for tax purposes. Most state tax websites also offer downloadable tax forms, or information on where to get them.)

Like federal taxes, state income taxes for members must often be paid in quarterly installments.

Estimating and Paying Your Taxes Quarterly

Anyone who earns income from a business must generally pay income taxes in quarterly installments over the course of the business year. Some businesspeople who expect to owe little or no income tax are exempt from these estimated payment requirements. At year end, if you've paid more than what you owe, you'll get a refund. On the other hand, if you didn't pay enough in your quarterly installments, you will owe more.

This system isn't all that different from the way taxes on employment wages are handled. From each paycheck, the federal (and often state) government requires an employer to withhold income taxes from each employee's wages based on the employee's expected annual salary or hourly pay. At year end, the employee calculates and reports a personal tax obligation based on how much money was actually earned during the year. Depending on the dollar amount of the tax obligation, the employee will either owe more money (if the employer didn't withhold enough) or be due a refund (if the employer withheld too much).

The IRS and state tax agencies collect withholdings or advance payment of estimated taxes for a simple, practical reason: They know that a sudden multi-thousand-dollar bill on April 15 can be difficult for anyone. Spreading out payments by wage withholding or estimated payments is the tax agencies' way of making your life a little easier—and making sure they get their money.

Unfortunately, it's much easier for an employer to figure out an employee's estimated tax burden based on individual yearly salary or hourly wage than it is for a small business owner to estimate taxes based on future income from a new and unproven business. Projecting future income in order to estimate your tax obligation can be a dicey task, especially for brand-new business owners whose income hasn't yet evened out into any predictable rhythm. To make matters worse, you'll be socked with a penalty if your estimates are off and you don't pay enough each quarter.

But here's the good news: You don't need to start making estimated tax payments until you earn enough income to subject you to a threshold quarterly payment requirement. This should give you enough time to get a pretty good feel for how much and how quickly money—and, by extension, taxable profits—are coming into your business. And even if you do underestimate your taxes and face a penalty of a few hundred dollars, you can at least take heart that you owe extra only because your business has become profitable sooner than you anticipated.

In addition to the IRS, many state tax agencies also require profitable businesses to make estimated tax payments. For the most part, these states' rules are similar to the federal one, but they use slightly different formulas. The rest of this section will address just the federal requirement; check with your state tax agency to find out its formula for estimating taxes. (Website addresses for each state's tax agency are included in Appendix A and on this book's companion page on Nolo.com.)

Who Must Pay Estimated Taxes?

Business owners have to pay federal estimated taxes if they expect to owe at least $1,000 in federal taxes for any particular year (including income taxes and self-employment taxes). Generally, this means you'll have to make estimated payments if your adjusted gross income (taxable net profits minus tax exemptions, deductions, and credits) will be between $3,000 and $6,000, depending on your tax bracket. The point here is, if your business is at all profitable, count on estimating and paying your taxes quarterly. On the other hand, if you're operating at a net business loss or making next to nothing, you may not have to make estimated payments.

EXAMPLE: On December 31, as part of a New Year's resolution, Jason quits his job as a computer salesman and opens a river rafting outfit called the Rapids Transit Company. For the first few months of the next year, every dollar he takes in pays for equipment, insurance, and marketing. At the rate he's going, he doesn't know if he'll make a profit at all that year, so he doesn't worry about estimated taxes. However, starting in June with the heavy tourist season, he starts clearing about $1,300 per month, after all deductions. He thinks he may have at least four more months like that before winter slows business down. If so, his annual profit will be about $6,500 ($1,300 x five months). Depending on his tax status, he'll probably owe between $1,000 and $2,000 in taxes at the end of the year. He realizes he'd better start making estimated quarterly payments to be safe, or risk a penalty.

Now for the nitty-gritty. The IRS has a relatively straightforward formula (okay, that may be stretching this just a bit) for determining whether you need to estimate and pay your taxes in installments. You'll have to pay estimated taxes if you expect:

- to owe at least $1,000 in federal taxes (including income taxes and self-employment taxes) for the current year, after subtracting any withheld taxes, and
- your withheld taxes and credits to be less than the smaller of:
  - 100% of your total tax owed for the previous year, or
  - 90% of your total tax obligation for the current year.

<table>
<tr><td>

Your Day Job May Help You Avoid Estimated Taxes

If, in addition to the business you own, you work at a job on which taxes are withheld from your income, you might not have to pay estimated taxes if your income from your business is not a significant part of your total income. This is because the taxes withheld from your job may cover you for any estimated taxes owed on your business income. In other words, the IRS wants to make sure that a certain portion of the total taxes you'll owe are paid in installments over the year, but it doesn't care whether those taxes are withheld from your paycheck or paid as estimated taxes. It's possible that the taxes withheld from your paycheck will be enough to meet your entire tax obligation. On the other hand, if your business is bringing in significant income, chances are that your wage withholding won't cover your tax bill.

</td></tr>
</table>

This formula sounds complicated, but it's not. First, it requires you to make estimated payments only if you expect to owe at least $1,000 to the IRS at year end, above and beyond any taxes withheld from wages. This translates to about $3,000 to $6,000 in adjusted gross income from your business, depending on your tax bracket. So if your business is barely breaking even, you probably won't have to make estimated payments.

Second, if you do expect to make at least that amount from your business, you may not have to pay estimated taxes on your business income if enough taxes are withheld from a paycheck (assuming you receive one). If the taxes that are withheld from your paycheck in the current year will add up to more than 90% of what you'll owe in taxes, you won't have to make estimated payments. Or, if that's not true, there's one more way you can escape making estimated tax payments: If the taxes withheld in the current year will add up to at least what your entire tax bill was for the previous year, you're free of the estimated tax requirement.

EXAMPLE: Nels works as a manager of an auto parts store, which pays him a salary and deducts federal and state taxes from each paycheck. He starts a sole proprietorship called Falcon's Auto Tow. In the first few months of his auto-towing business, Nels operates at a loss. Since his only taxable income during those months is from his paychecks, on which taxes are withheld, he doesn't have to worry about estimated payments. In the fifth month, he starts to turn a profit, at which point Nels starts to pay attention to whether he must pay estimated taxes. If he thinks his wage withholding will account for at least 90% of his total tax bill at the end of the year, he doesn't need to file and pay estimated taxes. In other words, if he thinks that taxes on his small business income will account for less than 10% of his total tax bill, he'll just file his taxes at year end like most people whose entire income is all subject to wage withholding.

Except for C corporations, a business must use the calendar year as its business year unless it gets permission from the IRS to choose a different starting and ending point. A bit of tax jargon is important here. Any one-year period other than the calendar year (ending on December 31) that a business uses for tax purposes is called a "fiscal year," a "tax year," or an "accounting period." The IRS allows sole proprietorships, partnerships, LLCs, and S corporations to use a fiscal year only if there is a valid business reason for it, such as significant seasonal fluctuations in business. Fiscal years must begin on the first day of a month and end on the last day of the previous month one year later. An unincorporated business that wants to use a fiscal year must submit Form 8716, *Election To Have a Tax Year Other Than a Required Tax Year*, to the IRS and have it approved.

 RESOURCE
Where to find IRS Form 8716. This form is included on this book's companion page on Nolo.com; the link is in Appendix B. You'll also find Form 8716 on www.irs.gov.

Most businesspeople, of course, anticipate becoming profitable eventually —preferably sooner than later—so at some point you'll need to start paying estimated taxes. In the real world, what usually happens is that once you become profitable and owe income taxes for the first time, your accountant will calculate the next year's estimated tax payments based upon what you owed the previous year. The accountant will likely even prepare the vouchers for you, so all you have to do is send in the payment with the voucher stub by the applicable deadline.

When to Make Estimated Tax Payments

As just discussed, you become subject to the federal estimated tax payment requirement when you expect to earn enough profit during a business year to trigger the payment requirement. Each quarterly payment must be filed a half-month after the end of the quarter. For federal estimated taxes, the quarterly due dates are as follows:

Income made during:	Tax installment due:
Jan. 1 through Mar. 31	April 15
Apr. 1 through May 31	June 15
June 1 through Aug. 31	September 15
Sept. 1 through Dec. 31	January 15 of the next year

If your business uses a fiscal rather than a calendar year, your payments will be due on the 15th day of the 4th, 6th, and 9th months of your fiscal year and the 1st month of the following fiscal year.

 CAUTION

Don't overlook your self-employment taxes. Self-employment taxes, like income taxes, are subject to the estimated tax payment requirement. Be sure to include them when figuring your estimated tax burden for the year.

For more information on federal estimated tax payments, refer to IRS Publication 505, *Tax Withholding and Estimated Tax,* available online at www.irs.gov.

City and County Taxes

Unlike the federal or state governments, many cities and counties impose taxes directly on your business, even if your business is a pass-through entity such as a sole proprietorship, partnership, or limited liability company. Of course, you, as the owner of the business, are personally liable for these financial obligations, but the difference is that your business itself—not merely the profits that flow through to you and any other owners—incurs taxes by local governments. Often, these taxes can be more of a burden than federal or state ones, because many of them are based on your business income before you deduct business costs and expenses. Some areas, for instance, impose a gross receipts tax, which calculates the tax based simply on how much total income your business brings in, without regard for your expenses.

Local taxes vary a lot from one area to the next, but your business can always expect to face some sort of "business taxes" from your city or county, which may include property taxes.

Business Taxes

The vague term "business taxes" simply refers to the tax your local government imposes on all businesses within the city or county limits. Businesses in rural areas will probably only deal with their county tax authority. Whether the tax is imposed by a city or a county tax authority, the information about business taxes provided in this section generally applies.

Unlike the IRS and most state tax agencies, which simply collect taxes after they're incurred, most local tax collectors require you to go through a tax registration process before you start your business. (Information on how the registration process generally works is provided in Chapter 7, Step 4.) Once you've registered, you'll obtain what's commonly called a "tax registration certificate" (or sometimes, inaccurately, a "business license"). Registration gives notice to your local tax authorities that your business exists and allows them to tax it, based on whatever method your locality has adopted for your type of business.

In many cities and counties, you actually start paying your local taxes when you purchase your business license or registration certificate. Often, a locality will base its registration fee on your expected local tax for the year. In some localities, your registration fee is like a prepaid tax that can be applied toward your total year-end tax. In other places, the registration cost is purely an administrative fee and cannot be applied to your tax bill. And in still other areas, part of the registration cost is a prepaid tax that can be credited toward your tax bill, and part is an administrative fee.

The taxing schemes used in various cities and counties are usually based on certain attributes of your business. Most localities divide businesses into a number of different categories or types, such as retail sales, wholesale sales, hotels/apartments, and service businesses. Each category uses a certain criterion to calculate taxes, usually called a tax base. A common tax base, for example, is "gross receipts" (total income, before expenses). Each category has a certain tax rate for each tax base.

For example, in Oakland, California, retail sales businesses (Code A) must pay $1.20 per $1,000 of gross receipts (the tax base). Recreation and entertainment businesses (Code G) in Oakland also have gross receipts as their tax base, but must pay $4.50 per $1,000. Other criteria used as tax bases include total payroll, number of employees, or number of company vehicles. Other tax bases exist as well. For instance, in Sacramento, California, certain professionals, such as accountants, attorneys, and podiatrists, pay taxes based on the number of years they have been licensed in the state. The moral of the story here is that local tax systems have just about as many ways of taxing your business as there are types of businesses.

Because rules vary widely from city to city and county to county, you'll need to check with your local tax agency to find out how it will tax your business. When searching for the appropriate tax agency, look online or in the government section of your telephone book under City Government (or County Government if you live in an unincorporated area) for names such as "Tax Collector," "Business Licenses and Permits," or "Business Tax Division." And, since local taxation of businesses is usually closely tied to start-up registration requirements, most businesses will automatically receive tax-filing information either when they register or soon after by mail. (For more information on start-up registration requirements, see Chapter 7.)

Property Taxes

Many localities impose taxes on certain kinds of business property, such as real estate, business equipment, furniture, and vehicles. Property tax reporting procedures vary considerably from area to area, but a common requirement is for businesses to provide their local tax authority with an itemized list of business property subject to tax. Check in your area to determine whether any property taxes apply to your business and how to go about paying them.

Sales Taxes

In many states, retail sales are subject to state, county, and local district sales taxes. They are often just referred to as state sales taxes, since they're often filed and paid to one state sales tax agency with just one return. In states that use this system, it's up to the state sales tax agency to distribute the collected taxes to the counties and districts across the state.

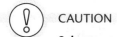 CAUTION

Sales tax rules are closely related to seller's permit requirements. Recall from Chapter 7 that most businesses that engage in retail sales must apply for a seller's permit. This can be true even if the business ultimately makes no taxable sales—for instance, if all sales fall into a tax-exempt category, like groceries. (See Chapter 7 for help in figuring out whether your business needs a seller's permit.)

Taxable Versus Nontaxable Sales

In most states that impose sales taxes, the general rule for whether a transaction is taxable is that the sale must:

- involve the sale of a tangible item, and
- be made to the final user of the item.

Tangible items are things you can touch, such as books, toys, or furniture. Nontangible items might include services, downloadable books, software, or intellectual property such as patents or copyrights.

A final user is a consumer—either an individual or a business—rather than a reseller (a wholesaler or distributor). Sales that are made directly to end users (consumers), rather than resellers, are retail sales (taxable). Sales to resellers are wholesale sales (nontaxable). This means that if you operate as a wholesaler and sell tangible goods to resellers who will in turn sell them to consumers, your sales are likely exempt from sales tax.

Keep in mind, however, that this rule is by no means uniform from state to state. For instance, some states may consider sales of software to be taxable sales of tangible items, but others do not. A common source of confusion is the fact that states often have unique (to put it delicately) definitions of the terms "tangible item," "final user," or whatever other terms apply within the state. For example, in the late 1990s, more than a few graphic artists in California were surprised to learn that the state did not consider their transactions to be services (which are not taxable in California), but instead to be taxable sales of tangible items, merely because the artists' work was given to the client on a physical piece of paper. The sales tax regulations were amended in 2002, resulting in more fair treatment of graphic artists' work. The point here is not to rely on common definitions, but to find out specifically how your state tax agency interprets sales tax terminology.

Sales Tax Exemptions

Part of the reason that the rules on sales taxes can be so convoluted is that the "rules" are clouded by swarms of exceptions and exemptions. Here are several examples of common exemptions from sales tax:

- most groceries (but not restaurant or take-out food)
- sales to out-of-state customers
- sales to the U.S. government, and
- some sales related to the entertainment industry.

Rules vary from state to state, so be sure to check with your state sales tax agency about which sales are exempt from sales tax. For general information, see The Sales Tax Clearinghouse, http://thestc.com.

Besides the fact that many states use broad definitions in deciding what is taxable, a few states diverge from the general rule described above. Unlike the majority of states, Hawaii, New Mexico, South Dakota, and West Virginia impose taxes on all or almost all services. Still other states charge taxes on certain services, and others tax services when they're performed along with a taxable sale of a tangible item, such as charges for delivering a taxable item. Again, the state rules regarding these sales tax situations are complex and fraught with exceptions, so it's crucial that you check with your state agency to find out the details that apply to your business. (Website addresses for state sales tax agencies are listed in Appendix A.)

 CAUTION

You may need a permit to sell tangible goods. As we mentioned earlier, businesses that sell tangible goods must typically obtain a seller's permit from the state before sales begin, even if the sales aren't taxable (such as wholesale sales, discussed below). Selling tangible goods without a seller's permit is a misdemeanor crime in some states, but, typically, the state sales tax agency will give you the opportunity to comply by getting a permit before it files any criminal charges. But keep in mind that if you made any sales that were taxable before you got your seller's permit, you may be required not only to get a permit, but to pay all back taxes that are due.

Online Sales and Nexus After *Wayfair*

In the pre-Internet economy, sales tax rules were more heavily affected by physical locations of businesses—specifically, whether or not they had a connection (or "nexus") in the form of a physical presence in the state where they conducted sales. The general rule was that businesses were required to collect sales taxes only on sales conducted within states where the business had a physical presence. This rule, established by the U.S. Supreme Court in *Quill v. North Dakota*, 504 U.S. 298 (1992), was the law of the land for 26 years—until the Supreme Court overturned it in a landmark 2018 case, *South Dakota v. Wayfair*, Inc., 138 S.Ct. 2080 (2018) (commonly known as *Wayfair*).

In the *Wayfair* decision, the Court ruled that states do have the authority to impose sales tax on sellers even if they have no physical location in the state where the sale was conducted. In the Court's words, "Physical presence is not necessary to create a substantial nexus."

Pre-*Wayfair*, simply shipping a product or a catalog to a customer in a certain state wasn't enough to establish a nexus in that state; you needed either a brick-and-mortar location there or an employee (such as a salesperson) based there. As online sales exploded, states understandably wanted to tax these transactions, and lots of legislative activity started happening to define nexus more broadly to include purely economic contacts. With the *Wayfair* case, nexus has been decoupled from physical location and may be present when remote sellers meet a minimum amount or number of sales in a state. The result is that many online sellers will now be considered to have a nexus within a state even if they have no office, building, employee, warehouse, affiliate, or other physical presence there.

With this more inclusive definition of nexus, many businesses will be subject to the sales tax laws of other states where they conduct sales. When that's the case, they must comply with any requirements for getting a seller's permit, as well as for collecting, reporting and paying the tax to the state.

Both the *Quill* and *Wayfair* opinions recognized the potential and actual complications involved in requiring sellers to comply with numerous state tax agencies and requirements, and they noted the importance of exempting some small sellers for whom compliance would be too burdensome. The South Dakota law at the heart of *Wayfair*, which is now in effect, is considered a model for laws that will pass legal muster; it exempts sellers with annual sales of less than $100,000 or fewer than 200 transactions.

By the time this book goes to print, many similar state laws will be newly effective, and many more are in legislative pipelines. The best way to make sure you understand and comply with the laws that apply to your sales and business operations is to talk with an accountant or bookkeeper who is familiar with sales taxes for online sales. Bear in mind that many legislative changes are still happening (including proposed federal legislation), and more court decisions are sure to follow. In fact, the *Wayfair* opinion acknowledged that the complicated tapestry of sales tax laws across the U.S. may warrant a legal revisiting of the issues related to taxation of online sales. As Justice Kennedy noted, "These issues are not before the Court in the instant case; but their potential to arise in some later case cannot justify retaining this artificial, anachronistic rule that deprives States of vast revenues from major businesses." So stay tuned for more developments.

RESOURCE

The Sales Tax Institute (www.sales taxinstitute.com) offers in-depth information, updates, and state-by-state guides on how to stay in compliance with state sales tax laws after *Wayfair*. Its "Remote Seller Nexus Chart" is regularly updated with new state legislation as it is passed

Sales to Final Users Versus Sales to Resellers

As mentioned above, states generally tax only sales to the final user. The idea behind this rule is to make sure that items are taxed only once. Rather than taxing the sale of a lamp, for instance, each time it is sold—from its manufacturer, to the wholesaler, to the final customer—it is taxed only when it is sold to the final consumer. (Some transactions that are exempt from sales tax, however, may be subject to a nearly identical tax—see "Use Taxes," below.)

How can you be sure that a customer is a final user? Customers who intend to resell your product should present you with a "resale certificate," which states that the product is being purchased for resale. Depending on your state's law, the certificate must usually contain certain information, including:

- the purchaser's name and address
- the number of the purchaser's seller's permit
- a description of the property to be purchased
- a statement that the property is being used for resale, in terms such as "will be resold" or "for resale" (language such as "nontaxable" or "exempt" is not enough)
- the date of the sale, and

- the signature of the purchaser or an authorized agent.

If you are not presented with such a certificate, you should assume the customer is the final user and treat the sale as taxable. If you sell to the same customer repeatedly, you'll usually need to collect only one resale certificate, which you should keep on file at your office. From then on, whenever you sell items to that company, you shouldn't have to collect another resale certificate.

Using Resale Certificates

Just as your customers can escape paying you sales taxes by presenting a resale certificate, you can use one to purchase goods and supplies free of sales tax as long as the goods and supplies are for legitimate resale. This applies whether you'll resell purchased goods as is, or whether you'll incorporate purchased supplies into your products. If you buy regularly from the same supplier, you should only have to present your resale certificate once.

This exception doesn't apply to goods and supplies that you don't plan to resell or use in manufacturing products. You must pay sales taxes on all items that you'll use in your business and not pass on to a customer. In other words, when you are actually the final user, you have to pay sales tax like anyone else. This includes sales tax on goods and supplies you use to

perform services or operate your business. For example, a hairdresser must pay sales tax on the shampoo used to wash hair. Similarly, if you purchase a computer to keep track of your sales, you should pay the sales tax on that purchase. When purchasing a combination of goods, only some of which you intend to resell, you should clearly indicate which items are for resale and pay sales taxes on the rest.

Use Taxes

Although some sales of tangible goods are exempt from sales tax, many of these transactions are actually subject to a use tax. In keeping with its name, a use tax is due when you use a tangible good on which you didn't pay sales tax.

Use taxes commonly apply to purchases of tangible goods from outside your state. For instance, if you order 20 computers, 20 chairs, and 20 desks for your office from an out-of-state mail order catalogue, you probably didn't pay sales taxes on those items, because most states don't require businesses to collect sales tax from out-of-state purchasers. But under use tax laws in many states, your state can collect use taxes from you, the buyer, to make up for the revenue it would have gotten if you had bought the equipment within the state.

Other transactions subject to use tax include purchases of items you originally intended to resell (and bought tax free because you used your resale certificate) but used for another purpose. Also, items that you buy to incorporate into a new product to sell, as well as items you lease, are subject to the use tax (assuming you bought them free from sales tax with a resale certificate). Inventory that you store for future resale is not subject to use tax.

To pay use taxes, you typically fill out a use tax return, which is often the same as or related to the one that your business will use for paying sales taxes to the state. Essentially, you'll enter information on the form about the purchases you made that are subject to use tax, and follow the form's instructions for calculating your tax. There's not much more to it than sending it off to the state sales tax office, along with a check (assuming you owe money).

There's a high blow-off factor when it comes to use taxes. Use taxes have largely been ignored by individuals and businesses, and the inherent difficulty of enforcing this tax allows virtually everyone to get away with it. However, some states that have traditionally been lax in enforcing and collecting use taxes are now stepping up their efforts to collect them. Particularly in today's environment of thriving e-commerce and state budget deficits, sales taxes on out-of-state purchases have become a red-hot issue. Keep an eye out for developments in this area, and don't get caught with your use taxes down.

Who Actually Owes Sales Taxes?

Despite the fact that most consumers pay sales taxes on a daily basis, there's a lot of misunderstanding out there over who really owes sales taxes—purchasers or sellers. Here's the deal: In most states, consumers are technically responsible for paying sales taxes. In these states, the retailer is essentially merely a collector for the sales tax owed by the consumer. In some states, however, the actual responsibility for sales taxes falls on the retailer. This sort of tax is sometimes called a "privilege tax," because businesses are taxed for the privilege of conducting retail sales.

Keep in mind that these are often technical distinctions without a whole lot of practical effect. For example, if consumers are legally responsible for paying sales taxes in a certain state, that doesn't mean that businesses can escape paying state sales taxes. Usually, all it means is that the business must state the selling price and the sales tax separately on receipts and invoices. That way, consumers see that they are in fact being charged sales tax.

Keeping Track of Your Sales

When you obtain a seller's permit in most states, you obligate yourself to file a sales (and use) tax return. This means that you'll need to keep careful records of both your sales and purchases. Most state sales tax agencies require that you keep:

- books or computer files recording your sales and purchases
- bills, receipts, invoices, contracts, or other documents (called "documents of original entry") that support your books, and
- schedules and working papers used in preparing your tax returns.

In addition, if you conduct business in more than one county, city, or other local tax district, you may need to keep separate records of sales made in each area.

Finally, your records should show all sales your business makes, even sales that aren't taxable.

Calculating, Filing, and Paying Sales Taxes

Sales taxes in many states are actually a combination of state, county, and city sales taxes. For example, an 8% sales tax may actually break down into a 5% state tax, a 2% county tax, and a 1% city tax. The sales taxes that apply to your business will often depend on where your taxable sales are being conducted. If you conduct taxable sales in more than one tax district, you may end up paying several different rates. Conveniently, many states allow businesses to file just one state tax return that includes all taxes for all applicable

districts. The return will usually ask you to identify where your sales were made so that the state can allocate the fair share of taxes to each tax district.

Businesses that have been issued a seller's permit will often receive their state sales tax return package automatically, along with an account number, due date, and filing instructions. Depending on your sales volume, you'll need to submit your sales tax return yearly, quarterly, or monthly. Contact your state agency for details.

Filling out the sales tax return is generally fairly straightforward and will vary only slightly in format depending on the form used by your state. Basically, you'll enter sales information for each tax district in your state where you conducted taxable sales and identify the tax rates that apply to each of these sales. The return will typically walk you through the calculations and will tell you whether and how much sales tax you owe. In most states, you can get telephone assistance if you're having trouble filling out your return. Consult your state sales tax agency (website addresses are included in Appendix A and on this book's companion page on Nolo. com; the link is also in Appendix A) for detailed instructions on filing your sales tax return.

CAUTION

Sellers may be required to file sales tax returns. If you applied for and received a seller's permit because you anticipated selling goods, you may need to submit your sales tax return even if you never made a sale. If you didn't make any taxable sales, you shouldn't owe any taxes, but you may still need to submit the form. If you don't, you may risk losing your seller's permit, which could mean you couldn't legally make any sales at all. Check with your state agency (listed in Appendix A) for its requirements.

Chapter 9 Checklist: Paying Your Taxes

☐ Become familiar with the general scheme of taxes faced by small businesses.

☐ Remember that you may have to pay estimated taxes in quarterly installments. Other taxes may also have to be paid more often than once a year, such as your state sales taxes. Make a calendar of important tax dates so you don't miss them and incur penalties.

☐ Keep careful track of your expenses so that you may deduct them.

☐ Consult a tax professional at least once a year to help you organize your books and keep your taxes to a minimum.

☐ File and pay your annual taxes each year, and other taxes as they become due.

Laws, Taxes, and Other Issues for Home Businesses

t's not an exaggeration to say that the explosion of home-based businesses has radically reshaped the small business landscape. By most accounts, the number of home-based businesses in the United States exceeds 15 million (more than half of all small businesses) and is growing strong. Along with the boom in home businesses, whole new industries have emerged, such as major office supply chains; home office networking equipment dealers; home business consultants; and a host of magazines, websites, mobile apps, and other media dedicated to home business issues. No question about it, home businesses—and the industries that have grown around them—are here to stay.

The home business sector has achieved a new level of respect in recent years. Entrepreneurs of all stripes and funding levels have discovered that setting up shop in a home can be a cost-efficient, flexible way to get a business venture off the ground. And an increasing number of home-based businesses are staying put at their founders' homes rather than moving into company digs. "Home business" no longer means Tupperware parties or shady multilevel marketing schemes. Even the most professional, reputable, and aggressively growth-minded companies are joining the ranks of home-based businesses.

It's no secret why the idea of starting a business from home is so attractive to so many. The convenience of working at home is a major draw, especially to parents who want to cut commute times and increase time with the family. Not having to pay rent for an external office helps the bottom line of any business—especially important in the start-up days. And thanks to fast, affordable Internet connections and wireless networks, it's never been easier to exchange documents, do research, send emails, teleconference, and otherwise be connected to the world from home.

In addition to communications and networking, a number of other technologies have advanced by leaps and bounds to help home businesses get firmly established. Prosumer—a hybrid of professional and consumer—imaging products, such as digital cameras, scanners and printers, and easy-to-use Web development software, allow home businesses to create professional-looking brochures, websites, and other marketing materials. With all this new technology, a home business can develop a much more professional image than was possible a decade ago.

Before you hang out your shingle, however, it's important to realize that a home business isn't immune to a number of the requirements that affect businesses in general. Similar to a business operated from a commercial office space, a business run from home must comply with zoning requirements in its area. And there are several special tax rules for home businesses, as well as insurance issues, that you should understand. All of this is discussed in this chapter.

Is a Home-Based Business Right for You?

Not all businesses lend themselves to being run out of a residence. Make sure you've considered whether using your home as your office is a good idea. Ask yourself the following questions:

- How will you deal with customers and suppliers? Will they be able to easily park and pick up or unload material if necessary?
- Will customers take you and your company seriously if you work out of your house?
- Will your business require a lot of space for performing services or storing supplies?
- Can you work productively in your home, considering potential distractions, such as kids, the couch, the refrigerator, and the TV?
- If you rent, will your landlord give your business the okay?

Businesses that require nothing but a small office and don't generate much traffic coming and going—such as graphic design, accounting, and Web development—and those in which most of the dirty work is routinely done offsite—such as construction and plumbing—are particularly well suited for home businesses.

Home Business Zoning Restrictions

As with leased office spaces, you need to make sure that the business activities you plan to carry on in your home are within the letter of your local zoning laws. You may also have to apply for a special "home occupation permit" before you begin. (Zoning laws typically refer to home businesses as "home occupations.")

If your home is in an area that's zoned for residential use only (some loft-type or urban apartments might be zoned for mixed use), the types of businesses allowed in your neighborhood will probably be pretty limited. A few areas actually forbid home businesses altogether. But most cities and counties allow home businesses that have little likelihood of causing noise or pollution, creating traffic, or otherwise disturbing the neighbors. Writers, artists, attorneys, accountants, architects, insurance brokers, and piano teachers are examples of businesspeople commonly allowed to work from home. Typically not allowed are retailers, automotive repair shops, cafés and bars, animal hospitals and breeders, or any type of adult-oriented businesses.

CAUTION

Watch out for private land use restrictions. If you live in a condo, co-op, planned subdivision, or rental property, you are likely subject to private land use restrictions in addition to your local laws. Condo regulations, for instance, often contain language restricting or sometimes even prohibiting business use of the premises. Or your apartment lease might prohibit business on the property. Check the documents governing your property to see if you are bound by any such rules.

Check With the Planning Department

To find out how your city or county deals with home businesses, call the planning department or visit its website if it has one. Ask or look for any information available on home businesses. Some areas have websites or pamphlets with information explaining home business restrictions and how to obtain any necessary permits. In other places, all that's available might be a grainy photocopy of the municipal code, which you'll have to decipher yourself. If there's no approval or permit process for home businesses in your area, it's generally up to you to comply with the local zoning codes. And those codes are subject to change; be sure to check with the local zoning offices for updates.

The most foolproof way to avoid trouble with zoning officials is to do your best to keep down your business's impact on the neighborhood. As long as you're not in flagrant violation of the zoning laws regarding home businesses and your neighbors are happy, you'll probably be fine.

TIP

Let your neighbors in on your business plans. Getting to know your neighbors can be a huge help in avoiding problems with zoning officials. For instance, if your business requires people to come and go from your house or packages to be delivered daily, your neighbors might jump to the nutty conclusion that you're a drug dealer and report you to the city. Even though you can show your drug of choice is vitamin C, the city might unearth technical zoning violations that never would have otherwise turned up. As preventive measures, communicating with your neighbors and dealing with their concerns about issues such as parking and noise will greatly reduce the likelihood that the zoning police will come knocking on your door.

Understand Common Restrictions

Assuming that your local zoning laws do allow your type of home business, they are likely to impose some restrictions, such as allowing only residents of your home to be employees, restricting the number of customers that may come to your house, limiting the percentage of your home's floor space that can be used for business, or prohibiting signs outside of your house that advertise the business. In Milwaukee, Wisconsin, for example, home businesses cannot employ anyone other than residents of the home, and the business may not use more than 25% of the usable floor area of the home, including the basement. In Austin, Texas, it is illegal for any equipment or materials associated with the home business to be visible from the street. And in Sacramento, California, home businesses may keep only one vehicle on premises, not larger than one ton.

In addition to these general limitations, cities often impose restrictions on specific types of home businesses. For instance, a city might forbid any type of home business from having a neon sign or it might have a special rule for landscapers that prohibits landscaping supplies from being kept at the home office. Be sure to find out from zoning officials or the local city hall whether there are special rules for your type of business.

Comply With Local Requirements

If you find out that your city does allow your type of home business in your area, you may have no further need to contact the zoning office. Many cities do not require any special permits, as long as a home business complies with all of the rules and restrictions contained in its planning code (as discussed above). Some cities, however, require all home business owners to get a "home occupation permit." Obtaining such a permit is usually a simple matter of filling out a form provided by the planning department and paying whatever fee may be required. If your business meets the restrictions your city imposes, your permit will be issued.

If you don't meet all of your city's rules for having a home occupation, or your area isn't zoned for your type of home business, you may be out of luck and simply not allowed to run your business from home. In some locales, however, a home business that meets most but not all of the city's restrictions may be allowed to operate, but only after obtaining a home occupation permit. In San Diego, for instance, no permit is required for home businesses that meet all of the city's criteria: no business signs, no nonresident employees on the premises, and so on. If the home business deviates from the criteria, the city may allow the business to proceed, but only with a permit. Acceptable deviations in San Diego include having one nonresident employee, having one client who visits your home office by appointment, and using more than one vehicle for business.

Keep in mind that the zoning agency is probably not the only land use regulatory agency in your area. Even though your activity might be okay with zoning officials, operating out of your home may not pass other departments' requirements. For example, if you're starting a catering business, chances are your county health department won't let you work out of your home kitchen. You may be allowed to convert your garage or another separate structure into a professional kitchen— but, of course, that is likely to necessitate securing building permits and passing county health inspections, in addition to zoning compliance or permission. (See Chapter 7 for more on permits for your specific business.)

The Home Business Tax Deduction

If your office is located in your home, you may be able to claim a portion of your home expenses—such as rent or depreciation, property taxes, utilities, and insurance—as a special deduction when reporting federal taxes. The IRS's general rule is that if your business qualifies (discussed below), you can deduct a pro rata share of home business expenses. "Pro rata" simply means a share that's proportional to the percentage of home

space that you use for your business. Alternatively, since tax year 2013, you can calculate your deduction using a simpler formula: the square footage of your home office multiplied by a rate specified by the IRS. We'll explain both of these methods of calculating your deduction below.

This section explains which businesses may qualify for the home business tax deduction, how the deduction is calculated, and other tax issues that apply. (For information on how businesses in general are taxed, see Chapter 9.)

 TIP

Many expenses are automatically fully deductible. Many taxpayers mistakenly believe that they need to qualify for the home business deduction before they can claim any expenses associated with a home-based business. But, in fact, you can deduct business expenses necessary for your business whether they're incurred in your home or anywhere else, even if you don't qualify for the home business deduction. For instance, you can always deduct the portion of your home long-distance phone bill that you spend on business-related calls. Other deductible business expenses might include office supplies, furniture, and equipment that you use in your home office, and the cost of bringing a second telephone line into your home for business use. As used in this chapter, "home business expenses" will refer to expenses that can only be claimed with the home business deduction.

IRS Requirements

Before tackling the nitty-gritty requirements, let's look at a couple of basics. First, the IRS definition of "home" is pretty broad, generally including any type of dwelling in which you can cook and sleep. This includes houses, condos, apartment units, mobile homes, boats, and wherever else you reside. Both renters and owners are eligible for taking the home tax deduction.

Moving on to the meat of the criteria, the IRS has two requirements for any business owner who wants to deduct expenses for using part of a home as a business:

- You must regularly use part of your home exclusively for a trade or business.
- You must be able to show that you:
  - use your home as your principal place of business, or
  - meet patients, clients, or customers at home, or
  - use a separate structure on your property exclusively for business purposes.

Each of these criteria is examined a bit more closely below.

Exclusive and Regular Use for Business

The IRS will allow you to deduct home business expenses only for space in your home that is 100% dedicated to business use. For example, a graphic designer who sometimes sits at the kitchen table to do illustrations can't claim business deductions for using the kitchen—assuming the kitchen is also sometimes used for nonbusiness purposes, such as cooking and eating. A spare room, however, that's set up as an office space and used only for business would probably meet the exclusive use test. But if the room contains a bed for the occasional overnight guest or doubles as storage space for clothing, then, technically, it wouldn't qualify.

The regular use test is generally pretty easy to pass. As long as you use your home business space for business on a frequent, continuing basis, rather than for a once-in-a-while garage sale or other sporadic business activity, you'll probably make the cut.

EXAMPLE 1: Stacey runs a hat-making business. She makes the hats in an extra room of her house in which she has a sewing machine and all her supplies, as well as a computer and a file cabinet containing her sales and other financial information. Because the only use of that room is for the hat-making business, it will meet the IRS's criteria of exclusive use. And since Stacey has made and sold hats for a couple of years, with consistent monthly sales, she'll have no trouble proving that she uses the space regularly for business.

EXAMPLE 2: Parisha has a full-time job at a plant nursery, but also does occasional freelance photography work. She has a darkroom in her basement that she uses to develop photos for her assignments. Her darkroom is dedicated to her photography business, but she spends most of her time working at the plant nursery and has only done one photo shoot in the last six months. Parisha would be ill-advised to claim her darkroom expenses as a home business deduction, because she doesn't regularly use it for business.

Exceptions to the Home Storage Exception

In its inimitable fashion, the IRS has created two exceptions to the home storage exception. First, you won't qualify for the deduction if you have an office or other business location outside your home. Second, you must store the products in a specific, identifiable space such as your garage, a closet, or extra room—not just stacked against the wall of your garage or in the corner of your basement. It's okay to use the storage space for other purposes as well, as long as you regularly use it for storing inventory or samples.

EXAMPLE: Mariana teaches ballet lessons to children at a studio in her home. She also sells instructional dance videos and regularly stores the inventory of DVDs in a large closet in her basement. Because Mariana has no other business location away from her home, she can claim a home business deduction for the basement closet. This is true even though she also stores other things in that closet such as skis and boxes of books. However, if Mariana ever opens a studio outside her home, she will not be able to deduct the expenses of the storage space.

There are two exceptions to the exclusive use rule: If your business use is either storing inventory or product samples, or running a qualified day care center, you don't have to meet the exclusive use test. In these two cases, the parts of the home you use for business—say, a closet for inventory storage or a living room for the day care center—may also be used for personal activities, and you will still qualify for the home business tax deduction. (See IRS Publication 587, *Business Use of Your Home*, for details. It's available online at www.irs.gov.)

Principal Place of Business

In addition to fulfilling the exclusive and regular use requirements, your home business space must also be the main place where you do business—with two exceptions, as explained below in "Meeting Clients or Customers" and "Home Business in a Separate Structure." Thankfully, the principal-place-of-business rule is fairly easy to satisfy. Your home office will qualify as the principal place of business if you:

- use the office to conduct administrative or management activities, and
- do not have an office or other business location outside your home set up to conduct these activities.

This rule is just as straightforward as it sounds. As long as you use your home office to keep track of your business files, do your bookkeeping and accounting, maintain your client databases, or conduct whatever other type of administration is required, and you don't have a space away from home set up for these activities, your home office will be considered your principal place of business.

Meeting Clients or Customers

If your home office doesn't qualify as your principal place of business under the test described above, you can still qualify for the home business deduction if you regularly and exclusively use your space to meet with clients or customers. As long as you regularly use the home space to meet clients—say, once or twice a week—and don't use the space for nonbusiness purposes, you can claim the deduction for the space even if you have an office away from home.

Home Business in a Separate Structure

Finally, another way to qualify for the home business deduction is to use an external structure on your property—a detached garage, shed, or in-law unit, for example— regularly and exclusively for your business. Again, this rule applies even if you have another business space, such as a storefront or an office, and regardless of whether you meet clients or customers there. If the space is used regularly and exclusively for business and is not physically connected to your house, you can deduct expenses for it.

CAUTION

Tax concerns for separate structures. If you use a separate structure on your property for your home business, beware of possible tax repercussions when you sell your home. When a separate structure is used, the business portion of the home will be subject to capital gains tax when sold. (Be sure to read "Tax Issues When You Sell Your Home," below.)

Tips on Establishing Home Business Use

Home business owners should make an effort to clearly establish their home offices as places of business. Here are some ways you can accomplish this:

- Take pictures of your home office that show its business character.
- Draw a diagram showing the floor plan of the house with the home office clearly defined. Include room dimensions, if possible.
- Keep a log of the times you work in the office.
- Keep a record of all client meetings at your office, including whom you met, when, and the subject of the meeting. Recording client visits to your home office is especially important if you also have an outside office.
- Have your business mail sent to your home.
- Get a separate phone line for the business.

Figuring Deductible Home Business Expenses

Once you've determined that you do in fact qualify for the home business tax deduction, you'll need to figure out exactly how much you can deduct. Obviously, you can't deduct all of your housing costs—only the expenses attributable to business purposes, as defined by the IRS, qualify.

The old standard method is to determine a "business percentage" for your home—simply, the percentage of your home that is used for business. Then you'll look at your home expenses and figure out to what extent they may be deducted.

Now, however, you can use a new, simplified method to calculate your home office deduction: Multiply the square footage of your home office by a prescribed rate set by the IRS. We'll describe this below, after going through the old method, which is still acceptable.

Calculating Business Percentage

You can calculate the percentage of your home used for business in one of two ways: the "square footage" method or the "number of rooms" method. Either approach is acceptable to the IRS.

The square footage method simply divides the square footage of the business space by the square footage of the whole house. For instance, if you use 250 square feet for business, and your entire house takes up 1,000 square feet, then your business space uses 25% (250 ÷ 1,000) of your home.

The number-of-rooms method is just as simple: If your house has five similarly sized rooms, and you use one of them for business, then the business uses 20% (1 ÷ 5) of your home.

Categorizing and Deducting Expenses

Once you have calculated a space percentage for your business, use it to calculate the portion of your home expenses that is deductible to the business. Home expenses fall into one of three categories, with different deductibility rules for each.

Unrelated expenses. Expenses that are unrelated to your business space are not deductible at all. For example, you can't deduct the cost of repainting your bedroom or replacing your dining room window.

Direct expenses. You can fully deduct expenses that directly affect your business space, such as the cost of installing new carpeting, replacing a broken window, or repairing the heating vent in your office space. Note that direct expenses for a day care center may not be fully deductible. (For more information, see IRS Publication 587, *Business Use of Your Home*, available online at www.irs.gov.)

Indirect expenses. Expenses that affect the whole house—called indirect expenses—

are deductible, but only partially so, based on the percentage of your home that is used for business. For instance, you can deduct a percentage of the cost of plumbing services, roof repairs, mortgage interest, real estate taxes, and utility bills.

To calculate the portion of indirect expenses attributable to your business, you generally multiply the indirect expense by your business percentage. Rent, for example, is an easy expense to prorate. If your business uses 25% of your home, and your rent is $2,000 per month, then $500 per month is a deductible home business expense (25% x $2,000). The same simple approach generally works for calculating the deductible business portion of many other indirect expenses, such as homeowners' insurance, mortgage interest, home utilities, and repairs.

> **CAUTION**
>
> **Repairs are generally deductible; permanent improvements are not.** The IRS won't let you deduct the cost of major projects it considers "permanent improvements"—those that increase the value of property, add to its life, or give it a new or different use. The cost of repairs, on the other hand, may be deducted—either fully if a direct expense or partially if an indirect expense. The IRS defines "repairs" as those that "keep your home in good working order over its useful life." (For more details on the IRS's distinction between repairs and permanent improvements, see IRS Publication 587, *Business Use of Your Home*, available online at www.irs.gov.)

Calculating Your Deduction with the Simplified Method

The simplified method for calculating your deduction does not change any rules regarding whether you're eligible for a home office deduction. It just offers a much simpler way to calculate your deduction.

Under the new rule, simply multiply the square footage of your home office by the IRS's prescribed rate: $5 per square foot, with a maximum footage allowed of 300 square feet. It's that simple.

Note that if you use the simplified method and you own your home, you cannot claim a depreciation deduction as described below. You still may claim deductions for mortgage interest and real estate taxes however, and you won't need to allocate these between your business and personal use.

For more information on the new simplified method, visit www.irs.gov (search "Simplified Option for Home Office Deduction").

>
> **RESOURCE**
>
> **For more on the home office deduction.** For more detailed information on tax deductions for home businesses, read *Home Business Tax Deductions: Keep What You Earn*, by Stephen Fishman (Nolo).

Calculating a Depreciation Deduction

If you own your home and you qualify for the home business tax deduction, an indirect expense that you may deduct is the depreciation of your home. Depreciation of your home is an allowance for the wear and tear inflicted upon it. And the home business depreciation deduction is simply a deduction for the business portion of this. Calculating this deduction is slightly more involved than the indirect expense deductions mentioned above. This section offers an overview of how to calculate the depreciation deduction; detailed instructions are included in IRS Publication 587, *Business Use of Your Home,* available online at www.irs.gov.

Keep in mind that depreciation is calculated for the building only—not the land. Property tax assessments usually show the breakdown of home value versus land value.

In a nutshell, calculating the depreciation deduction works like this:

1. To start, figure out the adjusted basis of your home (don't include land value) at the time you started using it for business. The adjusted basis of your home is generally its cost, plus the cost of any permanent improvements, minus any casualty losses (sudden losses from accidents such as a fire or damages from a falling tree) or depreciation deducted in earlier tax years. (The IRS explains adjusted basis in its Publication 551, *Basis of Assets,* available online at www.irs.gov.)

2. Next, figure out the fair market value of the home (again, not the land) at the time you started using the home office. The IRS defines fair market value as follows: "The price at which the property would change hands between a buyer and a seller, neither having to buy or sell, and both having reasonable knowledge of all necessary facts." Information such as appraisals or the selling price of similar homes in your area when you started using yours for business will help you determine its fair market value.

3. Next, calculate the portion of the cost of your home that can be depreciated. This amount is called the "depreciable basis." Calculate the depreciable basis by multiplying the percentage of your home used for business by the smaller of:
   - the adjusted basis of your home (excluding land) on the date you began using it for business, or
   - the fair market value of your home (excluding land) when you began using it for business. The result of this calculation—the depreciable basis—is the portion of the home's value attributable to the business.

4. Last, calculate the actual deduction that your home business will be able to claim. To oversimplify, this deduction is calculated by multiplying your depreciable basis by a certain percentage, set by the IRS. The percentage and specific depreciation method to use will depend on when you started your home business.

There are many more details involved than this book can cover, so you would be wise to consult the IRS publications mentioned before tackling the depreciation deduction on your own. Or consider handing the job over to an experienced business accountant. (See Chapter 17 for more on working with accountants and other professionals.)

Tax Issues When You Sell Your Home

Homeowners with home businesses face a couple of tax issues if they end up selling their homes: capital gains taxes and depreciation recapture. These concepts are widely misunderstood, with the result that many home business owners don't claim their rightful share of deductions for fear of the tax implications. Don't make this mistake. Not only are the rules relatively easy to understand, they're quite favorable to home business owners.

No Tax on Proportional Gain

Since 2002, when you sell your home at a gain, you do not need to allocate a portion of that gain to your home business. You can go ahead and claim all the home business tax deductions you're entitled to, without worrying that you'll be stuck with capital gains taxes for your home business portion. You'll only have to pay capital gains taxes if you exceeded the limits of $250,000 gain ($500,000 for married couples), which would apply whether or not you had a home business.

There's an important exception to the rule that you don't need to allocate gains from a home sale to your home business: Home businesses located in a separate structure will continue to be subject to capital gains taxes. So if you run your business from a separate, freestanding garage or shed, for example, you'll be stuck paying the gains taxes when you sell your home. To avoid this, stop claiming the home business tax deduction two years before you sell your home.

Recaptured Depreciation Tax

If you sell your home at a gain, while you do not need to allocate a portion of that gain to your home business, you are subject to what's known as "depreciation recapture," however. As in the past, home business owners who sell their homes must still pay taxes on the depreciation deductions they've taken over the years. In other words, if you claim depreciation deductions for a home business, the total of those deductions will be taxed—"recaptured," if you will—when you sell your house.

EXAMPLE: Patrice, a yoga instructor, sells her house at a gain of $200,000. Her home studio takes up 10% of her home. Under current IRS rules, she will not be subject to capital gains taxes for the 10% of her home used for business activities. However, Patrice must pay depreciation recapture tax on the total depreciation deductions she's taken in the five years of operating her home teaching studio.

This rule isn't really so bad when you consider the depreciation recapture rate is only 25%. Most business owners pay much more than this on income—self-employment tax at a rate of 15.3%, plus their federal personal tax rate of 15%, 28%, or higher, plus state tax rates—so that depreciation deductions can easily offer savings of 40% or more each year. The bottom line is that it's worth it to take the depreciation deductions, since you'll almost certainly save more in cumulative savings over the years than you'll end up paying when you sell your home.

Risks and Insurance

Just because you run a business from your home, don't make the mistake of taking risk management and insurance issues lightly. Home businesses are often just as vulnerable to theft, fire, personal liability claims, and other risks as businesses based in storefronts or office buildings— sometimes even more vulnerable. It can be a real catastrophe if your computer system is stolen or destroyed, or if a client trips and falls over your garden hose on the way up your front walk.

If you assume that your homeowners' policy will protect you against these risks, you may well find out the hard way that you're horribly wrong. Potentially even more important, home business owners need to make sure that none of their business pursuits jeopardize their regular homeowners' policy for nonbusiness-related claims.

This section discusses the insurance and risk management issues particular to home businesses. (Chapter 8 offers a full discussion of these topics as they apply to all businesses. Be sure to read that chapter in addition to the material below.)

RELATED TOPIC

Start by evaluating your risks.
All risk management and insurance decisions must begin with a realistic assessment of what risks your business faces. Only after you do this assessment will you be able to decide how to reduce your risks with insurance or other strategies. While some basic insurance protection for your business assets is never a bad idea, some home business owners may sensibly conclude that insurance is not necessary. (See Chapter 8.) Much of the discussion in this chapter presumes that you've decided some insurance is necessary.

Limitations of Homeowners' Policies

A common mistake among owners of home-based businesses is to assume that business losses will be covered by their homeowners' or renters' policies. This is a very dangerous assumption. While many insurance companies will extend homeowners' coverage to a home business, they'll often require an endorsement—sometimes called a "floater" or "rider"—to a policy that specifically authorizes the coverage. You'll generally have to pay an extra premium for such an endorsement. Without one, the insurance company may deny claims related to a home business.

TIP

Honesty is the best insurance policy.
You might wonder how an insurance company would find out that you are quietly operating a home business. Apart from the fact that trying to deceive your insurance company is just a foolish idea, the insurance company's suspicion can easily be aroused by claims involving major business assets such as high-end computer systems, machine equipment, or inventories that seem unsuited for home use. All it could take is a few questions or a visit from an insurance adjuster to blow your cover. When it comes to communicating with your insurer, the best advice is not to mess with the truth.

In addition to requiring home businesses to jump through extra hoops, some insurance companies exact harsh consequences if you run a business from home without informing them first. In some cases, an insurance company may terminate your coverage altogether—even for nonbusiness claims—if it discovers that you've been running a business from your home without its authorization. This is a sobering possibility.

And even when homeowners' policies do cover home businesses—either with or without an endorsement—the coverage may be only for property loss, not for other claims such as liability or business interruption. If a client is injured on your slippery floor, your business may have to pay for any damages awarded in a personal injury lawsuit, without any coverage from the homeowners' policy. And if your business records are destroyed in a fire, it's highly unlikely that your homeowners' policy would cover your inability to collect accounts receivable or your lost income from business downtime.

The bottom line is that no home business owner should make the mistake of finding out what is or isn't covered the hard way. If you have homeowners' or renters' insurance, contact the providing company and find out specifically how it deals with home businesses and what kinds of claims are covered. If you're like many home business owners, you'll likely find that your coverage isn't quite what you hoped it might be. Your next step will be to fill in those gaps, either by getting an endorsement to your existing homeowners' policy or purchasing separate coverage.

Finding and Purchasing Insurance Coverage

An increasing number of insurance companies are willing to insure home businesses, no doubt due to the massive growth of this market. And despite what you might fear, costs are generally not prohibitive. An endorsement for a home business is typically no more than $1,000 a year—and sometimes much less. Another option is a "home-business-type" policy that's becoming more common. These are distinct from homeowners' policies but aren't quite as robust as full commercial policies, and as a result are generally a good value. Larger businesses with significant assets or risks may need to look at full commercial policies, which may be somewhat more expensive.

If you have a homeowners' or renters' policy, start your search by contacting your current insurance provider. If an endorsement is required, the process is generally a simple matter of paying an extra premium and having documents drafted reflecting the home business coverage. Of course, you'll need to check that the coverage limits are sufficient to cover the value of your business equipment. Also find out whether liability or loss-of-income claims are covered. If not, and if these risks are a concern, you may need to purchase additional coverage.

If your current insurer doesn't offer the coverage you need, one possibility is to find a policy with a different company that meets your requirements. Another option, whether or not you have existing home coverage, is to look for a separate business policy. Business policies can get complicated and expensive, so it's a good idea to use a broker who can present you with options from a range of companies. (See Chapter 8 for general tips for buying insurance.)

Home business owners sometimes can get good deals through trade associations or other organizations that offer coverage options for their members. Organizations tend to get favorable group rates from insurance companies, so these resources are definitely worth a look.

Chapter 10 Checklist: Laws, Taxes, and Other Issues for Home Businesses

☐ Evaluate whether your business activities can be run well from your home.

☐ Find out whether any city or county restrictions apply to running a business at home—these are commonly called home occupation regulations—and obtain any necessary permits.

☐ To satisfy IRS requirements for the home business tax deduction, use your home business space exclusively for business and not for any personal uses. Review other IRS rules such as the "principal place of business" rule to make sure your home business qualifies for the tax deduction.

☐ Take photos of your home business space to establish its business use.

☐ Do not rely on homeowners' insurance to protect you against losses related to your home business. Even more important, make sure your homeowners' policy is not voided entirely—even for personal claims—by running a business from home.

Entering Into Contracts and Agreements

As a business owner, you'll often have to enter into contracts (legal agreements) with other businesses and people: suppliers, customers, creditors, and landlords, for example. While a few of these transactions will be simple enough to complete with a handshake, most will be sufficiently complicated, long-term, or financially important to require a written contract.

Thankfully—and contrary to what many people believe—a contract is often a fairly simple legal document. It sets out mutual promises to do specific acts: "A promises to pay B $1,000 if B delivers 50,000 twist-ties to A's warehouse on or before March 1, 20xx." A written contract will usually include the main terms of the agreement: the price of goods, important dates, and the time and place of delivery. For most contractual agreements, standard forms are readily available. Except in the relatively few instances in which lots of money or new legal issues are involved, you probably won't need a lawyer to complete your contract.

Simple as some types of contracts may be, you must remember that they are legally enforceable. If you fail to keep your end of the bargain, you can be sued and forced to pay damages to the other party or, in some circumstances, to do the things you promised in the contract.

This chapter explains some contract basics, including what makes a contract enforceable and which contracts are legally required to be in writing.

Contract Basics

Although lots of contracts are filled with mind-bending legal gibberish, there's no reason why this has to be true. For most contracts, legalese is not essential or even helpful. On the contrary, the agreements you'll want to put into a written contract are best expressed in simple, everyday English.

 TIP

Don't be afraid to redraft contract language. When reading a contract that has been presented to you, your first task is to make sure you understand all of its terms. It is just plain foolish to sign a contract if you're unclear on the meaning of any of its language. If a clause is poorly written, hard to understand, or doesn't accomplish your key goals, rewrite it to be clear. By refusing to sign at the "X" unless your goals are clearly met, you'll be less likely to find yourself in a breach-of-contract lawsuit later on. A breach of contract occurs when one party fails to live up to the terms or promises in the contract. (For more on changing contract language, see "Reading and Revising a Contract," below.)

Elements of a Valid Contract

A contract will be valid if all of the following are true:

- All parties are in agreement (after an offer has been made by one party and accepted by the other).
- Something of value has been exchanged, such as cash, services, or goods, for something else of value (or there is a promise to exchange an item for something else of value).
- In a few situations, such as the sale of real estate, the agreement must be in writing. (See "Oral Versus Written Contracts," below.) Of course, because oral contracts can be difficult or impossible to prove, it is wise to write out most agreements.

Each of these elements is described below in more detail.

Agreement Between Parties

Although it may seem like stating the obvious, an essential element of a valid contract is that all parties really do agree on all major issues. In real life, there are plenty of situations that blur the line between a full agreement and a preliminary discussion about the possibility of making an agreement. To help clarify these borderline cases, legal rules have developed to define when an agreement exists.

Advertisements as Offers

Generally speaking, an advertisement to the public does not count as an offer in the legal sense. In other words, if you advertised your catering services in your local weekly newspaper, and included a price quote of $300 for your standard menu serving 20 people, you would not be legally bound to live up to that service if someone called you and said, "I accept!" If, for instance, you were too busy with other catering jobs and unable to do the job for the eager caller, you could decline. Because your ad wasn't, legally speaking, an offer, the caller couldn't claim a legal acceptance of it to create a binding contract.

Despite this, however, you do need to watch what you say in your advertisements. Some states require retailers to stock enough of an advertised item to meet reasonably expected demand, or else your ad must state that stock is limited.

Of course, false or misleading advertising is always a bad idea. Federal laws regulating trade and state consumer protection laws prohibit deceptive advertising, even if no one was actually misled. And check your ad's facts; false advertising is illegal, even if you believed the ad to be truthful when you ran it.

The most basic rule of contract law is the "offer and acceptance" rule: A legal contract exists when one party makes an offer and the other party accepts it.

For most types of contracts, this can be done either orally or in writing. (For a few, discussed in "Oral Versus Written Contracts," below, the offer and acceptance must be made in writing.)

Let's say, for instance, you're shopping around for a print shop to produce brochures for your business. One printer confirms, either orally or in writing, that he'll print 5,000 two-color flyers for $200. This constitutes his offer. If you tell him to go ahead with the job, you've accepted his offer. In the eyes of the law, when you tell the printer to go ahead, you create a contract, which means you're liable for your side of the bargain—in this case, payment of $200. But if you tell the printer you're not sure and want to continue shopping around (or don't even respond, for that matter), you clearly haven't accepted his offer, and no agreement has been reached. Or, if you say his offer sounds great, except that you want three colors instead of two, no contract has been made, since you have not accepted all of the important terms of the offer—you've changed one. (Depending on your wording, you may have made a "counteroffer," which is discussed below.)

In real, day-to-day business, the seemingly simple steps of offer and acceptance can become quite convoluted. For instance, sometimes when you make an offer, it isn't quickly and unequivocally accepted; the other party may want to think about it for a while or try to get a better deal. And before your offer is accepted by anyone, you might change your mind and want to withdraw or amend it. Delaying acceptance of an offer, revoking an offer, and making a counteroffer are common situations in business transactions that often lead to confusion and conflict. To cut down on the potential for disputes, make sure you understand the following issues and rules:

- **How long an offer stays open.** Unless an offer includes a stated expiration date, it remains open for a "reasonable" period of time. What's "reasonable," of course, is open to interpretation and will depend on the type of business and the particular situation. Because the law in this area is so vague, if you want to accept someone else's offer, the best approach is to do it as soon as possible, while there's little doubt that the offer is still open. Keep in mind that until you accept, the person or company who made the offer—called the offeror—may revoke it.

  If you are the offeror, it's best to be very clear about how long your offer will remain open. The best way to do this is to include an expiration date in the offer. But to leave yourself room to revoke the offer, avoid wording such as, "This offer will remain open until December 31, 20xx." Instead, use language such as, "This offer will expire on December 31, 20xx."

> **TIP**
>
> **Include an expiration date clause.** In many types of businesses, from replacing roofs to redesigning websites, it is common to bid (in other words, to make an offer to create a contract) on lots more jobs than you really need or want. But sometimes this strategy can backfire. With lots of offers floating around, there is always the possibility that too many will be accepted, which could raise the embarrassing possibility that you might not be able to deliver on all the work. One easy way to eliminate this problem is to print right on your bid or offer form that all offers are good for only ten days (or some other relatively short period) unless extended in writing.

- **Revoking an offer.** Whoever makes an offer can revoke it as long as it hasn't yet been accepted. This means if you make an offer and the other party wants some time to think it through, you can revoke your original offer. If your offer is accepted while it is still open, however, you'll have a binding agreement. In other words, revocation must happen before acceptance.

- **Options.** Sometimes the offeror promises that an offer will remain open for a stated period of time—and that it cannot and will not be revoked during that time. This type of agreement is called an option, and options don't usually come for free. Say someone offers to sell you a forklift for $10,000, and you want to think the offer over without having to worry that the seller will revoke the offer or sell to someone else. You and the seller could agree that the offer will stay open for a certain period of time, say, 30 days. Often, however, the offeror will ask you to pay for this 30-day option—which is understandable because he or she can't sell to anyone else during the 30-day option period. But payment or no payment, when an option agreement exists, the offeror cannot revoke the offer until the time period ends.

- **Counteroffers.** Often when an offer is made, the other party will not accept the terms of the offer right off, but will start bargaining. Of course, haggling over price is the most common type of negotiating that occurs in business situations. When one party responds to an offer by proposing something different, this proposal is called a "counteroffer." When a counteroffer is made, the legal responsibility to accept or decline the offer or make another counteroffer shifts to the original offeror. For instance, if your printer (here, the original offeror) offers to print 5,000 brochures for you for $300, and you respond by saying you'll pay $250 for the job, you have not accepted his offer (no contract has been formed), but instead have made a counteroffer. It is then up to your printer to accept, decline, or make another counteroffer. If your printer agrees to do the job exactly as you have specified for $250, he's accepted your counteroffer and a legal contract has been formed.

Exchange of Things of Value

Even if both parties agree to the terms, a contract isn't valid unless the parties exchange something of value in anticipation of the completion of the contract. The "thing of value" being exchanged—called "consideration" in legal terms—is most often a promise to do something in the future, such as a promise to perform a certain job or a promise to pay a fee for that job. Returning to the example of the print job, once you and the printer agree on terms, there is an exchange of things of value (consideration): The printer has promised to print the 5,000 brochures, and you have promised to pay $250 for them.

This requirement helps differentiate a contract from generous statements and one-sided promises that are not enforceable by law. If your friend Leili offers you a favor, for instance, such as to help you move a pile of rocks without asking anything in return, that arrangement wouldn't count as a contract, because you didn't give or promise anything of value. If Leili never followed through with the favor, you would not be able to force her to keep that promise. If, however, in exchange for helping you move rocks on Saturday, you promise to help Leili weed a vegetable garden on Sunday, the two of you have a contract.

Although the exchange-of-value requirement is met in most business transactions by an exchange of promises ("I'll promise to pay money if you promise to paint my building next month"), actually doing the work or paying the money can also satisfy the rule. If, for instance, you leave your printer a voice mail message that you'll pay an extra $100 if your brochures are cut and stapled when you pick them up, the printer doesn't have to respond; he can create a binding contract by actually doing the cutting and stapling. And, once he does so, you can't weasel out of the deal by claiming you changed your mind.

Oral Versus Written Contracts

Before you learn more about which contracts have to be in writing to be legally enforceable, here's some advice: Put all of your contracts in writing. For compelling practical reasons, all contracts of more than a trivial nature should be written out and signed by both parties. Here is why:

- Writing down terms tends to make both parties review them more carefully, eliminating misunderstandings and incorrect assumptions right from the start.
- An oral agreement—no matter how honestly made—is hard to remember accurately.
- Oral agreements are subject to willful misinterpretation by a not-so-innocent party who wants to get out of the deal.
- Oral contracts are sometimes difficult, and often impossible, to prove, making them hard to enforce in court.

EXAMPLE: Kay opens a plant shop called The Green Scene. Because she needs specialized grow-lights for her extensive line of tropical plants, she checks with several contractors who install lighting systems. One company, Got a Light, says it will install a system for $3,000, including the cost of the lights themselves and installation charges. That quote is the lowest among the companies Kay has checked, so she tells Got a Light she'll accept the offer, but only with a written contract.

When Got a Light sends Kay a contract, she notices that it doesn't address rewiring her shop. She calls Got a Light and talks with Dan, who tells her that she needs to have an electrician add several new circuits and provide six specialized outlets before Got a Light can install the lighting system. Based on this discovery, Kay and Dan discuss exactly what needs to be done before Got a Light's work begins and include this new agreement in an additional contract clause. Dan recommends an electrician, whom Kay hires to do the rewiring. She also manages to negotiate a lower price with Got a Light, based on the fact that the rewiring will be done according to Got a Light's specifications, making the installation much easier.

The best advice is to get every contract in writing. Now here's what the law says: All states have laws that *require* certain contracts to be in writing. These laws often go by the name "statute of frauds" and are quite similar from state to state. They typically require the following types of contracts to be in writing:

- An agreement that by its terms can't be completed in a year or less. For example, a contract for a bakery to provide fresh bread to a restaurant for two years must be in writing. On the other hand, if the contract might take longer than a year to complete but could be completed within a year, it doesn't need to be in writing. For example, a contract for a gardener to landscape five big properties would not need to be written, because it is quite possible that the gardener would finish the work within one year. Similarly, a contract for a bakery to bake bread for a restaurant with no time period stated would not need to be in writing.

- A lease for a term (or time period) longer than one year, or an agreement authorizing an agent to execute such a lease on your behalf.

- Any sale of real estate (or of an interest in real estate), or an agreement authorizing an agent to purchase or sell it on your behalf.

- An agreement that by its terms will not be completed during the lifetime of one of the parties. This includes a promise to leave someone your business when you die.

- A promise to pay someone else's debt, such as a business partner's promise to pay your car payments or an agreement that the person who prints your brochure will also pay the cost of photographic work done at another shop.

In addition to the statute of frauds laws, each state has a special body of law on commercial issues called the Uniform Commercial Code (UCC). (Although Louisiana has not fully adopted the UCC, it has implemented some of its more important provisions.) Under the UCC,

a sale of goods for $500 or more requires at least a brief written note or memo indicating the agreement between the buyer and the seller. The note can be much less detailed than a normal contract; it needs only to show an agreement between the parties and the quantity of goods being sold. Other terms that are typically covered in contracts, such as the price of goods or the time and place of delivery, aren't required. This written memo usually has to be signed, although if one party doesn't object to the memo within ten days of receiving it, then that party's signature isn't required.

Now that you have an idea of which contracts must by law be in writing, it bears mentioning again that, in practice, written contracts are almost always preferable over oral ones—whether legally required or not.

Using Standard Contracts

By now you should understand that your contracts should be written, but you may still have no idea about how to write the ones you'll need. Luckily for you and most other businesspeople, virtually every type of business transaction is covered by a readily available standard contract. Service contracts, rental agreements, independent contractor agreements, contracts for sales of goods, and licensing agreements are just a few examples of blank-form contracts you should easily be able to find.

Special State Requirements for Contracts

Various state laws impose additional requirements for contracts involving particular businesses or certain kinds of transactions. In California, for instance, contracts for weight-loss services and dating services must be in writing. Plus, the law requires some contracts to include special language. For example, California dating service contracts must include the following language in at least 10-point boldface type:

"You, the buyer, may cancel this agreement, without any penalty or obligation, at any time prior to midnight of the original contract seller's third business day following the date of this contract, excluding Sundays and holidays. To cancel this agreement, mail or deliver a signed and dated notice, or send a telegram which states that you, the buyer, are canceling this agreement, or words of similar effect." (Cal. Civ. Code § 1694.2.)

Unfortunately, there's no centralized place where a business owner can learn if any special contract laws apply to a particular type of business. Talking with people in your line of business is one option. Another is to do research in a library or online.

If doing legal research to find any required contract language is too time-consuming or overwhelming for you, a good alternative is to use the limited help of a lawyer who's generally familiar with small business issues and, if possible, already works with businesses in your field (other plant nurseries, website designers, or restaurants, for example). Many small business lawyers are now more flexible in offering just as much or as little help as clients need, and they may offer coaching services to those who want to handle their simple legal affairs themselves. Using a legal coach is especially useful for small business owners, who often need answers to simple legal questions rather than full-blown attorney services. Chapter 17 discusses working with lawyers and finding one who's willing to coach you through simple legal matters.

Anyone who has ever picked up a fill-in-the-blanks lease or promissory note from an office supply store, torn a form out of a self-help law book, or downloaded one from a website is familiar with how this works. Blank rental agreements, for example, are widely available at office supply stores, through landlords' associations, at most public libraries, and from many other sources. Once you find the blank-form contract you need, you simply fill it in and, if necessary, modify it before signing.

If you can't easily find a blank-form contract that meets your needs, try the sources described here:

- Trade associations are excellent resources for fill-in-the-blanks contracts.
- Your competitors might be less than willing to share their contracts with you, but similar businesses in faraway locations (which you won't be competing with) might be willing to show you theirs.
- The Web has oceans of information for small businesses, including sample contracts. Try searching for terms particular to your type of business to find specific contracts you need.
- Nolo books offer many different blank-form agreements and Nolo. com includes many single-copy forms such as promissory notes. For general business contracts, two great resources are *Legal Forms for Starting & Running a Small Business,* by Fred S. Steingold and *Quicken Legal Business Pro.*

Once you've found a contract that generally fits your needs, you can amend it for your particular situation. It's entirely appropriate and often necessary to change clauses of a fill-in-the-blanks contract to suit your needs. Of course, it's crucial that you understand what you're doing. Don't just strike a clause because you don't understand what it means or add a clause without fully knowing the consequences of including it. To help you educate yourself about typical contract language, the next section explains which clauses commonly appear in contracts and what they mean.

How to Draft a Contract

If you can't find a form agreement, or if you find one that needs a load of revisions, you may need to write a clause or two—or possibly even the whole contract—from scratch. Don't be intimidated. Either way, your goal is simple: to state clearly what each party is agreeing to do and the specifics of how they'll do it (usually called the terms of the contract). Put another way, your written contract should be the most accurate reflection possible of the understanding you have with the other party.

This section explains the important things to include in most contracts and alerts you to the situations that might require more specialized provisions. The information provided here will help you in editing or drafting amendments to a standard contract, or in drafting a contract from scratch, if necessary. You'll also find examples of how to state certain terms—although, as mentioned above, clear English is really all that's usually necessary.

TIP

Don't get *too* specific. Although a good contract covers all the important aspects of a deal, you don't need to specify every tiny detail. For instance, if you hire a cleaning service, you probably don't need to specify what type of brushes it will use to scrub your floors. Better to put your energy into picking the right person or company to do the job and to leave some of the specifics of the actual work up to those who will do it. In deciding how much detail is enough, you'll simply have to judge for yourself which nitpicky details are so important that they should be covered in your contract, and which ones you can safely ignore. For example, if you need fresh salmon for a party at 6 p.m., the time of delivery and quality of the fish are extremely important points, but the exact weight of each fish or the method of delivery may be a lot less so. In short, don't micromanage in your contracts.

What to Include in a Basic Contract

So you've reached an agreement with another party and are ready to put it into writing. Before you start editing a form contract or writing one on your own, step back a moment to consider that the goals of all contracts are to:

- clearly outline what each party is agreeing to do (including timelines and payment arrangements)
- anticipate areas of confusion or points of potential conflict, and
- provide for recourse (a remedy) in case the agreement is not followed through to completion.

Good Ideas to Keep Your Contracts Crystal Clear

- Avoid the use of "he," "she," "they," or other pronouns in your contracts as they can easily lead to confusion over what parties you're talking about. Use either the actual names of the parties or their roles, such as "Landlord" and "Tenant." It might seem repetitive or clumsy to write this way, but your goal is to be clear—not to write beautiful prose.

- Stay away from legalistic words such as wherefore, herewith, or hereinafter. Far from making your contract sound more impressive, this type of language is simply unnecessary and outdated. Stick to modern, clear English. And don't include legal expressions you think you may have heard elsewhere. Legal-sounding jargon will not make your contract more binding—and if you get it wrong, you may be bound to terms you didn't want, or your contract may be void.

- Make at least a couple drafts of your contract. After the first draft, let it rest a day or so, and then reread it. Does it leave any questions in your mind? If it does, you need to fill in the gaps with more information.

The more you have at stake, the more carefully you should approach the task of putting together your contract. For example, if you're entering into a contract to buy a truckload of bicycle tires for $1,000, you won't need your agreement to be outlined nearly as meticulously as you would in a contract for the construction of a building.

 SEE AN EXPERT

For complex agreements, you may need an attorney. Complex contracts—especially those in areas unfamiliar to you—are often best handled with the help of a lawyer. Certainly, if a transaction is so huge or elaborate that it makes your head spin, you shouldn't go it alone. First, decide how much help you need. Rather than having an attorney draft your contract from start to finish, you could simply have an attorney review a contract that you or the other party has written. Ideally, you should hire a lawyer with some experience with small business, preferably your type of business. Even better would be an attorney who knows the ins and outs of your business based on a long-term working relationship. (See Chapter 17 for more information on getting legal assistance.)

Let's look at the information that most contracts include to fulfill these three goals. Except where noted below, you don't need to use any special language:

- **Title.** Generally, a contract will have a simple, to-the-point title such as "Contract for Printing Services" or "Agreement for Sale of Ball Bearings."
- **The names and addresses of all the parties.** It should be clear what role each party has in the contract, such as seller or buyer; landlord or tenant; client or service provider.

> **EXAMPLE:** Christopher Johnson ("Client") desires to enter into a contract ("contract") with Virgil's Printing ("Printer") for printing services for Client's newspaper.

The addresses of the parties generally appear at the end of the contract, in the section with the signatures.

- **A brief description of the background of the agreement (called "recitals").** While not always included, this type of information is often necessary to frame the contents of the agreement. Typically, this section includes a brief description of what kinds of businesses the parties run and the nature of the transaction covered in the contract.

> **EXAMPLE:** Client produces and distributes a free, weekly, 24-page newspaper called *El Norte* with a circulation of 40,000. Printer operates a full-service print shop. The subject of this Contract is an agreement that Printer shall print Client's newspaper each week in exchange for payment.

- **A full description of what each party is promising to do as part of the agreement.** This section, sometimes called the "specifications" or just "specs," describes the terms of the deal. If a product is being sold, describe the product and delivery terms. If a service is being performed, describe the job and then state when it will be completed, including any intermediate deadlines that must be met before the final completion date. If strict compliance with deadlines is necessary, throw in the phrase, "Time is of the essence." This is a standard phrase used in contracts. It simply means that deadlines will be enforced strictly.

If specifications are complicated (for example, intricate performance details for a software contract), they should normally be set out in attachments to the contract, which may include scale drawings, formulas, or other detailed information about the transaction.

> **EXAMPLE:** Client promises to upload PDF files ("Files") for printing to Printer's server no later than 10:00 a.m. each Wednesday morning. Printer promises to print, fold, and bundle 40,000 copies of Client's newspaper and have them ready for Client to pick up from Printer's shop by 8:00 p.m. that same Wednesday. Time is of the essence regarding this contract. If, however, Client fails to upload Files to Printer by 10:00 a.m. Wednesday morning, Printer may take extra time to complete the job. The amount of extra time will depend on how late Client is in uploading the Files and on Printer's schedule of other jobs, but in no case shall be longer than 24 hours after uploading of the Files.

- **The price of the product or service.** This section states how much one party will pay for the other party's goods or services. If the price may vary (say, based on the time or quality of performance) or if it will be established later, a description of how it will be calculated should be included.

  > **EXAMPLE:** Client will pay Printer $1,000 for every 10,000 24-page newspapers printed, up to 50,000 newspapers. The price will be renegotiated if Client orders more than 50,000 newspapers, or if the number of pages per newspaper changes.

- **Payment arrangements.** This section should explain when payment is due, whether it will be paid all at once or in installments, and whether interest will be charged if payments are late. Also include any other special requirements, such as whether payment must be by certified or cashier's check. Otherwise, a garden-variety check will normally suffice. Again, if strict compliance with payment deadlines is necessary, use the phrase "Time is of the essence."

  > **EXAMPLE:** Client will pay Printer the full amount of each week's printing cost within three days of picking up the completed newspapers.

Automatic Warranties

Under the Uniform Commercial Code, which is adopted in some form in all 50 states, all sales of products are automatically covered by some warranties whether or not the seller promised anything to the buyer. These warranties are called "implied warranties" and include two guarantees: that the product is fit for its ordinary use and that it is fit for any special purpose for which the seller knows the buyer wants to use it. For example, the sale of a kitchen knife comes with an implied warranty that the knife will work in ordinary kitchen uses. If the buyer asked the retailer to help pick out a knife that would cut through heavy beef bones, then whatever knife the retailer sold would come with a warranty that it would work for cutting heavy beef bones. This is true regardless of whether or not the knife came with an express, written warranty that it could be used for heavy butcher work.

Be aware of the existence of implied warranties when drafting your contracts. Even if you don't make specific promises in your contracts, you will still be legally bound by the two kinds of implied warranties described above: fitness for ordinary use and fitness for a particular purpose. The law regarding warranties can be complex. You may want to consult an attorney for more detailed information about your obligations as a seller.

- **A statement of any warranties made by either party regarding the product or service being provided.** A warranty is essentially a guarantee made by one party to another that a product or service will meet certain standards. If either party gives a warranty, the contract should state what will happen if the guarantee isn't satisfied—for instance, if certain standards aren't met, the party who got the raw end of the deal will be given a refund or may give the other party another chance to do the job right at no additional cost.

  EXAMPLE: Printer warrants that the completed newspapers shall be free from printing defects or errors attributable to Printer. In case such errors do occur, Printer and Client may negotiate a discount not to exceed actual damages suffered by Client.

- **A statement of whether either party may transfer the contract to an outside party.** Transferring contract rights is also called assigning. If you have chosen a company to provide products or services because of particular characteristics, such as good personal service or artistic detail, you may not want that company to be able to hand off the job to someone else, who may not do as good a job.

EXAMPLE: Neither Printer nor Client may assign this Contract or any part of it to another party.

- **The contract term.** This section establishes how long the contract will be in effect.

EXAMPLE: This Contract will remain in effect for a period of one year, or until it is terminated by one of the parties, whichever is first.

- **A description of any conditions under which either party may terminate the agreement.** It's not uncommon to allow either party to terminate the contract with a certain amount of notice, say 30 or 60 days. Some lawyers call this "termination for convenience" since it essentially allows the parties to terminate for any reason whatsoever, no questions asked.

EXAMPLE: Either Printer or Client may terminate this Contract upon 30 days' written notice. Email notice is sufficient for this provision.

In other cases you and the other party may prefer to discourage termination, and limit it to circumstances such as insolvency (a party goes bankrupt) or breach of contract. This is often called "termination for cause."

EXAMPLE: Either Printer or Client may terminate this Contract effective immediately if the other party (i) commits any material breach or default of this Contract and does not remedy such breach within 30 days of receiving notice from the other party; (ii) becomes the subject of any voluntary or involuntary proceeding under the U.S. Bankruptcy Code or state insolvency proceeding and such proceeding is not terminated within sixty (60) days of its commencement; or (iii) ceases to be actively engaged in business and has not assigned this Contract.

No matter which reasons you allow for termination, you should include language clarifying how you will handle payments for services performed but not yet paid for, or for payments made but services not yet performed.

EXAMPLE: If upon termination of this Contract, either party has provided services that have not yet been paid for, or payments for which services have not yet been performed, the parties agree to provide payments or refunds based upon a good-faith estimate of the pro rata value owed to the other party.

- **An outline of how you will deal with a breach-of-contract situation.** Though signing a contract may not head off a subsequent dispute, it can channel the dispute in ways that will allow it to be resolved as quickly and cheaply as possible. There are a number of different approaches you can take.

You can decide, in advance, the amount of damages (financial compensation) a breaching party will have to pay to avoid the often lengthy and contentious process of calculating a party's damages after the other party breaches the contract. When damages are preset in a contract, they are called liquidated damages. In order for a liquidated damages clause to be valid, the dollar amount of damages that you set must be a reasonable estimate of what actual damages would be, not merely a preset penalty for breaking the contract.

Another option is for both parties to agree in the contract to try mediation and, if that fails, arbitration to settle a dispute as an alternative to going to court.

EXAMPLE: If any dispute arises under the terms of this Contract, the parties agree to select a mutually agreeable, neutral third party to help them mediate it. The costs of mediation will be shared equally. If the dispute is not resolved after 30 days in mediation, the parties agree to choose a mutually agreeable arbitrator who will arbitrate the dispute. The costs of arbitration will be assigned to the parties by the arbitrator. The results of any arbitration will be binding and final.

If one or both of you prefers going to court, you can provide in the contract that the losing party in a dispute must pay the other party's legal fees, or you can establish that each party is responsible for individual legal fees regardless of who prevails. Note that for some commercial transactions, neither party in a lawsuit can collect attorneys' fees from the other unless it is provided for in a written contract.

- **For contracts with out-of-state entities, a statement of which state's laws apply to the transaction.** Although contract law in all states is very similar, using the law in your state will generally be the simplest for you, since you'll have more resources at your disposal, including law libraries and local attorneys.

    EXAMPLE: This Contract is governed by and interpreted under the laws of New Mexico.

- **Signatures, dates, and addresses.** Your signature section should always include room for the date the contract was signed, as well as the addresses of the parties.

Jennifer F. Mahoney, owner of an illustration service in Northern California, (www.candraw.net):
My creativity is exercised just as much by drawing up a good agreement with a client as it is by the way I create art for that client.

RESOURCE

More on business contracts.
For detailed advice on how to write contract provisions, find out what a particular contract term such as indemnity means, or make sure you can enforce important business agreements down the road, see *Contracts: The Essential Business Desk Reference*, by Richard Stim (Nolo).

Putting Your Contract Together

In addition to making sure your contract includes all the necessary information, you'll need to present it in an easy-to-follow, professional format. Generally, contract clauses are organized in numbered paragraphs for easy reference to specific terms.

If your agreement includes any hard-to-articulate details, such as the specifications of a software product, a drawing of a company logo, or architectural blueprints, you can include them as attachments to the main contract. If you do include an attachment, be sure to label it and refer to it in the main contract. To officially make it a part of the contract, state somewhere in the main contract that you "include the Attachment in the contract" or that you "incorporate the Attachment into the contract."

EXAMPLE 1: Company agrees to pay Artist $100 for use of logo. Logo is attached to this Contract as Attachment A and is included in this Contract.

EXAMPLE 2: Contractor agrees to complete remodeling within one year. The final plans are attached to this Contract as Exhibit B and are incorporated into this Contract.

Reading and Revising a Contract

If you don't like certain terms of a contract that's presented to you, you can propose changes. By doing this, you are technically making a counteroffer. Contracts are commonly negotiated back and forth (offer and counteroffer) this way until all the terms are accepted by both parties. Remember, if the parties aren't in agreement, there's no contract—oral or otherwise.

Changes to a contract—whether to a form contract or one drafted from scratch—can be made in a number of ways. You can simply cross out language and fill in new language directly on the contract itself. Both parties should initial any such changes to show that they approve of them, then sign the contract as a whole.

In today's world, however, it's more than likely that there will be an electronic copy of the contract on someone's computer. If so, it makes much more sense to make the necessary changes directly in the digital file and then print out a clean copy for both parties to sign. However some industries (such as the real estate industry) commonly use a separate document when making a counteroffer that states the desired changes and refers back to the original offer. In that case, both the original offer and the counteroffer together form the contract.

A contract can also be amended at a later date with a separate document, called an addendum. The addendum should state that its terms prevail over the terms of the original contract, especially if the terms are in direct conflict, such as when the price or completion time for a job is changed. Both parties should sign the addendum.

Electronic Contracts

While the basics covered so far generally apply to any contract regardless of form—whether the contract is printed in a formal document, scratched on a cocktail napkin, or just spoken and sealed with a handshake—there are new and emerging rules that apply specifically to contracts created online. Before you read the very general overview of the special issues involved in electronic contracts, keep in mind that law in this area is rapidly evolving.

What Is an Electronic Contract?

An "electronic contract" is essentially any agreement that is created and executed in electronic form—in other words,

no paper or other hard copies are used. Typically, electronic agreements are created either via email or on interactive webpages. For instance, many companies use interactive forms at their websites that users must complete to purchase goods or software, join a membership organization, participate in a mail listserver, or do whatever else the company is offering. In addition to asking the user to enter various items of personal information, these forms typically display the terms of the contract between the company and the user, and ask the user to agree to the terms by clicking on a button such as "I Accept."

Here's another example of an electronic contract: A business associate of yours emails you a request to purchase a specified number of items you sell, at a named price, for immediate delivery. If you email back to the associate that you agree to all the proposed terms, you've probably just entered into a legally enforceable electronic contract. Why the "probably"? Because there is no way for you to sign the contract with pen and ink, and states vary in how they treat digital signatures. Read on.

Taking Traditional Contract Principles Online

As mentioned above, contract law has only recently begun to grapple with the details of these types of paperless agreements. When electronic contracts have been challenged, courts have had a difficult time determining whether an actual binding contract existed, since it can be unclear whether all the traditional elements of contract formation were met.

Shortcut Contracts for E-Commerce

When it comes to small transactions in which you pay for goods by credit card, most sites get around the issue of whether a valid contract has been formed by saying that if you are dissatisfied for any reason, they will give you your money back. This is another way of saying that if you don't want a contract to exist, it doesn't. Or put another way, the company concedes in advance that it won't try to enforce the contract. This trust-the-customer approach works well for small transactions but has obvious limitations when it comes to major purchases—a car, for example, or significant business-to-business transactions. In these situations, a real signature on an enforceable contract is needed.

Clickwrap Agreements

Some businesses and industries have traditionally used standard contracts that aren't open to negotiation; customers have to either accept the contract as is or not complete the transaction. Examples might include a car purchase contract or an agreement to rent a moving truck,

in which a consumer who insisted on changing any of the terms of the company's standard contract would not be able to buy the car or rent the truck. Over the years, these types of contracts have been challenged on the grounds that they are not fair to the consumer, because they are typically presented in a take-it-or-leave-it manner, giving the consumer little or no power to amend a contract that is often highly favorable to the seller. Whether or not these types of contracts (sometimes called contracts of adhesion, because consumers are forced to "adhere" to the contract) are valid has long been a contentious area of contract law. Generally, adhesion contracts are held to be valid, as long as the terms are clear to the consumer and not grossly unreasonable.

Today, Internet click-to-agree contracts (often called clickwrap, webwrap, or browsewrap agreements) are facing similar challenges. So are other nonnegotiated agreements, such as the software licenses included with packaged software, sometimes called shrinkwrap agreements. While these types of agreements have generally been found valid, courts have refused to enforce certain terms that are deemed too burdensome or unfair to the consumer.

A federal case decided in 2002 sheds some light on the question of when a clickwrap agreement may be deemed invalid. In that case, an Internet user who downloaded software from a website operated by the Netscape company later sued Netscape, claiming that the software license was not binding. To download the software, the user had simply clicked a "Download" button and was not required to view the software license or click any button such as "I Agree" to indicate consent to license terms. To view the license, the user would have had to scroll below the Download button and click on another link to a separate page where the license terms were posted.

The U.S. Court of Appeals for the Second Circuit ruled in favor of the user, based on the principle that for a contract to be binding, both parties must assent to be bound. The court found that the structure of Netscape's software download page "with license terms on a submerged screen" and no button to clearly indicate consent was not sufficient to create a binding contract with the user. (*Specht v. Netscape Communications Corp.*, 306 F.3d 17 (2d Cir. 2002).)

The *Netscape* case establishes that downloading alone does not indicate acceptance of license terms. To make sure a clickwrap agreement is binding, the site must be set up to ensure that a user can clearly indicate consent to the license terms of any downloads. Keep this in mind if you plan to use any clickwrap agreements with your business.

Legislative Attempts to Solve Clickwrap Issues

Over the past several years, some state legislatures have tried to deal with the problems raised by clickwrap agreements. However, state laws governing electronic contracts are not consistent, and state courts that have ruled on electronic contract cases have come up with different decisions. The result is that checking an "I accept" box may create a contract in one state but not in another. This lack of uniformity has been a real thorn in the side of e-commerce, which, of course, recognizes no state boundaries.

In response, the National Conference of Commissioners on Uniform State Laws (NCCUSL) decided to tackle the problem by drafting model legislation for adoption by the states. One of these proposed laws, the Uniform Computer Information Transactions Act (UCITA), addresses the issue of clickwrap and shrinkwrap agreements, essentially making these types of contracts valid and binding.

But in the several years since the UCITA was drafted, hardly any states have adopted it. One reason may be that many consumer advocates, as well as more than 25 state attorneys general, have argued that the UCITA is biased in favor of software vendors and information services providers, leaving consumers with significantly less protection than they have under current law. An online search of the term "UCITA" will lead you to many sites with updated information on the act—and an almost universally negative take on it.

Electronic and Digital Signatures

One of the stickier issues involving electronic contracts has to do with whether agreements executed in a purely online environment have been "signed" (outside of clickwrap agreements, discussed above). For many centuries, the traditional way to indicate your acceptance of contracts (and most other binding documents) has been to sign with your unique signature. But electronic contracts can't be signed this way. Instead, people use other means to indicate they accept the terms of a contract, such as simply typing their names into the signature areas of the documents. But, increasingly, better technological approaches to the problem of signing contracts online are being developed, such as fingerprint or iris scanning, or a cryptographic technology known as public key infrastructure (PKI). These methods are collectively known as electronic signatures. The term "digital signature" refers specifically to cryptographic signature methods such as PKI.

Until relatively recently, most states didn't have any laws stating which of these ways to "sign" an electronic document was legally acceptable. In response, the NCCUSL drafted another model law, the Uniform Electronic Transactions Act (UETA), which specifically addresses electronic signatures. In a nutshell, the UETA provides that electronic signatures (in all their forms) and contracts are just as valid and legally binding as their paper counterparts. As of late 2019, all states had enacted the UETA except Illinois, New York, and Washington (although those states have adopted similar laws making electronic signatures legally enforceable).

What Is PKI?

Security experts currently favor the cryptographic signature method known as public key infrastructure (PKI) as the most secure and reliable method of signing contracts online. Without going too deeply into the technical details, PKI involves using an algorithm to encrypt the document so that only the parties will be able to modify it or "sign" it. The process of encrypting the document is known as creating a digital signature. Each party will have a "key" allowing it to read and sign the document, thus ensuring that no one else will be able to sign it fraudulently. PKI standards are still evolving, but the technology is already widely accepted as the best electronic signature method currently available.

Federal Law on Electronic Signatures

Fortunately, as the states were mulling over whether to adopt the UETA, the UCITA, or both, the U.S. Congress forged ahead and passed federal legislation establishing the validity of electronic signatures nationwide. This bill, known as the Electronic Signatures in Global and National Commerce Act, was signed into law in June 2000 and became effective on October 1, 2000. The law applies to all states that had not already adopted the UETA or a similar electronic signature law by mid-2000. In this way, the law finally gave some much-needed consistency to the way states treat electronic signatures in online transactions.

This law is similar to the model UETA in that it makes electronic signatures and contracts (including clickwrap agreements) just as valid as paper ones. While certain transactions are exempted from this law and must still be completed on paper (wills, cancellation of utility services, court orders, and other official court documents, among others), the law allows an enormous range of business and consumer transactions to be completed totally online. In essence, it throws the door wide open for all types of e-commerce, allowing businesses and consumers to create (in theory, at least) reliable, binding contracts online, without the inconvenience of shuttling paper documents back and forth.

Tips for Creating Contracts Online

While the federal e-signature law, along with the UETA, create a solid legal frame-work for online contracts, electronic signature technology is still evolving, which means the reality of online contracts still falls somewhat short of its promise. Like the UETA, the e-signature law does not specify any particular technology for electronic signatures, leaving that up to software companies and the free market to establish. As mentioned above, PKI technology is currently favored by security experts, though its standards aren't completely nailed down or ready for common use. As developments in PKI and other electronic signature methods create solid, worldwide standards, e-commerce will only become more efficient and widespread.

While waiting for reliable standards to develop, it will be important to approach online contracts carefully. Of particular concern is the possibility for fraud, especially since there is no set standard for what constitutes an electronic signature. Until the technology is airtight, make sure that you trust the other party and are comfortable with the type of electronic signature that you're using. If you're not comfortable creating a contract online, you may want to stay lower tech and stick with paper contracts, either faxed back and forth or sent by overnight mail.

The nonprofit Consumers Union, which publishes *Consumer Reports* magazine, has issued a set of tips to follow when using electronic signatures and creating online contracts:

- Don't consent to using an online contract if you are uncomfortable using a computer or do not under-stand how to use email.

- Don't agree to use an online contract or to receive electronic documents until you are sure that your computer's software and hardware will be able to read and use the documents provided.
- Remember that the electronic signatures law allows you to opt to receive documents on paper instead of electronically if you prefer.
- Keep backup paper copies of the electronic documents you receive, and keep a list of the businesses with which you agree to exchange electronic documents.
- Notify the businesses of any changes that may affect your ability to receive and read email and attachments, such as changing your email address, your hardware, or your software.
- Close any unused email accounts.
- Don't give out your email address to any business if you don't want to receive email notices from it.
- Notify the business right away if you have any problems receiving its emails or opening its documents.

CAUTION

Beware of e-viruses. Never open attachments to email if you aren't expecting the email or don't know who it's from. Nasty viruses are often spread through email attachments, so it's good policy to just throw away suspicious mail as soon as you see it. Even when you know the sender of the email, you need to be cautious. Some viruses use a computer user's email address book to replicate themselves, by sending themselves out to everyone in the book. This means that if you get an email with an attachment from your friend Steve Smith, there's a chance that Steve Smith didn't actually send the email. For this reason, you shouldn't open attachments unless you're expecting them.

Chapter 11 Checklist: Entering Into Contracts and Agreements

☐ Become familiar with the legal basics of contracts.

☐ Put all your contracts into writing whenever possible. (Contracts created online or by email are considered to be "in writing.")

☐ Try to respond to offers promptly, and, when making an offer, include an expiration date.

☐ When you need to draft a contract from scratch, try using standard form contracts to get started.

☐ Be thorough in your contracts. Make sure that any points of potential conflict are clearly spelled out.

☐ Use caution when entering into electronic contracts (also sometimes called online contracts or digital contracts). If you're uncomfortable creating a contract online or by email, don't do it—opt for a paper contract.

Bookkeeping, Accounting, and Financial Management

Perhaps the hardest part of accounting is getting over the psychological hang-up that most people seem to have about it. Many of us hate to balance our checkbooks on a regular basis, much less keep detailed accounts of how our money comes and goes. In truth, you don't need to be a financial wizard to start a small business; you just need a comfortable working knowledge of the basics.

If you read Chapter 4, "Drafting an Effective Business Plan," some of this material may be a review. That chapter explained how to generate financial projections using sales and expense estimates to see if your business is likely to turn a profit. The financial tools used in business planning—particularly profit/loss analysis and cash flow projection—are the same tools used in accounting, just employed slightly differently. Instead of making financial projections, we'll focus on how to track actual, current financial data for your business.

This chapter will give an overview of what's involved in bookkeeping and the basic concepts business owners need to understand. We'll explain what receipts and records your business should keep and describe simple ways to organize them. We'll also explain how bookkeeping software works, including setting it up, entering your income and expense data, and generating reports showing how well (or poorly) your business is doing financially. Generating reports from your income and expense data will also help you manage the cash that flows through your business so that you can pay your important bills on time.

While this chapter provides important, basic financial management information that every business owner should understand, keep in mind that it often makes sense to use a professional bookkeeper to handle data entry and financial management tasks. Retail stores, for example, with dozens or hundreds of transactions every day, would likely want to have a part- or full-time bookkeeper on staff to keep the books continually updated. Smaller businesses like consultants or freelancers might simply do the data entry themselves, or contract with a bookkeeper to do data entry once a month. And even if you plan to do all the data entry and financial management yourself, it's still a good idea to have at least a consulting session or two with an experienced bookkeeper when you start your business to make sure you set up a solid financial management system from the very beginning. An experienced bookkeeper can be a huge help in getting off on the right foot, from clarifying what records you should keep to setting up your bookkeeping software and understanding how to use it.

Fortunately for today's entrepreneurs, inexpensive, powerful, and easy-to-use software is available that vastly simplifies financial management tasks. Programs such as *Quicken* and *QuickBooks* have several different versions to meet the needs of all sizes and types of businesses, making this once unsavory task much more palatable. Once your income and expenses are entered into the software, you can easily generate sophisticated financial reports that would have taken many hours and considerable skill to create just a decade ago. In fact, these programs are so affordable (generally under $400, and often far less) and user friendly, it really doesn't make sense to track your finances by hand, which is not only much more time-consuming but also more prone to errors.

Bookkeepers and Accountants: What Is the Difference?

In a nutshell, bookkeepers specialize in the day-to-day tasks of tracking a business's income and expenses, often being in charge of data entry and generating reports such as monthly profit/loss statements (explained later in this chapter). In addition, bookkeepers are often hired to prepare payroll (including determining how much tax to withhold from employees' checks, issuing the checks, and managing payroll tax deposits), file statements for property or unemployment taxes, and related bureaucratic tasks.

Accountants, on the other hand, specialize in making sense of your financial data and handling tasks such as filing tax returns and managing tax-savings strategies for businesses. Accountants can analyze your financial data and give advice on questions such as whether it's a good time to expand your business, or how to set up employee benefits to maximize tax savings. Since accountants typically have deeper knowledge of tax rules than bookkeepers, they are usually in the best position to answer any gray-area tax questions, such as whether certain types of transactions are subject to state sales tax. (See Chapter 17 for more information on different kinds of accountants, such as certified public accountants.)

There's typically a big cost difference between accountants and bookkeepers—accountants usually charge significantly more—so you'll want to hire the right one for the right tasks. It's generally advised for all small businesses to hire an accountant at least once a year to prepare your business's tax return. (Tax basics are discussed in Chapter 9.) For smaller, day-to-day tasks and routine filings, you'll be better off hiring a bookkeeper. Bookkeepers can also be a big help in establishing an effective record-keeping system, including choosing the best financial management software for your business, setting it up, and showing you how it works.

CAUTION

Report cash payments above $10,000.
Someone in a trade or business has 15 days to report receiving more than $10,000 in cash in one transaction or related transactions. A "transaction" includes the purchase of property or services, the payment of debt, and even holding cash for someone for more than 15 days as part of a deal. "Cash" includes any combination of U.S. and foreign coins and bills and a cashier's check, money order, bank draft, or travelers' check (but not a personal check) with a face amount of $10,000 or more—unless it comes from a bank loan. To report, the business owner must file Form 8300 (*Report of Cash Payments Over $10,000 Received in a Trade or Business*) with the IRS and the Financial Crimes Enforcement Network (FinCEN). Breaking up one transaction into many little ones to avoid this reporting requirement can lead to prison and heavy fines. Check with your accountant or lawyer if you find yourself with this kind of cash.

TIP

Don't expect accounting software to do all your work for you. You shouldn't simply rely on the numbers that your software program spits out if you don't fully understand them. The accounting concepts and processes described in this chapter are the same whether done manually or by accounting software—and you should take the time to learn them. Though accounting software makes it much easier to manipulate the numbers you've entered and to generate informative financial reports, you still need to understand what all the numbers mean in order to use them to make meaningful business decisions.

Accounting Basics

If you are intimidated or just plain overwhelmed by the prospect of managing your business's finances, it can be helpful to get back to basics and consider the big picture. Carefully tracking income and expenses helps you in the following two primary ways:

- **You'll improve your chances of making a profit.** Having a firm handle on your income and expenses is essential to making smart business decisions that lead to profitability.
- **You'll have well-organized financial information that is necessary to file your various tax returns and local tax registration papers.** There's no worse nightmare than facing a tax deadline and having months' worth of unorganized receipts that haven't been entered into your record-keeping system (or worse yet: not having a record-keeping system in place at all).

Sounds pretty simple, no? All the intricacies of financial management basically boil down to these two points. You should also be reassured to know that there is no requirement that your records be kept in any specific organizational system. There is a requirement, however, that some businesses use a certain method of crediting their accounts. (See "Cash Versus Accrual Accounting," below.) In other words, there's no official system or

Accounting Glossary

A big part of understanding the financial side of your business consists of nothing more than learning the language of accounting. Once you're familiar with some common terms, such as the ones listed below, you'll be better able to make sense of basic written reports and to communicate with others about important financial information. And you'll also be well positioned to cope with a common business problem: people who use key financial terms imprecisely or even incorrectly, needlessly confusing themselves and others.

- **Accounting** refers to the process of tracking your business's income and expenses, then using these numbers in various calculations and formulas to answer specific questions about the financial and tax status of the business.
- **Bookkeeping** refers to the task of recording the amount, date, and source of all business revenues and expenses. Bookkeeping is essentially the starting point of the accounting process. Only with accurate bookkeeping can there be meaningful accounting.
- An **invoice** is a written record of a transaction, often submitted to a customer or client when requesting payment. Invoices are sometimes called *bills* or *statements*, though statement has its own technical meaning. (See below.)
- A **statement** is a written summary of an account. Unlike an invoice, a statement is not generally used as a formal request

for payment, but is used to outline the details of an account.
- A **ledger** is a collection of related financial information, such as revenues, expenditures, accounts receivable, and accounts payable. Ledgers used to be kept in books preprinted with lined ledger paper (which explains why a business's financial information is often referred to as the "books"), but are now commonly kept electronically using various software programs.
- An **account** is a collection of financial information grouped according to customer or purpose. For example, if you have a regular customer, your information regarding that customer's purchases, payments, and debts would be called his or her "account." A written record of an account is called a *statement*.
- A **receipt** is a written record of a transaction. A buyer receives a receipt to show that he or she paid for an item. The seller keeps a copy of the receipt to show that he or she received payment for the item.
- **Accounts payable** are amounts that your business owes. For example, unpaid utility bills and purchases your business makes on credit are included in your accounts payable.
- **Accounts receivable** are amounts owed to your business that you expect to receive, including sales your business makes on credit.

format to organize your books. As long as your records accurately reflect your business's income and expenses, the IRS will find them acceptable.

TIP

Organization is everything. One thing that all good bookkeeping systems have in common is organization. A well-organized system with accessible, reasonably neat files (including both hard-copy and electronic records) not only will be a godsend in the event of an audit, but will help you keep track of your business as well.

Benefits of Well-Maintained Financial Records

Are you beginning to believe that you don't need to be afraid of accounting? Good, because it's something you absolutely need to embrace as part of running any business. Failing to keep track of income and expenses is one of the surest ways to run any business off a cliff. Here are a few more details on how a well-maintained bookkeeping system will help your business:

- **You'll be able to price your goods and services more competitively.** Only by staying on top of your business's income and expenses will you know how much money you'll need to bring in each week, month, or year to make a profit. This knowledge is essential to allow you to price your goods and

services appropriately. For instance, if you don't know your break-even point, you will only be able to guess at how much you should charge your customers for products or services, with the likely result that you'll charge too little (and make an inadequate profit) or too much (and alienate customers).

- **You'll be able to trim costs strategically.** Having updated and categorized expense data will allow you to see your spending patterns and spot areas where you can reduce your costs to improve your bottom line. For example, you may see the need to cut back on travel expenses or on outsourced services that aren't sufficiently helping generate income.

- **You'll be able to pace your growth more effectively.** A good set of books will give you the information you need to decide when and how to expand your business. If your numbers tell you that sales and profits have been growing consistently for several months, that may be a signal that it's time to hire additional employees or enter into a new market—or both. Without meaningful financial numbers, making any decisions about growth can be a gamble. For example, just because your business has a lot of money in its checking account doesn't necessarily mean you're making good money.

(You might have received several big payments from past sales, while current sales are actually slowing down.)

- **You may be able to reduce taxes.** Knowing your company's finances inside and out will help you save money when tax time comes around. For example, if the end of the year is nearing and your up-to-date records clearly show the year to be profitable, you can purchase needed supplies or equipment before the end of the year and write off these expenses, reducing your taxable income. Also, keeping careful track of your expenses will remind you to claim them as deductions at year-end. Businesses that are sloppy about bookkeeping often miss opportunities for saving tax dollars. Don't be one of them.

- **You'll avoid tax penalties.** In addition to helping you legally save tax dollars, responsible bookkeeping will help you avoid errors in your tax returns that can subject you to fines and other penalties. If your business is audited, the IRS can be really nasty if it finds your books in bad shape. In extreme situations, it may even refuse to recognize perfectly legitimate expenses. In short, neglecting your responsibility to maintain basic, accurate records is likely to result in the kind of trouble with the IRS that you might not wish on even your worst enemy.

The Financial Management Process

At the most basic level, you can break down the process of financial management into three broad steps. We'll discuss these in more detail later in the chapter; for now let's just look at an overview:

1. **Keep records.** The process starts with keeping records (basic receipts, usually) of all the money the business spends (expenses) and all the money it earns (income). This means carefully keeping and organizing your expense receipts (that is, receipts from the office supply store, bills from your accountant and lawyer, records of payments to your employees and freelancers, and so on) and your income receipts (such as a cash register tape of your clothing store's income, check stubs from your client's payment checks, or your invoices to clients marked "Paid").

2. **Enter information into a bookkeeping system.** Next, on some periodic basis—say monthly for a small consulting business, or daily for a busy retail store—you'll enter the information from the income and expense receipts into a bookkeeping system. More often than not this will be some sort of financial management software such as *QuickBooks*. (In the old days, this was done by entering the income and expenses into a ledger.)

3. **Generate financial reports.** Finally, with up-to-date information entered into your bookkeeping system, you'll generate reports such as a profit/loss report or an accounts receivable report to reveal how your business is doing. These reports summarize the data you've entered to show you different aspects of your business's financial situation. For example, a profit/loss report shows whether you made a profit in a given time period (usually monthly), while an accounts receivable report shows how much your clients owe you at any given time. Generating reports should be done on some periodic basis, with some reports following different schedules than others. For example, most businesses should generate a profit/loss report each month, as well as quarterly and annually.

CAUTION

Do not neglect to open a business bank account! Using your personal bank account for business deposits and expenses is a huge mistake for a number of reasons. One is that if you hoped to protect your personal assets by creating an LLC or a corporation, you'll basically throw any such protection out the window by commingling personal and business funds. And on a more important day-to-day level, mixing your business transactions with personal transactions will make

it impossible to do the types of simple financial management described in this chapter. Run, do not walk, to your local community bank and open a business bank account as soon as you're ready to launch.

Cash Versus Accrual Accounting

Before turning to several simple systems for keeping your records, you need to understand the two principal methods of keeping track of a business's income and expenses: cash method and accrual method accounting (sometimes called cash basis and accrual basis accounting). In a nutshell, the difference between these methods has to do with the timing of when transactions—both sales and purchases—are credited to or debited from your accounts. In short:

- Under the cash method, income is counted when cash (or a check) is actually received, not necessarily when the sale occurs; expenses are counted when they are actually paid, not necessarily when you made the purchase.
- Under the accrual method, transactions are counted when they happen —for example, when you complete a sale, or make a purchase—regardless of when the money is actually received or paid. You don't have to wait until

you receive the money, or until you actually pay money out of your checking account, to record the transaction.

For example, say you hire a branding firm to redesign some of your product packaging, and they complete the new designs and all other terms of the contract in mid-December 2019. The contract specifies that you will pay within 30 days of project completion and invoice, so you pay the full balance of $2,500 in mid-January 2020. Using cash method accounting, you would record a $2,500 expense in January 2020, when the money was actually paid. But under the accrual method, the $2,500 payment would be recorded in December 2019, when the job was completed and you became obligated to pay for it. Similarly, if your computer installation business finished a job in November 2019 and didn't get paid until January 2020, you'd record the payment in January 2020 if you used the cash method. Under the accrual method, the income would be recorded in your books in November 2019.

Note that expenses paid with a credit card can be deducted at the time when incurred. The IRS allows a business to take deductions for business credit card purchases before you've paid the credit card bill, even if you're using cash basis accounting. For more details on this and other exceptions and gray areas, talk with a bookkeeper.

TIP

Timing can be tricky. Some sales aren't completed all at once. If you use accrual accounting, you may sometimes wonder exactly when you can enter the transaction into your books. For instance, say someone buys two CDs from your record store but also makes a special order for another CD, and pays for all three at once. Or, say your landscaping company finishes a large project, except for the last step of applying a final lawn fertilizing treatment two weeks after laying the sod. The key date here is the job completion date. Don't count the transaction until you deliver all of the goods, finish all parts of a service, or otherwise meet all terms of a contract. If a job is mostly completed but will take another few days to add the finishing touches, it doesn't go on your books until it is completely done. In situations like these, the help of an experienced bookkeeper can be a godsend.

TIP

Both methods can produce the same results. As you can see, the results produced by the cash and accrual accounting methods will only be different if you do some transactions on credit. If all your transactions are paid in cash as soon as completed, including your sales and purchases, then your books will look the same regardless of the method you use.

Accounting Methods and Taxes

The most significant way your business is affected by the accounting method you choose involves the tax year in which income and expense items will be counted. (See "Tax Years and Accounting Periods," below.) For instance, if you use the cash method, and you incur expenses in the 2020 tax year but don't pay them until the 2021 tax year, you won't be able to claim them on your 2020 tax return. But you will be able to claim them in 2020 if you use the accrual method, since that system records transactions when they occur, not when money actually changes hands.

EXAMPLE 1: Zara runs a small flower shop called ZuZu's Petals. On December 22, 2020, Zara buys a number of office supplies for which she will be billed $400. She takes the supplies that day but, according to the terms of the purchase, doesn't pay for them for 30 days. Under her accrual system of accounting, she counts the $400 expense during the December 2020 accounting period, even though she didn't actually write the check until January of the next year. This means that Zara can deduct the $400 from her taxable income of 2020.

EXAMPLE 2: Scott and Lisa operate A Stitch in Hide, a leather repair shop. They're hired to repair an antique leather couch, and they finish their job on December 15, 2020. They bill the customer $750, which they receive on January 20, 2021. Because they use the accrual method of accounting, Scott and Lisa count the $750 income in December 2020, because that's when they earned the money by finishing the job. This income must be reported on their 2020 tax return, even though they didn't receive the money that year.

Tax Years and Accounting Periods

Income and expenses must be reported to the IRS for a specific period of time, alternately called your "tax year," "accounting period," or "fiscal year." Unless you have a valid business reason to use a different period, or unless your business is a corporation, you'll have to use the calendar year, beginning on January 1 and ending on December 31. Most business owners do use the calendar year for their tax years, simply because they find it easy and natural to use. But if you want to use a different period, you must request permission from the IRS by filing Form 8716, *Election To Have a Tax Year Other Than a Required Tax Year.* (A copy of this form is included on this book's companion page on Nolo.com, and the link is in Appendix B.) Also, your fiscal year can't begin and end on just any day of the month; it must begin on the first day of a month and end on the last day of the previous month one year later.

Which Method to Use

In choosing a method, first consider the IRS rules that may dictate your choice. The general rule as of 2018 is that corporations and partnerships with average annual gross receipts for the three preceding tax years of $25 million or less (indexed for inflation) qualify as a "small business" and can use the cash method. Note that the rules for accounting for inventories can be slightly more complicated, so it's a good idea to ask an accountant for advice.

Perhaps even more important than the IRS rules is to consider which method will give you the most control over your business's finances. In general, the cash method is simpler and may be the best route for freelancers and small firms. However, the cash method does not give as accurate a picture of your operational profitability as does the accrual method. Under the cash method, for instance, your books may show a three-month period to be spectacularly profitable because a lot of credit customers paid their bills in that period, when actually sales have been slow. Because the accrual method shows the ebb and flow of business income and debts more accurately, it is generally recommended for all but the smallest businesses.

Whichever method you use, it's important to realize that either one gives you only a partial picture of the financial status of your business. To have a true understanding of your business's finances, you need more than just a collection of monthly totals; you need to understand what your numbers mean and how to use them to answer specific financial questions, as discussed in the rest of this chapter.

Step 1: Keeping and Organizing Receipts

Comprehensive summaries of your business's income and expenses are the heart of the accounting process. But unless you want to flirt with tax fraud, you can't just make up the information in your books. Each of your business's sales and expenditures must be backed up by some type of record containing the amount, the date, and other relevant information about that transaction. The best way to stay organized is to have a system in place—in other words, a set of files, folders, cash register receipts, or whatever else that you use consistently over time, so that you always know where to find the information you need.

From a legal point of view, your method of keeping receipts can range from slips kept in a cigar box to a sophisticated cash register–based system; this may include point-of-sale (POS) software, which typically goes beyond tracking transactions to managing categories and subcategories, inventory, and more. Practically, you'll want to choose a system that fits your business needs. For example, a small service business that handles only relatively few jobs may get by with a bare-bones approach. But the more sales and expenditures your business makes, the more sophisticated your system needs to be. Whether your needs are simple or complex, the important thing is to make sure that you and any staff know the system and use it consistently. If your records aren't accurate, the financial statements you make from them won't be, either.

This section discusses common ways of keeping your receipts. The bottom line is to choose or adapt one to suit your needs.

Income Receipts

Every time your business brings in money, you need a record of it. Most of your revenue will come from sales of your products or services, but keep in mind that some may come from loans or capital contributions. How you keep track of sales will vary a great deal, depending on what type of business you run and how many sales you make. Businesses such as grocery stores that make hundreds or even thousands of sales a day will likely need a cash register (and possibly an integrated POS system) to record each sale. Other businesses with slower sales, such as hair salons or auto shops, may get by simply writing out a receipt for each sale from a receipt book. Freelancers and consultants generally use their invoices marked "Paid" as income receipts.

Regardless of how you generate income receipts, they should always include the date, a brief description of the goods or services sold, an indication of how payment was made, whether the sale was

subject to sales tax, and if so, the amount of sales tax separate from the total.

If any of your sales are subject to a state or local sales tax, it's critical that your income receipts distinguish a pretax total from the amount of sales tax charged (if any). Your income records must reflect whether a sale is taxable, and if so, the amount of sales tax. If any of your sales are subject to local or state sales taxes, you'll need this information to compute and file your state sales tax returns.

If you use a cash register, taxable sales will generally be marked as such by the push of a button at the time of each sale, and tax amounts will be shown separately. If you write out a receipt of each sale by hand, be sure to show any sales tax separately, not just as part of a total. If the sale is nontaxable, make that clear by writing "no tax," "nontaxable," or the like.

Finally, make sure to document any income your business receives from sources other than sales and keep these receipts separate from your sales receipts. If you get a loan or contribute your own personal money to the business, record this fact with some sort of receipt or promissory note. Be sure your written records adequately describe the source of income so you'll know whether to count it as taxable income or not (see "Taxable Sales Versus Taxable Income," below). Most income generated from sales of your products or services, for example, will be taxed at the end of the year, while income that you personally contribute to the business will not.

TIP

While it's good business practice to give receipts to customers who purchase goods or services, it's a legal requirement that you keep a copy for yourself. Therefore, if you write out your own receipts, you'll need to make two copies—one for you, and one for the customer. Cash registers and most receipt books make each record in duplicate.

Taxable Sales Versus Taxable Income

As discussed in this section (and in more detail under "Sales Taxes," in Chapter 9) many sales of goods are subject to sales tax, which retailers must pay to the state. But other large categories of sales are often exempt from sales tax, such as sales of services, sales to out-of-state residents, or sales to resellers. So, some sales income is taxable, and some is not.

However, whether a sale is taxable for *sales tax* purposes is a different issue from whether income is taxable or not for *income tax* purposes. Generally, taxable income—that is, money you take in that is subject to income taxes at the end of the year— includes any money earned by your business, minus certain deductions. All of this income must be reported on your year-end income tax return, whether or not it is subject to state sales tax.

Expenditure Receipts

Ever hear the business wisdom that the key to small business success is to keep your costs down? Though this isn't the only thing a successful business owner needs to do, watching those pennies is always a good idea. The first step in keeping costs down is keeping accurate track of what they are. Just as you keep a record of each individual sale, you need to keep a record each time you spend money for your business. Business expenditures include paychecks to employees; money spent on supplies, office rent, and telephone bills; payments on loans; and all other costs associated with your business. Legally and practically, each and every one of these expenses must be recorded.

The easiest way to ensure you track every expense is to make sure to get a written receipt for every transaction in which you spend money for the business. Each expenditure receipt should include the date, the amount, the method of payment, who was paid and—most important—a description of what type of expense it was, such as rent, supplies, or utilities. The description is important because later, when you enter your expenses into your bookkeeping software, you'll need to assign one or more categories to each expense. These categories—such as rent, advertising, supplies, utilities, meals, travel, and taxes— are important for tax purposes, because different types of expenses have different rules for deductibility. If any important information isn't included on the receipt, write it in. Later, when entering receipts into your bookkeeping system, you'll be glad you made sure to note the important information.

Bear in mind that you'll often have a number of receipts for just one purchase: a credit card slip, a register receipt, and an itemized statement, for example. If you throw all three receipts into your files to be posted later, you run the risk of counting all three separately. Ditto if you have a checkbook register entry plus a register receipt. To avoid counting transactions more than once, either discard multiple copies of receipts immediately after the transaction or staple them all together. It's also a great idea to write the last four digits of the credit card number on the cash register receipt so you can easily cross-check when entering receipts into your software.

Step 2: Entering Receipts Into Bookkeeping Software

On some regular basis—every day, once a week, or once a month at a minimum—you should transfer ("post") the amounts from your income and expenditure receipts into your bookkeeping software. (Entering income and expense receipts could also be described as entering transactions.) Later, you'll use the data you've entered to answer specific financial questions about your business, such as whether you're making a profit and, if so, how much.

Generally speaking, the more sales you make, the more often you should enter your receipts. A busy retail operation that does hundreds of sales every day should post daily, while smaller, slower businesses with just a few large transactions per month would probably be fine posting weekly or even monthly. With a high sales volume, it's particularly important to see what's happening every day and not to fall behind with the paperwork. For this reason, most busy, high-volume businesses will have a modern cash register that's programmed to automatically "dump" the day's information into the bookkeeping software at the end of each day.

When entering information into your bookkeeping software, remember the adage "garbage in, garbage out." If the information you enter isn't accurate or the software isn't set up correctly in the first place, you won't be able to generate the meaningful financial reports that are so crucial to any business. Take the time early on to learn how your software works, configure it correctly, and enter data carefully to minimize errors.

Let's take a look at some of the details involved in setting up your bookkeeping

software and entering transactions.
Remember, once the transactions are
entered, accounting software makes
preparing monthly and yearly financial
reports incredibly easy.

TIP

**Learn the concepts behind the
numbers.** Even though bookkeeping software
allows you to generate sophisticated financial
reports with a few mouse clicks, you should still
take the time to understand how the numbers
fit together and what they mean. The more you
know about your numbers and the relationships
between various figures, the better able you'll
be to make positive and profitable business
decisions.

Creating Accounts

When setting up your bookkeeping
software, one of the first things to do is
set up accounts to mirror the business
accounts you have in real life: a checking
account and a credit card account, for
instance. It's critical to post transactions
to the appropriate accounts, so that you
can reconcile your bookkeeping records
against the bank or credit card statements.
Reconciling each month is an important
way to make sure your records are complete
and accurate; we'll describe the reconciling
process in a bit more detail below.

TIP

**Create a "catch-all" account for
business expenses paid for with personal
accounts.** Inevitably, business owners occasionally
spend money from their personal accounts (either
using cash or a debit or credit card) on business
expenses. While you should strive to avoid this,
it just happens from time to time—for example,
you bought some business books among a bunch
of personal books paid for with your personal
debit card; or you bought a work uniform along
with personal clothes and paid for it all with your
personal checking account. One good way to
account for these stragglers is to create a "general
register" account in your bookkeeping software
as a catch-all account that will include any
transactions (usually expenditures, not income)
that for whatever reason weren't made from an
official business checking or credit account.

Depending on your circumstances
and how your accountant or bookkeeper
advises you, there are other accounts you
can create to track your business's finances.
Common examples include separate
accounts for receivables (amounts owed to
you) and payables (amounts you owe to
others), or accounts to track depreciable
assets, such as computers or vehicles.
Again, a bookkeeper can be quite useful
in helping you figure out which accounts
to set up.

Creating Income and Expense Categories

Besides creating accounts, an important part of setting up your bookkeeping software is creating categories for income and expenses. As mentioned above, different types of income and expenses are treated differently for tax purposes, so it's essential that they are tracked separately in your bookkeeping system. As we discuss in more detail in Chapter 9, some expenditures can be deducted right away in full, others may be deducted only over several years (referred to as "depreciating expenses"), while other costs may not be deductible at all.

Income categories will typically include "taxable sales," "sales tax," and "nontaxable sales" categories and possibly others—say, "travel reimbursement," "loan," or "interest income." Businesses typically have many different categories for expenses such as rent, utilities, computer equipment, employee wages, legal fees, postage, or travel, to name a few.

 **RESOURCE**

The IRS has oceans of rules. For more information on different types of business expenses and their deductibility, read *Deduct It! Lower Your Small Business Taxes*, by Stephen Fishman (Nolo). Reading the rules issued by the IRS isn't a bad idea, either. IRS Publication 334, *Tax Guide for Small Business*, is a good place to start. It's available at www.irs.gov.

Typical Expense Categories

As a general reference, here's a list of common expense categories:
- advertising
- automobile
- bank charges
- cleaning services
- copying
- delivery/freight/shipping
- dues and fees
- education (classes, workshops, and so on)
- employee wages
- equipment/furniture/computers
- equipment rental
- insurance
- interest on business debt
- legal and professional fees
- meals (business related)
- membership
- office expenses/supplies
- office rent
- online services
- postage
- publications (books, magazines, and so on)
- software
- tax preparation fees
- taxes
- telephone
- travel, and
- utilities (gas and electric).

Besides categorizing income and expenses to account for different tax treatment, there's another essential reason to categorize expenses: Careful, strategic categorization will allow you to generate financial reports that reveal which aspects of your business contribute the most (or least) to your bottom line, which in turn will allow you to make adjustments to maximize profits. We'll discuss the details of financial reports in the next section, but the point here is that the categorization is essential. Without tracking income and expenses by category, you won't be able to generate meaningful financial reports later on.

EXAMPLE: Shane is launching a photography studio that will focus on weddings, baby portraits, and professional head shots. When setting up the bookkeeping system (with the help of a trusted bookkeeper), Shane makes sure to include separate categories for income from these three separate services. This way, he will be able to generate reports showing which services bring in the most gross income. In addition, Shane makes sure to categorize expenses so that he will be able to generate reports showing the expenses associated with each of the services, as well as reports comparing income to expenses for each service.

After six months in business, the financial reports show that the weddings consistently generate the most gross income. The profitability picture is different, however. When expenses associated with each service are factored in, Shane sees that baby portraits are actually the most profitable service, because there are much lower costs associated with them than with the weddings. Shane decides to put some effort into lowering the costs associated with weddings in order to make them more profitable. If Shane had not created separate income and expense categories for weddings, baby portraits,

and professional head shots, the financial records would not have revealed the revenue and profit trends, and Shane would have missed out on the opportunity to tweak his marketing and pricing in order to boost profits.

When deciding what categories to create and track, keep in mind the distinction between fixed costs and variable costs. Variable costs, you may remember from Chapter 4, are tied to your products or services, while fixed costs (overhead) more or less stay the same regardless of your production and sales volume. Without keeping careful track of variable costs, you won't know how profitable your individual products or services are, or whether your pricing is too high, too low, or just right. Fixed costs are also crucial to track, in large part because they can be such a drain when business is slow.

There's something of an art to defining the categories that are relevant for your business. You want them to be tightly defined—but not so narrow that you end up with dozens of tiny groups. For example, a handyman would likely use categories such as lumber, paint/sealants, hardware, and equipment rentals, but wouldn't go so far as to have a separate category for nails versus screws. A hair stylist might use categories like booth rental, cutting tools, and hair products; depending on her circumstances, she might want to further subcategorize the hair products into shampoos, conditioners, and styling products. An experienced bookkeeper familiar with your field can be extremely helpful in setting up your categories and subcategories in a way that will help you generate the most meaningful reports for your business.

As for actually setting up the categories in your bookkeeping software, all programs make this really easy. Generally speaking, you'll create the categories when you set up the software; later, when you enter your transactions, you'll choose from the list of categories you've created. Undoubtedly, over time you'll refine your bookkeeping system and your categories, and all bookkeeping software allows you to add, edit, and delete your categories whenever you want.

Entering Transactions

When it comes time to enter the information from your receipts (in other words, entering your transactions), you'll find that most bookkeeping software has an interface similar to a checkbook: Each transaction, whether an income or expense, is entered into a "register" where you'll include information including date, check number, payee, description, amount, category(ies), and any notes. With income transactions, remember to show any sales tax amounts separately from the total income. Bookkeeping software generally allows you to do this by "splitting" a transaction, showing

a pretax subtotal separate from the sales tax amount.

 TIP

Some states require nontaxable sales to be broken down into certain categories, such as wholesale sales, services, sales to out-of-state customers, or freight charges. Check with your state sales tax agency to find out which, if any, nontaxable subcategories you must use in your record keeping. As mentioned above, creating custom categories and subcategories in your bookkeeping software is incredibly easy.

When you have entered a receipt, mark the receipt as entered. Use whatever system works for you; you could hand-write an "E" on the receipt, use a stamp that says "Posted" or something similar. Then file the receipt away, ideally in a well-organized file system that will allow you easily to find a receipt should any questions arise later.

Finally, keep your bookkeeping records safe and regularly back them up. They will be essential to create financial reports revealing your business's financial health (explained in "Generating Financial Reports," below), and to complete your local, state, and federal tax returns. Losing your financial records can be an expensive disaster—dealing with an IRS audit without them is just one nightmare scenario—so be sure to treat them as the important business documents that they are.

TIP
Treat credit card purchases like cash. Even though the cash method of accounting records expenditures when they are paid, not when incurred, you should record purchases made with a credit card as if they were paid with cash. For whatever reason, the IRS considers credit card purchases paid on the date of purchase, not when payment is made on the credit card.

Step 3: Generating Financial Reports

Financial reports pull together various financial data to answer specific questions about your business's financial situation. For example, a profit and loss report compares monthly income to monthly expenses to show whether your business is making enough sales of products or services to cover costs each month. A cash flow projection shows similar information, but includes other sources of income such as capital contributions from owners or loans (that is, not just revenues from sales), and organizes the information slightly differently to show you whether the timing of your income is adequate to pay your bills on time.

The financial reports discussed in this section are easily generated from your bookkeeping software—assuming that you've entered data consistently and correctly. When income and expenses have been entered and categorized accurately, you'll be ready to create the following reports showing you the financial health (or illness) of your business.

Profit and Loss Statement

If the typical owners of a small business start-up got a nickel for every time they asked themselves, "Will my business make a profit?" they'd probably be rich enough to retire before the doors were even open. A profit and loss statement (also called a P & L, or an income statement) is designed to answer this very question. Chapter 4 discussed creating a profit and loss forecast with projected numbers. This section explains how to do a P & L after you've opened your doors and have actual numbers to work with.

A P & L shows you pretty much what the name implies: how much profit or loss your business is making in a given period of time. You'll typically generate a profit and loss statement each month, as well as quarterly and annual summaries. We'll use a monthly period when describing the process of creating a P & L, below.

In the most basic terms, a P & L is made by totaling your monthly revenues and then subtracting your monthly expenses from that total. If you use accounting software, it will generate a P & L at the click of a button based on the income and expense data you've already entered. For each month, you'll be able to see whether your revenues are higher or lower than your expenses and by how much. The monthly results are totaled to obtain your annual profit or loss.

An important detail involved in profit/loss calculations is that fixed costs need to be considered separately from variable costs. Fixed costs (also called overhead) are the costs associated with running your business in general, not with individual products or services themselves. Examples include rent, utilities, and insurance. Variable costs (also sometimes called costs of goods sold, or COGS) are the expenses that are directly tied to the product or service that you're selling. Examples include the costs of materials, packaging, and labor costs directly tied to producing the product or service (but note that labor costs can be tricky; see Tip below).

For example, say your business produces and sells greeting cards. Your variable costs would include the costs of the paper, printing costs, costs for packaging and labels, and the labor cost for the workers that package and distribute them. As the name implies, these costs will vary depending on the amount and type of product you make and sell or service you perform. For example, if you produce more or less of a particular greeting card or if you emboss or use a heavier grade of card stock, your variable expenses will be affected.

 TIP

Labor costs: sometimes variable, sometimes fixed. If you ask a group of accountants whether the labor costs associated with making a product are fixed or variable, you're likely to get conflicting answers. Some argue that, as long as the workers will get paid regardless of whether they're working on that product, their salaries should be considered fixed, like rent or utilities. Others say that, to have accurate financial records, you need to reflect the cost of the labor that goes into a product. You or your accountant can decide how your business will categorize labor costs for making a product. Labor costs for providing services, on the other hand, are almost always treated as variable costs.

But other costs—your fixed costs—will not go up or down depending on the products you make or the services you perform. These costs, such as your rent, office utility bills, and insurance for your company vehicles, will be more or less the same, regardless of the amount or type of greeting cards you make. This is exactly why age-old business wisdom says to keep your overhead costs as low as you can. In times of slow sales, you want to be saddled with as few fixed costs as possible.

Now that you know the distinction between variable and fixed costs, you need to understand how they're each subtracted from your revenue on a typical profit and loss statement.

1. A profit and loss statement starts with your total sales revenues, then subtracts your variable costs. The result is called your *gross profit*—how much money you've earned from sales of your products or services over and above their cost to you.

2. Next you subtract your fixed costs from your gross profit. Any money you're left with is usually called *net profit*, but is sometimes called net income or pretax profit. Other than the various taxes you'll need to pay on this income, this is your (and any other business owners') money.

To sum up, the formula used in a profit and loss statement is basically as follows:

	Sales revenue
−	Variable costs (costs of sale)
=	Gross profit (gross margin)
−	Fixed costs
=	Net profit

A typical P & L is shown below.

A P & L not only will tell you whether you're making or losing money, but also will help you identify which aspects of your business need adjusting in order to boost profits. Often, a profitability

20xx Profit/Loss Statement								
	Jan	**Feb**	**Mar**	**April**	**May**		**Dec**	**Year Total**
Sales Revenues	$1,900	$1,950	$2,000	$1,850	$2,000		$2,100	$23,550
Variable Costs	(300)	(310)	(350)	(300)	(325)		(350)	(3,840)
Gross Profit	1,600	1,640	1,650	1,550	1,675		1,750	19,710
Fixed Expenses								
Rent	(700)	(700)	(700)	(700)	(700)		(700)	(8,400)
Supplies	(150)	(100)	(75)	(90)	(125)		(100)	(1,220)
Utilities	(200)	(200)	(200)	(200)	(200)		(200)	(2,400)
Advertising	(150)	(150)	(150)	(150)	(150)		(150)	(1,800)
Misc.	(75)	(80)	(65)	(70)	(75)		(85)	(830)
Total Fixed Expenses	(1,275)	(1,230)	(1,190)	(1,210)	(1,250)		(1,235)	(14,650)
Net Income (Loss)	$325	$410	$460	$340	$425		$515	$5,060

problem can be found in your expenses. Being able to see the totals of each of your various expense categories over the course of several months, all on one report, can help you pinpoint areas in which you're spending too much money (and help give you the courage to do something about it). And, of course, accurately tracking income totals month by month will help you quickly spot a downturn in revenue and prompt you to take action to boost sales.

Cash Flow Projection

Chapter 4 discussed cash flow projections as a way to determine whether your business will be able to pay its bills once it gets started. A cash flow projection is also a crucial tool to use in your ongoing business, as it tells you whether you'll have enough cash available at any given time to pay your operating costs. Having lots of customers and thriving sales isn't enough, especially if you sell on credit. If your customers pay you in 90 days, but you must pay your expenses in 30 days or even immediately, you may face a situation where, even though your financial statement says you are making a profit, you can't pay your staff, rent, utilities, insurance, delivery services, or other key bills. If you see the cash crunch well in advance, you'll usually be able to juggle expenses or take other measures, such as taking out a loan or a line of credit to get through the squeeze. But if the cash

crisis sneaks up on you without warning, you may not have enough time to react, possibly even forcing you to close up shop.

Helping you understand why you may not be able to pay your bills despite being profitable—and how to take steps to avoid this—is the role of a cash flow projection. A cash flow projection focuses on the actual cash payments made to and by your business. These payments are called cash-ins and cash-outs (or inflows and outflows) to differentiate them from sales and expenses, which may not be paid right away. Estimating your cash-ins and cash-outs for upcoming months can help you predict when you might run short, allowing you to take action early, such as by tightening up on your credit terms, raising more capital, getting a loan or line of credit, or putting more effort into collecting accounts receivable.

Your cash flow projection will use most of the same numbers as your profit and loss statement, along with a few new ones. The big difference is that your cash flow projection will include all of your sources of income—not just sales income—and only income that's paid in cash (not credit). In other words, while your profit and loss statement is concerned with how much revenue your business is earning through sales of its products or services, your cash flow projection is designed to show you how much cash you will have on hand from all sources, including paid sales, loans, interest from investments, transfers from your personal accounts, lottery winnings, whatever. That's because when it comes to paying bills, the bottom line is whether you have enough money, period. Similarly, your cash flow projection will include all money you pay out of the business, whether for supplies, taxes (including any estimated taxes you owe; see Chapter 9), loan repayments, or any other expenditure.

The basic formula for cash flow analysis is:

	Cash in bank at beginning of month
+	Cash receipts for the month
−	Cash disbursements for the month
=	Cash in bank at end of month

In a cash flow projection, each month starts with the amount of money you have in the bank. (This will generally be the same amount that's left over from the previous month.) Next, you'll add any cash that came in during the month in all relevant categories, such as sales income, loans, interest earned, and any personal money you put into the business—your total cash-ins for the month. Next, subtract the money you spent during the month: your cash-outs. The result is the cash left at the end of the month. Enter that figure into the beginning of the next month's column, and do the same process for the next month. If you use accounting software, a cash flow spreadsheet can be generated automatically once you've entered figures for income and expenses.

Now that you see the basic formula behind cash flow analysis, you need to understand that the real power of this tool is not in tracking actual cash-ins and cash-outs, but in predicting future cash flows. Periodically, say once a month or every couple of months, you should use your actual figures to help make estimates for upcoming months and complete a cash flow projection for the future, generally up to one year. Hopefully, you'll see that you will have enough cash to cover your expenses each month. If not, don't panic. First, pat yourself on the back for doing a cash flow analysis and figuring out ahead of time that you won't be able to cover all your expenses. Then come up with a plan—either put off some expenses that can wait; get more money (perhaps through collecting accounts receivable or getting a short-term loan or line of credit); or sell, sell, sell more product, or services.

Especially when you're in the early stages of a business and don't have much of a business history, predicting cash-ins and cash-outs for future months isn't easy (though cash-outs are often easier to predict than cash-ins, because you have more control over them and many costs recur each month). You'll need to make estimates of how much income will come in and what expenses must be covered—a task that may seem only slightly easier than reading tea leaves.

Cash Flow Projection, Completed April, 20xx

	January	February	Mar	April	May
Cash at Beginning of Month	$2,000	$1,250	$600	$700	$350
Cash-Ins Sales Paid	15,000	14,750	15,500	14,750	15,500
Loans and Transfers	0	0	0	0	0
Total Cash-Ins	15,000	14,750	15,500	14,750	15,500
Cash-Outs Variable Costs	3,000	3,100	3,500	3,000	3,250
Rent	7,000	7,000	7,000	7,000	7,000
Supplies	1,500	1,000	750	900	1,250
Utilities	2,000	2,000	2,000	2,000	2,000
Loan Payments	1,500	1,500	1,500	1,500	1,500
Misc.	750	800	650	700	750
Total Cash-Outs	15,750	15,400	15,400	15,100	15,750
Cash at End of Month	$1,250	$600	$700	$350	$100

The key is to do your best—with an emphasis on "do." Accept the fact that your estimates won't be 100% accurate, but make them anyway. As the months tick by and the flow of cash into and out from your business settles into daily, weekly, and monthly patterns, making estimates will inevitably become easier, and you'll find them increasingly more accurate.

An example of a cash flow projection you can do on a simple spreadsheet is shown above.

As you can see, arranging income and expense information into a cash flow projection reveals a lot about the financial workings of a business. For example, the sample cash flow forecast shows that cash is tight each and every month (look at the "Cash at End of Month" row), so the business owner might consider ways to cut costs or to tighten credit terms.

Cash Flow Projection, Completed April, 20xx (continued)

June	July	August	September	October	November	December
$100	($300)	$150	$0	$0	($550)	$300
15,000	16,100	16,250	15,500	15,250	16,750	16,900
0	0	0	0	0	0	0
15,000	16,100	16,250	15,500	15,250	16,750	16,900
3,150	3,450	3,500	3,250	3,300	3,400	3,550
7,000	7,000	7,000	7,000	7,000	7,000	7,000
900	1,100	850	1,000	1,100	950	900
2,000	2,000	2,000	2,000	2,000	2,000	2,000
1,500	1,500	1,500	1,500	1,500	1,500	1,500
850	600	1,550	750	900	1,050	850
15,400	15,650	16,400	15,500	15,800	15,900	15,800
($300)	$150	$0	$0	($550)	$300	$1,400

TIP

Compare your projection to reality. Each month, replace your projections with actual results from your accounting system. It's a great way to see how good a job of projecting you're doing.

Of more pressing importance is the projected cash shortfall starting in June. Knowing a few months in advance that a shortage is likely will help a business owner figure out what to do while there's still time to take action. The owner could contribute some personal money to the business (note that the cash flow didn't include any loans or personal transfers to the business) or could try to cut some nonessential expenses, at least until later in the year when there will be a bit (but only a small bit) more cash available.

Who Needs to Do a Cash Flow Analysis?

David Rothenberg, a CPA, gives the following advice: "If your business is wildly profitable, you have little or no debt, you are not planning on expanding your business anytime soon, and you don't grant your customers a long time to pay, you probably don't need to do a cash flow analysis—you already know you'll have plenty of cash to meet your needs. But if this doesn't sound like your business, then you probably will benefit from keeping a close eye on your cash flow. Remember, the cash flow statement isn't for the IRS, and it isn't for the bank; it's for you! That's right, YOU! You're the one who won't sleep at night if your bank account is empty. So what are you waiting for? Get out there and start projecting!"

Balance Sheet

A balance sheet is a financial report showing the net worth of your business at a particular point in time. Businesses typically generate balance sheets monthly, quarterly, and annually. In a nutshell, a balance sheet shows a complete picture of a business's financial situation by summarizing its assets, liabilities, and owner equity (sometimes called net worth) in the business. The general formula is:

$$\text{Assets} - \text{Liabilities} = \text{Equity}$$

Or, put another way:

$$\text{Assets} = \text{Liabilities} + \text{Equity}$$

As you'll see in the following example, the structure of a balance sheet reflects this second formulation. But they both mean the same thing, as described below.

The value of a balance sheet is that it provides a view into the business's financial position. It will reveal whether a business is, on one hand, overleveraged with too much debt, or perhaps on the other hand, in a good position for expansion. In short, it offers a snapshot of the financial health of a company.

While balance sheets aren't quite as intuitive to read for the uninitiated, the elements that are included and how they relate to each other aren't that complicated. As with the other financial reports described in this section, a balance sheet can easily be generated from your bookkeeping software, assuming all transactions have been entered and categorized correctly. But it's worth going through each element of a balance sheet so that you truly understand what it means and how to decipher one, rather than just relying on your software to spit one out for you without grasping the full meaning of the information it summarizes.

As mentioned above, a balance sheet reflects a business's assets, liabilities, and equity. In other words, when you subtract a business's liabilities from its assets, the result is the net equity the business owner(s) have in the business. This report is called a balance sheet because it reflects the balance between assets, on one side of the equation, and liabilities plus equity on the other side. When the data in your bookkeeping software are accurate, the assets will equal (or "balance") liabilities plus equity.

Let's look at each of these elements in a bit more detail.

Assets include anything of monetary value that your business owns. The standard balance sheet format lists assets in decreasing order of liquidity—in other words, how easy it is to convert the asset to cash. The following categories are typically used to reflect this breakdown:

- **Current assets** are those that can be converted to cash within one year. These include cash (of course), checking accounts, money market accounts, accounts receivable, and inventory.
- **Noncurrent assets** (sometimes called capital, long-term, or fixed assets) are defined as things with a useful business life of more than one year. These include land, buildings, vehicles, business equipment, and furniture. With the exception of land, tangible noncurrent assets depreciate, which means they lose

value each year; this is reflected as a "depreciation expense" in the balance sheet. If all assets are entered correctly into your bookkeeping software, including the type of asset and when it was purchased, the software should automatically calculate this overall depreciation figure for you. Other assets that would be considered noncurrent include intellectual property, such as patents, trade secrets, copyrights, trademarks, customer lists or even company goodwill. Valuing these intangibles can be difficult, and they are typically heavily discounted on a balance sheet if included at all.

Liabilities are things that your business owes to others. Like assets, liabilities are typically divided into current and noncurrent:

- **Current liabilities** include debts your company owes within the next year. Examples include accounts payable, payroll owed to employees but not yet paid, accrued but unpaid taxes, loans that need to be repaid within the year, and credit card debt.
- **Noncurrent liabilities** include debts payable over a term longer than one year. This includes mortgages or other debts due more than one year from the date the balance sheet is prepared.

Balance Sheet				
	Current 4/1/20xx	Previous Year 4/1/20xx	$ Change	% Change
Assets				
Current Assets				
Cash in bank	$15,700	$14,050	$1,650	11.74%
Accounts receivable	2,350	1,800	550	30.56%
Inventory	5,500	3,900	1,600	41.03%
Other current assets	0	0	0	0.00%
Total Current Assets	$23,550	$19,750	$3,800	19.24%
Fixed Assets				
Machinery & equipment	$13,500	$11,075	$2,425	21.90%
Furniture & fixtures	2,500	2,000	500	25.00%
Land & buildings	0	0	0	0.00%
Other fixed assets	0	0	0	0.00%
(Accumulated depreciation on all fixed assets)	(7,350)	(7,155)	(195)	2.73%
Total Fixed Assets (net of depreciation)	$8,650	$5,920	$2,730	46.11%
Other Assets				
Intangibles	$0	$0	$0	0.00%
Goodwill	$0	$0	$0	0.00%
Other	$0	$0	$0	0.00%
Total Other Assets	$0	$0	$0	0.00%
Total Assets	$32,200	$25,670	$6,530	25.44%
Liabilities and Equity				
Current Liabilities				
Accounts payable	$4,250	$2,985	$1,265	42.38%
Payroll unpaid	$0	$0	$0	0.00%
Taxes payable	1,700	985	715	72.59%
Short-term debt (due within 12 months)	$0	$0	$0	0.00%
Credit card debt	$0	$0	$0	0.00%
Other current liabilities	$0	$0	$0	0.00%
Total Current Liabilities	$5,950	$3,970	$1,980	49.87%

Balance Sheet (continued)				
	Current 4/1/20xx	Previous Year 4/1/20xx	$ Change	% Change
Long-Term Debt				
Bank loans payable	$0	$0	$0	0.00%
Other long-term debt	$0	$0	$0	0.00%
Total Long-Term Debt	$0	$0	$0	0.00%
Total Liabilities	$5,950	$3,970	$1,980	49.87%
Owners' Equity				
Invested capital	$15,000	$15,000	$0	0.00%
Retained earnings	11,250	6,700	4,550	67.91%
Total Owners' Equity	$26,250	$21,700	$4,550	20.97%
Total Liabilities & Equity	$32,200	$25,670	$6,530	25.44%

Equity is what's left over when you subtract liabilities from assets. This is the net worth of the business, which is essentially the amount that would be paid out to the owner(s) if the business liquidated. It includes:

- Any **capital contributions** to business, including money contributed by the owners and any stock sold to the public.
- Any **retained earnings**, which is the total of all annual profits since the beginning of the business (including the current year) that haven't been paid out to the owner(s) in draws or dividends.

Below is an example of how a balance sheet typically presents this information. A copy is included on the Nolo website; see Appendix B for the link.

Using Technology to Manage Money, Inventory, and Projects

As mentioned throughout this chapter, bookkeeping and accounting software makes the job of managing your business's finances easier and enables you to do much more sophisticated reports than you'd normally be able to do manually.

In addition to bookkeeping software, other software and hardware products help business owners manage the money and operations of a business. These include spreadsheets, point of sales (POS) systems, project management software, appointment scheduling software, and customer relationship management (CRM) software.

Bear in mind that many business management applications are essentially databases that have already been customized for a specific purpose. They may be called "off-the-shelf" solutions, to differentiate them from more general database applications that need to be customized for your needs. For example, you could purchase a database program, such as *FileMaker Pro* or Microsoft *Access*, and customize it (likely with the help of a database specialist) to manage your consulting projects, including tracking hours, recording expenses, and generating client invoices. Or, you could purchase an off-the-shelf project management application such as *Billings Pro* or *Asana* that have these functions preprogrammed. (Note that *Asana* is a "cloud" application. We discuss cloud apps in the sidebar below.)

Also note that the lines between different types of business management software are becoming blurry. The features, functions, and add-on capabilities of business management applications change frequently as software companies try to offer more and "be everything" to attract more customers. For example, project management applications may add CRM features or introduce companion CRM software; likewise, CRM software may add project management tasks to its feature set. *QuickBooks* is a perfect example of this trend: It offers an ever-growing list of functions and add-ons to handle everything from project management to CRM and inventory control, aiming to be a one-stop, turnkey solution for virtually any business. Other software companies are trying to do the same thing, but *QuickBooks* is way ahead of the game.

Let's take a closer look at bookkeeping software; then we'll review the other applications and databases that you might consider using to manage your business.

Bookkeeping Software

As discussed throughout this chapter, bookkeeping software is so powerful because it automates the process of generating financial reports, such as cash flow projections and balance sheets. If you take care to enter and categorize your income and expense records regularly, you can easily crunch that data and answer important questions about your business, such as how much profit (or loss) you're making, how much you're spending on certain expenses, or how much money your customers owe you.

Cloud Apps Can Streamline Your Systems

While many of the technology products discussed in this section are huge productivity assets for small businesses, they also can create headaches—for example, you'll need to keep your software up to date and you may face the nightmare of "technology difficulties" when things go wrong.

Enter cloud applications which you use online for monthly fees, instead of installing software on your own computer. With cloud apps, you'll typically use a browser to log into your account and access your data. Most cloud apps allow you to export data which you can then store on your own computers or hard drives. There are cloud apps—sometimes called "hosted solutions"—for bookkeeping, project management, and many more business needs.

One of the most compelling benefits of using cloud apps is that you won't need to deal with installation or updates on your company computers or network. This can be a serious and stressful time drain for small companies, which is one reason cloud apps are so popular.

Another big plus is that you can access your data anywhere you have Internet access. Related to this, remote teams can easily collaborate which each other, even if they're on opposite sides of the globe. If you've ever dealt with the headaches of emailing files among multiple team members, you'll appreciate the value of real-time editing of documents in the cloud. Many apps are geared for mobile devices, allowing your team to keep projects moving forward even if they're on the go.

QuickBooks is by far the most popular bookkeeping software; it offers different products for different sizes and types of businesses, including an online version that stores all your information on its servers. Another option for businesses at the small end of the spectrum is *Quicken*, which focuses more on personal finances but offers a *Home & Business* version with plenty of features for small operators.

When choosing bookkeeping software, pick a product that offers the features you need, keeping in mind what information you need to track and what reports you need to generate. For instance, if you need to manage multiple categories of inventory, and regularly must deal with returns from retailers, make sure the software and the version you choose makes it easy to enter and categorize inventory, and to generate reports such as a yearly summary of returns by category or by a particular retailer. *QuickBooks* offers dozens of add-on products, including many industry-specific applications to help you manage certain kinds of businesses, such as restaurants, retail, or manufacturing.

Finally, make sure your bookkeeper and accountant can work with whatever software you choose. Virtually all financial management professionals work with the various *QuickBooks* products.

Spreadsheet Software

A spreadsheet is a document that allows you to store information in rows and columns, making it easy to sort the information in different ways. For example, a spreadsheet containing information about your clients could have column headers of "First Name," "Last Name," "Business Name," "Business Address," "Business Phone Number," and so on, with each row containing that information about one of your clients. If you had 50 clients, you'd have 50 rows of data, and you'd be able to sort the list by first name, last name, business name, or any other of the columns.

Beyond sorting, the real power of spreadsheets is in their ability to do mathematical formulas. This makes them particularly useful for doing budgets, project estimates, and projections, in which you'd use estimates instead of actual financial data. (To track actual data you'll probably use bookkeeping software, as described above.)

For example, you could use a spreadsheet to cost out a landscaping project, entering individual expenses in separate lines: Dirt; Gravel; Weed barrier; Plants; and so on. You could define one cell to display the sum total of all the individual expenses, so when you tweak individual line items the total will be automatically updated. Using a spreadsheet in this way makes the budgeting process much easier and faster than if you had to manually add together the expenses each time you made a change.

In essence, a spreadsheet is like a mini-database, which is software specifically for managing lots of pieces of information. (Databases are discussed separately below.) Like databases, spreadsheets allow you to do mathematical formulas and functions, as well as sorting and filtering of text data.

To do sophisticated or complex formulas, sorting, or filtering, you'll probably want to go with a true database that will typically have more robust reporting functions already built in and require much less customization. For example, you could easily customize a client and project database to create a report showing what clients were signed in a specific year, with a list of projects you completed for each of those clients, sorted by the total amount of project fees. You could track similar information with a spreadsheet and create a similar report, but it would typically take considerably more work to do so. In addition, if you have a lot of data, using a database is preferable to scrolling through hundreds of lines of a spreadsheet.

If you don't use databases for whatever reason—perhaps your business needs are simple, or you can't afford to buy and customize a database at the moment—

Integrating Applications and Databases With Bookkeeping Software

If a feature isn't built in to your bookkeeping software, and there's not an add-on product that achieves what you need, it's possible that your business will need an external application or database to manage that information. For example, if you need to carefully track the hours and expenses of your consulting projects, you may want to use project management software (discussed below) in addition to your bookkeeping software. I discuss different types of management applications below.

With many types of business applications and databases, it makes sense to integrate them with your bookkeeping software so that the programs can share information, rather than having to enter information into both systems. For example, if your project management software is integrated with your bookkeeping software, when you create a client invoice within the project management software and mark it "paid," it will automatically enter a payment into your bookkeeping system.

This saves time and avoids the potential for errors and inconsistencies when entering the same data into two different systems.

When considering whether you need to integrate various databases with your bookkeeping system, you'll simply need to weigh the improved and streamlined operations that integration offers, versus the cost. Integrating applications and databases with bookkeeping software typically requires the help of an experienced consultant and may be relatively expensive, often in the thousands or tens of thousands of dollars. For larger or growing businesses, the benefits of streamlining your operations may be well worth this expense.

If you want to integrate multiple applications, you'll need to make sure they're all technically compatible. The vast majority of external applications and databases have *QuickBooks* compatibility.

---

spreadsheets are a great alternative. They're cheap, easy to use, and quite powerful for a wide variety of applications. Besides budgeting and job-costing, they can be great for tracking project hours or maintaining client or vendor lists.

The most common spreadsheet software is Microsoft *Excel*, which you may already own as part of a Microsoft *Office* package. Another very cool option these days is

to use Google spreadsheets, which are Web-based and allow multiple users. For example, a small sales team could use a Google spreadsheet to manage its list of prospects. Whenever a sales person contacted a prospect, she could enter the encounter information into the Google spreadsheet, which would automatically be visible to all other members of the team (who could also edit the spreadsheet).

Point of Sales (POS) Systems

Generally speaking, a point of sales (POS) system is a system for tracking and managing retail sales and inventory. While a handwritten receipt book could in theory be called a POS system, what is usually meant by this term is a computerized cash register system that handles each sales transaction as it is made; calculates the sales total and any sales tax; tracks inventory by SKU (stock-keeping unit) and automatically updates inventory databases; and generates detailed sales and inventory reports.

POS systems vary widely in what hardware and software they use; hardware often includes a computer and terminal or an electronic cash register, a bar code scanner, and a credit card swiping machine. The software varies in the complexity of the information it can track and report. You'll typically integrate the POS software with your bookkeeping software so that sales are automatically recorded into your books.

While *QuickBooks* and other bookkeeping software offer some inventory management functions, POS systems generally allow for more advanced management and reporting. More complex POS systems can manage inventory across multiple stores. Many POS systems are tailored for specific industries such as hair salons, medical offices, grocery stores, or restaurants.

To find the right POS system for your operation, start with some online research. There is no shortage of discussions online among business owners sharing their good and bad experiences with various POS systems. Offline, ask other business owners for their experiences.

> **TIP**
>
> **Don't be shy about asking other businesses what technologies they use.** While you might find it difficult or awkward to approach other businesses who may be your competitors, you'd be surprised how easy it is to stop into a store similar to yours and strike up a conversation with the clerk or business owner (whoever is there) about your similar businesses. A direct question, "What kind of POS system do you guys use?" is likely to get a direct response, and possibly a conversation about their experiences. This information can be incredibly valuable. Of course this approach may not be advisable if competition is fierce between you and another business. Use your judgment.

Project Management Platforms

Service firms, consultants, and freelancers can often benefit from using project management software. Platforms such as *Asana*, *Trello*, *Basecamp*, and *Slack* help with a variety of details involved in managing projects; depending on the platform, this can include coordinating project team members, sharing files, sharing calendars/schedules, tracking billable hours, managing different billable rates, tracking project expenses, and invoicing clients. Freelancers often find the time-tracking and invoicing features particularly useful in preparing professional-looking invoices automatically, based on hours and billable rates entered into the system.

Each project management application may have a particular focus or strength in certain features and be less strong in others. Choose an application that handles the aspects of projects that will be important to you. As mentioned above, find out from other business owners (either directly or by reading comments online) what they like and don't like about the software. Features may include:

- scheduling, including shared calendars
- budgeting and estimating projects and components
- time tracking
- billing and invoicing
- establishing different rates for different types of work
- file sharing and document distribution, and
- messaging and chat.

Project management software may be integrated with your bookkeeping software

if the two applications are compatible. If you plan to integrate these applications, make sure to confirm compatibility before purchasing.

Most project management software is pretty affordable. How you pay will depend on whether you purchase and install software, or use an online version. Overall, yearly costs start at around $100 for small businesses with just one user. Larger businesses and multiple users might end up paying a few thousand dollars a year.

Appointment Scheduling Software

Scheduling is a huge time sink for many of us, and it only becomes more of a burden the busier you get with a small business. If earning income from client meetings is a part of your business model, emailing back and forth with potential clients to find a time that works can be a huge drain on your productivity. Similarly, scheduling meetings with partners, collaborators or other business associates can eat up a lot of time and emails.

Enter appointment scheduling software. Apps like *Acuity Scheduling*, *Calendly*, or *TimeTrade* allow those who want to meet with you to book with you—and pay, if applicable—online. You set available times in the system, and the calendar will be accessible online to people you choose; typically you can provide your contacts a scheduling link, or embed your calendar at a "Scheduling" page at your website. When appointments are booked you'll get an email notification. Brilliant!

Consultants, lawyers, massage therapists, salon stylists, and anyone else who relies on client bookings should consider using one of these online appointment scheduling apps. Rates range from $10 a month to $50 per month or more for multiple users, and will be well worth the operational efficiency if you book even a few clients per month.

Customer Relationship Management (CRM) Software

Customer relationship management, or CRM, software helps a business manage potential and existing customers with the general goals of finding and retaining customers and reducing marketing costs. It started out as a tool to help salespeople —often a sales department—manage prospects, accounts, and territories, including tracking what types of outreach and communications had been made to individual contacts. Today, CRM has grown into a more comprehensive strategy for managing customer service and marketing efforts.

CRM software is essentially a database that contains key information about current and prospective customers. From a sales point of view, the CRM application should identify the best prospects and provide key information about their needs in order to help the sales team turn them into paying customers. The CRM database can also support customer service operations by including all information that may help a representative effectively assist the customer, such as what products or services were purchased, details of previous service calls, warranty expiration dates, and login information for the customer's online accounts, for example. Data in a CRM system can also be helpful to marketing departments in identifying trends and evaluating the popularity of the company's products and services. This in turn helps the marketing team develop marketing campaigns and messages.

As with other types of business management software, CRM software can be integrated with your bookkeeping application, depending on compatibility. If integration will be important for your business, make sure your choices are compatible before purchasing.

A popular CRM application is *SalesForce*, which can be integrated with *QuickBooks*. Other reputable products include *SAP CRM* and *SugarCRM*. Most of these applications have different versions, some installed and some cloud hosted, with a wide variation in cost. Very generally speaking, a basic version for a small or one-person company might cost a few hundred dollars per year; a large company might spend tens of thousands of dollars a year for robust data functions and multiple users.

Customized Databases

Boil them down, and much of the technology we've been talking about in the sections above are essentially databases. A database is simply software that helps you manage information. You can use databases to manage all kinds of information, such as clients, vendors, products, parts, employees, and more. Bookkeeping software is really nothing more than a database that has been customized to handle financial information; CRM software is essentially a database that's tailored for customer data.

When your business has complex tracking or reporting needs that can't be handled by an off-the-shelf solution, you may need to create a customized database from the ground up. With database software like *Filemaker Pro* or Microsoft *Access*, you can customize a management solution to handle your data and generate reports to suit your unique business needs.

Of course, customization from scratch comes with costs. While purchasing database software isn't terribly expensive in itself, hiring a consultant to customize it for you can easily run into the tens of thousands of dollars. You'll also need to maintain the database including making changes as needed and dealing with bugs and problems, so you'll need a maintenance budget of probably at least a couple thousand dollars a year, maybe considerably more. Make sure there's not an off-the-shelf product that could meet your needs—likely at a significantly lower cost—before committing to the expense of a customized database.

> **TIP**
>
> **Ask your bookkeeper and other business owners what software they recommend.** Talk to people within your network who might know of industry-specific applications with features customized for your type of business. A bookkeeper can also help you set up the software and show you how to use it. You can usually test-drive these applications at their websites or with a trial version of the software. If there's not an industry-specific application for your type of business, *QuickBooks* offers several different versions to meet the needs of all sizes and types of businesses.

Chapter 12 Checklist:
Bookkeeping, Accounting,
and Financial Management

☐ Decide whether to use the cash or accrual system of accounting.

☐ Keep records of all payments to and from your business. Create an organized system for keeping your receipts.

☐ Enter your income and expense information into bookkeeping software on a regular basis. Businesses with high volumes of sales or expenses should do this frequently—daily or weekly. If appropriate for your business, hire a part- or full-time bookkeeper to keep up with this task.

☐ On some regular basis—typically monthly, quarterly, and annually— generate financial reports such as a profit/loss statement and a cash flow analysis to show you the big picture of how your business is doing financially.

☐ Consult with an accountant or tax professional at least once a year to keep your system on track.

Small Business Marketing 101

So you've got a great product or service and have built a solid business infrastructure to support it. How will you get customers to buy it? The process of reaching out to potential customers and trying to attract them to your business is what's known as marketing. Some business owners look forward to the marketing process and enjoy the creative aspects of it; others find it intimidating and bewildering. The good news is that marketing your business does not have to be terribly time-consuming, complicated, or expensive. In fact, the best marketing methods are often the simplest and cheapest.

For example, encouraging good word of mouth and networking within a well-defined target audience will cost you little (if anything) and will greatly help your business develop name recognition and build a potential customer base. In fact, generating positive word of mouth—both online and off—is one of the most powerful ways for a business to develop its reputation and attract customers. Other inexpensive marketing methods, such as being active on social media, sending out press releases, and fostering media coverage, can generate far better exposure than spending a fortune on advertising.

Before we dive into the nuts and bolts of marketing, keep in mind an important and often misunderstood distinction: Marketing is not synonymous with advertising. Paid advertising can be part of a marketing strategy, but it seldom makes sense for a small business to invest precious resources on ads. Paid advertising is much more expensive—and less effective—than many cheaper (or even free) methods of getting exposure. More efficient ways to promote your business include:

- networking with potential customers, other business owners, government officials, and community leaders
- creating incentives for your customers to pass good word of mouth about your business to others
- pitching stories about your business to local media
- organizing or participating in special events, such as a grand opening party, product demonstration, trade show, or informational seminar
- creating a website and promoting it
- engaging in thoughtful email outreach
- engaging with current and potential customers on social media
- distributing brochures, flyers, or other literature, and
- listing your business in local directories.

This chapter outlines a simple, affordable, and effective approach to marketing your business. The strategies and tips described here will help get your marketing machine up and running and can be expanded as your business grows. Chapter 14 focuses specifically on online marketing.

TIP

Valuable marketing lessons are all around you. We live in a world saturated by marketing appeals. As annoying as it is to be relentlessly courted by thousands of companies each day, constant exposure to marketing messages does have a bright side: Whether you've "studied" marketing or not, you've unwittingly absorbed some basic marketing know-how. As an experienced marketing target, you probably know more about marketing than you think you do. Use this knowledge to turn the tables—to think like a marketer, rather than a "marketee."

Defining Your Market

Your very first concern when marketing your business is making sure you understand who and what your market is. In fact, defining and learning about your market is a fundamental step in planning your business, period. You've probably heard this advice before, but what exactly does it mean to "know your market"? It's helpful to break the concept of "market" down into three components:

- your potential and actual customers
- your competition, and
- your industry.

Often, the term "market" is used as shorthand for your customer base. But it's crucial to understand that knowing your market also means knowing who your competition is, and what the trends are in your industry. When you have a clear vision and understanding of all three—

customers, competition, and industry— you'll be well positioned not only to tailor your business to a profitable customer base, but also to reach that customer base with effective marketing strategies.

Let's look at each of the components of your market in a bit more detail.

Who Are Your Target Customers?

When you've come up with an idea for a business, one of the first questions you need to consider is whether there are enough potential customers to support the business. If there aren't enough people or other businesses willing to buy the product or service you plan to offer, you'll obviously have a hard time turning a profit.

To evaluate your potential customer base, start by putting careful thought into exactly whom you expect to be your most likely customers—in other words, your target customers. Part of the process of defining your target customers is learning as much as you can about them for a number of reasons: so you can make sure they are in fact a profitable customer base, so you can tailor your products or services to better suit their needs and desires, and so you can plan the most effective marketing outreach. We'll discuss methods of researching and learning about your target customers in "Learning About Your Market: Market Research," below. For now, we'll focus on why defining your target customers is so important, and on how to develop a target customer profile.

Common Marketing Terms

So many terms are thrown around when people are referring to marketing efforts—it can be hard to understand the distinctions among specific types of marketing, such as publicity, public relations, and media relations. Truth be told, there's often only a fuzzy line between these categories. Here's a quick definition of some of the most common marketing terms as they are used in this chapter.

Marketing means just about any promotional activity: advertising, special events, direct mail, online discounts and promotions, and the like. Marketing includes all ways of promoting your business.

Branding refers to the process of developing positive and specific associations in your target customers' minds regarding your business, above and beyond the basics of what products or services you provide. When a company has a well-developed brand, customers have an emotional tie to the company and a feeling of connection to the brand. For example, McDonald's is typically understood to be family friendly, cheerful, and fun. Volvo conveys the feeling of safety and quality. Levi Strauss & Co. projects a hip-yet-timeless vibe.

Advertising means buying print or digital space or airtime to deliver a promotional message designed to reach the general public, through print media, television, radio, the Internet—or even the sides of buses and park benches.

Listings or directories include business directories and other specialized publications, both in print and online. Some, such as a directory of film production companies in a city, are highly targeted; others are very broad. As with advertising, you must pay for a listing. But, unlike most ads, directories often serve as valuable resources that are used again and again, which means they can be much more effective than typical display ads.

Public relations is another broad term that can refer to many different types of outreach efforts. In this chapter, public relations means a coordinated, multifaceted effort, often called a "campaign," to get your business's message out to the public. A public relations campaign might include sponsoring events, pitching stories to the media, inviting key people to participate in conferences, public speaking, and advertising—all coordinated to ensure clarity and consistency of message.

Media relations refers to contacting the media and pitching story ideas in hopes of obtaining editorial coverage—coverage in articles or feature stories not tied to advertising. Most commonly, media relations involves sending press releases to newspaper editors, reporters, and television producers to announce an event or provide information that could be the subject of a news story. Another media relations technique is to hold a press conference at which your business conveys a specific (and newsworthy) message to invited members of the press.

Publicity means exposure in the media and in public generated via a variety of methods, such as holding or participating in events, or making media appearances.

TIP

Defining your target customers and learning about your market can be a circular process. Typically you'll start by identifying your best customer prospects based on your observations and intuition about your market (remember, your market includes not only customers, but also your competition and industry). Next, you'll want to do research to learn more about your market, such as what your target customers' buying habits are, what your competition is doing, or whether there are important industry trends. Based on this research, you may want to refine your target customer definition or refine your business idea to make the most of an unmet demand in the market. Also, remember that learning about your market and adjusting your business plan accordingly is an ongoing process, and lies at the heart of running a business. Successful business owners constantly monitor market conditions and make adjustments to their businesses in order to stay profitable.

Every business needs to have a clear idea of its most promising and likely customers. Without having a clear vision of your expected customer base, you will seriously diminish your business's chances of success for a number of reasons:

- You may fail to realize there are not enough potential customers for your business (in other words, there is not enough demand for your products or services).

- You may miss opportunities to tweak your business idea to better meet the needs of a potential customer base.
- You won't know how to reach your most promising prospects, which is another way of saying you won't know where to target your marketing efforts.
- You won't be able to craft your marketing messages appropriately— using the right tone, language, and attitude to appeal to your best prospects.

In a nutshell, defining your target customers means identifying specific characteristics of the people or businesses who you believe are most likely to actually buy your product or service. These characteristics are sometimes called a demographic profile. Common characteristics used to classify customers include:

- age
- gender
- income level
- buying habits
- occupation or industry
- marital status
- family status (children or no children)
- geographic location
- ethnic group
- political affiliations or leanings, and
- hobbies and interests.

Use these criteria to draw a profile of your most promising potential customers, those who have a real need or desire for your products or services. A maternity store specializing in professional wear, for example, may identify its target customer as 25- to 40-year-old pregnant, married women in the legal, financial, and real estate industries, within a ten-mile radius of the store. A bike shop with a focus on single-track mountain biking gear might define its target customer as 18- to 25-year-old single males living within two miles of the local university.

Deciding how narrowly to define your target customer is more of an art than a science, but in general it helps to err on the side of being more specific. It's far more common for business owners to make the mistake of envisioning their customer base too broadly, making it very difficult to engage in effective marketing efforts. Remember: A solid definition of your target customer serves as a foundation for all your marketing activities. The more carefully you've defined your target market, the more likely your marketing efforts—even simple, low-cost methods—will bear fruit.

TIP

Defining a target market will not limit your business. New entrepreneurs sometimes resist defining a target customer base, thinking that it will somehow limit the business or reduce the number of potential customers. This is a misconception. For starters, identifying target customers in no way prevents a business from accepting customers that might not fit in the target. If a customer who completely does not fit your target profile walks through your door and wants to buy your product or service, great. But what's crucial to understand is this: Unless you have unlimited marketing resources, it's much more effective to focus your marketing efforts on potential customers who you have determined are *likely* to buy your product or service—and not waste your time and money courting the vast world of prospects who merely *could* become customers.

Bear in mind that some businesses may focus on selling to other businesses rather than individuals. Selling products or services to other businesses (sometimes called B2B, for "business to business") can be lucrative because businesses usually buy in larger quantities than individuals. For example, a soap manufacturer might sell 50 bars of soap to individual customers via its website in a given month, but could sell 500 bars in just one sale to a hotel. If your business is targeting other businesses, you should still define your target customer, using characteristics such as:

- industry (i.e., restaurants, construction, banking, arts/culture, etc.)
- size, by number of employees or annual sales, and
- geographic location.

Defining a Niche

The term "niche" is somewhat of a buzzword in business. A niche is essentially a relatively narrow or specialized market—for example, a maternity clothing boutique specializing in corporate/professional wear or a law firm that specializes in immigration cases. In a crowded marketplace, a niche serves the critical function of distinguishing you from your competitors.

Focusing on a niche can be an effective and profitable strategy for small businesses because it is often too difficult and costly to try to cater to very broad audiences. Instead of trying to appeal to everyone, a small business usually will do better to develop a specialty in an area that is not being fully served by other businesses, and exploit that niche with cost-effective marketing strategies. Think of a niche as a hook that will help you reel in the potential customers that you have identified as the most profitable and likely prospects for your business.

There are two aspects of defining a niche: an operational aspect and a marketing aspect. Operationally, you'll have to decide to what degree your business will tailor its products or services for the target customer base. This is separate from the question of how you'll market your business to this target market. Targeting a niche usually involves both, to varying degrees—tailoring your products or services for a specific market segment, and actively reaching out to this segment with your marketing efforts—and it's up to you how you balance the two aspects

For example, a vegan catering business is a business that is heavy on the operational component of defining its niche: Its services (providing vegan meals) are completely dictated by its aim to appeal to the vegan market. Of course, it will also focus its marketing efforts on outreach to vegans.

In contrast, consider a day spa that mostly caters to local residents, but that recognizes an opportunity to boost business from the sizable number of tourists that come to its city. Though the spa's massage and other services might not be highly specialized for tourists, it could focus its marketing efforts on this niche by reaching out to the city's hotels, tour group companies, and travel agents. While its operations might not be wholly dictated by its goal of attracting tourists, it might make small operational tweaks, such as offering a free shuttle service to local hotels or including maps of local tourist attractions in its lobby area.

The point to understand here is that marketing to a niche usually involves some combination of operational adjustments to appeal to a target audience, along with focusing your marketing outreach to this audience. When you do both well, you'll be on your way to carving out a niche for your business.

Niches are by definition narrow, but not so narrow that they don't contain enough customers to sustain your business. The key to defining a profitable niche is to find an area where there is an unmet demand, and to fill that need with your products or services.

Evaluate Your Competition

Another crucial part of your market is your competition: the other businesses that are trying to sell similar products or services to roughly the same customers as you are. Knowing your competitors is just as essential as understanding your potential customers; you need to know who they are and what they are doing to help you establish and maintain a competitive edge. Further, the more precisely that another business targets your specific customer base, the more important it is for you to develop compelling reasons for customers to choose your business instead of theirs.

When evaluating your competition, start with the businesses that are your closest, most direct competitors—the ones that target the same customers as you do. If you want to focus on a specific niche, you'll need to know whether other businesses are doing the same thing. If so, that niche may not have room for another business and you may want to find a different angle.

Niches that have little competition offer good opportunities for your business to be profitable. But keep in mind that a profitable niche that has little or no competition will likely not stay that way for long—you should expect competition to arise in any market that proves to be profitable. Sometimes, in fact, being the first business in a profitable niche isn't an advantage. Other businesses can observe and learn from the experiences of a "pioneer" business and improve upon the business model, sometimes beating out the original pioneer. The moral here is that profitable markets will either already have competition or will develop competition in the future. To keep your competitive edge, you'll need to stay current on what customers want and what the competition is offering. In addition, you'll want to know about industry trends, which we'll discuss next.

Know Your Industry

Anticipating change is essential for all businesses, and staying abreast of industry trends is an important way to stay ahead of the curve. Your industry is not the same as your competition—rather, it's the broad world of businesses that operate in your general field, some of which may be competitors. Learning about industry trends helps a business improve its competitive edge by incorporating trends that aren't being adopted by its competition. It also helps a business avoid trouble by knowing about trends that may pose a threat to the business.

For example, any restaurant should know about trends in the restaurant industry, which may include learning about what is happening in New York and

Los Angeles restaurants. For a restaurant in Austin, Texas, the New York and Los Angeles restaurants would not be actual competitors, but the Austin restaurant might want to read about their practices and experiences in order to learn valuable information about the restaurant industry. A trend such as eliminating foie gras from menus because of inhumane farming practices might be happening in New York and getting positive reactions from diners, but not happening at all in the Austin area. A smart Austin restaurant owner who is familiar with the trend could be the first to cut foie gras from the menu and reap valuable positive publicity.

Some trends can threaten entire industries, so being aware of them might be essential. The low-carb trend of the last several years was a serious blow for bakeries, pasta makers, and anyone serving or manufacturing carbohydrate products. The smart businesses learned about the trend and adapted their business strategies appropriately. Many restaurants began making rice or pasta optional in certain dishes, or offering burgers with gluten-free buns. For some businesses like bakeries, the best way to respond was to offer other products like expanded coffee and tea menus, or deli items heavy on meat and cheese. Others responded not by changing their product offerings but with marketing messages trying to convince customers

that not all carbs are bad. Whatever the strategy, the key was to recognize the trend in the first place and respond in time rather than be blindsided by it.

General economic conditions are also important to your business. General forecasts for your city or region can give you an idea of whether economic upturns or downturns are on the horizon. The health of other key industries may also have a big effect on your business, even if you're in a completely different industry. For example, if you run a restaurant in an area where a major hospital is facing huge layoffs or closing, that will certainly impact your business. Keep a broad view when evaluating market conditions that can affect your bottom line.

 TIP

A profitable niche may exist in bucking a trend. For example, a technology might become obsolete (technology businesses are particularly vulnerable to trends and market changes), which could open a possible niche of serving the few customers who continue to use the obsolete technology. If you're the only electronics shop in town that fixes or sells turntables, you may have a profitable niche with little competition, even though turntables and vinyl records (while seeing a resurgence) are hardly a major growth industry. As with any niche, the trick is to make sure it is big enough.

Learning About Your Market: Market Research

Effective marketing starts with knowing key information about your market—your potential customers, competition, and industry. Doing market research is an important and effective way of testing your assumptions and answering any questions you may have about your market. For example, if you want to open a coffee shop, you may be confident that the university area would be a great location, but not sure whether the students will be willing to pay a bit more for fair trade coffee. Market research will help you test your assumption about the location, and answer your question about pricing—and in turn give you valuable information upon which to base important business decisions.

The term "market research" tends to scare business owners who think it means hiring pricey firms and conducting complicated demographic studies. In fact, market research can be much simpler and just as effective. Most small businesses can do their own market research with a very limited budget. Large business ventures might hire a firm to do more extensive market research studies, but the simpler approach usually makes more sense for small to medium start-ups.

Market research can include primary and secondary research. Primary research involves doing studies with potential customers to find out how they feel about your product or service and your competitors' offerings, and to answer a myriad of other questions about their shopping habits and preferences. Secondary research involves studying what others have learned about your market; typically this involves reading trade journals, other business publications, or reports generated from studies that others have commissioned. Small businesses often focus on secondary research because they find primary research intimidating. But as described below, small businesses can easily and inexpensively tackle primary research—and there's no substitute for the information you get directly from your target prospects.

Clarifying Your Research Objectives

The first step in doing market research is figuring out exactly what questions you want to have answered: What specifically do you want to learn about your market? A very helpful way to go about this is to approach each aspect of your market—potential customers, competition, and industry—separately.

The table below offers a breakdown of the types of questions and research methods that would be appropriate for each group. It's not an exhaustive list, but is meant to illustrate how your inquiry will shift depending on what you're researching and what you're trying to answer.

Market Research Questions and Methods		
Subject	**Questions to Answer**	**Methods**
Customers	• Who are your target customers? • What products/services do they need or want? • Where/how do they buy products/services? • What do they typically pay for your type of products/services?	**Primary Research Methods:** • Surveys and questionnaires • Focus groups • One-on-one interviews or inquiries of trusted contacts **Secondary Research Methods:** • Magazine or trade journal articles • Reports from previously conducted studies
Competition	• What do they offer? • What do they charge? • How do they provide the products/services? • Who are their customers? • What is their competitive edge?	• Primary sources (marketing materials, websites, and so on) • Trade shows • Networking • Magazine or trade journal articles
Industry	• What are standard practices? • What are the latest trends? • What does the future hold?	• Magazine or trade journal articles • Trade shows • Books

With a clear outline of what questions you want answered, you'll be in a good position to choose the best research methods. The best approach is to conduct both primary and secondary research—getting information from actual prospects (primary) and reading what others have to say about your market (secondary).

Primary Research Tools

Though primary research may not be quite as easy as reading a trade magazine, it's very doable and will generally yield much more valuable information because it comes directly from your prospects. The specific way that you'll ask questions of those prospects will depend on your type of business and the product or service you're offering, but in general, there are three options: surveys and questionnaires, interviews, and focus groups. Let's look at each of these.

Using Surveys and Questionnaires

Presenting your target customers with surveys or questionnaires is a great way to answer specific questions you have about them. Start by identifying exactly what you want to learn; you can call these your research questions. Based on these research questions, you'll draft the actual survey questions themselves. It's a subtle but important distinction: Your research questions are not exactly the same as the survey questions. Instead, the survey questions should be crafted so they yield results that will help you answer your research questions. Your research questions will be more general than your survey questions, and you want your survey questions to be as specific as possible.

EXAMPLE: Solange plans to open a massage studio in San Francisco. She'd like to open it in the Nob Hill neighborhood because she thinks this neighborhood would appeal to her target customer base. To test her assumption, she creates a survey and distributes it via email to her contacts who fit her target customer profile. Solange's research question is: "Is Nob Hill a good location for a massage studio?" To help her answer this fairly general and subjective question, Solange drafts more specific questions for the survey, such as:

- "Do you consider parking in Nob Hill to be a problem?"
- "Do you currently get massage services in Nob Hill, and if so, where?"
- "What massage services are currently lacking in Nob Hill?"
- "What would be the ideal neighborhood for you to get massage services?"

The survey responses indicate that there is a great desire for a massage studio in Nob Hill, and only mild concern about parking. The primary complaint about the existing massage services is that they don't offer enough different massage styles such as hot stone therapy. The survey results solidify Solange's decision to open her studio in Nob Hill, and help her tailor the services to her target audience.

You can send surveys in hard copy via mail, in plain text format via email, or— even better—by using a Web-based service, many of which are free. At sites such as SurveyMonkey (www.surveymonkey.com) and Zoomerang (www.zoomerang.com), you can create professional-looking online surveys, invite your prospects by email, and tabulate the results in useful ways, all for free. More features are available if you upgrade to a paying account, but the excellent free versions are a great place to start.

Interviewing Prospects One-on-One

There are a few different ways of getting information directly from individuals. One way is simply to set up interviews with people whom you trust and who may have relevant opinions. For example, if you want to start a child care referral service, you could meet with people you know who have young children and ask them about their experiences. Or if you're starting a software company that will focus on data management for construction companies, set up lunch meetings with people you know in the construction business and pick their brains about their data management challenges.

Another way to interview people is to canvass them at locations where you are likely to encounter people within your target profile. A good example is going to a trade show related to your industry, standing in a high-traffic area, and asking people if they could answer a few short questions. The key here is to have just a few short questions that passers-by could answer quickly with concise answers ("yes" or "no" or a numerical answer, for example) that you can easily record on a clipboard or laptop computer. Other locations might include special events that appeal to your target audience.

Working With Focus Groups

A focus group is simply an event at which you provide a presentation or demonstration to potential customers and solicit their feedback. Often, feedback is gathered via a survey or questionnaire prepared in advance. Feedback is also obtained though oral question-and-answer sessions and discussions among the group, which are recorded by someone taking careful notes. Examples of focus groups might include:

- a food manufacturer holding taste tests of a new salsa, asking participants to rate flavor and texture and to compare the new salsa to the competitors' versions
- a software company having users test their new time management application, asking them to rate it on ease of use and timing them on how long it takes to complete certain tasks with the software
- a nail salon demonstrating its signature pedicure on focus group participants, asking them for feedback on their experience during the pedicure and on the results.

While there's nothing inherently complex or expensive about conducting a focus group, it will require at least a nominal commitment of your time. If you don't have a retail or other space, you may need to rent an appropriate venue. Because of the preparation and possible expense involved, be sure to start the invitation process early enough to ensure that you get enough confirmed participants to justify the time and expense of doing the focus group.

Getting Started: A Basic Approach to Primary Research

Now that you have an overview of primary research tools, here's a simple approach to help get you started:

1. **Start by identifying the questions that you want answered—your research questions.** In other words, specify exactly what you want to learn.

2. **Decide the best way to get those questions answered.** As described above, the basic methods include surveys, interviews, and focus groups (usually in conjunction with a survey or questionnaire). The methods you choose will largely depend on the types of questions you want answered and the nature of your product or service.

3. **If you'll be using a survey or questionnaire, you'll need to draft the questions.** Your goal is to craft questions that will yield responses that will help you answer your research questions.

4. **Identify and invite your study's participants.** Start with your list of contacts and include people who fit your target customer profile. Build and expand your list by asking trusted contacts to suggest others that would be appropriate. Developing your list of contacts—particularly before you've started your business—is often a matter of networking, unless you want to pay for mailing lists. Networking is discussed under "Cost-Effective Marketing Tools," below.

5. **After conducting the study, compile the results.** Remember, doing market research is all about obtaining data, so don't neglect the essential task of assembling and analyzing your results.

Once this is done, you'll be poised to make business decisions based on the information you've learned.

Secondary Research Tools

Doing secondary research is generally as simple as reading trade journals and other business publications. It's something that all businesses should regularly do. Most businesses have at least one trade publication (many have several); identify the ones most relevant for you and read them as often as you can. Note that trade magazines do tend to be expensive, so read them at your local library if it's not in your budget. Also, particularly if your business will mostly have local customers, read your local newspapers and other media to keep an eye on your local economy.

 TIP

Read beyond the business pages. Valuable industry and other information is often found in other sections of your local newspaper. For instance, if you run a garden supply company, the home and garden section will have lots of information on trends and may feature other companies in your market. And an owner of a clothing store might find out about interesting fashion trends in the arts and culture section.

Effective Marketing Starts With a Solid Organization

Lots of small businesses fail to understand the importance of having an efficient, organized operation in place *before* they start their marketing efforts. After all, you'll want to be ready to handle the heightened attention your marketing will bring to your business. For example, a restaurant should not start a big marketing campaign without already having a good chef and enough waitstaff in place to handle a surge of diners. Otherwise, the unprepared restaurant's marketing efforts will likely result in unhappy diners and bad publicity.

Here's another way of saying this: Before you decide *how* to market, pay attention to *what* you're marketing. Make sure your house is in order before you worry about how to call attention to it.

Cost-Effective Marketing Tools

There are endless ways to market your business—the key is to pick the methods that will give the most bang for the buck. Forget about the mega-budget strategies of the big businesses you see advertising on TV. The best bet for small to midsized businesses is to focus instead on building an excellent reputation and encouraging great word of mouth. Think about it: How did you choose a hair salon, plumber,

or auto mechanic? Chances are that you asked your friends and acquaintances for a recommendation. Likewise, you want your customers to recommend your business to their contacts. The more that you can motivate your customers and clients to rave about your business, the more likely your business will be a success.

This section provides an overview of the many ways you can market your business, focusing on some key, tried-and-true methods: networking, media relations, special events, and listing your business in directories.

Networking

Key contacts are essential to every business and the best way to develop these contacts is through networking. Networking involves actively cultivating relationships with people, businesses, community leaders, and others who present possible opportunities for your business—not just as potential customers, but also as vendors, partners, investors, or other roles. Networking is not the same thing as sales: Rather than the simple goal of making a sale, a huge goal of networking is to inform other businesspeople and influential people about what you do in hopes that they will recommend your business to their circle of contacts.

Lots of folks new to the world of business fear that successful networking requires unsavory schmoozing or pandering. These concerns are unfounded. In fact, if you adopt a sleazy wheeler-dealer approach, you risk alienating the very people whom you want to make your allies. Instead, successful networking is little more than sincere communication with others about what you do. You are "networking" every time you attend an event held by a local trade association, get to know other business owners and community leaders, write a letter to the editor, participate in an online discussion group, or have lunch with another local business owner.

> **TIP**
>
> **Forge relationships with contacts before you need help from them.** For example, if you need the support of a local politician on an upcoming city zoning decision, you'll have a better chance of getting the politician's vote if he or she already knows you and thinks favorably of your business than if you place a call to his or her office out of the blue.

While it may be easiest to meet someone at an event, introducing yourself to a potentially useful contact can be as simple as picking up the phone, writing a letter, or sending an email. In making your initial contact, you should be as formal or informal as is appropriate for the person with whom you are making contact. A letter of introduction on attractive letterhead might be best for an influential politician, for example, but a phone call might be fine to introduce yourself to a local business owner. In your letter, email, or phone call, explain who you are, what your business does, and why you thought that person might be interested in your products or services. Try to conclude by encouraging further communication in the future, such as inviting the contact to an event or asking if he or she would be interested in receiving email updates from your business. If you talk to someone on the phone, a follow-up email or letter thanking the contact for his or her time is always a smart idea.

> **TIP**
>
> **Check out online networking.** Social media, such as LinkedIn and Facebook, offer lots of opportunities for networking. See "Social Media: Facebook, Twitter, and More," in Chapter 14, for details.

Media Relations

Another excellent—and inexpensive— way to promote your business is to generate media coverage in newspapers or magazines, or on radio, television, or the Internet. Your goal is to get "editorial" coverage, meaning some mention of your business or event in news or feature stories (as opposed to paid advertising). Because editorial coverage is far more credible than advertisements or paid publicity, it will have a greater impact. For example, a local newspaper article about your business being awarded a lucrative state contract will almost always generate a more favorable and lasting impression than any advertising.

The term "media relations" means the process of attempting to obtain editorial coverage. It is a fairly simple process: You contact the media on behalf of your business and encourage an editor, producer, or reporter to write or produce a story about your particular subject. As with most marketing efforts, the more specific and targeted your message, the more impact it will have. For example, you'll be much more likely to interest an editor in your business's recent expansion and opening of a new facility than of the very general fact that your business exists.

The basic steps for conducting media relations are as follows:

1. **Write a press release.** A press release is a key tool to use when pitching a story idea. Typically, a press release is a one-page announcement outlining the information you want the media to cover. You have two main goals in writing a press release: 1) to capture the journalist's attention, and 2) to make it easy for the journalist to write the story you want published. Stylistically, press releases are usually written like news stories, offering journalists an example of the story you want them to produce. (See "Elements of a Strong Press Release," below, for more details on how to put together a winning pitch.)

2. **Make initial contact with the journalist by phone.** Make a preliminary phone call before sending a press release, so your release doesn't get lost in the shuffle. If you don't know which reporter would be likely to cover your story, call the news department, briefly describe the nature of your press release, and ask who might be the best person for you to contact. Once you have a name of a reporter, an editor, or a producer, give that person a call to introduce yourself and your business, briefly explain the nature of your news story, and tell the person you will be sending a press release. If you can't reach the journalist by phone (as is often the case), don't let it hold you up: Leave a message and send out your press release. While you could make this initial contact by email, a phone call makes a stronger impression. And creating lasting relationships with individual reporters is the best way to get positive coverage over the long term.

Elements of a Strong Press Release

The better your press release, the more likely a journalist will write about your business, giving you valuable exposure in the press. Reporters, editors, and producers are chronically busy and squeezed by deadlines; they need good story ideas and clear information to get their jobs done. The easier you can make it for them to cover your story, the more likely they are to oblige. If you write a strong, clear press release, they may even use parts of it verbatim. But you'll need to keep your press release as succinct as possible.

Here are some tips on how to construct a compelling press release that is likely to generate media placements:

- **Start with a news hook.** Like a news story, your press release should have a strong first sentence, known as the story's "lead" (sometimes spelled "lede"). What is the most important point you want to get across? Write it in a clear, straightforward style and you will have your lead.
- **Date, time, and location information should be easy to find.** If your press release is promoting an event, don't bury important information deep within long paragraphs. Include important event details such as date, location, and registration deadlines in the first sentence or two or summarized in bullet points at the end.
- **Include the most important information first.** Your press release should include all important details up front, then work toward more general or background information in later paragraphs.

- **Include quotes from yourself or other key people.** Reporters like to include quotes from real people in their stories, so include at least one or two catchy quotes in your press release. If you are the best person to offer a quote, don't be shy about quoting yourself! It may feel strange, but it's perfectly appropriate. Remember, you're offering the media a sample of the story you want them to write, so include a quote as if an outside reporter interviewed you.
- **Include a separate section with contact information.** The journalists who receive your release may have additional questions to ask you. Choose a point person who will be available to field any such questions and include his or her contact information clearly at the end of the release.
- **Create a news angle.** If it is appropriate and possible, tie your release into a topic that's currently in the news. For example, if your press release is announcing your furniture manufacturing company starting a new line featuring environmentally friendly materials, you'd certainly want to include a reference to the rapid growth of "green" businesses—a hot news topic.
- **Use statistics.** Reporters love statistics that show how prevalent a problem is or how many people are affected by an issue. Using the previous example, you could include recent statistics that 35% of people surveyed would be willing to pay a premium for environmentally friendly products.

Sample Press Release

FOR IMMEDIATE RELEASE
May 6, 2020

State of Illinois Contracts with Data Solutions, Inc. for Data Communications Equipment and Services

CHICAGO, Illinois—The state of Illinois has entered into a purchasing contract with Data Solutions, Inc. for a wide array of data communications equipment, related software, and Data Solutions' award-winning network management services. Under this agreement, the equipment and services provided by Data Solutions will be available at special volume pricing to all Illinois state agencies, municipalities, and educational institutions.

"We are thrilled that the state of Illinois has chosen Data Solutions to fill its data communications needs," said Data Solutions CEO Steven Dutch. "As a growing Illinois company, we are proud to play a role in keeping technology money in the Illinois economy."

Illinois' contract with Data Solutions will allow state procurement agencies to support and enhance their data communications networks with the highest-quality products and support services. In addition to the data communications equipment included in the purchasing agreement, Data Solutions' engineers will be available under this contract to provide analysis, design, installation, training, and maintenance services for the equipment included in the contract.

The agreement will be effective until December 31, 2022.

About Data Solutions

Data Solutions is a privately held Illinois-based company specializing in the design, implementation, support, and management of voice, video, and data communications infrastructures. Data Solutions offers unparalleled expertise in IP-based networking, including LAN, WAN, and IP multiservice technology. Data Solutions is headquartered in Chicago and has a second site in Milwaukee, Wisconsin. More information about Data Solutions and its award-winning products and services is available at www.datasolutionswebsite.com.

Contact Information

Steven Dutch, CEO
Data Solutions, Inc.
312-555-1212 ext. 123
sdutch@datasolutionswebsite.com

Polly Harvey, Media Relations
Clarity Media
312-555-9876
polly@claritymedia.com

3. **Send the press release by email, both as a PDF attachment and in the body of the email.** Years ago, press releases were sent by mail. Then, for years it was all about delivery by fax. Today, it's typical to send press releases via email, ideally as a both a PDF attachment and as plain text in the body of the email. Emailed press releases work because reporters like having an electronic copy from which to cut and paste when writing their stories.

4. **Follow up after you send the press release.** Shortly after sending your press release—a few hours or a day later, depending on the timing of your announcement—follow up with another phone call or email to make sure your press contact received the release and to answer any questions he or she may have.

An example of a press release is shown above.

Some people feel timid about contacting the media and asking them to cover a specific story. While you shouldn't be a pest, you also shouldn't feel shy about pushing your story idea persistently. To do their jobs, journalists must come up with a constant stream of interesting new story ideas. Local business journalists are often particularly challenged in finding newsworthy business stories. Just as you need their help, they need yours. Because you will often know more than reporters do about a particular story, you can offer valuable information that they can use. If you are honest and reliable, you will usually be treated with respect.

If you don't get a response after an introductory phone call, a press release via email, and a follow-up call, let the particular story idea rest; this will help you preserve your reputation as a pleasant, professional person to deal with the next time you want to pitch a story. A journalist may not cover your story because he or she does not think it is newsworthy or because there are other stories that take precedence. A few months later, when you try again, you may be pleasantly surprised to find that you've pitched the right story on the right day.

 TIP

Relationships with media people are gold. The most effective media relations come from relationships you build with reporters, editors, producers, and other media contacts. Because you are more likely to get news coverage from a reporter with whom you've worked before than from someone who's never heard of you, you should always treat your relationships with people in the media as the valuable resource they are.

Finally, keep in mind that having a story written about your business isn't the only way to get media coverage. Another great way to get exposure is to be interviewed and quoted for articles on subjects in which you have expertise. Ideally, you'll develop relationships with reporters who will understand you to be an expert in a certain area, so that they call you for a quote when covering that topic. Similarly you might be invited to participate in a local TV show on a topic within your expertise. Foster this type of coverage by making sure your reporter contacts understand your area of expertise, and that you are willing to offer your opinions and information if they need them for a story.

Special Events

Holding events such as a grand opening party, a product demonstration, an informational workshop, or a holiday gala will help you forge a closer bond with your customers, while simultaneously generating valuable publicity for your business. Special events tend to grab the attention of the media, making them a particularly effective marketing method. The icing on the cake is that events can (and should!) be fun, for both you and your customers.

One reason that special events are such effective publicity tools is that the media is generally more responsive to specific, time-sensitive activities or events than to the business in the abstract. An event is an easy hook, particularly if there is any educational or public interest component to your event. For example, if your housewares store offers a half-day workshop on

how to make your home more green, a reporter might well be able to craft a story around the event and discuss the timely topic of sustainable living.

Even if your event isn't newsworthy enough to merit a whole story, most events can be listed in local business calendars, usually for free. Most daily papers have a business section with events listings, and submitting your event is an easy way to get a dose of publicity.

Listings or Directories

Getting your business listed in appropriate directories is a great way to boost your visibility with your target customers. Listings work so well because consumers who consult a particular directory or directory category have already determined that they are looking for a specific type of business. In addition to every city's phone books, most communities have other types of directories—for example, the local chamber of commerce membership directory, a directory of women-owned businesses, or the African American business league's directory. Some directories are published in hard copy, though many directories are posted online.

Most business directories charge fees. You'll have to evaluate whether the fees fit into your budget and whether the directory exposes your business to the right audience. While most directory fees are modest, some are prohibitively expensive; these are not worth considering unless the audience you're trying to reach is extremely narrow and desirable, and the directory is highly targeted to that audience.

Note also that some membership organizations include a directory listing as a benefit of membership. Chambers of commerce, for example, will typically list member businesses in their directories—print, online, or both. As with regular directory fees, you'll have to judge whether the directory listing (plus any other benefits) are worth the membership fee.

With any kind of directory, the most important consideration is what audience the listing will reach. Ask about how and where the directory will be distributed, how many copies are printed, and how often a new edition is published.

To find all of the directories in which you should list your business, you'll have to do some homework. Looking online is a good start, but you should also check with local resources, such as local government offices, chambers of commerce, economic development organizations, and trade associations.

Sponsorships

Sponsoring an event, sports team, nonprofit organization, or public television or radio station is a great way to develop your brand. Sponsorships are a lot like advertising in the sense that you pay money in exchange for having your business recognized in some way, usually with a display of your logo and sometimes a short marketing message. But unlike advertising in traditional media like newspapers or television, a sponsorship does more than just communicate your marketing message: It also conveys a sense of connection to whatever you are sponsoring and thus creates more positive associations in your potential customers' minds.

For example, if you sponsor a local golf tournament and have your logo prominently displayed on signs, event schedules, and other materials, the golf-oriented attendees will start to see your business as an ally and begin to develop an emotional connection to your business. Similarly, a business that sponsors a gay and lesbian film festival will develop a connection to the gay and lesbian community.

Sponsorship opportunities tend to fall in a few categories:

- **Events.** This includes events such as sport tournaments, film festivals, trade shows, street fairs, concerts, and just about any other event open to the public. Event organizers often want businesses to help fund their events in exchange for recognition, usually on signs, in printed materials, and in TV or radio ads.

- **Facilities.** New building projects, such as sports arenas, courthouses, or university buildings, sometimes ask for corporate and business sponsors, who are often recognized on a plaque, statue, or other sign in the building. Being recognized in this way helps show your business is a pillar in the community.
- **Nonprofit organizations.** Most nonprofits welcome sponsorship funds from businesses and will have specific benefits available for different levels of financial support. Sponsoring a nonprofit is an excellent way to build your reputation in the community served by and involved with the nonprofit.
- **Public television and radio.** While public TV and radio sponsorships are beginning to blur into the more traditional commercials, there still is a distinct difference in the perception of sponsors of public media. You'll also typically reach a more affluent, educated demographic via public media than with commercial stations.

Email Outreach

First off, we're not talking about spam here. While unsolicited junk mail is a huge problem, there is also a legitimate way to send out emails to your target customers to let them know about upcoming promotions, events, and other business information. This approach involves sending useful information to a list of people who have indicated a desire for your emails. See "Email Marketing" in Chapter 14 for an in-depth look at email promotions.

Direct Mail

Besides sending out email promotions, you can send out hard copy marketing materials by U.S. mail—a process that's called direct mail. People often perceive direct mail campaigns to be complex and expensive, and they can be both. However, direct mail campaigns can also be simple, targeted mailings that are effective without costing a fortune. If you keep the materials simple and develop your own mailing list instead of paying a firm for a list, you can engage in a direct mail campaign that's both thrifty and effective.

First, decide what the goal and subject of your direct mail campaign will be. As with most types of marketing outreach, the more specific your message, the better. Instead of sending out a general brochure about your printing business, for example, send out a postcard offering a 50% discount off the first order for new customers. Special promotions, discounts, or giveaways are the best way to capture people's attention amid all the junk mail.

You can take different approaches in developing your mailing lists, from simply compiling names of everyone you know and looking up their addresses to hiring a mailing list firm and paying a fee for a list. You may be surprised at how many names you can come up with on your own. Start with the people within your target customer profile and work outward. Ask your friends for names of people they know who might be interested in your business. If you'll be targeting other businesses, scan other directories for their contact information.

Creating the printed materials for your mailing can be more affordable than you might expect. You don't need to produce a high-end direct mail package like the ones you get in your own mailbox, printed in full color on heavy paper with special die-cut shapes and other frills. Instead, focus on creating simple layouts of text and graphics on standard-sized pages or postcards. Ideally, you, a partner, or an employee can design your materials in-house, using relatively inexpensive software such as Adobe *InDesign*. Alternatively, a professional graphic designer can be immensely helpful, particularly if no one in your business has graphic design skills.

Samples

Everyone loves stuff for free. If you have a product that lends itself to being sampled, consider setting up a table at a trade show or another venue and offering freebies to the public. Sure, you'll always end up giving things away to people who have no intention of buying your product, but it's usually worth it to forge a connection with even a few potential buyers. Some examples of offering samples effectively include:

- a handmade soap maker offering small slices of their beautiful soaps at a table in the health food store
- a coffee shop offering small free cups of their house-roasted coffee at a street fair, and
- a massage studio offering free five-minute massages at a local trade show.

When offering samples, prepare in advance to ensure that you make a powerful and positive first impression. Have your business name and logo prominently displayed. And remember to have business cards or brochures available so that the people sampling your product or service can find you later.

Customer Loyalty Programs

The phrase "customer loyalty program" sounds much more involved than it really is. What we're talking about here is implementing ways to keep your current customers coming back for more. Here are a couple of ideas:

- **Offer punch cards for repeat customers.** Coffee shops often use these, but plenty of other businesses can use them too. After a number of purchases—measured either in units or dollar increments—the customer gets something free. For example, a coffee shop might offer a customer a free cup of coffee after they had purchased ten cups, tracked on the punch card. Or a record shop might punch the card for every $10 spent, and after $100 is reached the customers might get $10 off their next purchase.
- **Include freebies with each sale.** A shoe store, for example, could include a small tin of shoe polish with every order. A baby store could include a free rubber duckie with each sale. It's amazing how much customer goodwill you can generate by including something worth about 10¢ in each sale.

Print Materials

Brochures, business cards, flyers, letterhead, and other printed materials can help you spread the word about your business. It might be worth hiring a professional graphic designer to create these materials to ensure they convey a professional image. It's also important that your logo and other imagery remain consistent across all the media you produce, both in print and online.

Websites and Social Media

As described in detail in Chapter 14, every business should have at least a simple website with basic marketing information. These days, if customers Google your business and come up empty-handed, they might think your business isn't very professional or stable and might keep looking, choosing one of your competitors that does have a useful site. In addition, there are endless ways to network online, including social media such as Facebook, YouTube, and countless others. Read Chapter 14 for guidance on how to establish your business online and effectively network within online communities.

Publishing Articles or Newsletters

Publishing substantive information is a great way to establish your credibility and enhance your reputation, particularly for professional service businesses. Accountants and lawyers, for example, are perfect candidates for newsletters because the heart of their businesses is information. Newsletters—both print and email versions (discussed in Chapter 14)—are powerful marketing vehicles, helping to strengthen the relationship with existing clients and to broaden the customer base when existing customers pass on the newsletter to their friends and family.

On the flip side, newsletters do require a fairly sizable time commitment, and possible expenses if you need to hire someone to help. Writing and editing are time-consuming tasks (even for professional writers), and you might need to hire a designer for the layout work if you plan to distribute a hard copy version.

Also bear in mind that by its nature, a newsletter is distributed periodically, so if you can't commit to whatever time frame—typically weekly, monthly, or quarterly—then don't do it at all. Starting to send a monthly newsletter and then have it disappear after six months will give a much poorer impression than never offering a newsletter in the first place.

If you really want to publish but can't commit to a newsletter, consider publishing occasional articles on topics of your expertise. There are often opportunities available online (for example, some lawyer directories include articles by lawyers who have signed up for the directory). Or consider sticking with marketing copy rather than substantive information. Putting out regular flyers or emails highlighting your products or services and any special events at your store is much easier than a substantive newsletter, and might be all you need.

Chapter 13 Checklist: Small Business Marketing 101

☐ Define your target market—potential customers, competition, and industry—and learn everything you can about it. Based on what you learn, you might decide to tweak your target market or aspects of your business operations in order to better appeal to a profitable customer base.

☐ Engage in primary market research to get information directly from your potential customers. Web-based surveys are excellent tools to use.

☐ Have an efficient, organized operation in place before you start your marketing efforts.

☐ Focus on marketing strategies other than advertising—particularly on ways to encourage good word of mouth—that are usually less expensive and just as effective.

☐ Network by cultivating relationships with other businesses, community leaders, and others.

☐ Develop relationships with reporters and editors and pitch newsworthy stories about your business to them. Make your expertise clear to media people so that they contact you for quotes or interviews when writing stories on certain topics.

☐ Maintain at least a simple website and network online.

E-Business: Selling and Marketing Online

E-business these days encompasses much more than just creating a website. In many ways, today's possibilities for online business are incredibly exciting—new technologies are emerging every day that allow businesses to promote themselves and sell products and services online in novel and amazing ways. The downside is that the e-business landscape is constantly shifting and evolving, making it a real challenge to keep up with what's current and to separate the true opportunities from the hype.

Despite how bewildering the world of e-business can be, don't stick your head in the sand. Every business needs to consider to what degree it will operate online. At a minimum, a business should create at least a basic online presence to let the e-world know it exists; often this involves creating just a simple website as an "online business card" of sorts for a bricks-and-mortar business. At the other end of the spectrum, some businesses operate entirely online, with all revenues generated from online sales. In this situation, the website itself and its e-commerce functions will certainly need to be more complex, and it will be more important to implement a sophisticated online marketing strategy to drive traffic to the e-commerce operation.

In between having a basic marketing site and running a full e-commerce operation, there is a wide world of options for doing business—and in particular, promoting your business—online. Blogs and social media are transforming the way that businesses interact and develop relationships with potential customers online. And strategies for boosting your business's ranking with search engines such as Google (and thus driving more traffic to your site) have become a whole industry unto itself, known as search engine optimization or SEO.

What's true for all businesses is that taking your business online needs to be approached strategically. Most importantly, you need to establish how your e-business activities will fit into your overall business strategy, and do so before you start developing your site or other online ventures. For example, if you hire a Web developer to create a website and a blog without first giving careful thought to your e-business strategy, you might end up with a site that is ineffective—or worse, one that unexpectedly drains your business's valuable resources.

Even when your strategy is clear, creating a website can be tricky. It's incredibly common for business owners to think the site they envision is simple or basic, when in truth it is anything but. Some business owners are tempted to build the site themselves to save money, but quickly discover they're out of their depth. Others decide to hire outside Web developers, but find they're at the mercy of programmers who push technologies the business doesn't need or who lack business savvy, resulting in sites that don't achieve business goals.

In this chapter, the term "e-business" refers to the broad range of ways your business can operate online beyond simply maintaining a website. This chapter demystifies the process of taking your business online—starting by helping you clarify your strategy and understanding the range of opportunities online. We'll discuss a wide range of e-business issues, including:

- creating a website
- developing a social media presence
- selling your products online
- driving traffic to your site through SEO
- how to find and work with Web developers
- how to evaluate alternatives, such as template-based website builder services and opening an affiliate store within e-commerce sites like Amazon, eBay, or Etsy
- the process of developing a website methodically, from strategy and concept to programming and testing, and
- domain name, copyright, and other intellectual property issues.

Defining Your Strategy and Goals

Way before you start thinking about the cool features or content you want to include at your website, or how you'll promote your business on Facebook, put careful thought into your broad strategy for e-business and how it fits into your overall business strategy. In particular, you want to make sure that your online activities serve your business strategy and not the other way around. For example, don't let a Web developer talk you into an online store or a blog if they don't directly serve your business needs or fit within your resources.

If your business was originally conceived as an online business—for example, an online-only athletic equipment retailer or an electronic publication—you probably already have a clear idea that online activities will be your focus. But if you are planning a website for an offline business, such as a bakery, retail store, interior design business, or consulting firm, it's important to take the time to be clear about how your website or other online activities fit into your bigger business plan. Bricks-and-mortar businesses are vulnerable to stumbling into bigger e-business activities than they can handle. If you will be conducting business online, then you need to make sure that you have adequately accounted for these online operations in your business plan. If not, you'll need either to scale back your e-business plans or revise your business plan accordingly.

Internet Jargon: Defined

To help stay clear about what's what online, here are definitions of some of the most common terms related to online marketing:

- **Blog** is short for "weblog," a website using a format of short posts, ordered in reverse chronological order (as in, the most recent post at the top of the page), which often include links to other sites. Blogs are regularly updated—often several times daily—with new information by one or more contributors, called bloggers. Blogs started out as largely personal communication vehicles, but an increasing number of reputable businesses and online publications are using the blog format.
- **Crowdfunding** is a method of raising money online directly from your social media network and other supporters. Crowdfunding websites (also called "platforms") like Kickstarter or IndieGoGo make it easy for users to create fundraising campaigns that can easily be promoted among social media networks, such as Facebook or Twitter. See the "Crowdfunding and Social Media" section in Chapter 5 for more on the subject.
- **E-commerce** refers to an online sales operation, generally via a website that is set up to allow online orders and process credit card or other types of payments.
- **Email lists** are compilations of email addresses of people who have expressed interest in receiving promotional emails from a business. (If the content of the email is substantive in nature the email would usually be called an e-newsletter.) For example, your business could send emails about special promotions or events to an email list. It's critical that the recipients included in an email list have clearly expressed interest in receiving the emails. As you're probably aware, unsolicited marketing emails are known as spam and frowned upon by savvy businesspeople and their recipients alike.
- **Listservs** are essentially email discussion groups about specific topics that allow people who have signed up to them to share information with each other. Any subscriber can send an email to the listserv, and that email will automatically be sent to all other listserv subscribers. This differentiates a listserv from an email list, in which communications are typically only one-way from the administrator to the list.
- **Online presence** refers to the broad collection of ways a business is represented in the electronic world. For instance, in addition to having a website, you could maintain a blog; manage Facebook, Twitter, and Instagram pages; be listed in numerous online directories; be a regular commentator on other blogs and online forums; have a regular email newsletter; supply informative articles to other websites; or moderate a listserv. The sum of all these activities is often called your online presence.

Internet Jargon: Defined (continued)

- **Social media** is a general term referring to networks of users such, as Facebook, Twitter, Instagram or LinkedIn. Businesses can promote themselves and develop their brands by strategically engaging in these channels.
- **Web developers** specialize in all aspects of creating websites, including organizing the information, graphic design, and programming. Avoid the term "Web designer" when referring to these individuals because graphic design is only one aspect of creating a website. Another acceptable term for Web developer is Web builder. Although some Web developers work alone as independent contractors, they typically involve teams to create a website: information architects, graphic designers, content developers, and programmers.

It's all too easy to be seduced by the latest interactive features and other Web-based applications—online sales and publishing are common examples—and to lose the focus of your core business operations. Online sales in particular tend to involve a whole new set of details you'll need to handle, such as managing online sales reports, shipping, and online customer service. If these activities weren't included in your original business plan, you might quickly find yourself overwhelmed and unable to keep customers happy—a bad situation for any business. With careful strategic thinking before launching a website or other e-business activities, you can plan for the resources you'll need and avoid this mistake.

EXAMPLE: Michele is planning to open a store selling handmade jewelry. She wants to create a website and starts talking to Web developers to get an idea of what a site would cost. Many of the developers she talks with encourage her to create an online store to help increase sales. Without having put much thought into the website, Michele initially likes the idea. She figures that if the site generates even a few sales per month, it would be welcome additional income.

When Michele takes the time to think more about an online jewelry store, though, she realizes she has several questions about how it would work. She calls back some of the developers she's talked to and asks about details such as how the site would be updated with photos of current pieces and how other tasks would be handled, such as shipping, billing, inventory control, and customer service. She learns that indeed, while some tasks such as billing can be somewhat automated, other tasks would have to be handled either by her, an employee, or a subcontractor, such as the Web developer.

Michele realizes that her business plan did not account for the logistics involved in online sales, and that she'd rather stick with her original plan and make sure to run her shop well, as she originally planned. In keeping with this, she decides to keep her website strategy simple, with a basic marketing website used to promote her real-world business, not for online sales.

Beyond identifying an overall strategy for how your site and other online activities will fit within your business, you also need to define specific goals for your online efforts. All too often, business owners fail to do this with any specificity; many think the goal is simply to "increase business." However, goals can and should be more specific so that your e-business efforts are well-tailored to them.

Typical goals for many small business owners would include:

- building recognition of the business and its brand
- attracting new clients and customers, either to come to a physical business or to call the business
- collecting email addresses or other contact information for marketing efforts
- showing work samples and portfolio items

- selling products online—otherwise known as e-commerce
- answering common customer questions to decrease customer service phone calls
- attracting investors, and
- publishing late-breaking information, such as news about the latest trends in craft brewing or recent technology releases.

By clearly defining goals, you'll be better able to decide what information is important to communicate to your audience. In addition, your specific goals will play a big part in determining how information is organized at your site. Content that is closely tied to high-priority goals should be featured prominently.

A Website: Your Online Base Camp

A few years ago, the concept of e-business was more or less synonymous with having a website. But as we enter the third decade of the 2000s, doing business online is much more expansive. A website is no longer one and the same as your e-business operations—rather, think of a website as the base camp for your e-business activities. Besides maintaining a site, you might: maintain a Facebook page and actively network it among hundreds of "friends"; post photos to Instagram of your latest products; send out Twitter updates with business news or customer service tips; host a YouTube channel where you post informative or entertaining videos related to your business; and send out periodic promotional emails announcing special sales or other company news. Your website is still important as a central repository for business information and possibly a revenue center, if you have an online store. But these days, a website typically does not work solo but, rather, in sync with a wider range of online activities that collectively serve to generate business.

As mentioned above, every business needs to evaluate its overall strategy to figure out to what degree it will engage in doing business online. If heavy social media networking doesn't make sense for your business, the conventional wisdom is that you still should have at least a simple website—for instance, one that includes basic information about what the business does and contact information. In some cases, this might be nothing more than a one-page site, similar to a listing in the yellow pages. Whether to create a more extensive site or integrate it with other forms of online marketing (such as a social media outreach strategy) will depend on the specifics of your business.

Generally, even an ultrabasic site will offer several benefits to your business. Here are some of the main things it will help you do:

- **Project a professional image.** Some customers consider businesses that don't have websites to be less serious or less stable than businesses that have them.

- **Reach the ever-growing number of consumers who look for businesses online.** This is true for all kinds of businesses, not just e-commerce ones. In our increasingly Internet-reliant population, a growing number of people start their searches for a local plumber, a café, a clothing store, or any other type of business online.

- **Communicate more information than you can typically fit on a business card or brochure.** When you include the Internet address (called the URL, for "uniform resource locator") on your business cards, brochures, or other printed materials, potential customers can go to your site for more in-depth information, such as product details or portfolio pieces.

- **Create a permanent place where you can post information that potential customers can always refer to—unlike brochures or business cards that often get thrown away or lost.** This can be helpful to current customers or clients who may need to look up your phone number or payment mailing address.

- **Facilitate word-of-mouth marketing.** Your happy customers will easily be able to share information about your business to their friends and family simply by sharing your URL.
- **Market your business without paying print costs.** This can save you a lot of money if the information you want to communicate is lengthy or changes frequently, such as sales, specials, and new product arrivals. And of course, your website can use full color, which can be quite expensive to print.
- **Develop and refine your marketing messages before committing them to print.** For example, you could create a simple three-page site with information about your services, your professional biography, and contact information—and refine these pieces of content for a month or two until you're satisfied with them; then create a print brochure with the information from the website.
- **Create a central place where all your marketing activities—both online and offline—can be referenced and linked.** For instance, your site can (and should) offer links to your Facebook, YouTube, and Twitter pages; a sign-up form for your email list; and a calendar of special events or workshops your business is hosting.

Keep in mind that a website might offer even more opportunities for your particular business, such as the potential for profits from e-commerce and innovative customer service. The bottom line is that even the simplest website will be an asset to your business. If more expansive online engagement efforts fit into your business strategy, then a website will serve as an important base of online operations.

The following sections discuss online marketing, blogging, social media, e-commerce, and other ways you can create an online presence for your business.

Online Outreach Methods

Though a website is often the centerpiece of a business's online presence, there is an ever-expanding list of other online methods of communicating with potential customers. It's important to consider the big picture of how you plan to interact with potential customers beyond simply maintaining a website. The subsections below discuss the methods businesses commonly use these days to promote themselves online. Bear in mind that these methods are constantly evolving as new technologies are developed, so it's important to monitor trends and adapt your approach as circumstances warrant.

Email Marketing

Email marketing is a huge component of many companies' marketing efforts, while for other businesses, it is nonexistent. Staying in touch with your customers and potential customers via email offers loads of possibilities and potential, but it also requires a commitment to ongoing outreach. If, like many business owners, you find you don't have the resources to regularly engage in email marketing, you're not alone. What I'll describe in this section is a basic approach to work towards, which you can build upon as your resources grow.

One of the first questions to consider is what kind of information you want to send to your current and potential customers. Broadly speaking, you can send either purely "marketing" information or more substantive information. True "marketing" information tends to be things like promotions, coupons, and other information that is closely targeted towards a sale. Substantive information, on the other hand, tends to be lengthier informational material that is of interest to your customer base; this is often called an e-newsletter. Of course, the line between marketing and substantive information can get pretty blurry, so here are some tips on how to communicate both types most effectively.

When emailing any type of information to your customers who have signed up for it, make sure that they receive the type of information they expected when they gave you their email address. In particular, don't send purely marketing information to customers who are expecting a more substantive newsletter with topic-based articles. Send marketing emails only to customers who have willingly signed up for that information.

Along these same lines, make sure anything that you call a "newsletter" actually lives up to its name. A newsletter —either in print or via email—does not have to be lengthy. In fact, short blurbs of useful information are generally more popular and reader friendly than lengthy articles. But a so-called newsletter that is little more than promotional copy for products and services will disappoint any customers expecting more substantive information. Considering how little tolerance people have for spammy marketing emails, be particularly careful not to send e-newsletters unless they contain truly useful information and are not just thinly disguised marketing copy. Some marketing information is fine in a newsletter, as long as substantive information is the focus. The best way to include marketing information in a newsletter is at the end of the more substantive information that offers some information of value to your readers.

⊘ CAUTION

Publishing an e-newsletter or other substantive material requires a higher level of commitment. Publishing-oriented websites differ from marketing websites in that they focus on substantive information, such as articles or reports, not promotional copy. Be careful if you're considering an online newsletter or other publishing activities; they will require a higher commitment and higher quality standards for the information you publish, as well as more frequent updating.

What is appropriate content for a newsletter will vary significantly from one business to the next. It will largely depend on the expectations of your audience. Newsletters traditionally contain topic-based articles, but for some businesses it may be sufficient simply to announce upcoming events. For example, an e-newsletter for an independent cinema may send out a monthly newsletter with schedules and descriptions of upcoming screenings. Considering that the film screening schedules are the customers' primary interest, they would likely find that content valuable and happily accept that as an e-newsletter. But a monthly "e-newsletter" from a clothing store that had no content other than sales and specials would likely seem like just another marketing email and irritate its recipients. Instead, a short article or two each month about current fashion trends might be more appealing to interested

readers. Or, the clothing store might reasonably conclude that an e-newsletter just isn't a good fit for its business, and simply be clear with customers that its email announcements will consist of sales specials, and other marketing information from the business.

True newsletters, particularly when they are done well, can take a fair amount of time to create. Though email newsletters may be simpler to create than print newsletters, don't underestimate the hours it will take you to write, edit, proofread, and send them. Similarly, don't underestimate the importance of well-written text that is free from errors and typos.

In addition, when you commit to publishing a newsletter, it means that you commit to putting one out regularly, usually once a month or at least once a quarter. Make a realistic evaluation of whether you or a staffer has the writing skills and the time to be able to reliably create a quality newsletter. If not, then it's best to put off your newsletter plans until you have the resources in place.

When sending out any type of email to your customers, keep in mind the following tips:

- **Use the blind copy function to keep email addresses private.** By putting all the addresses in your email list in the blind copy, or "Bcc" fields, the recipients will not be able to see all the other recipients' email addresses.

Failing to do this risks irritating the members of your lists and making your business appear unprofessional.

- **Manage your email list scrupulously.** Managing hundreds or thousands of email addresses—including dealing with returned mail, address change requests, and unsubscribe requests—is no easy task. Using an email marketing service such as MailChimp (www.mailchimp.com) or Constant Contact (www.constantcontact.com) will help avoid mistakes that can cost you customer goodwill. Be careful, however, and don't use shady, unethical services that really are just spam companies. Stick with the well-known, trusted companies.

CAUTION

Avoid spam at all costs. To avoid being perceived as a spammer, send mass emails only to customers who have requested to be included on your list. Even better, use a "double opt-in" system. In it, customers opt in the first time by indicating a willingness to receive your email communications—perhaps they signed up for your list at your website or signed a sheet at a tradeshow event. Then, you send an email to individual recipients asking them to confirm that they want to be included on your list. A double opt-in system shows your commitment not to send spam—and ensures that the folks receiving your emails actually want them.

Blogging

Blogs are easy, effective ways to communicate late-breaking information. A blog is basically just a website composed of chronologically ordered posts with the most recent entries at the top, much like an online journal. Photos or images are often included with individual posts. Posts tend to be short and almost always include one or more links to related information at other websites. In addition, many blogs allow readers to post comments. Inexpensive and free blog software (WordPress being one of the primary ones these days) makes it easy to add new posts—much easier than it used to be to add new content to nonblog-oriented websites.

Early blogs tended to be more like personal journals, but now blogs have been fully embraced by businesses, media outlets, and issue-oriented websites seeking new ways to connect with audiences. A number of characteristics have made blogs attractive to the masses:

- They are easy to update.
- They allow an informal, friendly voice and more flexible coverage of topics.
- Readers can easily comment on blogs, helping forge a connection between the blogger (that is, your business) and its readership (your potential customers).

The trick to a successful business blog is to offer information that's interesting to your potential customers and that favorably inclines them toward your business and products or services, without being too self-serving or marketing heavy. Doing so is a powerful way to build your brand and solidify your relationship with current and potential customers. For example, if all your business blog posts are about how great your business is—and even worse, if it's all in marketing speak—you'll quickly turn off readers. But if you present interesting topics or beautiful photos to your readers in a sincerely helpful, information-sharing way, you'll be more likely to attract regular readers who develop a favorable impression of your business. This may even mean occasionally linking to competitors, if appropriate.

Blogs that allow users to post comments tend to develop a more loyal readership. Keep in mind, however, that allowing reader posts means you will have to monitor those comments for offensive, libelous, off-topic, or otherwise unacceptable material. It's up to you what line to draw, but inevitably you won't please everyone. If you leave offensive posts untouched, visitors will likely be turned off; while if you edit posts, people are sure to complain that you're censoring them. Still, allowing user posts is a great way to connect with your audience. Just strive to be fair in your policies in editing the posts.

A few examples of business blogging that could be done successfully include:

- a bakery's blog offering baking techniques and tips, allowing comments from readers and encouraging readers to submit photos of their results
- a yoga studio's blog about the health benefits of yoga and tips for doing various poses correctly, as well as links to external articles and studies about yoga's role in healthful living, and
- a landscaping company's blog sharing its experiences and projects, with photos of gardens as they grow, tips on gardening and landscaping, and links to sites with helpful information and/or quality products (such as seeds or landscaping materials).

Remember, the best blogs offer helpful, practical tips and tidbits for readers—not straight-up marketing appeals. Rather than boosting sales directly, blogging is more likely to yield the indirect benefit of developing your brand as a reputable company that's in the know regarding industry developments. Keep this in mind when evaluating your expected results from a planned business blog.

Even more important are some fundamental realities to look at when considering a business blog. At a minimum, don't overlook the following:

- **The blog needs to be regularly updated, ideally a couple of times per week or more.** Don't start a blog unless you're sure that you or someone at your business has the time to keep it updated.

- **The blogger needs to be well-informed on the topic and Internet savvy.** Though the blogger doesn't have to be the world's top authority on your topic, he or she needs to know enough to create posts that are interesting and helpful to others seeking information on that topic. Part of this is being able to ferret out useful information online and provide links to that info.

- **The blogger needs to have some basic writing skills.** An informal, lively writing style is best on blogs. Avoid dry, academic writing or copy that sounds like a sales pitch.

Social Media: Facebook, Twitter, and More

It's hard to remember the pre–social media world, when the Internet was more of a one-directional flow of information from publishers to readers. When social media came onto the scene in the early 2000s, the shift towards sites featuring user-generated content was a brand new thing. These days, social media dominates activity online. Sites like Facebook, Twitter, Instagram, and YouTube are the dominant features of the online landscape, with tens of millions of users posting and engaging every day.

In the broadest strokes, social media sites differ from traditional, old-school websites in that they consist almost entirely of content contributed by site users like you and me. After creating a user account, you can post all sorts of content including text, photos, videos and other multimedia. These sites are "social" in that users typically create networks of friends or followers, and in this way build online communities within which they share information.

While some social media sites like LinkedIn are geared specifically toward professional and business networking, many others such as Facebook and YouTube began as vehicles for largely personal interaction among friends. (Facebook started as an online network for Harvard students.) But just about every sort of social media site has now been infiltrated (for better or worse) by businesses that have developed ways to use these sites to promote themselves and their brands. As you can imagine, some do it more effectively than others.

Very generally speaking, a business engages in social media by creating an account in the name of the business, then networking in whatever ways are appropriate within that community. There are endless ways to do this—so many, unfortunately, that the topic way exceeds the scope of this chapter. Without getting into details, here's a condensed outline of some tips, ideas, and examples to get you on the right track.

Monitoring Your Reputation Online

Even if you don't have the resources to participate heavily in social media, you at least need to keep tabs on what others are saying about you online—good and bad. One of the downsides of social media is that people can complain about your business online—and when they do so, it's often done loudly and bitterly. Both online and off, people tend to voice complaints much more loudly than praise; it's just human nature. But online complaints are particularly problematic for businesses because they reach so many more people than just someone kvetching to their friends and social circles. Unfortunately, this means every business—whether it has much of an online presence or not—needs to be proactive about damage control and at least periodically check out what (if anything) is being said about it online.

If there are particular sites where your customers are likely to post reviews of your business (for example, TripAdvisor for hotels/motels, or Yelp for restaurants), be sure to review those sites at least every month or so. Also use Google to search for your business and any mention of it in blogs. Better yet, set up a Google Alert for your business name (and any other relevant terms, such as names of your main products, or your personal name); that way you'll get an email notification any time your business (or its products, services,

employees, and so on) is mentioned online. Go to www.google.com/alerts to sign up for this free service.

If you do find instances of online customer complaints about your business, respond carefully and thoughtfully. First off, you don't need to respond to every minor complaint that you might read. Overreacting can make your business look desperate and petty. This is especially true if you have mostly positive reviews, with just a sprinkling of mildly negative comments. Potential customers are savvy enough to know that there will always be complainers, so if most online reviews are positive they'll likely believe the majority's opinion.

If, however, there are serious complaints, or a large number of them, you'd likely benefit with a response. Don't just give an empty apology; look into the problem before you respond and take whatever action is appropriate. Then respond with a brief apology and explanation of how you remedied the situation. In particularly egregious circumstances you might even want to offer that user some sort of a refund, either in the public forum or in a private email. The bottom line is to take your customer relations seriously and respond in a way that the customer—and the rest of the world reading that thread—understands you truly want to make the situation right.

Implement a Comprehensive Social Media Strategy

As with any type of marketing, using social media to promote your business is best done with a well-thought-out plan and a clear idea of where you'll focus your efforts. Figure out which social media sites will work best for your business and what your communication goals are before jumping in. Keeping your strategy firmly in focus will also help you avoid being swayed by overhyped technologies that may not be a good fit.

Use Social Media Sites That Your Audience Uses

While sites like Facebook have enormous and broad audiences, others may be more specific—and valuable—to certain industries or business types. If you run a B&B or a hotel, for example, you absolutely should strongly keep an eye on TripAdvisor.com, where users rate their stays at hotels, motels, B&Bs, and vacation rentals worldwide. The content on this website is generated by users, not the hotels themselves, allowing you to see what TripAdvisor users are saying about you and your competitors. And, as discussed in the sidebar "Monitoring Your Reputation Online," below, it's critical that you respond to any serious problems posted online by disgruntled guests. If your head is in the sand and you never visit TripAdvisor, you'd be at a serious disadvantage.

Similarly, if you're a freelance photographer, you should strongly consider having an Instagram or Flickr account. Because photographers tend to congregate at these sites, knowledgeable clients (say, wedding planners or PR agencies) often go there to find good photographers and check out their work. If you don't have an account with photos showing your best work, you'll be missing some potential opportunities.

Understand the Ins and Outs of the Online Community(ies) You're Thinking About Joining

Create a user account for yourself personally to learn how the community operates. Learning the conventions and customs that others use will help you avoid making any faux pas—more than just embarrassing, these kinds of missteps can damage your business's reputation and cost you customer goodwill.

Be Creative!

From creating a hilarious or insanely clever YouTube video that goes viral to finding novel ways to use Twitter for customer service, there's no limit to the ways you can use social media for your business.

Keep an Eye on the Horizon and Shifting Trends

A social media hub that's red-hot with millions of users can quickly become deserted when the next big thing comes around. Remember MySpace? It was the top social media site for a few years, only to become something of a ghost town. Many musicians and bands still have MySpace pages, but by 2010 or so, the rest of the world of social media users largely jumped ship to Facebook. In 2010 and 2011, online coupons and daily deal sites like Groupon were extraordinarily popular, both with users and venture capital firms that helped them scale up hugely. Now they are largely forgotten about. In 2016, Periscope was the hot new social media tool du jour, featuring live videocasting. Now? Not so much.

The point is to keep an ear to the ground so that your investments in social media don't languish. Only you can decide if and when it's time to expand to a new site and/or abandon efforts at sites where you're already established. But you won't be able to make those decisions if you don't stay current with trends, at least at a minimal level.

Forums and Listservs

Many business owners establish their expertise and spread the word about their businesses by posting comments and engaging in threads in forums, Facebook groups, and other discussion areas online about topics related to their businesses. The key is to share information as an expert, not hustle for business. Including your business name and contact info may be okay depending on the customs of the forum; actively soliciting business is generally a no-no.

If discussion groups exist about your business area, start there. If you can't find any, one option is to start a forum at your own website or create a Facebook group—but keep in mind that building even a small online community and moderating it will require a considerable time investment.

A listserv is similar to an email list, in that people who have signed up for the listserv receive emails. However, with a listserv, the emails can be sent by anyone who is part of the listserv, not just by the manager of the listserv. For example, someone who reads a listserv email could respond to the whole group by sending an email to the listserv, which would be distributed to all recipients of the listserv. In contrast, email lists are one-directional, from the business to the list.

Listservs are most common in nonprofit organizations and schools, but some businesses also have customers who want to engage in an ongoing email discussion group. Business listservs tend to be appropriate only when a business's customer base has a compelling desire to interact, such as with software companies whose customers like to share user tips with each other. Yes, listservs are pretty old-school, but if there is an established one in your industry it could be a great place to have a presence.

E-Commerce: What's Involved?

If you're planning to open a traditional brick-and-mortar store, you may see your website as a great way to expand sales. Or perhaps you have an idea for an online-only operation, such as selling vintage posters on your website. But keep in mind that selling products or services online adds complexity and cost to your website. (And don't forget the related logistical details your business will need to handle such as shipping and customer service.)

From a technical standpoint, your site will need to install "shopping cart" software that handles, at a minimum, the functions of the shopper's selecting products and proceeding to checkout. Some shopping cart software does much more, such as allow you to provide discount codes, create custom categories of products, manage inventory, and more.

Besides shopping cart software, an e-commerce operation generally requires that your business have a "merchant account," which is essentially a business bank account specifically set up to accept credit and debit card payments. It's the same thing that a brick-and-mortar business needs to have in order to accept credit cards.

In addition, an e-commerce site needs something called a "payment gateway," which is the service that securely processes the transfer of money from the buyer's payment instrument to the seller's merchant account. Think of the payment gateway as analogous to the credit card swipe machine that's used in brick-and-mortar businesses.

Each of these services charges its own set of fees. These can include an application fee, annual and/or monthly fees, and per-transaction fees, which may be a set amount or a percentage of the transaction total. With the hundreds of shopping carts, merchant accounts, and payment gateway services available, and the complicated mix of fees they charge, picking the best suite of services for your e-commerce can be confusing, to say the least.

The good news is that there are a few standout e-commerce services have become well established. Services like Shopify,

PayPal, Squarespace, and Google Checkout are particularly popular, as they offer bundled services, including shopping carts, merchant accounts, and payment gateways. Each of these services offers a variety of options, but they simplify the process for customers by offering a streamlined, integrated suite of components rather than forcing you to research and choose them on your own.

If you don't use a bundled service, you'll need to choose shopping cart software (popular carts include Magento, WooCommerce, and Zen Cart, but there are many, many others), set up a merchant account (it's not a bad idea to start by inquiring with your existing business bank), and choose a payment gateway (Authorize. Net is a well-established and popular choice). Your shopping cart software, merchant account, and payment gateway need to be compatible with each other and with any other technology used at your website, such as a content management system (like Wordpress or Joomla). The best bet is to ask your Web developer (discussed below) for recommendations, and ask other business owners you know for their experiences with various service providers. If you are interested in setting up an online store with Amazon, eBay, or Etsy, see "Website Builder Services and Affiliate Stores: Do or Don't?" below.

Website Builder Services and Affiliate Stores: Do or Don't?

A common question for small business owners embarking on their e-business plans is whether, instead of hiring a Web developer (discussed below), they could use one of the many template-based website builder services currently available that cost significantly less than typical Web developer fees. Considering that many of these services can be quite inexpensive— say, as low as $50 or even $25 per month compared to a typical minimum $3,000 for a basic site built by a developer—it's certainly understandable that they are appealing to cash-strapped start-ups. Another attractive alternative is to create an affiliate store at an e-commerce site like Amazon, eBay, or Etsy.

There are a few different types of services here, so let's talk about them separately. First we'll look at template-driven sites created with website builder software. Then we'll consider options such as Amazon, eBay, and Etsy, which similarly allow you to do business online without having to hire a developer.

Using a Hosted Website Builder Service

Services such as Wix, Weebly, and Squarespace allow you to build a site using a simple browser-based interface that does not require any technical knowledge or skills. You will generally choose a prebuilt design template and customize it with menu headers, images, and text. Fees, which typically include hosting, can be as low as $10 per month or even free, but these lowest-end fees are generally only for personal websites. Business sites can usually expect to pay in the range of $25 per month and up.

Generally speaking, these template-driven services might be appropriate for only the smallest of businesses who are truly pressed to get a minimal presence online. The biggest drawback is that these types of sites are seriously limited both in terms of design and functionality. While there may be hundreds of design templates to choose from, it can be difficult or impossible to implement a specific design, or to add features that you want such as calendars, blogs, e-commerce, or interactive features. If it is possible to add these features at all, it will usually be only with whatever plug-in that the service provider has created for its template site, which may be primitive at best.

Another downside of using do-it-yourself template sites is that they usually take more time, effort, and skill than these services claim. At the very least, inexperienced users will typically find they'll need to spend a fair amount of time learning the site building system, often through trial and error, before being able to get a site up and running. When considering a website builder service, be sure to look for user comments (often at websites separate from the builder service) to get a sense of how easy or difficult others found the service to use.

Even if you are able to figure out the builder software fairly easily, another issue to consider is that a lack of experience in designing a website will often result in a poorly organized site. Deciding what content to include and how to break up and organize that content at the site can be more complicated than you think. An experienced Web professional can make a huge difference in developing carefully considered content and organization—resulting in a site that's more tightly aligned with your strategic goals.

With all those downsides in mind, let's consider the positives: cost and convenience. Web builder services will significantly reduce the up-front cost of creating a site and minimize the complicated decisions and maintenance that are required when building your own site. These services generally include hosting and will usually handle software upgrades for free. Not having to deal with these issues can be a true relief for new business owners who are swamped by the many other details of getting their businesses off the ground.

A final note: This field of template-driven, do-it-yourself sites is growing rapidly, and designs and features are definitely improving. Expect to see more and better options in coming years.

Opening an Affiliate Store: Amazon, eBay, Etsy, and Others

Another alternative to hiring a Web developer to build your site is to open a store within an existing e-commerce site, such as Amazon, Etsy, or eBay. Creating a store within one of these mega e-commerce portals is definitely a quicker, easier, and less expensive way to get started selling your products online. Typically, the registration and set-up processes are easy to complete; as long as you have good photos of and copy about your products, you can be up and running in a day or two. (Again, remember this doesn't include the very important tasks of doing solid business planning to ensure your venture will be a success.)

There are downsides, however, to having just a store at Amazon or eBay and not your own website. The main drawback could perhaps best be described as getting lost within the shopping mall. Instead of developing name recognition for your business and its domain name, customers will have to find you amongst the thousands and thousands of other Amazon or eBay sellers. Anyone who has shopped at Amazon and other similar e-commerce sites can testify that finding a store or product can be like finding a needle in a haystack. Even if you give your store a specific name, shoppers within sites like Amazon are much less likely to remember your store name than if you had a custom-built store with its own domain name and the ability to use the site design and content to develop your brand more strongly.

Another aspect to consider is that having a store within a big e-commerce operation restricts the content, design, and functions you can offer—and by extension, your ability to control and develop your brand image. With your own site built by a developer, you can use design elements to reinforce your brand, and develop creative, strategic content to draw traffic—say, with a blog, an interactive customer service area, or other unique content. While stores within Amazon, Etsy, eBay, and others do allow you to offer some customized design and content, you'll be much more limited. Bear in mind that you can avoid this issue by having an affiliate store in addition to your own website that you use to develop your brand.

Planning a Website Project

After putting careful thought into your e-business strategy, including the methods that appear best suited for your specific goals, it's time to make some plans to implement your website and any related outreach activities. It's best to tackle some of the planning and preparation tasks before you contact a Web developer. If you take the time and effort to consider the issues discussed below before your first meeting, it will help create an efficient workflow, and help you clearly convey to the developer what you want. Of course, it's normal to have some unresolved questions when you initially contact a Web developer and begin to work with him or her in refining your overall goals. The point is to do at least some planning and preparation in advance to get the most out of the working relationship.

If you want to take an alternative route by using a website builder service (like Weebly) or creating an affiliate store at a site like Amazon or eBay, read "Website Builder Services and Affiliate Stores: Do or Don't?" above. As we discuss in that section, there are several drawbacks to relying on these types of services to establish your online presence. In a nutshell, creating your own website will always give you more control over developing your brand online.

Identify Participants

Define early on which people in your company will be involved in the website project—in particular, who will have the authority to make decisions. With small start-ups, this is usually pretty straightforward: The business owners typically are involved, meaning they help to set goals, review the site in various stages of development, and have approval authority. However, if there are several business owners and one or more are not involved from the beginning, the possibility exists that they may raise objections down the line, after significant time and resources have already been spent on the site. To avoid this, make sure all business owners agree from the beginning who will have decision-making authority and what approval process will be followed.

> **CAUTION**
>
> **If you outsource your site, retain control of strategic decisions.** Unless someone involved with your business has experience creating websites, it's generally best to outsource most aspects of the website creation process. (See "The Website Development Process," below, for details.) Do not, however, give a consultant or Web development company complete discretion over your overall strategy for e-business. Even if you know and trust the developer you hire, you and any other business owners must be involved in these important strategic questions.

Research Other Sites

One of the best ways to educate yourself about the world of possibilities online and to generate specific ideas for features, designs, content, and other elements to include at your site is to browse the Web and look for examples of sites you like and don't like. Even if a site is very different from how you envision yours, there may be elements that could work for your site—for example, the color scheme, fonts, graphic images, or the organization of the information. Most Web developers will ask you for such examples, so it's a good idea to do this research before meeting with a developer.

Learn About Content Management Systems

A content management system (CMS) is the software that manages content at a website. In recent years, CMSs have evolved quite a bit so that nontechnical people can easily maintain a site after it has been built, including updating or adding content and even changing the structure and/or layout of the site. WordPress is one of, if not the most popular, CMS these days; others include Squarespace (for very simple sites), and Joomla and Drupal (for much more robust sites).

When you have a content management system in place, you'll use it via a browser such as Chrome, Firefox, or Safari. You'll log in with a username and password, then will be able to access and edit the content at your site. Generally speaking, you can add as many users as you want and set administrative privileges for each user so that certain people can make deep-level changes (such as to the administrative settings or the structure of the site), while others only have access to certain types of content, or are merely able to submit content but not publish live.

Besides making it easy to update content, CMSs also offer the benefit of being based on technology that is constantly updated and improved. Security is typically a top concern for the companies that maintain CMSs, so you'll regularly be notified of updates to the underlying technology to keep your site safe. Sometimes these updates happen without your involvement; sometimes you'll have to install an update yourself.

So, what content management system should you choose for your site? The answer depends on your strategy and needs for your website. If your entire business will operate online, chances are you will need robust features that integrate marketing and sales, and/or can be highly customized to meet your unique needs. If, on the other hand, your business is primarily a bricks-and-mortar "real-world" business with your website operating as a marketing channel, you may not need all the functionality and customization options of the most feature-rich CMSs.

With that as context, the most popular CMS these days is WordPress which offers a powerful combination of user-friendliness with a huge world of options for features and customization. It is a great choice for a wide range of businesses, from solo operators to businesses with 50 employees or more. If your business needs even more customizable features, you might want to consider Joomla or Drupal.

Another alternative, as discussed above, is to use a hosted CMS like Squarespace, Wix, or Weebly. These offer an inexpensive and quick way to get online without a lot of hassle, but will limit the functions and customization of your site.

 TIP

WordPress isn't just for bloggers anymore. Originally, WordPress was developed as a CMS specifically for blogging. It offered clean templates and an exceptionally easy-to-use back-end interface making it incredibly popular off the bat. Over the years as more and more features have been added to the WordPress platform and it has gotten increasingly customizable, more and more small businesses are turning to WordPress as the platform for their websites. People have discovered how easy it is to use the WordPress CMS to create a robust site that doesn't look anything like a blog, but like a "regular" small business site. It's incredibly easy to maintain and update a WordPress site on your own—most folks find it considerably easier than Joomla or Drupal sites.

 TIP

Some Web developers specialize in certain CMSs. As you interview potential Web developers, ask them what CMS they recommend and why. Beware, however, that some developers may not have experience with some CMSs and may therefore express a bias against them. Make sure that whatever developer you choose uses a CMS that is relatively common; otherwise you may end up with a site built with technology that hardly anyone else knows how to work with— not a good situation if you ever want to hire a different developer down the road. We discuss more tips for choosing a Web developer, below.

Set a Realistic Budget

You don't need to spend a fortune creating a website, but you certainly can—and you can do so either by choice, or by letting costs spiral out of control. An essential step in preventing costs from smothering your best intentions is to set a budget for what your business can realistically afford for website creation and maintenance. It's best to do this before you start talking to Web developers, to get a clear answer from those you contact about whether they can do what you want within your budget. You'll likely get quite a wide range of fees and rates from different developers, which often are affected by how many years they've been in business and what technologies they use. As long as your budget is realistic to begin with, you'll likely be able to find someone who can create something close to the site you want within your budget.

When attempting to set a realistic budget, keep a few parameters in mind. Very generally speaking, a basic CMS-based site will typically cost somewhere between $3,000 and $5,000. To build any additional features—e-commerce functions, a photo gallery, a graphical calendar, an online registration system, a blog, and so on—the price will go up. Remember also that there are often third-party fees beyond what the Web developer charges, such as payment processing and security certificate fees for e-commerce sites, and domain name and hosting fees. The bottom line is that the more features and functionality a site has, the more it will cost. Major, complex websites can cost in the tens or hundreds of thousands of dollars to create.

 TIP

You get what you pay for. Even simple websites require several components: information architecture, graphic design, content creation, and programming. To have all these done well, you'll generally need a bare minimum budget of $3,000. You are not likely to get a quality, professional site—even a simple one—for $1,000. It's better to pay a bit more for a site that is customized for you and that has a professional look and feel.

In addition, it's essential to consider the cost of maintaining your site after it has been created. Assuming you create a site with a content management system, you should be able to handle a significant portion of updating on your own. But don't underestimate the time commitment required—you'll need to define an updating schedule, establish who will be doing the updating work, and make realistic estimates for the time it will take to get the updates done.

Even with a CMS, you may want to hire a Web developer to make deeper technical changes, say to add a calendar function or change the layout of your pages or templates. With Web developer fees ranging from $50 to $150 an hour, outsourcing maintenance can get expensive.

Finally, remember that every site should have a periodic software and security update. Content management systems like WordPress, Drupal, Joomla, and others continually release new versions to address bugs or security issues, and to add functionality. You should plan on reviewing, or hiring a developer to review, your site for necessary updates at least once or twice a year.

Besides software and security updates, the following maintenance and updating tasks are typical:

- writing new content
- adding, removing, or editing products and descriptions in an online store
- taking new photographs—particularly for e-commerce operations when new products are added
- responding to emails from site visitors
- generating and analyzing traffic or sales reports, and
- promoting and marketing the website.

Establish a Schedule

For some business owners, the timing of the launch of their website is crucial—say, it absolutely needs to go live before an important trade show, or before a grand opening. For others, it may not matter very much at all. The point is to consider whether the timing of your website project is an important issue, and if so, schedule accordingly.

It typically takes at least a few months from the start of the website project until the site's launch, and often longer—for complex sites, considerably longer. If holiday online sales are a big part of your business strategy, get the ball rolling in time to get your site up and running by mid-October; this means at a bare minimum getting a contract signed with a developer by September, which means starting your search for a developer and other preparations in early summer. Of course, even this is cutting it close, considering the time it takes to market a site and gain exposure for it. The essential thing is to start the process well before you need your site to be launched.

Also, consider your own busy schedule when planning a Web project. Web developers typically need a fair amount of input from you during the development process, which may require several meetings. For example, you'll likely need to review and approve diagrams or design mock-ups and provide guidance on site content. Definitely do not assume that once you start the project, the Web developer will just run with it and finish it off; you'll absolutely need to account for the time necessary to participate, review, and provide information to the developer.

Finally, your cash flow can be an issue in timing your Web project. Make sure you'll have the necessary cash or credit for any advance deposits and other payments.

Draft an Outline of Site Content

Drafting at least a rough outline of the content you want to feature at your site is a good idea for a few reasons. The most compelling reason is that your site content should be closely related to your site strategy and goals—and because you know these best, it's wise not to turn this task over entirely to a developer. In addition, drafting the initial content outline may help to reduce costs by reducing the work that a Web developer will have to do. Finally, it generally makes sense for you to take the first stab at outlining content because you know best what kind of content exists or can easily be created for your business. Your Web developer can—and likely will—help you refine a content outline, but you are in the best position to make the first draft.

What to Include

A content outline is pretty much what it sounds like. It's not the content itself, but an organized list of topics and subsections that you envision for the site.

When deciding on what to include, focus on the content that will directly help you achieve your goals for the website. For example, if you are creating a simple marketing site with a goal of motivating clients to call you, effective content might include a well-presented portfolio and testimonials from customers, which will impress site visitors about the quality of your work. If you want to create a successful online store, you will want to make it easy for customers to choose among your products; make sure to include important information like dimensions, specifications, installation instructions, or other informative text that will make customers feel confident in choosing a product. If your goal is to attract investors, a downloadable PDF of your business plan would be an obvious piece of valuable content, as would your business history and resumes of the owners.

In addition to your substantive content, always include easy-to-find contact information, including your phone number, email address, and location. Or, if a site goal is to reduce customer service calls, then only include an email address. Again, think strategically and include content that fits with your strategy.

Tips on Drafting

In drafting your content outline, just use the same approach you learned in school: List sections and subsections, and possibly third-level or fourth-level subsections. For example, a website for a photography studio might look something like this:

1. Home page
2. Services
3. About the studio
    a. History
    b. Photographer bios

4. Location and map

5. Portfolio

    a. Weddings

    b. Graduation photos

    c. Professional head shots

6. Tips for great photos

Keep in mind that each section may or may not correspond to its own separate webpage. At this stage of the game, don't worry too much about the specifics of each section or the details of whether certain information will be grouped on one page or on separate pages. And definitely don't get sidetracked into details regarding fonts, colors, or design —not yet. Instead, focus on the overall scope of the site and which sections will be offered. Later, as you work with your Web developer, you'll refine your outline into a more detailed blueprint for the website.

Choosing and Working With a Web Developer

Ironically, lots of Web developers are poor communicators and tend to drown potential clients in tech-speak, making it hard to discern whether they understand what you want or what they're offering. Obviously, you want a developer who is easy to communicate with and who clearly understands your vision, and who does quality, professional work.

This section offers advice on how to find a Web developer—and gives tips on what to consider when choosing one.

Starting Your Search

Just as when you are looking for any professional, the best way to find a Web developer is to ask other business owners for recommendations. In addition, look for examples of good local websites and find out who built them. Sometimes a website will include a credit saying who built it; other times you may have to ask the business owner.

Keep in mind that in the last few years, Web developers have multiplied like little tech-savvy rabbits. Lots of talented developers—and plenty not so talented—operate under the radar, often with no advertising presence. You really need to ask around and talk with plenty of other business owners to get the word on the street about who does great work, at a reasonable price.

What to Look for in a Web Developer

Before you consider hiring any Web developer, visit other sites that he or she has created. Web developers' own websites will usually have online portfolios showing websites they've done. Visit those sites and poke around to make sure they work well. Ideally, the developer will have experience with sites and features that are similar to what you want. Even better, the developer has experience working with businesses similar to yours. As discussed earlier in this chapter, strategic considerations are critical in website projects, so the more your developer understands your business and the strategies driving it, the better.

Specific Technical and Creative Skills

Web development involves several different components and skills. Ideally, you'll find a Web development firm that can offer a team with skills in the following areas:

- designing the organization of the information at your site, also called information architecture
- designing the graphical elements of your site, including choosing a color palette, fonts, and images
- programming the site, and
- creating and finalizing necessary content, including text and images.

Some individual Web developers may say they can handle all these tasks on their own—but this is usually a risky way to go. You'll almost always get a better result from a firm that employs or contracts with specialists such as information architects, graphic designers, programmers, and content developers. This isn't to say that each task absolutely needs to be handled by a separate person, just that it's important that the folks handling the variety of tasks have the right specific skills.

Ask directly about whether professional information architects, graphic designers, programmers, and writers will be used. If the person or firm pitching services to you has loads of expertise in one element such as graphic design or programming, but not in other important aspects of Web development, such as user interface design or content development, it may be wise to keep looking.

If you plan to handle certain aspects of Web development in-house, another consideration is to find a Web developer who can work collaboratively with you. For example, if you want your in-house graphic designer to create the design templates for the site, make this fact clear to the prospective developer and evaluate whether that type of working relationship will be successful.

Use of Technologies and Standards

Some Web developers use specialized development platforms and other technologies that are proprietary or difficult for others to use. So if you end up parting ways with your developer, you might get stuck with a website that is difficult or nearly impossible for others to maintain and update.

When considering Web developers, ask them what technologies they use and whether they are widely supported, and what difficulties might arise for other developers in maintaining the site. You may feel uncomfortable asking this, but it's a perfectly legitimate question that the developer should answer clearly.

In addition, ask whether the developer conforms to Web standards—specifically, the standards established by the World Wide Web Consortium, otherwise known as W3C. Generally, think of Web standards as guidelines that help ensure the best accessibility and compatibility for websites that conform to them. The benefits of conforming to W3C standards are multifold: The website will be compatible with more browsers; it will be easier and cheaper to modify; it will be accessible on other devices, such as cell phones and handheld devices; and people with disabilities such as vision limitations will be able to access your content.

Professional Project Management

An important but often overlooked issue is how well a Web developer manages and coordinates all the various aspects of the project—such as defining the information organization, doing the graphic design, creating the content, and programming the site—to ensure a smooth process. The developer's overall communication skills and responsiveness are important, too.

Web developers should have a clear process in which you, the business owner, are asked to approve the Web developer's progress at various stages. For example, if a Web developer does not follow a methodical process and does not obtain your approval of early stages of site development, you may find yourself presented with a nearly finished site that has no resemblance to what you envisioned. If this happens, the developer may virtually have to start all over again—a situation that could have been averted if approvals had been requested along the way. They may also try to charge you for their extra work, even if it was their poor project management skills that were to blame.

Don't find out the hard way how time-consuming —and sometimes, costly— a poorly managed website project can be. Make sure your developer uses a systematic, methodical approach with a clear review and approval process. If you get the sense that a developer's approach is to "wing it," it's not a good sign.

"The Website Development Process," below, offers a broad-strokes outline of a sensible process for Web development. While it's not intended to be a definitive, end-all approach, it should give you a general idea of how the process should go. Use it as a general model when asking Web developers about their processes and approaches.

Proposals, Quotes, and Contracts

After you have met with a few potential developers and have narrowed your list down to a few prospects, ask each of them to give you a proposal and quote in writing. Generally speaking, it's best to get at least two or three proposals or quotes to compare. Some developers might give a bare-bones quote focused on numbers; others will give more of a proposal that outlines their planned approach. Though an exhaustive, novel-length proposal isn't necessary, a proposal with even just a bit of descriptive text is better than a strictly numbers-oriented quote, because it will demonstrate whether the developer understands your specific needs and has come up with the right solution for you.

Also, watch out for developers who balk at putting a quote or proposal in writing, or who merely want to give you a total quote without a breakdown of services and fees. At the very least, a quote should show what specific services will be offered; ideally the cost will be broken down into line items.

Once you choose a developer, it's essential that you write and sign a contract clearly outlining the project. At a minimum, that contract should include:

- **An overview of the scope of services.** Make sure that you and the Web developer are on the same page regarding who will be responsible for what tasks. Don't assume he or she

will create or edit content for you. Web developers typically will work with your text and photographs, but will not write text from scratch or take photographs without charging extra.

- **A list of deliverables.** In other words, anything the developer will deliver to you, such as a site map, a color mock-up, an HTML template, or anything else that he or she promises to deliver as the project progresses and at the end of the project should be included.

- **A clear schedule.** This should show deadlines for various aspects of the project, often tied to deliverables.

- **Intellectual property provisions.** These detail who will own the materials developed in the project—including graphic designs, templates, written content, photographs, software programming, and any other material subject to intellectual property protection. (Intellectual property is discussed in more detail later in this chapter.)

- **Compensation and payment terms.** Include specifics on how fees will be calculated if work goes beyond the scope originally anticipated.

- **Termination provisions.** Detail what will happen if the working relationship falls apart or either party wants to end the project.

CAUTION

Get it in writing. This advice cannot be overstated: Do not work with a Web developer without a contract. If the developer is reluctant to create or sign a written contract, it's a clear sign that he or she lacks the professional standards that you want. Even worse, without a contract, the Web developer may own copyright to the code, content, or other aspects of your site that he or she creates. Avoid this at all costs by insisting on a contract that addresses intellectual property ownership. For more on this crucial issue, see "Intellectual Property: Who Owns Your Website?" later in this chapter.

The Website Development Process

As has been mentioned previously, an efficient, methodical process will go a long way toward making your website a success. This is true whether you create a website in-house or hire a Web developer to help you. This section outlines a simple, generalized approach that will help ensure an efficient workflow between the Web developer and your business, including all the participants involved in the project. Keep in mind these steps aren't written in stone; there's always a certain amount of fluidity in Web development projects.

In particular, be aware that it's common for Web projects to get a bit circular at times, and that you may need to revisit earlier steps to make modifications. For example, you may need to refine your site's information architecture after you create content if some of that content does not fit into your original design. This is normal, as long as it's not chronic and extensive. The reality is that following a methodical process will improve efficiency. Even if you're planning a small, simple site, following a process similar to the one described here will help increase your chances of success.

The planning process will generally involve the following steps, many of which have been discussed earlier in this chapter—and each of which is outlined below. Those steps include:

- clarifying strategy and goals
- defining content and organization, or information architecture
- defining design elements or the look and feel of the site
- creating content, including text and graphics
- building the website, including any necessary HTML coding, database creation, or programming, and
- testing the site to ensure it functions smoothly before being unleashed on the public.

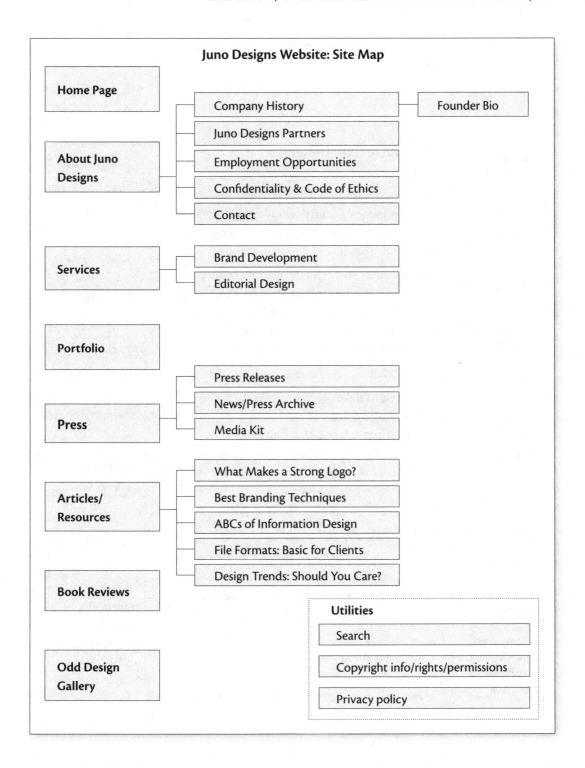

Juno Designs Website: Site Map

Home Page

About Juno Designs
- Company History — Founder Bio
- Juno Designs Partners
- Employment Opportunities
- Confidentiality & Code of Ethics
- Contact

Services
- Brand Development
- Editorial Design

Portfolio

Press
- Press Releases
- News/Press Archive
- Media Kit

Articles/ Resources
- What Makes a Strong Logo?
- Best Branding Techniques
- ABCs of Information Design
- File Formats: Basic for Clients
- Design Trends: Should You Care?

Book Reviews

Odd Design Gallery

Utilities
- Search
- Copyright info/rights/permissions
- Privacy policy

Juno Designs Website: UI Diagram

Juno Designs
logo

image

Search site

Company Information

Home

About

Services

Portfolio

Press

Juno Designs
555 Main St.
Palm Springs,
CA 12345
555-987-6543
info@juno
designs.com

Partner Sites

Spitz Software

Smart Dog Printing

Main Street Independent Business Alliance

Welcome to Juno Designs

Juno Designs is a graphic design firm specializing in brand development and editorial design. We have helped businesses, nonprofits, trade associations, and others define their brands, develop compelling company images, and produce award-winning collateral.

The links at the left offer information about our company and services. The links at the right offer a wide range of informational resources on graphic design issues. Please feel free to contact us directly at 555-987-6543 or drop an email to info@junodesigns.com.

**Featured Article:
What Makes a Strong Logo?**
A strong logo helps develop your brand and ingrains your business in the minds of customers. This short article outlines some principles driving effective logo design. More ...

Featured Projects

image

Annual Report Design. Client: AAA Corp. Juno Designs recently completed a project designing a 150-page report for AAA Corp. More ...

Home | About | Services | Portfolio | Press
Books | Articles | Odd Design Gallery
Search | Site Map

© 2015 Juno Designs. | All rights reserved Privacy Policy | Terms of Use

---

Books

Image

Reviews of the best art and design titles

Articles

Informational articles on design strategies

Odd Design Gallery

Image

Old ads, trademarks, and other odd designs of today and yesteryear

Clarify Your Strategy and Goals

All website projects should start by clearly identifying strategy and goals. (See "Defining Your Strategy and Goals," above.) It's crucial in this early stage that you and your Web developer have open and clear communication about these issues.

It's usually helpful to have workshop-type meetings in which your business's website project participants—and possibly other staffers or associates—contribute ideas. And it's often a good idea to solicit comments from a wide range of people in the early stage, even if those people won't be involved in the project as it progresses. Soliciting feedback from people who will be affected by the website—such as your customer service team or some trusted potential customers—helps ensure that you will include a wide range of perspectives and avoid tunnel vision.

Define Information Architecture and Templates

The term "information architecture" may sound like tech-speak, but it's actually an accurate description of an important, fundamental aspect of all websites: how the information is organized. This is also sometimes called information design or content mapping. In all websites, defining the information architecture is the first step in actually starting to build the site.

Ultimately, you'll develop layouts, called templates, for each unique area of your site. If every page will have the same layout then you'll have one template. If different sections have different layouts, you'll have additional templates.

A basic tool in defining information architecture is called a site map. Closely related to a simple content outline, a site map is a visual representation of content modules and how they are related to one other.

Another fundamental tool is called a user interface diagram, or UI diagram, which is a mock layout of how content and other elements, such as links and images, will be organized on the site pages, which is another way of saying how the pages will look to users. A UI diagram is nearly analogous to an architectural blueprint for a building.

To help understand the difference between a site map and a UI diagram, bear in mind that a site map shows what content will be at a site, and a UI diagram shows how it will be displayed to site users.

On the preceding pages, you'll find examples of both a site map and a UI diagram for a fictional site (Juno Designs).

Web developers vary quite a bit in which types of diagrams they use. At a minimum the developer should offer you some sort of visual diagram showing all the templates that will be used—in other words, all the proposed layouts for the main areas of the site.

Define the Website's Look and Feel

Once the template diagrams are approved, the developer will usually start working on the graphic design and other visual elements of the website, which as a whole are generally called the site's "look and feel." Color palettes and typefaces are major elements to consider, as well as images and composition. Web developers will typically ask you for some initial direction, such as whether you want your site to appear traditional, modern, funky, high tech, or whimsical. You'll also usually be asked about what colors you envision at the site. Your input at this stage is important so that the site conveys the right message and strikes the right tone for your business. Then, based on your guidance, the developer will usually make mock webpages, sometimes called color comprehensives, for you to review and approve.

Create Content

With information architecture and visual elements approved, you can get started on creating the content that will populate the website's pages. You may have already spent some time developing brochures, flyers, or other written information about your business. Don't reinvent the wheel: Use what you have as a basis for your website's content. You may need to rework the existing content to make it shorter and more concise for the website, but it's still much easier to adapt something that's already written than to start from scratch.

If you don't have any written materials, someone will need to start writing. Generally speaking, less is more when it comes to online content. Due to the space constraints of computer screens—especially on mobile devices—as well as the ever-shortening attention spans of some computer users, nothing will turn visitors away from your website faster than dense, lengthy paragraphs. The best online content is concise and easy to digest, so don't be afraid to get right to the point and condense information into lists, bullet points, and short blurbs.

If you decide to publish longer material—for example, a user manual or an industry report—either break it up into sections or provide the document in a downloadable format, such as a PDF, or Portable Document Format, file. Better yet, offer both an HTML version searchable and navigable by section and a downloadable version, so that your visitors can read the document in whatever manner they prefer.

Finally, make sure that at least two people are involved in creating the website's content to make sure that it is clear, concise, and free from errors. At a minimum, one person should write the material and another person should review and edit it. Even if the writer is experienced, a second set of eyes can really make a difference. A little bit of care in these areas will go a long way toward giving a professional look and tone to your site and enhancing the credibility of your business.

When you're done creating and formatting your content, it's up to you (and what's in your contract) whether you or the developer enters it into the CMS. If the developer will do it, make sure the content is formatted so that the developer can easily see which information belongs in a header, where paragraphs should break, which information belongs in bullet points, and so on. You'll need to review the content again once it's on the site to be sure the formats look clean and the information flows well and logically.

Build the Website

Often, while the content is being written and photographed, the programmer is busy building the site based on the approved site architecture diagrams and design mockups. When the build is complete, it will be ready for the content (both text and images) to be entered into the CMS. Depending on your contract, either the Web developer or you will do the content entry. If you do it, you'll likely need some guidance as to how to use the CMS first, which may be a mini-training in addition to the full training done at the conclusion of the project. (See "Train the Site Administrators," below.)

Though your Web developer may build the site on a test server, he or she may prefer to build the site on the Web server where it will ultimately have its home. If so, you'll need to tackle domain name registration and Web hosting before the build is begun. (See "Domain Names and Hosting," below.)

Test the Website

When your site is complete, it should be thoroughly and methodically tested, and all glitches—or bugs—fixed. It's normal and not a bad reflection on the Web developer if the site contains some bugs. What's important is to find them and fix them before launching your site to the public. Professional Web developers should include a testing phase. Once it is completed and all bugs reported and corrected, the site is ready to be launched.

Train the Site Administrators

When the site is finished, the Web developer will generally offer a one- to three-hour training to whoever at your company will be in charge of maintaining the site (the site administrators). If you'll be outsourcing maintenance to the Web developer or an experienced outside contractor, the training may not be necessary.

Driving Traffic to Your Site

There are a number of ways to market your site and drive traffic to it. The extent of your website marketing activities will depend on how your website fits into your overall marketing strategy for your business. If you're planning an e-commerce site that will be the sole source of sales and income for your business, then marketing your site will be critical. If, on the other hand, your website is a basic marketing site that isn't a significant source of referrals and doesn't play a major role in marketing your business, don't worry too much about actively promoting it. That said, all businesses should do simple things such as including their website URL on their business cards, flyers, any ads they run, and other materials they produce.

If driving traffic to your site is a priority, one of the best approaches is to develop inbound links to your site. Besides the obvious traffic-boosting effect of having many other sites link to yours, another benefit is that sites with many inbound links will rank more highly in search engine results, as discussed below.

Developing Content and an SEO Strategy

Creating content at your site that other sites will want to link to is key. Taking this a step further, you can share your site's content by licensing it to other sites with a requirement that the other site provide a link back to your site.

When developing your content, there are a couple of things to keep in mind regarding how well your site ranks in search engine results. The practice of trying to improve your site's search engine results ranking is called search engine optimization, or SEO. While SEO is a complex and constantly evolving topic, there are a few basic strategies you can use to boost your site's rankings in search engine results. In a nutshell, your content affords you two simple SEO opportunities:

- **Developing inbound links.** Quality content that results in other sites' linking to your site does more than just boost site traffic. Having many inbound links will have a strong effect on how well your site ranks with search engines.
- **Relevant keywords.** Content that contains appropriate words and phrases will also improve your search engine results.

Let's discuss each of these in a bit more detail.

Inbound Links

One of the most powerful ways to rank highly with search engines is to have lots of other sites link to yours—in other words, to have a lot of inbound links. This concept is sometimes called "link popularity." Search engines have developed complex formulas to determine how many inbound links a site has, and, all things being equal, sites that have more inbound links will rank higher than other sites. The thinking goes, if other reputable sites find the content at a website useful, then that is a powerful indicator that the site is a quality one that deserves to rank highly for relevant searches.

How this relates to site content is pretty simple: Sites with quality content tend to have more inbound links than sites with meager or inferior content. For example, consider two websites that both sell tennis equipment. One is a straightforward e-commerce site that sells tennis rackets, shoes, tennis balls, and other equipment. The second site sells similar equipment, but also has informative how-to articles and a few streaming videos showing techniques, such as a primer on serving and a demonstration of different backhand techniques. Hundreds of other tennis- and sport-related websites link to the second, content-rich site for its informative content, while far fewer link to the first e-commerce site. So, when people search for "tennis," "rackets," or make other tennis-related searches, the second site ranks way above the first site in Google's search engine results.

As you can see, quality content has a doubly powerful effect on bringing traffic to your site: Besides merely attracting more visitors by virtue of being useful or compelling, content that many other sites have linked to will also raise a site's visibility by helping to improve its search engine rankings.

To attract links (and plain old traffic) to your site, include content that is useful, entertaining, or otherwise interesting to your target audience. Blogs that allow user comments can be very effective at drawing traffic. How-to articles are always popular, as are lists such as "Top Ten Ways to Make Your Home Greener," or "Five Tips to Improve Your Forehand."

TIP

Search engines include the quality of the inbound links in their algorithms. To favorably influence your search engine rankings, the inbound links must come from other reputable sites—not from shady sites such as "link farms," which are meaningless webpages with hundreds or thousands of links created by unethical Web marketing firms trying to trick search engines. Quality inbound links are from legitimate sites like online publications, trade associations, or other businesses in related industries.

Keywords

When creating content, you'll also want to use certain words and phrases—called keywords—that potential customers are likely to use when searching for your site. Including appropriate keywords in your site content should help improve its search engine rankings.

When choosing keywords, put yourself in the mind of potential customers: What words and phrases would they use when searching online for a business such as yours? For example, if you own an electronics store selling audio and video equipment, typical keywords (which should include single words and multiple-word phrases) might include: audio, video, home audio, home video, home entertainment, stereo, surround sound, CD player, MP3 player, speakers, DVD player, DVR, television, TV, plasma TV, LCD TV, flat screen TV.

The trick is to identify appropriate keywords, then use them in your site content so that they read naturally. Don't create awkward text that is crammed with keywords; site visitors can usually see through this tactic or at the very least will be turned off by your poorly written copy.

Besides looking for keywords in your site's content, search engines also look at the page titles for relevant keywords. The title is what appears in the top bar of the browser window. Title text is set in the HTML code for a webpage; assuming you're hiring a Web developer to create your site, he or she will know how to set the page title text. If your Web developer has expertise in search engine optimization he or she can be a big help in choosing keywords and drafting title text; otherwise it's fairly simple for you as the business owner to do it.

Page titles should generally not be much longer than 80 characters, so you should include your most important, strategic keywords here. Ideally you'll have custom keywords for each individual page. For example, instead of having the same title for every page of your plumbing supply e-commerce website, each page's title should accurately describe what's on the page. The home page title could be, "McGee's Plumbing Supply—Clawfoot Faucets, Restoration Hardware, Vintage Accessories," while the title on the Faucets category page could be, "Clawfoot Faucets: Wall Mount, Tub Mount, Gooseneck; Hand Showers; Bronze, Chrome, Brass." Again, put yourself in the mind of your potential customers and think of words or phrases they would use when looking for your products or services.

Using Social Media to Drive Traffic to Your Site

Using social media channels like Facebook, Twitter, or YouTube can be a great way to drive traffic to your site. As mentioned earlier in this chapter, the key is to use the channels that are frequented by your customers and potential customers, and to engage with them via entertaining or helpful content. Remember, being too self-promotional on social media can backfire, so make sure you proceed cautiously to ensure your substance and tone are appropriate.

Facebook is an important channel for many businesses and offers some great opportunities to connect with your audience and steer them to your site. There are also frustrating aspects, such as Facebook's trend toward requiring payment to boost the visibility of your page and its posts. Users are largely at the mercy of Facebook as to these and other rules or algorithms that often change without notice. But, if you hold your nose and dive in, you may find that Facebook can really help your site's traffic.

Interactions on Facebook tend to be quick, casual and informal, so it's generally fairly easy to maintain a page—usually considerably easier than maintaining your own blog, for instance. Make sure to include the URL for your main business website in the "Info" area of your Facebook page, and include links to it in your posts when appropriate; this will allow Facebook friends of your business to click through to your main site, where you'll likely have much fuller information about your business's products and/or services.

Similarly, creating a Twitter, Instagram, YouTube, or other social media account for your business opens opportunities to get your brand noticed and steer traffic towards your site. As always, focus on the channels that your audience tends to use. Also make sure to be thoughtful and strategic before creating accounts. For example, don't create a YouTube channel if you're not sure you can actually produce at least a couple videos a month or so.

Other Traffic-Boosting Tips

Here are a few more ways to steer traffic to your site.

Write for other sites. If you have expertise in a certain area, find online publications that are looking for writers—you'd be surprised how many there are. You may not get paid for your writing but can usually get a link to your site. Remember that it's best to be brief when writing for websites, so you usually won't need to write much more than 500 words, often less.

Submit press releases to online newswires. As discussed in Chapter 13, sending press releases to local reporters and editors is a great way to get exposure for your business. On the Web, you can submit press releases to distribution services such as PRWeb (www.prweb.com) or SourceWire (www.sourcewire.com), which, for a fee, can get your release picked up by Google News and Yahoo! News as well as hundreds of other news outlets. When your press release includes one or more links back to your website, this can result in quality inbound links.

List your business in online directories. There are loads of directories online, grouped by industry type, location, or other criteria. As long as the directories are fairly reputable and not link farms (see Tip, above), this can be a great way to develop inbound links. Some directories charge fees, so do some research before deciding where to list. Pick the ones that look like they get the most traffic and that fit into your budget.

Join membership organizations that provide an online directory listing. Related to the above, keep in mind that some organizations such as your local chamber of commerce or other trade organizations will list your business in their online and print directories as a benefit of membership. Again, evaluate the membership fees and estimated distribution of the directories before deciding on which ones to join.

Clare Zurawski, Albuquerque regional manager of WESST, a New Mexico nonprofit dedicated to helping people start or grow their own businesses (www.wesst.org):

Although there are aspects of search marketing that do involve meticulous technical details, in general, SEO strategy is coming full circle to align with good old-fashioned target marketing and public relations. There are no shortcuts anymore. Essentially, an optimized website must contain relevant content that's well presented in the eyes of your customers.

RESOURCE

For more on search engine optimization, see these books and websites:

- *Search Engine Optimization: An Hour a Day*, by Jennifer Grappone and Gradiva Couzin (Sybex), is a detailed and practical book that's aimed at busy business owners who are short on time but who need to take search engine optimization seriously. The authors maintain a blog at www.yourseoplan.com to offer the latest-breaking information.
- Search Engine Watch (searchenginewatch. com) is a website devoted to tracking the latest developments, trends, and tips for search engine optimization.
- The SEO for Growth blog (http://seofor growth.com/blog/) by leading online marketing experts John Jantsch and Phil Singleton offers practical, detailed, and up-to-date posts full of winning SEO tips and strategies.

Domain Names and Hosting

Before you can post your webpages for the world to see, you must register a domain name and sign up with a Web hosting company. Your domain name is part of the address visitors will use to access your site, such as nolo.com or amazon.com. Your Web host is the company that keeps your site pages on computer servers that are connected to the Internet 24 hours a day, so the pages are always available for visitors to view.

Choosing and Registering a Domain Name

Your first task is to choose an available domain name—that is, a name that is not currently registered to, or being used by, another group. (See "Choosing a Domain Name," in Chapter 2.)

Your domain name has tremendous potential marketing value, so you should take the time to choose it carefully. Remember that it may not be just your business name that attracts customers; names of your popular products and services are also good candidates for domain names. Considering how inexpensive domain name registration is—roughly $10 per year—it makes little sense not to register multiple names if they are appropriate for your business.

It also often makes sense to register your domain name in multiple domains (in addition to .com) in order to establish the widest presence possible for your domain name. Beyond the most common .com domain, the .biz and .net domains are appropriate for for-profit businesses. However, don't make the mistake of registering a .org address for a for-profit business. The .org domain is intended for nonprofit organizations only. Even though this rule is not enforced by the .org registry, it's misleading and inappropriate to use a .org address for your for-profit

business. At the very least, using a .org address will make your business look ignorant of domain name rules; at worst, customers will think you are trying to mislead them into believing you are a nonprofit.

Once you select an available name, register it online at a domain name registrar. There are hundreds of options out there. If you'd like to do some comparison shopping, you can find a list of approved registrars at www.internic.org.

RESOURCE

How one domain name registrar works. One popular registrar is Namecheap at www.namecheap.com. Here's how the process works: At the Namecheap website, you will first be prompted to enter your proposed domain name to see if it has already been registered. If not, you will be allowed to proceed and register the name yourself.

Fees vary depending on the options you choose; all are generally affordable. Registering one name for one year through Namecheap costs under $10. Once you've chosen your options, simply enter information about your business and provide credit card information.

Although registering a domain name is pretty simple, there are a few potential pitfalls. In particular, if you allow your Web host to take care of domain name registration or renewal—a common practice—you must make sure it lists your business or an authorized representative as the domain name registrant and administrative contact. If anyone but an authorized representative of your business is listed as the domain name registrant, you might find that your control over your domain name is seriously compromised. Web host companies have developed a nasty habit of registering their clients' domain names under the host company's name, rather than the name of the client. This creates serious domain name ownership and control issues.

For example, if your Web host handles the domain name registration process for your business and lists itself as the registrant of the domain name you've chosen, you might not be able to make any changes to your host account or even your domain name account, because you are not listed as the registrant. In this way, the Web host company can hold your domain name hostage, preventing you from switching hosts or otherwise managing this crucial part of your business's identity.

Your domain name is an asset, and the people or organizations listed in the domain name registration have varying degrees of authority over the asset. Be particularly careful about whom you list as:

- **Registrant.** The registrant is the legal owner of the domain name. Use your business's legal name, not your Web host company's name.

- **Administrative contact.** The administrative contact should be someone in your business who has authority to make policy decisions, particularly with regard to the domain name. Again, you should not list your Web host company here.

- **Technical contact.** This is the person the registrar may contact with technical issues. You may list your Web host company here.

If your Web host handles domain name registration or renewal, make sure it uses the names you want. Otherwise, it may cost you many times the original registration fee to get the registration back in your rightful name.

Choosing a Web Host

A Web host is a company that maintains servers, which are simply high-performance computers that are connected to the Internet continuously, serving the webpages stored on it to the world. When your website files have been uploaded to the host's server and your Web host has configured your domain name correctly, your website will be live and all the information it offers will be available to visitors around the globe, 24 hours a day, 365 days a year.

To choose from the many Web hosts out there, get recommendations from other business owners to find one that offers reliable servers and good customer service. Make sure there are reasonable customer service hours during which you can talk to an actual human. More than a few host companies offer no live-person customer service, which can be infuriating if you're experiencing any problems.

Web hosts may charge by the month or by the year. Fees are based on how much data you need the server to store—that is, the size of your website in disk space—or how much data you transfer to and from your website each month.

Intellectual Property: Who Owns Your Website?

Intellectual property laws establish ownership rights and other rules for various types of works such as text and artwork protected by copyright, marks used in business protected by trademark, and inventions protected by patents. Copyright is of particular importance in Web development projects, as many of the components of websites are protected by copyright. (It is also a huge issue on social media where most people don't think twice before sharing creative works owned by someone else. See below for details on avoiding trouble on social media.)

As mentioned earlier, it's crucial that your contract with a Web developer includes clear, detailed terms on ownership and permissions for any materials developed for the website protected by copyright. Other intellectual property laws, such as trademark or patent, also may come into play, though not as often.

Copyrightable materials include text, photos, artwork, and designs, as well as technology developed for your site, such as databases and programming. As you can imagine, serious troubles can arise if ownership of any aspect of your website is in dispute. The way to avoid this is by including clear copyright terms in your contract with the Web developer. This section gives a quick overview of copyright basics and the specific issues that arise in Web development projects, to help you head off any copyright conflict.

RESOURCE

In-depth resources on copyright and intellectual property issues. For the full treatment on copyright and the permissions process, see *Getting Permission: How to License & Clear Copyrighted Materials Online & Off*, by Richard Stim (Nolo). For lots of free articles on intellectual property, see the Patent, Copyright & Trademark section of Nolo.com.

Copyright Basics

When someone owns copyright to certain works, it means that others may not reproduce, modify, distribute, or sell the works without the copyright owner's permission. In legal terms, permission to use someone else's copyrighted content is known as a license. When you license content, you do not own it; you simply obtain the right to use it in specific circumstances. In contrast, buying the copyrights to a creative work, known in legal terms as an assignment, gives you all the rights to the work as if you were the original copyright owner.

The general rule is that the person who creates content owns the copyright. However, if the work qualifies as a "work for hire," then the hiring party, not the creator, legally owns the copyright to it. The rules regarding what constitutes a work for hire vary depending on whether the work is created by an employee or an independent contractor.

Rules for Employees

When an employee creates any work in the course of employment, the work is considered a work for hire, so that the employer—not the employee—owns the copyright to that work. Having your website created by employees, not contractors, is the simplest and most straightforward way for your business to make sure that it owns copyright in all aspects of the site.

Unfortunately, this isn't an option for many start-up businesses. But fortunately, there are other ways to make the work a work for hire, even if it is created by an independent contractor, not an employee.

Rules for Independent Contractors

When an independent contractor creates certain types of content, the hiring party owns the copyright in the work if the contractor and hiring party have made a written agreement stating that the work is a work for hire. The written agreement is essential: Work-for-hire agreements are necessary whenever a nonemployee creates the work. Without a written work-for-hire agreement, the nonemployee Web developer owns copyright to the materials he or she develops for the website.

But there's an important wrinkle: You cannot turn every kind of creative work into a work for hire using a written agreement. According to copyright law, a work-for-hire agreement will give copyright to the hiring party only if the content is:

- part of a larger literary work, such as an article in a magazine or a poem or story in an anthology
- part of a motion picture or other audiovisual work, such as a screenplay
- a translation
- a supplementary work, such as an afterword, introduction, chart, editorial note, bibliography, appendix, or index
- a compilation
- an instructional text

- a test or answer material for a test, or
- an atlas.

Without trying to puzzle through how on earth lawyers came up with these categories, it's important to understand that depending on whom you ask, the categories may not include the components of websites. This naturally raises the question: If website materials cannot be the subject of work-for-hire agreements, how can you obtain ownership from a Web development contractor? The answer is that you'll need to have a written and signed copyright assignment—an outright sale of all copyright from the contractor to your business. Though it's possible that website materials might legally fall into one of the work-for-hire categories, the safest route is to assume they do not, and to handle ownership transfer with a copyright assignment.

To sum up, to obtain ownership of materials created by a Web developer for your website, you'll need to:

- hire the creator as an employee—which usually is not a practical option, unless you already planned to hire a Web developer on staff, or
- have a written copyright assignment, signed by both you and the developer, usually within your website development contract.

Employee or Independent Contractor?

A number of laws govern whether a worker is an independent contractor (IC) or an employee, and each of these laws has a different way of looking at the issue. For example, the IRS has one method of determining whether a person is an independent contractor, but your state workers' compensation board may use a different test. Because of all these different laws, often referred to as "worker classification" rules, the issue of whether a worker is an IC is not always straightforward.

The IRS is probably the most important agency to satisfy when it comes to classifying a worker as an IC. Under the IRS's test, workers are considered employees if the company they work for has the right to direct and control the way they work—including the details of when, where, and how the job is accomplished. In contrast, the IRS will consider workers independent contractors if the company they work for does not manage how they work except to accept or reject their final result. (See "Employees Versus Independent Contractors," in Chapter 16, for a more complete discussion of distinguishing between these types of workers.)

Protecting Your Interests

It's obviously in your interest to own all aspects of your website so that you have the legal right to do anything you want with the site. For example, if you fail to obtain a copyright to the site's text content from the Web developer, the developer could potentially prevent you from making any changes to the text on the site. The same is true for images, graphic designs, and technologies created by the Web developer for the website. This may sound far-fetched to you now, but consider what might happen if you and the developer ever got into a conflict and decided to part ways. A developer with a bone to pick who owns any rights to your site could deal a serious blow to your online business.

Be aware that sometimes a Web developer will not want to assign copyright ownership to your company for certain aspects of the site. As discussed below, this may be perfectly legitimate. What's crucial in this situation is for you to get permission—legally, a license—from the Web developer to use his or her copyrighted work as necessary for you to get the full benefits of your website. Without such permission, you'll be at the mercy of your Web developer when you want to edit content or make changes to technology owned by the developer—a situation you definitely want to avoid.

There are a number of situations in which it might make sense for a Web

developer to retain ownership. Developers sometimes will not transfer ownership of technology that they have developed such as content management systems, shopping carts, or other functions. Developing Web applications and using them for multiple clients is the lifeblood of some Web firms, so they naturally are not willing to transfer ownership of that programming code to your company. Instead, they'll give your business permission, or a license, to use the technology in specified ways. This is perfectly legitimate, but you'll need to be careful about a couple of things:

- **You need to protect your company's ability to make changes to the site down the road.** You should always think about—and ask prospective developers about—what will happen if you end your relationship with the developer in the future. If the developer creates the site with proprietary technology, you may find it difficult or impossible to make changes without using the original developer. It's not uncommon for a business to learn this lesson the hard way and have to create a new website from scratch after ending its relationship with a previous developer who refused to grant permission to the business to make changes to the code the developer owned.

- **If you are hiring the developer to create functions or other programming code that will give your business a competitive edge online, then you'll want to obtain full ownership of that code so that it can't be used for other businesses.** This isn't usually the case with small, basic websites that simply want to establish an online presence. But if you are paying a developer to create an innovative shopping cart or search function that will help distinguish you from your online competition, it's essential that you own that code when it's complete so that it can't be used by anyone else without your permission (and possible licensing fees paid to you). Don't be surprised to be charged a premium for this type of full transfer of rights.

At the end of the day, the important thing is that you and the developer are on the same page about who owns what. Consider another possible scenario: Say your business has only a tiny budget for photographs for the site, and cannot afford the rates a developer would charge to take photos and transfer all rights to your company. As an alternative, your website development contract could specify that the developer will retain all rights to any photos it takes for the site, and that the developer grants your company a license (permission) to post the photos at the site indefinitely. In this case, your contract should state specifically how you are allowed to use the photos—and you must abide by the license agreement. With an agreement like this, you typically will not be allowed to use the photos in advertisements, on T-shirts, or in any other ways. As long as having broad use of the photos isn't important to you, letting the developer retain copyright is a good way to keep your website project costs down.

EXAMPLE: Marina is negotiating contract terms with the Web developer she chose to create her pottery store's website. To keep costs down, Marina and the developer agree that Marina will be responsible for taking photos. However, they also agree that the developer may take photos for the site, and that he will retain the copyright to those photographs. To make sure she retains control over the website, Marina gets a provision in the contract granting her business a license to display any of the developer's photos at her website indefinitely. In addition, Marina asks the developer if he would be willing to include a license allowing her to modify the size and the brightness of the photos in case they ever need such adjustments. The developer agrees to a license to modify that is limited to size and brightness, but no other modifications.

In deciding what ownership or licensing arrangements will work for your business, keep in mind the following rule: The more important content or technology is to your site, the more crucial it is that you either get ownership or a broad license to use and possibly modify those materials. This is true whether or not the Web developer has a valid reason to retain ownership. If it's essential that you own copyright ownership in a database or other technology, don't enter into an agreement that won't confer the rights you need.

Avoiding Copyright Troubles on Social Media

With these general rules as background regarding what copyright protects and who owns what parts of your website, it's important to understand that copyright rules also extend to uses on social media. In an age of fast and furious sharing of photos, videos, quotes, and more, there's no question that copyright rules are often completely forgotten. Many people who would never dream of using someone else's photograph without permission on their website, would share it on Facebook without a second thought.

Of course, it's undeniable that the customs of Facebook and Twitter encourage a sharing mentality, and that this is often okay with owners of copyrightable material. For example, when someone creates a funny meme (a clever photo or video with text, meant to go viral), by posting it in the first place, it's

clear they want it to be shared without any expectation of payment or credit to the creator. Note that some memes do include a URL or another type of watermark on the image, in which case it's clear the online creator wants that credit info to be included with the image. Removing the URL or watermark violates the clear intention of the creator, yet the likelihood of consequences are low. The bottom line is that on social media, while rules may seem fuzzier, the intention of the creator is an important consideration.

Moving beyond memes, using photos (or text, or anything subject to IP protection) that you find online and sharing them in any of your business's activities is a very bad idea if you don't have permission. It's one thing when an individual shares things recklessly, but when a business does it, it is attempting to profit commercially with the infringement, making it more egregious. Don't—as in, DO NOT—feel free to use photos you find on Instagram, Flickr, or other social media unless you use them within the rules. If the photo does not include special licensing terms, then general copyright rules apply. Sometimes photographers include generous licensing terms within the information about the photo, such as permission to use it for noncommercial (or even sometimes commercial) uses, as long as credit is provided.

Other issues that can arise include using photos (or other copyrightable material) on social media that you paid a contractor for, but for a different use. Say, for example, you hired a photographer for photos of your café's food for its menu. Your contract with the photographer specified the photos were for the menu, but did not address social media use. If you then start posting those food photos on Instagram, the photographer might be peeved—and have a case for infringement.

Since the possible uses of photos and other creative works on social media is so endless, and so potentially high profile, you should make it a point to be on the same page with anyone you hire for creative work about whether and what social media uses are allowed. Many photographers would be happy for you to share their work on social media (assuming they've been paid, etc.), but often want to be credited. Giving credit is easy to do, and can actually help the reach of that social media post by potentially tapping into the photographer's followers.

On the flip side, be crystal clear: Giving credit does *not* get you out of infringement trouble if you're, in fact, using something without permission.

Chapter 14 Checklist: E-Business: Selling and Marketing Online

☐ Assess your strategy and goals for your site and any other e-business activities, and how they fit into your overall business plan.

☐ Consider the wide range of ways your business can reach out to customers online, such as with a blog, email lists, e-newsletters, listservs, e-commerce, social media, and others when crafting an e-business plan.

☐ Research other sites to get examples of organization, design, content, and features that might work well for your site.

☐ Choose a Web developer who has strong project management skills.

☐ Develop compelling content that will attract traffic to your site and actively encourage inbound links to that content.

☐ Insist upon a written contract with your Web developer, and make sure your business will obtain copyright ownership of most, if not all, content and technology developed for the site.

☐ When marketing your site using social media, make sure to avoid copyright infringement claims. Ask for permission before sharing anything that you or your business don't own.

Planning for Changes in Ownership

As discussed in Chapter 1, choosing a legal structure is a fundamental task for every new business owner. Whether you operate as a sole proprietorship, a partnership, an LLC, or a corporation has important implications for liability issues and taxes—two areas definitely worthy of your close attention.

For businesses with more than one owner, there's another important and related concern: how to handle any future changes in business ownership. It probably won't be top of mind in your early, exciting start-up days, but the fact is that businesses commonly face situations that raise serious—and often unexpected— ownership questions. An incapacitating illness or untimely death are just two of the more extreme situations that call the business's ownership into question. What if an incapacitated owner wants to sell to someone the other owners don't like? Will a deceased owner's child inherit the ownership interest and become an active owner of the business? Plenty of other situations can also have an impact on the ownership of the business; they're discussed later in this chapter.

The best way to handle all these situations is to make an agreement about how the business will deal with them. This type of agreement is known as a buy-sell agreement; the phrase "buy-sell" refers to the rules it outlines for how a company's ownership shares may be bought or sold. By anticipating certain events and defining what will happen if they arise, a buy-sell agreement can lessen the chaos that ownership changes can inflict on a business.

Busy as you may be with the details and concerns of starting up your business, it makes the best sense to address these issues even before you get up and running. Since buy-sell provisions generally limit what owners can and cannot do with their ownership interests, it's crucial to create fair, impartial rules while everyone is on equal footing. If you wait until something happens that puts ownership on the brink of change—for example, one owner becomes incapacitated and desperate to sell out—you'll have a much harder time imposing rules that are comfortable for everyone involved. And addressing buy-sell provisions early on is one of the best ways to build and maintain harmonious relationships among business co-owners.

This chapter starts by explaining who should consider drafting a buy-sell agreement and why. Then it defines buy-sell agreements, explaining the essential provisions you'll typically find. Finally, it offers sample buy-sell provisions to help you get started in drafting your own agreement.

RESOURCE

For more in-depth information.
While you'll learn the basic, essential elements of buy-sell agreements in this chapter, *Business Buyout Agreements: Plan Now for All Types of Business Transitions*, by Bethany Laurence and Anthony Mancuso (Nolo), covers much more ground. It walks you through the process of drafting a comprehensive buy-sell agreement that addresses a wide range of issues such as structuring and funding buyouts, and tax and estate planning concerns.

When You Need a Written Buy-Sell Agreement

If your business—whether partnership, LLC, or corporation—has more than one owner, you would be wise to have a written buy-sell agreement in place. Although hopeful co-owners of a new business usually want to think their alliance will last forever, this attitude is unrealistic. Even the most compatible, fair-minded business owners commonly face all sorts of life events that can bring ownership into question: death, divorce, illness, bankruptcy, or simply a decision to change life's direction. Rather than let ownership changes sneak up on you and wreak havoc on your company, it's much smarter to accept that the ownership will likely change at some point, and plan for that day.

If you still need convincing, consider some common situations and how they can impact a business.

An Owner Leaves or Retires

It's often said that being a co-owner of a business is like being in a marriage—and the pressures of running the business can lead to a bitter break-up. But even when co-owners get along famously, one of them may simply want to retire or do something different. Perhaps the business didn't provide an owner with the satisfaction anticipated, prompting a decision to change course and leave the business.

Whatever the circumstances, the potential departure of an owner raises serious questions. What if an owner decides to stop working for the company but refuses to sell the share in the business, hoping to earn income without contributing to it? Assuming an owner does plan to sell the interest in the business, can the sale be to anyone at all? Clearly, the remaining co-owners would not be happy to learn the departing owner sold out to someone they all detest. How will the price of the departing owner's interest be determined if offered for sale? Valuing the company and determining share price can be quite contentious, particularly when continuing owners want to purchase the share.

On the flip side, consider what would happen if you wanted to retire. What if you couldn't find someone to buy your interest, and your co-owners didn't want or couldn't afford to buy your share? Would you be stuck, unable to cash out? Failing to address these issues early in the life of your company can result in a real quagmire if they arise in real life.

An Owner Becomes Disabled

If one owner has a debilitating stroke, is paralyzed in a car accident, or suffers some other incapacitating illness, the remaining owners face some big questions: Can they force the disabled owner to sell out? Can the departing owner sell to whomever he or she pleases? If the sale is to the continuing owners, what price must they pay for that share?

Again, the issues shift a bit for the person who becomes disabled and wants— or, more likely, needs—to sell. If you find yourself in this situation, you'd likely be concerned about being able to sell your ownership interest for cash to help pay medical bills and get through the tough time. Truth is, it's often difficult for small business owners to find outside buyers, especially for a minority ownership interest. If your co-owners are uninterested or unable to buy you out and you have no buy-sell agreement in place, you could find yourself in a really tight spot.

An Owner Dies

The death of a co-owner is sure to be traumatic for everyone in the business. In the midst of it, the co-owners will be faced with the burden of figuring out who will own the deceased owner's share. For example, will they be forced to accept anyone who inherits the ownership interest as a new, active owner? What if the person who inherits the share wants to sell it for cash to the current owners, or to an outside buyer?

Similarly, if you die, these questions will be dropped into the minds of your grieving family members or the people who may take over your ownership share. They may need money for funeral expenses, not to mention living expenses once you aren't earning any income.

A buy-sell agreement can anticipate and provide a clear plan for these emotionally laden situations. Without an agreement, the trauma of losing an owner can go from bad to worse if the current owners and the deceased owner's successors can't agree.

An Owner Divorces

You don't need to be reminded that divorce is a possibility, even when marital harmony and bliss seem certain. Roughly half of all marriages end in divorce, so you absolutely must deal with the question of how a marital split might affect your business.

The most glaring possibility is that when a co-owner gets divorced, the ex can become a new owner of the business. Except when a premarital agreement or "prenup" prevents it—and, in reality, many prenups are hard to enforce—spouses of business partners often have a legal interest in the business. This legal right is most clear in community property states—including Arizona, California, Idaho, Nevada, New Mexico, Texas, and Wisconsin—in which each spouse owns half of the couple's community property, usually most of the property gained during the marriage. But even in noncommunity property states, laws often require that a couple's property be divided fairly during divorce.

Having an ex suddenly on board can, of course, be a true disaster, especially if former spouses each have an ownership share and must run the business together. Even if the original co-owner sells out of the business and the ex remains an owner, there's a huge potential for drama and trouble—particularly if the divorce was a nasty one. If the divorce was friendly, an ex who has no business experience or is just plain incompetent may still be unwelcome as an owner. In short, there are ample and compelling reasons to preemptively avoid these situations by implementing a sound buy-sell agreement.

Specific contract language is discussed below in "Sample Buy-Sell Provisions." For now, keep in mind that to avoid the situations outlined above, all the spouses of current business owners should read and sign the buy-sell agreement.

An Owner Becomes a Liability

Sometimes conflict with a business owner goes beyond the occasional squabbling and sniping typical of many business relationships. In extreme cases, the conflict crosses the line and some of the owners agree that it's time to push out one of the other owners. This situation can arise for all kinds of reasons: The owner may be inherently unreasonable and difficult, suffering from alcoholism or substance abuse, mentally ill, or engaged in criminal behavior.

Whatever the root cause, once things have deteriorated to an intolerable level, it's important to have a mechanism in place to expel an owner. Having rules—for instance, outlining the situations that call for expulsion—will help make this nasty situation a little less nasty.

To sum up, when any of these often painful situations occurs, you can depend on a buy-sell agreement to dictate an orderly transfer of ownership interests according to rules all have consented to beforehand. As discussed in more detail below, a buy-sell agreement can outline straightforward rules about when ownership shares can or must be sold, to whom they may be sold, and how to determine the share's selling price.

Buy-Sell Agreement Basics

A buy-sell agreement is a contract among a business's owners that spells out, in varying degrees of detail, some or all of the following issues:

- who can buy a departing owner's interest
- when the owners can force another owner to sell a share of the business
- when one owner can force the other owners to buy a share
- what price will be paid for a departing owner's share, and
- how a buyout will actually happen, including specific payment terms.

In practice, a buy-sell agreement typically has a few standard provisions to handle these issues. Buy-sell provisions can either be assembled into their own stand-alone agreement or inserted into other business documents, such as your partnership agreement, LLC operating agreement, or corporate bylaws. The term buy-sell agreement in this chapter includes any buy-sell provisions your company has adopted, whether they're in a separate agreement or included in another business document.

The three provisions at the heart of buy-sell agreements establish:

- transfer of ownership interests with the right of first refusal
- the right to force buyouts, and
- a set price or a formula to determine share price.

Limiting Ownership Transfers

When an owner wants to leave a business and sell an ownership interest, it can create real and lasting chaos if the share is sold to someone the other owners don't want as a co-owner. But if there is a buy-sell agreement that establishes limits on the transfers of ownership shares, this possibility can be avoided.

The best way to avoid unwanted outsiders gaining ownership of your business is with a provision known as a "right of first refusal." This provision gives the company or the remaining co-owners the right to buy a departing owner's interest before it's transferred—that is, sold or given—to an outsider.

It works like this: A departing owner who receives an offer to purchase his or her interest from an outsider may not accept it outright. Instead, the right of first refusal requires the departing owner to give written notice to the company stating the intention to sell the shares and describing the terms of the proposed sale. At that point, the company and the continuing owners have the option to buy the departing owner's interest. Depending on how you structure your right of first refusal, the company and continuing owners will be entitled to purchase the shares either at the same price as the outsider offered or at a price previously agreed upon and included in the agreement. If the co-owners don't want to buy the ownership interest at those terms, then the departing owner has 60 days to sell it to the outsider according to the terms outlined in the notice.

The right of first refusal focuses on preventing unwanted outsiders from gaining ownership interest in your company. Since this is a fundamental issue, it is important for all business owners to put this provision in place.

But you can also include solutions such as the following for dealing with related issues in the right of first refusal:

- **Extend the right to potential sales to current owners.** If the right of first refusal is structured this way, when a departing owner offers a share to another current owner, all the co-owners must be given the option to buy it. The main reason to use this arrangement is to prevent one or more co-owners from seizing control of the business by buying a departing owner's share.

- **Create different rules for gifts or transfers to trusts.** It's possible to have the right of first refusal apply to sales of ownership shares, as described above, but not to other types of transfers, such as gifts or transfers to trusts. Generally, giving ownership shares to family members or putting them in a trust is done for estate planning purposes—to save estate taxes and

avoid probate. If you and your co-owners want more freedom to engage in estate planning techniques with your ownership shares, you may not want the right of first refusal provisions to apply to gifts and transfers to trusts.

- **Prohibit all transfers.** Current owners may keep the tightest grip on control of company ownership by banning all ownership transfers outright. However, since this approach is so rigid and unhelpful to owners who may really need to sell out of a business, it is generally not a good idea.

 FORM

You can find suggested language for a right of first refusal in "Sample Buy-Sell Agreement Provisions," below, and on the agreement included on this book's companion page on Nolo.com (see Appendix B for the link).

Forcing Buyouts

In addition to controlling who owns a business, an important function of a buy-sell agreement is to provide answers to the questions that can arise when the ownership setup is thrown into question. What if one of your co-owners dies? Will the heirs become co-owners in your business? What if a co-owner slides into crippling alcoholism or substance abuse? Will you be stuck with an inebriated business partner? What if your co-owner gets divorced and the dreaded ex-spouse gets an ownership share as part of the divorce settlement? Is there anything you can do?

You can remove the uncertainty from all of these situations by taking preventive action. By adopting forced buyout provisions in a buy-sell agreement, you'll establish rules for different scenarios, such as death, divorce, bankruptcy, retirement, and other business-disrupting events. When the rules are triggered by specific events, an owner can be forced to sell shares, or continuing owners can be forced to buy out a departing owner's share. Forced buyout rules help keep the business stable during difficult times and make ownership transitions as smooth as possible.

As you can imagine, a crucial fact about forced buyout provisions is that they must be agreed to well in advance of any situation that will trigger them. It goes without saying that the situations that trigger these provisions—such as death, disease, and divorce—often cause emotions to run high. You and your co-owners should discuss the possible scenarios and come to a consensus on what rules will apply in those situations before any owner is personally affected.

In a nutshell, there are two different kinds of forced buyouts: Either an owner can be forced to sell out, or a departing owner can force the other owners to buy the departing owner's share.

Forcing Owners to Sell

Business owners can force an owner or other person who has obtained an interest in the business to sell out of it—and sell the shares back to the company or the continuing owners at a specified price. They do it by including an option-to-purchase provision in the buy-sell agreement.

This provision can force any of the following people to sell back to the continuing owners:

- any one of the owners—for specified reasons such as retirement, disability, bankruptcy, loss of professional license, or misconduct
- the executor or administrator of a deceased owner's estate, and
- an owner's ex-spouse who gains an interest in the business through a divorce settlement.

The rules vary depending on which situation triggers the forced buyout, but the overall goal is the same: to keep control over the company's ownership and keep out anyone unacceptable to the continuing owners. This includes people who stand to gain ownership through inheritance, divorce, or bankruptcy—as well as current owners whom other owners want to push out.

All options to purchase should also address the price at which the shares will be sold. Usually this is accomplished by referring to the "Agreement Price" outlined in a separate buy-sell provision. (Price provisions are discussed in "Establishing the Price for Sales: How to Value the Business," below.)

Forcing Owners to Buy

The flip side of an option-to-purchase provision is the right to force a sale. Without a right-to-force-a-sale provision, an owner who wants to sell out might be stuck if the current owners don't want— or don't have the funds—to purchase his or her share. But with a forced buyout provision, anyone with an ownership interest in the business can force the other owners to buy that interest at a specified price. Common scenarios include an owner who's retiring or becomes disabled who wants to sell out of the business, or a deceased owner's survivors who want to cash out the ownership interest they got in a will.

Beware that while a forced buyout provision protects owners from being stuck in a business, it also has the potential to seriously damage a company that doesn't have the means to pay out departing owners, particularly when business isn't so hot.

But there is a way to both protect business owners who don't want to be chained to the business forever and to protect the business from bleeding money from cashing out owners. Your right-to-force-a-sale clause can allow owners to cash out of the business only after a certain time, by which you expect your business to be stable and profitable enough to pay out a departing owner. Anyone who chooses to cash out before that time—for example, three or five years—will only receive a fraction of the value of ownership share— say, 50%. This creates a disincentive for any owner to leave early in the life of the business, when cash reserves may be crucial.

 FORM

You can find suggested language for a forced buyout in "Sample Buy-Sell Agreement Provisions," below, and on this book's companion page on Nolo.com (see Appendix B for the link).

Negotiations can easily get tangled up on price issues, so it's important that the right to force a sale provision addresses the price at which the shares will be sold. Generally it will refer to a separate pricing provision, which is discussed next.

CAUTION

Wrinkles for co-owners with unequal shares. If your company has one controlling owner and one or more owners with small minority shares, the controlling owner may not want to be subject to the same rules as the minority owners. For example, say a company has a majority owner who is very identified with the company and who has played the primary role in building it over many years. The majority owner may balk at the idea that the minority owners could force his or her children to sell their shares, elevating the minority owners to control the company. Majority owners should consider consulting an experienced business lawyer before signing a buy-sell agreement. Before doing that, it's a good idea to read *Business Buyout Agreements: Plan Now for Retirement, Death, Divorce or Owner Disagreements*, by Bethany Laurence and Anthony Mancuso (Nolo), which explains the subtleties of buy-sell agreements in much greater detail than this chapter.

Establishing the Price for Sales: How to Value the Business

In addition to spelling out ownership transfer rules for specific situations, a buy-sell agreement should outline how to set the price for shares being sold. In essence, this determines how to value the company. It's all too common for departing and continuing owners to have significantly different ideas about a company's value. Without a consensus as to how to determine the company's value and the price of its shares, negotiations can be stymied or sunk.

In addition, a buy-sell agreement can define details of the ownership transfer such as how it will be funded, payment terms, and other specifics.

Equipment, property, and accounts receivable are simple enough to total, but it's much harder to put a price tag on intangibles such as business reputation or customer lists. When owners don't agree on how to establish a company's value, the haggling involved in an ownership transfer can get gnarly. If the ownership transfer is due to death, divorce, or some other wrenching event, you can count on the negotiations being even tougher.

To avoid these conflicts, a buy-sell agreement establishes in advance a value for the company or a formula that will be used to determine it. Any owner's share can then be calculated by multiplying the ownership percentage by the overall company value.

There are several different ways to value a business, and you can include any of them in your buy-sell agreement.

One approach is to establish a preset value for the company. Though the simplicity of this approach may be attractive, the obvious weakness is that the fixed price is likely to become outdated and may not accurately reflect the current value of the business—particularly if the business is growing or shrinking rapidly. One way to remedy this is to update the fixed price periodically, say, every year.

A better approach is to use a valuation formula in your agreement. With a formula, you and your co-owners will have a clearly defined way to figure out the value of the business and, by extension, the ownership shares up for sale. Even better, the value generated by a formula will be more meaningful than a fixed value, since the formula will be based on up-to-date data such as current assets or income.

There are a few different valuation formulas and methods possible. Here is a look at the most common ones.

Book Value

A company's book value is simply its assets minus its liabilities, the same as the information on a balance sheet. Because the figures used to calculate book value are readily available from various financial statements, this is an easy formula to use and to understand. Although book value does not include intangibles such as reputation, earnings potential, or customer goodwill, this may not be a big issue for new businesses that haven't had the time or luck to develop much of a reputation or goodwill. Another issue is that this method uses the depreciated value of assets, which

typically results in a low value overall. As your business grows, you may be wise to switch to a valuation method that reflects more and provides a higher buyout price.

Multiple of Book Value

This method is based on the book value approach, but goes further and includes intangible assets such as customer goodwill, a solid client base, a desirable location, a recently implemented marketing campaign, and intellectual property owned by the business. The overall value is reached by taking the business's book value and multiplying it by a predetermined number, aptly called a multiplier. The co-owners will need to choose a multiplier to include in the buy-sell agreement—and choosing is more of an art than a science. You'll find a wide range of multipliers used, from just over one to six or more. Do some research into your particular industry before choosing a multiplier.

Capitalization of Earnings

Also called "multiple of earnings," the capitalization of earnings method bases a company's value on its record of profits. Because brand-new businesses won't have a profit record, do not use this method until you develop an earnings history.

The valuation begins with the company's annual profit (gross revenues minus costs) multiplied by a predetermined number—a multiplier, sometimes called a capitalization rate. Co-owners will choose a multiplier based on several factors, including general economic conditions, type of business, business age, risk involved in business, or multipliers of similar businesses. Multipliers for the capitalization of earnings method can go as high as ten in some cases.

Appraisal Value

Rather than doing it yourselves, you can hire a professional business appraiser to determine a business's value once an ownership transfer is imminent. That certainly makes things easier for the co-owners, but it's not without drawbacks. One is cost: Appraisers don't come cheap. Expect to pay at least $1,000 for an appraisal of a small company, and up to $10,000 for large businesses with annual sales into the millions. Appraisals can also take valuable time, which may be an issue when an owner is eager to sell.

At the end of the day, you'll need to choose the valuation method that works best for your company. As a general rule, methods based on book value tend not to be good choices for service businesses that may have few assets. For such businesses, basing valuation on earnings history makes more sense.

TIP

Address other issues, such as payment terms and the funding source. Because ownership shares can involve big sums of money, buyouts cannot always be paid for all at once. It's a good idea to outline specific payment terms in your agreement—for instance, monthly payments of principal and interest, or some other arrangement. It's also wise to address where the money will come from in the case of a buyout. Businesses commonly need to take out a loan to pay departing owners, or to use proceeds from life or disability insurance. If you don't plan in advance how you'll fund buyouts, you might find there's not enough time to scramble the money together once something triggers a buyout.

FORM

You can find suggested language for agreement prices in "Sample Buy-Sell Agreement Provisions," below, and on this book's companion page on Nolo.com (see Appendix B for the link).

Implementing Buy-Sell Provisions

In general, buy-sell provisions either can be assembled into their own document, or can be added to your existing business-governing document. For corporations, this is the bylaws; for LLCs, it's the operating agreement; for partnerships, it's the partnership agreement. If you want to use the sample provisions provided below, it is best that you insert them into your existing business-governing document, because only the basic clauses are provided in the template included here.

To insert clauses into the existing document that governs your business, either type or cut and paste the clauses into your document file, preferably near the end. Be sure to renumber the sections as needed to conform with the existing numbering of your document.

Note that many of the standard clauses in the sample agreement have multiple options with checkboxes. Feel free either to copy and paste all the possible options and use the checkboxes to indicate your choices, or to copy and paste only the clauses you choose to use. However, it is not a good idea to select partial language; instead, choose among the clearly defined alternative options.

Before finalizing your agreement, you must tackle an important legal task: a consistency check. This requires scrutinizing whether any of the buy-sell provisions conflict with any existing business documents. Essentially, you need to make sure that your existing documents don't contain any language contradicting any of the buy-sell provisions. Generally, if there are no clauses in your existing document that explicitly contradict the buy-sell provisions, then you may be in

the clear. Still, analyzing the provisions for conflict can be confusing, and you may want simply to pay a lawyer to review the existing document and the buy-sell provisions.

CAUTION

Consistency checks are important business. Often, inconsistencies in documents will be obvious, even to a nonlawyer. For example, say your existing LLC operating agreement states that any person who is at the receiving end of an ownership transfer will have economic rights only—as in, no voting rights or management authority. Your buy-sell provisions, on the other hand, are based on the assumption that full ownership rights are being transferred, including voting and management rights. This should trigger alarm bells. One option is to delete the limited-ownership-rights provision from your existing operating agreement. Or, if you'd prefer, see a lawyer who can make the necessary changes for you.

Sample Buy-Sell Provisions

Sample buy-sell clauses are provided below for you to use as a starting point when drafting your own agreement. The sample clauses are also included in the agreement on this book's companion page on Nolo.com.

The sample agreement begins with one basic provision that may be necessary in some states: a statement that the company does not terminate when an owner transfers an interest, dies, withdraws, files for bankruptcy, is expelled, or otherwise leaves the company. Under some state laws, the legal default is that a partnership or LLC automatically dissolves once an owner is "dissociated"—in other words, when an owner sells an interest, dies, withdraws, or otherwise no longer holds an ownership interest—unless the remaining owners vote to continue the business. The introductory provision included here ensures that your business won't legally dissolve whenever an ownership transfer is triggered under your buy-sell provisions. As mentioned, make sure there is no statement to the contrary elsewhere in your partnership or operating agreement.

Moving on to the real meat of the buy-sell agreement, you'll find samples of the three most important clauses:

- a limitation on the transfer of ownership interests, or right of first refusal
- a right to force buyouts, and
- a method to determine share price.

You'll also find a fourth provision: payment terms, which outlines a few alternatives for how a buyout will be paid.

Keep in mind that these sample provisions stick to the basics and should be seen as a skeletal version of a full buy-sell agreement. There are many other details and issues you should consider once you're serious about putting your agreement together. All business owners would be wise to take these issues seriously from the get-go; it's especially important for businesses that have accumulated significant assets, and for business owners who are concerned about estate planning.

RESOURCE

Getting help with the details. For a more detailed agreement that anticipates a comprehensive range of issues and potential situations, consult *Business Buyout Agreements: Plan Now for All Types of Business Transitions*, by Bethany Laurence and Anthony Mancuso (Nolo).

SEE AN EXPERT

Run your buy-sell agreement by an expert. Although buy-sell basics aren't hard to understand, it may be a good idea to have an attorney or business consultant review yours once you've drafted it. The expert may be able to point out potential additional issues that are not covered in any depth in this chapter, such as tax and estate planning considerations.

Sample Buy-Sell Agreement Provisions

Section 1: Introduction

The legal existence of the company shall not terminate upon the addition of a new owner or the transfer of an owner's interest under this agreement, or the death, withdrawal, bankruptcy, or expulsion of an owner.

Section 2: Limiting the Transfer of Ownership Interests

Right of First Refusal

(a) No owner ("transferring owner") shall have the right to sell, transfer, or dispose of any or all of an ownership interest, for consideration or otherwise, unless he or she delivers to the company written Notice of Intent to Transfer the interest stating the name and the address of the proposed transferee and the terms and conditions of the proposed transfer. Delivery of this notice shall be deemed an offer by the transferring owner to sell to the company and the continuing owners the interest proposed to be transferred.

   If the proposed transfer is a sale of the owner's interest, these terms shall include the price to be paid for the interest by the proposed transferee, and a copy of the offer to purchase the interest on these terms, dated and signed by the proposed transferee, shall be attached to the notice.

(b) The company and the nontransferring owners then have an option, but not an obligation (unless otherwise stated in this agreement), to purchase the interest proposed for transfer, and may do so within 60 days after the date on which the company receives notice or becomes aware of the event triggering the Option to Purchase.

   If the company and the nontransferring owners do not elect to purchase all of the interest stated in the notice, the transferring owner may then transfer his or her interest to the proposed transferee stated in the notice within 60 days after the nontransferring owners' purchase option ends.

(c) Price and terms:
   [*Check either Option 1a or Option 1b below.*]
   ☐ **Option 1a: Price and terms in offer**

   The company and the nontransferring owners shall have the right to purchase the interest of the transferring owner only at the purchase price and payment terms stated in the Notice of Intent to Transfer submitted to the company by the transferring owner. The price and terms in this notice override the general Agreement Price selected in the "Agreement Price" and "Payment Terms" sections of this agreement.

☐ **Option 1b: Price and terms in agreement**

The company and the nontransferring owners shall have the right to purchase the interest of the transferring owner at the Agreement Price and payment terms selected in the "Agreement Price" and "Payment Terms" sections of this agreement.

Section 3: Providing the Right to Force Buyouts

Scenario 1. When an Active Owner Retires or Quits the Company's Employ

[You may check Option 1, Option 2, both, or neither below. Check Option 1 if you want the company and continuing owners to have the option to buy a retiring owner's interest.]

☐ **Option 1: Option of Company and Continuing Owners to Purchase a Retiring Owner's Interest**

An owner who voluntarily retires or quits the company's employ is deemed to have offered his or her ownership interest to the company and the continuing owners for sale. The company and the continuing owners shall then have an option, but not an obligation (unless otherwise stated in this agreement), to purchase all or part of the ownership interest within 60 days after the date on which the company receives notice or becomes aware of the event triggering the Option to Purchase. The price to be paid, the manner of payments, and other terms of the purchase shall be according to the "Agreement Price" and "Payment Terms" sections of this agreement. An owner who stops working for the company is referred to as a "retiring owner" below.

[Check Option 2 if you want a retiring owner to be able to force the company to buy his or her interest. This right can be in addition to Option 1 (company and continuing owners' option to purchase) above.]

☐ **Option 2: Right of Retiring Owner to Force a Sale**

An owner who voluntarily retires or quits the company's employ can require the company and the continuing owners to buy all, but not less than all, of his or her ownership interest by delivering to the company at least 60 days before departing a notice of intention to force a sale ("Notice of Intent to Force a Sale"). The notice shall include the date of departure, the name and address of the owner, a description and amount of the owner's interest in the company, and a statement that the owner wishes to force a sale due to the owner's retirement as provided in this provision. The price to be paid, the manner of payments, and other terms of the purchase shall be according to this section and the "Agreement Price" and "Payment Terms" sections of this agreement. An owner who requests that an interest be purchased is referred to as a "retiring owner" below.

Scenario 2. When an Owner Becomes Disabled

[*You may check Option 1, Option 2, both, or neither below. Check Option 1 if you want the company and continuing owners to have the option to buy a disabled owner's interest. If you check Option 1, insert the amount of time an owner must be disabled before the company or the continuing owners can purchase the available interest.*]

☐ **Option 1: Option of Company and Continuing Owners to Purchase a Disabled Owner's Interest**

An owner who becomes permanently and totally disabled, and such disability lasts at least _____ months (the "waiting period"), either consecutively or cumulatively, is deemed to have offered his or her ownership interest to the company and the continuing owners for sale. The company and the continuing owners shall then have an option, but not an obligation (unless otherwise stated in this agreement), to purchase all or part of the ownership interest within 60 days after the date on which the company receives notice or becomes aware of the event triggering the Option to Purchase. The price to be paid, the manner of payments, and other terms of the purchase shall be according to this section and the "Agreement Price" and "Payment Terms" sections of this agreement.

An owner who is unable to perform his or her regular duties is considered disabled. If disability insurance is used to fund a buyout under this provision, the insurance company shall establish whether an owner is disabled; without disability insurance, the owner's doctor will establish whether an owner is disabled. An owner who becomes disabled according to this section is referred to as a "disabled owner" below.

[*Check Option 2 if you want a disabled owner to be able to force the company to buy his or her interest. This right can be in addition to Option 1 (company and continuing owners' option to purchase) above. If you check Option 2, insert the amount of time an owner must be disabled before forcing the company to purchase an interest.*]

☐ **Option 2: Right of Disabled Owner to Force a Sale**

An owner who becomes permanently and totally disabled, and such disability lasts at least _____ months (the "waiting period"), either consecutively or cumulatively, can require the company and the continuing owners to buy all, but not less than all, of his or her ownership interest by delivering to the company, within 30 days of the expiration of the waiting period, a notice of intention to force a sale ("Notice of Intent to Force a Sale") in writing. The notice shall include the name and address of the owner, a description and amount of the owner's interest in the company, and a statement that the owner wishes to force a sale due to disability as provided in this provision. The price to be paid, the manner of payments, and other terms of the purchase shall be according to this section and the "Agreement Price" and "Payment Terms" sections of this agreement.

An owner is who is unable to perform his or her regular duties is considered disabled. If disability insurance is used to fund a buyout under this provision, the insurance company shall establish whether an owner is disabled; without disability insurance, the owner's doctor will establish whether an owner is disabled. An owner who becomes disabled according to this section is referred to as a "disabled owner" below.

Scenario 3. When an Owner Dies

[*You may check Option 1, Option 2, both, or neither below. Check Option 1 if you want the company and continuing owners to have the right to buy a deceased owner's interest.*]

☐ **Option 1: Option of Company and Continuing Owners to Purchase a Deceased Owner's Interest**

An owner who dies and the executor or administrator of the estate or the trustee of a trust holding the ownership interest are deemed to have offered the deceased owner's interest to the company and the continuing owners for sale as of the date of the notice of death received orally or in writing by the company. The company and the continuing owners shall then have an option, but not an obligation (unless otherwise stated in this agreement), to purchase all or part of the ownership interest within 60 days after the date on which the company receives notice or becomes aware of the death. The price to be paid, the manner of payments, and other terms of the purchase shall be according to the "Agreement Price" and "Payment Terms" sections of this agreement. An owner who has died is referred to as a "deceased owner" below.

[*Check Option 2 below if you want the estate, trust, or inheritors of a deceased owner to be able to force the company to buy his or her interest. This right can be in addition to Option 1 (company and continuing owners' right to purchase) above.*]

☐ **Option 2: Right of Estate, Trust, or Inheritors to Force a Sale**

When an owner dies, the executor or administrator of the deceased owner's estate, the trustee of a trust holding the deceased owner's ownership interest, or the deceased owner's inheritors can require the company and the continuing owners to buy all, but not less than all, of the deceased owner's interest by delivering to the company within 60 days a notice of intention to force a sale ("Notice of Intent to Force a Sale") in writing. The notice shall include the name and address of the deceased owner, the date of death, a description and amount of the owner's interest in the company, the name and address of the person exercising the right to force the sale, and a statement that this person wishes to force a sale of the interest due to the owner's death as provided in this provision. The price to be paid, the manner of payments, and other terms of the purchase shall be according to the "Agreement Price" and "Payment Terms" sections of this agreement. An owner who has died is referred to as a "deceased owner" below.

Scenario 4. When an Owner's Interest Is Transferred to His or Her Former Spouse

[*Check Option 1 if you want the company and owners to have the right to buy a divorced owner's interest from his or her former spouse.*]

☐ **Option 1: Option of Company and Continuing Owners to Purchase Former Spouse's Interest**

(a) If, in connection with the divorce or dissolution of the marriage of an owner, a court issues a decree or order that transfers, confirms, or awards part or all of an ownership interest to a divorced owner's former spouse, the former spouse is deemed to have offered the newly acquired ownership interest to the divorced owner for purchase on the date of the court award or settlement, according to the terms of this agreement. If the divorced owner does not elect to make such purchase within 30 days of the date of the court award or settlement, the former spouse of the divorced owner is deemed to have offered the newly acquired ownership interest to the company and the co-owners (including the divorced owner) for purchase, according to the terms of this agreement. The divorced owner must send notice to the company, in writing, that his or her former spouse now owns an ownership interest in the company. The notice shall state the name and address of the owner, the name and address of the divorced owner's former spouse, a description and amount of the interest awarded to the former spouse, and the date of the court award. If the company does not receive notice from the divorced owner, an offer to the company and the co-owners is deemed to have occurred when the company actually receives notice orally or in writing of the court award or settlement transferring the divorced owner's interest to the owner's former spouse. The company and the co-owners (including the divorced owner) shall then have an option, but not an obligation (unless otherwise stated in this agreement), to purchase all or part of the ownership interest within 60 days after the date on which the company receives notice or becomes aware of the event triggering the Option to Purchase. The price to be paid, the manner of payments, and other terms of the purchase shall be according to the "Agreement Price" and "Payment Terms" sections of this agreement.

(b)   A former spouse who sells an ownership interest back to the company or continuing owners agrees to be responsible for any taxes owed on those sales proceeds.

Scenario 5. Expulsion of Owner

[*Check Option 1 below if you want to give the company and the continuing owners the option to purchase an expelled owner's interest. If you check Option 1, also check and fill in Options 1a through 1f.*]

☐   **Option 1: Option of Company and Continuing Owners to Purchase an Expelled Owner's Interest**

(a)   When the company has three or more owners, situations may arise in which a group of owners wishes to expel another owner. An owner may be expelled upon a unanimous vote of all other owners for adequate cause. Upon such expulsion, the expelled owner is deemed to have offered to sell all of his or her interest to the company and the continuing owners. The company and the continuing owners shall then have an option, but not an obligation (unless otherwise stated in this agreement), to purchase all or part of the ownership interest within 30 days after the vote to expel the owner. The price to be paid shall be as specified in this section; if not so specified, then according to the "Agreement Price" section of this agreement. The manner of payments and other terms of the purchase shall be according to the "Payment Terms" section of this agreement. An owner who has been expelled is referred to as an "expelled owner" below.

(b)   Adequate cause includes, but is not limited to:

☐   **Option 1a: Any criminal conduct against the company (such as embezzlement)**

☐   **Option 1b: A serious breach of the owner's duties or of any written policy of the company**

☐   **Option 1c:** _____

(c)   If an owner is expelled for a reason listed in subsection (b), the price that the company or the continuing owners will pay for the expelled owner's ownership interest will be:

☐   **Option 1d: The full Agreement Price according to the "Agreement Price" section of this agreement**

☐   **Option 1e: Decided by an independent appraisal, according to the Appraised Value Method in the "Agreement Price" section of this agreement**

☐   **Option 1f: The Agreement Price as established in the "Agreement Price" section of this agreement, decreased by _____%**

Section 4: Agreement Price

Unless otherwise provided in this agreement, the undersigned agree that the method checked below for valuing the company shall be used to determine a price for ownership interests under this agreement.

[*You must check one and only one of the valuation methods below:*]

☐ **Valuation Method 1: Agreed Value**

The agreed value of the company shall be $ _____ , or such other amount as fixed by all owners of the company after the date this agreement is adopted as specified in a written statement signed by each owner of the company. If more than one such statement is signed by the owners after this agreement is adopted, the statement with the latest date shall control for purposes of fixing a price for the purchase of ownership interests under this agreement. The value of an individual owner's interest shall be the entire value for the company as determined under this paragraph, multiplied by his or her ownership percentage.

☐ **Valuation Method 2: Book Value**

The value of the company shall be its book value (its assets minus its liabilities as shown on the balance sheet of the company) as of the end of the most recent fiscal year prior to the purchase of an ownership interest under this agreement. The value of an individual owner's interest shall be the entire value for the company as determined under this paragraph, multiplied by his or her ownership percentage.

☐ **Valuation Method 3: Multiple of Book Value**

The value of the company shall be _____ times its book value (its assets minus its liabilities as shown on the balance sheet of the company) as of the end of the most recent fiscal year prior to the purchase of an ownership interest under this agreement. The value of an individual owner's interest shall be the entire value for the company as determined under this paragraph, multiplied by his or her ownership percentage.

☐ **Valuation Method 4: Capitalization of Earnings (Adjusted for Income Taxes)**

The value of the company shall be determined on the basis of _____ times the average net earnings (annual gross revenues of the company minus annual expenses and minus any annual federal, state, and local income taxes payable by the company) for the _____ fiscal years of the company (or the number of fiscal years the company has been in existence, if fewer) that have occurred prior to the purchase of an ownership interest under this agreement. The value of an individual owner's interest shall be the entire value for the company as determined under this paragraph, multiplied by his or her ownership percentage.

☐ **Valuation Method 5: Appraised Value**

The value of the company shall be its fair market value as determined by an independent appraiser mutually selected by the Buyer(s) and Seller of the ownership interest subject to purchase under this agreement. If the Buyer(s) and Seller are unable to agree upon an independent appraiser within 30 days, within the next 10 days, each shall select an independent appraiser. If the selected appraisers are unable, within 60 days, to agree on the fair market value of the company, then the appraisers shall select an additional independent appraiser within the next 10 days, who shall, within 30 days, determine the fair market value of the company. The Buyer(s) and Seller shall equally share all costs of an appraiser mutually selected by the Buyer(s) and Seller or of an additional appraiser. All costs of an individually selected appraiser shall be paid by the party selecting the appraiser. The value of an individual owner's interest shall be the entire value for the company as determined under this paragraph, multiplied by his or her ownership percentage.

Section 5: Payment Terms

Unless otherwise provided in this agreement, the undersigned agree that the payment terms checked below shall be used for the purchase of ownership interests.

[You must check one and only one of the payment terms alternatives below.]

☐ **Payment Terms Alternative 1: Full Cash Payment**

Cash payment for the Seller's ownership interest shall be made by the Buyer(s) to the Seller within _____ days of the date the company provides a Notice of Intent to Purchase to the Seller under this agreement.

☐ **Payment Terms Alternative 2: Monthly Installments of Principal and Interest**

The Buyer(s) shall pay the Seller the purchase price for an ownership interest in equal installments over a term of _____ months, with interest added to the amount of each installment computed at an annual rate of _____ and compounded annually on the unpaid continuing balance of the purchase price of the ownership interest. The buyer shall make the first installment payment to the Seller by _____, and the continuing payments shall be made on the _____ of every month, until the full purchase price, together with any interest owed, is paid in full.

☐ **Payment Terms Alternative 3: Customized Schedule for Payment for Ownership Interest**

The Buyer(s) shall pay the Seller the purchase price for the ownership interest according to the schedule and other terms included below:

_____

_____

_____

Section 6: Signatures

_____

Chapter 15 Checklist: Planning for Changes in Ownership

☐ If your business will have more than one owner, consider the various situations that may raise ownership questions: retirement, illness, disability, death, divorce, or conflict among business owners.

☐ To control the transfer of ownership shares in your business, include buy-sell provisions in your business formation document such as your partnership agreement or LLC operating agreement, or in a separate agreement. (The sample clauses in this chapter are to be used in your existing business formation document.)

☐ To limit the ability of a business owner to sell a business interest to an outsider, use a right of first refusal clause.

☐ To force an owner or someone who has acquired an interest in the business to sell the interest to the current owners, use an option to purchase clause.

☐ To force the other owners of the business to purchase a departing owner's share, include a forced buyout clause.

☐ Remember to include provisions for how the price will be set for ownership shares being sold, and payment terms.

Building Your Business and Hiring Workers

If all your careful planning, hard work, and good karma pay off, you may soon find yourself needing help to handle your thriving business. While part of you will surely be happy that your business is taking off, another, more practical side of you may worry about what's involved in hiring help. This chapter offers a broad overview of the many legal requirements that apply to businesses that have one or more employees. If you're thinking about hiring an employee but aren't sure about how or whether to do it, the information here should help you understand what you're getting into—and help you figure out if there's a better way to go.

In addition to the practical and financial concerns involved in hiring one or more people to work for your business, you need to be aware of several legal rules that apply to businesses with outside workers. First of all, you'll need to understand the difference between the two types of workers: employees and independent contractors. This distinction is crucial, because different rules will apply to your business depending on what kind of workers you hire. If the government considers your workers to be employees, you'll have to follow a number of state and federal laws and pay employment-related taxes. If, on the other hand, your workers can be characterized as independent contractors, you'll be spared many— but not all—of these financial and legal requirements.

Employees Versus Independent Contractors

Anyone who works for your business (other than a business owner) is either an employee or an independent contractor (IC). In a nutshell, an employee is someone who works for you, on your site, with your tools and equipment, and according to your rules and procedures. Independent contractors, on the other hand, are in business for themselves; they work on their own time and with their own tools, and perform services for a number of different clients.

This is not a distinction to be taken lightly. Businesspeople who hire employees owe a number of employment taxes, such as payroll tax and unemployment tax, while those who hire only independent contractors do not owe these taxes. If you treat an employee as an independent contractor and fail to pay employment taxes, you risk subjecting yourself to a huge back-tax bill, plus interest and other state and federal penalties. More than a few businesses have been torpedoed and sunk into bankruptcy after making this mistake.

With that warning in mind, here's the lowdown on classifying your workers.

The Agencies That Matter

Because paying taxes is the main drawback to classifying workers as employees, it shouldn't surprise you to learn that the

IRS takes a great interest in whether your workers are classified properly. At the federal level, the IRS will take swift and severe action if it finds out that you're treating a worker as an independent contractor when in fact that worker meets the criteria of an being an employee. At the state level, there are rules for classifying workers that may be stricter than or otherwise different from the IRS rules. The penalties at the state level can be at least as harsh as those imposed by the IRS, so be sure you understand the rules in your state. The state agency in charge of worker status rules and enforcement is generally an employment agency, tax department, unemployment office, or other employment-related bureau.

 RESOURCE

Where to find your state unemployment agency. Website addresses for the state agencies in charge of worker classification —the unemployment compensation agencies— are included in Appendix A, and on this book's companion page on Nolo.com; the link is in Appendix A.

IRS Criteria

The IRS's Publication 15-A, *Employer's Supplemental Tax Guide*, offers information and examples to help you determine whether a worker is in fact an independent contractor or an employee. It is available online at www.irs.gov.

A worker should normally be considered an employee, not an independent contractor, when he or she:

- works only for you and not for any other business
- works on your premises
- uses your tools and equipment
- follows work hours you set
- follows your instructions on how to complete a job
- receives reimbursement for expenses incurred in doing a job
- supervises any of your other workers, or
- receives any employee benefits, such as holiday pay, vacation time, or health insurance.

On the flip side, a worker should probably be considered an independent contractor if he or she:

- works for a number of different businesses or clients
- has a personal office, studio, garage, or other permanent place to work
- owns equipment and tools used for the work
- sets his or her own hours
- uses independent judgment as to how best to complete a job
- doesn't get reimbursed for expenses incurred in doing a job, or
- advertises services to the public.

Of course, a worker you hire might display some characteristics of both categories, which makes it harder to say for sure how that worker should be classified. Ultimately, you'll need to consider these factors all together and weigh them against each other to decide whether a worker should be classified as an employee or as an independent contractor.

EXAMPLE 1: Bob does a lot of freelance proofreading for a publisher of books on alternative health, Wholeness Press. He often works for Wholeness Press (about ten projects per year), but he also does four or five jobs per year for other publishers. He always works at home, receives minimal instructions as to how to do his work, and does his proofreading whenever he feels like it. Bob can probably be categorized as an independent contractor.

EXAMPLE 2: Susan programs almost exclusively for one software developer, Fizz Games, but she also does approximately one outside project per year. She sometimes works from home but often uses a computer at Fizz Games' office. She works closely with the software development team at Fizz Games, following instructions from some of the developers while training some of the newer workers in programming techniques. The government is likely to see Susan as an employee. It would be risky to try to treat her as an independent contractor.

In borderline situations, it's safer to treat a worker as an employee than risk the penalties that may result if the IRS or your state decides you've misclassified an employee as an independent contractor. Keep in mind that the IRS and most state authorities tend to disfavor independent contractor status. They'd much rather see borderline workers classified as employees so that they can collect taxes on them.

If you can't decide how one of your workers should be classified, there are a few ways you can proceed. One is to consult a lawyer or an accountant who understands business tax laws. Another option is to go straight to the horse's mouth and ask the IRS or your state agency to tell you how they would classify a certain worker. You can file Form SS-8, *Determination of Worker Status for Purposes of Federal Employment Taxes and Income Tax Withholding,* to request a formal ruling from the IRS on a worker's status. You can get this form from an IRS office or from the agency's website at www.irs.gov. As already mentioned, however, don't be surprised if the IRS classifies your worker as an employee.

For a state determination, contact your state employment or other agency that governs worker classification and find out what procedure it uses. Like the IRS does, it's common for states to classify workers as employees rather than independent contractors. You'll have to decide for yourself whether it makes sense to leave the determination up to these agencies, or whether you feel confident enough to classify your workers on your own.

Classifying Workers: Don't Make the Same Mistake Microsoft Did

Who would think that lowly temporary workers would be able to beat Microsoft, one of the world's mightiest (at the time) economic juggernauts? But that's just what they did, which should be a lesson to all businesses that hire independent contractors. Like many software companies, Microsoft supplemented its regular core of employees with a pool of workers it classified as "freelancers," paying them cash compensation (sometimes more than its employees) but providing them with none of the fringe benefits available to regular employees. Microsoft had the workers sign agreements specifying that they were ICs, which meant Microsoft wouldn't give them fringe benefits or withhold or pay any taxes for them.

The problem with Microsoft's designation of these workers as ICs was that it failed to treat them like ICs—that is, people running their own independent businesses. Instead, Microsoft integrated the workers into its workforce: They often worked on teams along with regular employees, sharing the same supervisors, performing identical functions, and working the same core hours. And because Microsoft required that they work onsite, they received admittance card keys, office equipment, and supplies from the company. Microsoft's treatment of the workers clearly spelled out "employee," not IC.

When the IRS audited the company's payroll tax accounts in 1989 and 1990, it determined that Microsoft treated the workers as employees—not ICs, who control the manner and means of how their services are performed—and therefore, owed employment taxes for them. Microsoft agreed with the IRS and admitted that the workers should have been classified as employees for tax purposes. The company paid back-payroll taxes and overtime for the workers and moved some of them to permanent employee status.

Upon learning of the IRS's decision, eight of the formerly misclassified workers sued Microsoft for full employee benefits for the time they worked as independent contractors. The workers finally won their lawsuit, and Microsoft had to pay a small fortune to its misclassified workers. (*Vizcaino v. Microsoft Corp.*, 120 F.3d 1006 (9th Cir. 1997).)

This case demonstrates that merely having a worker sign an agreement that he or she is an IC will not change the worker's status in the eyes of the law. Rather, the worker must be treated like an IC on the job. Because the penalties for misclassification can be severe, make sure that everyone who deals with ICs in your company understands that they can't be supervised or otherwise controlled in the same way as employees.

SKIP AHEAD

For businesses with ICs only.
If you decide that all of your workers will be independent contractors, the rest of the rules in this chapter won't apply to you. You may still want to read on, however, if you'd like to get an overview of the regulations that apply to businesses with employees.

CAUTION

Hiring ICs triggers some require-ments. For instance, if you pay any independent contractor over $600 in a year, you need to report those payments on IRS Form 1099-MISC, *Miscellaneous Income*, then send it to the worker and to the IRS. For in-depth information about hiring independent contractors, see *Working With Independent Contractors*, by Stephen Fishman (Nolo).

Special Hurdles for Employers

As soon as you hire your first employee, you unleash a swarm of legal requirements that apply specifically to employers. Not only will you have to pay a number of employment taxes, but you'll also need to register with certain government agencies, pay for certain types of insurance, and comply with various laws, such as those requiring you to keep a smoke-free workplace, and to post certain notices at your business premises.

Though the many laws that apply to employers are beyond the scope of this book, here's an overview of the major requirements that apply to businesses with employees. If you can't meet your needs by hiring an independent contractor and you must hire an employee, you'll need to consult additional resources to make sure you comply with the many state and federal laws governing employers. (Some additional resources are included below.)

In general, owners of businesses with one or more employees are required to take a number of steps:

- Report all new hires to your state's employment department within 20 days of the employee's first day of work.

- Obtain workers' compensation insurance, and follow the rules on notifying employees of their rights to workers' compensation benefits. You may purchase this insurance from a state fund or, in most states, from a private insurance company.

- Comply with state and federal job safety laws, administered by the federal Occupational Safety and Health Administration (OSHA) and the agency in your state that governs workplace safety. This includes filing an illness and injury prevention plan, reporting work-related injuries and illnesses that result in lost work time, and keeping a log of all work-related injuries and illnesses. For more information about OSHA regulations, visit the OSHA website at www.osha.gov.

- Withhold federal income taxes and FICA taxes (which basically consist of Social Security and Medicare taxes) from employees' paychecks, and periodically report and send these withheld taxes to the IRS. See IRS Publication 15 Circular E, *Employer's Tax Guide*, for details.
- Report wages and withholding to each employee and to the IRS with Form W-2.
- Pay the employer's portion of Social Security and Medicare tax for each employee, based on the employee's wages. The employer's portion is the same amount as the employee's share: 7.65% of the employee's wages up to $132,900, and 1.45% of wages in excess of that amount, according to rates for the year 2019.
- Withhold state income taxes from employees' paychecks, and periodically deposit them with your state income tax agency. (A list of state tax agencies is included in Appendix A and on this book's companion page on Nolo.com.)
- Pay federal unemployment taxes. It's the sole responsibility of the employer to pay the Federal Unemployment Tax (FUTA) directly to the IRS; you may not deduct it from employees' paychecks. The general rule is that you must pay FUTA taxes if you paid a total of $1,500 or more in wages in any calendar quarter or if you had one or more employees for at least some part of a day in each of 20 or more calendar weeks (not necessarily consecutive) during the year. The FUTA tax is reported annually on IRS Form 940, *Employer's Annual Federal Unemployment (FUTA) Tax Return,* available online at www.irs.gov.
- Pay state unemployment taxes, in many states. Most states require employers to pay unemployment taxes, which go toward a state unemployment insurance fund. Generally, you can take a credit against the federal unemployment tax for amounts you paid on time into state unemployment funds. A list of state unemployment tax agencies is available in IRS Publication 926, *Household Employer's Tax Guide,* available from the IRS's website at www.irs.gov.
- Pay or withhold other employment-related taxes that may be required by your state, such as disability insurance.
- Confirm employee eligibility to work in the United States by completing U.S. Citizenship and Immigration Services (USCIS) Form I-9 (available at www.uscis.gov).

! CAUTION

Make payroll taxes a top priority expense. The owner of a cash-strapped small business might be tempted to put off paying payroll taxes for a quarter, or a year. "This happens all the time, but it is a huge mistake. It can lead to jail time," says David Rothenberg, a CPA. You must include payroll taxes in your cash flow planning and then pay those taxes regularly.

Thinking twice about becoming an employer? There's no way around it: Adding employees to your business will greatly complicate your life. (And this is even without considering many other possibilities, such as providing optional benefits, including health insurance and 401(k) plans.) If there's a way to meet your needs with independent contractors rather than employees, it may be a much more practical road to take. At the very least, you shouldn't jump into hiring employees without having a clear reason to do so.

 RESOURCE

For more information on being an employer. As noted above, you'll need to check several government agencies (including the IRS, OSHA, USCIS, and your state employment department and income tax agency) to comply with legal requirements that apply to employers. If you want all the information in one place, see *The Employer's Legal Handbook*, by Fred S. Steingold (Nolo), an indispensable, comprehensive reference for employers that covers the legal rules on hiring, firing, taxes, workplace safety, and much more. And for lots of free articles, see the Employment Law section of Nolo.com.

Hiring and Managing Staff

If you've decided you're ready to take the leap and hire one or more employees, it's essential to hire and manage them with care. Obviously, it's important to hire only those people who can achieve the goals set for them. (This presumes that goals have been set for workers before you start the hiring process—as discussed in more detail below.) These workers will also need ongoing management to make sure they're doing a good job and dealing with any obstacles along the way.

This section outlines a simple, systematic approach to recruiting people to work for your business. The focus of this approach is on creating clearly defined positions and organizing them into an efficient structure.

Determine What Tasks Need to Be Done

The first step in hiring staff is to clearly define what needs to be done. Do you need help answering phones? Managing a retail store? Making donuts? The clearer you are about what needs to be done, the easier it will be for workers to meet these expectations.

Defining tasks can be somewhat overwhelming for business owners in the start-up stage. When considering what you need help with, your initial reaction will probably be, "Everything!" The best way to clear this hurdle is to evaluate your business plan and make sure to develop solid systems for all aspects of your business. For example, you'll want a well-established system or procedure for how the business will provide its products or services, how it will track inventory, what records it will keep and how it will keep them, how it will track employees' time, and so on. When you have sketched out a system for each of the essential tasks of your business, it will be much easier to see specifically what tasks need to be handled. This is where your needs for one or more employees will come into sharper focus.

Create Positions and Job Descriptions

With a solid and realistic task list in hand, the next step is to group tasks together for each position. Certain activities will fall together naturally. For instance, the tasks of answering phones, updating databases, managing office supplies, and doing very basic bookkeeping might combine well into one position. Ordering inventory and managing retail sales might similarly fall into a distinct task set.

Once tasks are grouped together, you can create job positions to handle those areas. The office tasks mentioned above, for instance, could go to an office manager. Tasks such as ordering inventory and managing sales might well be headed by a sales manager. Obviously, how you define specific positions for your business will depend on many different factors.

It's also important to write out a formal job description for each permanent position. Creating a job description for each position not only will help in the hiring process but will also be valuable when it's time to review the employee's performance. Fortunately, writing job descriptions should be easy if you have created the position from a task-based to-do list; the job description can simply restate the list in slightly more polished form.

Develop Staff Hierarchies

Progressive-minded folks sometimes look at staff hierarchies as undemocratic or somehow oppressive. Without getting into a treatise on the virtues or evils of various types of power structures, suffice it to say that a little structure goes a long way toward ensuring the efficient operation of any organization. That's not to say that it's necessary to create a multilayered, command-and-control reporting system. If your business will have five or more regular employees, however, it's important to take the time to designate clear lines of authority and accountability. In small businesses, this often means that everyone reports to one of the business owners. As the business grows, you'll probably want to add a second layer of managerial accountability—for example, to require marketing associates to report to the sales and marketing manager, not directly to the business owner.

Create Review Procedures

Every business should implement an evaluation procedure before hiring anyone. That way, new employees know what to expect from the very first day. The review procedure needn't be complex; it might simply identify who will participate in reviews, when they will occur, and the criteria by which staff will be measured.

Create an Employee Handbook

A handbook for employees serves a vital role, giving everyone ready access to important information about their jobs. Even more important, creating an employee handbook is a powerful way to minimize the risks posed by anyone that works for your business. As discussed in more detail in Chapter 8, a business's potential risk of a liability or contract lawsuit go way up as soon as you hire even one employee. Not only can that worker potentially harm someone and expose the business to a lawsuit, but he or she also could sue the business for a host of discrimination, wrongful termination, or other claims.

Creating a guidebook that outlines clear policies for employees will go a long way toward minimizing these risks. To create a handbook, the business owner or high-level manager will have to spend some time coming up with a set of rules for employees to follow and procedures the business will use in dealing with workers. Facing and answering these questions will help ensure that your employment practices are sound. And compiling these policies in a guidebook promotes positive staff relations by demonstrating your business's commitment to fair treatment for all workers, according to the same set of rules. By offering clearly stated expectations and procedures for treating employees consistently, a handbook provides a powerful deterrent to future workplace trouble.

Employee handbooks typically include information on:

- hiring
- hours and flextime
- sick and vacation leave

- parental leave
- employee benefits
- performance review procedures
- workplace behavior
- health and safety
- employee privacy
- conflicts of interest
- discrimination and harassment
- grievance procedures, and
- termination.

Lots of new business owners find the prospect of creating a staff handbook too overwhelming in their harried early days. While this is understandable, it's a good idea to tackle the task earlier rather than later—it will be easier to create a handbook before the staff grows large and complex. It's simply unwise to have more than a few employees without a written policy manual.

RESOURCE

Resource for creating your employee handbook. All businesses with employees would be wise to take this task seriously. An excellent guide is Nolo's *Create Your Own Employee Handbook,* by Lisa Guerin and Amy DelPo. This book walks you step-by-step through creating an employee handbook, explaining the issues and offering sample language you can modify to fit your workplace.

Orient New Employees

When employees come on board, it's important to take some time to introduce them to your world. For efficiency's sake, it's a great idea to create a standard orientation process—it could be a short meeting and video shown in a conference room, a walk-through of the office, or a get-together at your house—to explain the ins and outs of working for the business. If and when you have several employees coming on board at once, you can save time by orienting them as a group.

All new hires should receive basic information about the business, but you'll want to provide a more extensive orientation for higher-level positions. For example, you may want to spend a significant amount of time with a general manager—say, a series of meetings over a few days—to make sure he or she really understands what the business is about and how you want it to be run. This might include discussing the business's history and any past problems that you do not want to see repeated. For regular employees, on the other hand, this much information would be overkill. The point here is to keep those whom you are orienting in mind when deciding what information to include in your orientation sessions.

A good starting point is to provide each new employee with a copy of your employee handbook. Beyond that, the type of orientation may well depend on how many staffers are involved. If you're starting out with just a handful of employees, perhaps a couple hours of orientation followed by lunch might work. As your staff grows, you may want to have new hires attend presentations by a manager or supervisor. Pairing new employees with experienced ones for a mentorship period is also a good way to bring newcomers on board.

Chapter 16 Checklist: Building Your Business and Hiring Workers

☐ Become familiar with the legal differences between employees and independent contractors.

☐ Before hiring help, determine whether you need to hire employees or whether you could use independent contractors instead.

☐ Don't avoid the obligations of having employees by misclassifying your workers as independent contractors. If the IRS decides your workers are really employees, you can face serious penalties, including payment of back payroll taxes.

☐ Make sure you're ready to take care of all the legal, bureaucratic, and tax requirements that apply to businesses with employees before hiring your first one.

Getting Legal and Other Professional Help

Most business owners, especially sole proprietors and partners in general partnerships, won't need to rely on professional help for the vast majority of their day-to-day business affairs. As the chapters in this book have shown, the legal tasks required to start a business, as well as many of those relating to its ongoing operation, involve nothing more than complying with simple bureaucratic requirements, filling out standard forms, and paying fees.

But life's not always so simple, of course. From time to time, you may find yourself feeling like you're in over your head. Maybe you're struggling to decide whether it's a good time, financially speaking, to expand your business. Or perhaps there's a dispute brewing between you and a business partner. These are just a couple of examples of the types of situations where an expert can come in handy.

Even when things are running smoothly, virtually every business should at least occasionally consult an accountant or other tax expert for help in preparing tax returns. A tax professional can also help you manage your business's finances in order to minimize your taxes. Making contact with a lawyer and a tax professional early in your business life is often a sensible step. As your business grows, you'll be able to consult these experts for help with ongoing questions.

Once you decide you want to hire a professional, your next question very likely will be, "How do I find someone I can trust?" This chapter offers strategies that will help you find and hire a professional such as a lawyer or an accountant who's competent and aboveboard.

Working With Lawyers

Despite all the attorneys out there, a good lawyer can be hard to find. This section explains how to find a lawyer who meets your needs and how to make sure you're getting the most for your hard-earned money.

What to Look for in a Lawyer

You want to make sure to find an attorney who has some experience with small business issues, preferably for your type of small business. Plus, you want someone who's intelligent and competent—two qualities that don't necessarily go hand in hand with having a law degree. And, of course, you want a lawyer whom you can trust.

In today's world of ever-increasing specialization, lawyers often focus their areas of expertise rather narrowly. For example, an expert negotiator may not be an effective courtroom lawyer, and vice versa. Make sure that your lawyer can handle the particular type of problem you're facing, in terms of both its subject matter and the type of work involved.

In addition to finding a lawyer with the skills and experience relevant to your situation, it's important that you and the lawyer get along on a personal level. If an otherwise perfect lawyer—smart, experienced, and trustworthy—is condescending or rude, you should keep looking for someone with better personal skills. This general rule is especially true for small business owners, who will ideally develop a long-term relationship with a lawyer. The better an attorney knows you and your business, the better equipped he or she will be to provide the best advice and assistance for your specific situation.

Finally, you may want to make a special effort to find a lawyer who is willing to work with you collaboratively on certain matters that you can handle at least partially on your own. Handling some routine legal issues, such as amending your partnership agreement or executing a contract for services, may be well within your abilities, though you may be more comfortable having a lawyer review your work or give you limited advice. Some lawyers will agree to act as coaches for their clients, giving only as much service as the client wants. If you'd like to be more involved with your

business's legal matters and minimize the attorneys' fees you'll owe, be sure to ask the lawyer directly whether he or she is willing to have this kind of working relationship with you. (See "Using a Lawyer as a Coach," below.)

How to Find a Lawyer

Unfortunately, the easiest and quickest ways to find a lawyer are usually the least effective. Sure, you'll find hundreds of lawyers' names in the yellow pages, but how will you choose among them? You'll have the same problem if you look in legal newspapers for attorney ads or check out lawyer referral services operated by bar associations because you don't always know what you're getting in terms of the lawyer's expertise and skills. By the way, flashy, aggressive advertising is not necessarily a good indicator of quality legal services.

The best way to find a good lawyer is to get a personal referral, such as from your accountant or banker, but preferably from someone who runs a small business. Even better is a referral from someone who owns a business that's similar to yours. Book publishers, for instance, face different types of legal issues than do auto repair shops, and would be best served by a lawyer familiar with legal areas such as copyright and freedom of speech.

RESOURCE

Looking for a lawyer? Asking for a referral to an attorney from someone you trust can be a good way to find legal help. Someone looking to hire a lawyer, even if only for consultation, can also try these excellent and free resources:

- **Nolo's Lawyer Directory.** Nolo has an easy-to-use online directory of lawyers, organized by location and area of expertise. You can find the directory and its comprehensive profiles at www.nolo.com/lawyers.

- **Lawyers.com.** At Lawyers.com, you'll find a user-friendly search tool that allows you to tailor results by area of law and geography. You can also search for attorneys by name. Attorney profiles prominently display contact information, list topics of expertise, and show ratings—by both clients and other legal professionals.

- **Martindale.com.** Martindale.com offers an advanced search option that allows you to sort not only by practice area and location, but also by criteria like law school. Whether you look for lawyers by name or expertise, you'll find listings with detailed background information, peer and client ratings, and even profile visibility.

If you just can't find anyone who can give you a personal referral, try investigating lawyers who work in your industry. One good way to do this is to keep your eyes and ears open for names of attorneys who have worked on cases in your field. For example, a trade magazine might have an article about a current lawsuit involving a business similar to yours that mentions the names of the attorneys working on it. You can also contact organizations and visit websites that focus on your type of business. They can often direct you to lawyers who have worked in your industry. Once you get some names, try calling these lawyers and asking if they're available. If not, there's a good chance they will know someone else who might be able to help you.

TIP

Speak with the lawyer personally. You can probably get a good idea of how an attorney operates by paying close attention to the way your call is handled. Is the lawyer available right away, and, if not, is your call promptly returned? Is the lawyer willing to spend at least a few minutes talking with you to determine whether the two of you are good fits? Do you get a good feeling from your conversation? How you're treated during your initial call can be a good indicator of how the lawyer treats clients in general.

Using a Lawyer as a Coach

In a traditional attorney/client relationship, a client hires an attorney to take care of a legal problem and then hands over all responsibility for—and control over—the matter to the lawyer. Though some clients like it this way, many would rather be more involved in their cases, both to maintain some control and to save money on legal fees. But until relatively recently, limited legal help from a lawyer wasn't much of an option. Most lawyers wouldn't take cases unless they could handle them fully on their own.

A different model of legal services has finally emerged. In this approach, sometimes called "legal coaching" or "unbundled legal services," a lawyer provides only the services that a client wants, and nothing more. For example, a client who wants legal help in drafting a contract can arrange a short consultation with a lawyer to get answers to general questions, go home and draft the contract, then fax it to the lawyer, who will review it and suggest changes. Or, a client who wants to represent himself or herself in small claims court can use a lawyer to help draft motions and prepare for hearings but otherwise pursue the case alone.

For a small business owner, using a lawyer as a coach can be especially useful. More often than not, the legal issues that arise in the course of business are relatively simple, and—with a bit of good legal advice—most businesspeople can handle them. Many times, a business owner needs nothing more than some guidance through the bureaucratic maze that small businesses need to navigate. For instance, a businessperson facing a zoning conflict may be perfectly served by a five-minute explanation from a legal coach on the process of appealing a planning commission's decision. Rather than hiring an attorney for upwards of $1,000 to deal with the problem, using a coach might cost $50 and enable the business owner to proceed alone.

Despite the good sense to this approach, it still can take some effort to find a lawyer who is willing to be just a coach. To find a legal coach, use the same strategies discussed above (personal referrals, for example), but take the extra step of asking the lawyer directly whether he or she is willing to help you in your efforts to solve your own legal problems. If you don't find one right away, be persistent. In today's increasingly competitive legal marketplace, it's becoming easier to find lawyers who are willing to be flexible in the services they offer.

Dealing With Bills and Payments

Before you hire any lawyer, be sure you fully understand how your fees will be calculated. All too often, clients are unpleasantly surprised by their bills because they didn't pay enough attention to the billing terms when they hired the lawyer. For instance, make sure you understand who's responsible for paying for things such as court fees, copy fees, transcription costs, and phone bills. These costs aren't trivial and can quickly send your otherwise affordable bill into the keep-you-awake-at-night range.

Lawyers generally use one of the following methods of calculating fees for their services:

- **Hourly fees.** This arrangement works just like it sounds: You pay the attorney's hourly rate for the number of hours the attorney spends on your case. Simple as this system is, there are some details to consider. First, find out what hourly increments the lawyer uses for billing. For instance, if an attorney bills in half-hour increments, you'll be charged for a full half-hour even if you talk for just five minutes. That can easily total $100 or more for a five-minute phone call—a rate that would make even AT&T blush. You'd be better off if your lawyer uses 10- or 15-minute periods, though not all attorneys break down their time into such small increments.

    Another issue to ask about is whether all time spent on the case— even if the attorney isn't doing the work—is billed at the attorney's regular rate. For example, it's reasonable to expect a discounted rate for time spent by the attorney's administrative staff on making copies or organizing paperwork. Make sure that the hourly fee for the attorney applies only to the work of the actual attorney.

    Hourly fees for attorneys range from $100 or so to over $400 per hour. High rates may reflect a lawyer's extensive experience—or they might simply reflect a need to pay for a swank office. Don't pay the highest rates unless you feel the lawyer's expertise—not that Armani suit— is worth it.

- **Flat fees.** For some types of cases, attorneys will charge a flat fee for a specific task, such as negotiating a contract or filing articles of incorporation. As long as the job goes as expected, you'll pay only the agreed price, regardless of how many hours the lawyer spent on the job. If the lawyer hits a snag, however, or if the case becomes convoluted for some reason, the price may go up. Be sure you and the lawyer are on the same page regarding the situations that may result in a higher fee. Also, find out if any expenses, such as court costs or copy fees, are charged in addition to the flat fee.

- **Contingency fees.** In a contingency fee arrangement, you pay an attorney's fee only if the lawyer wins money for you through a court judgment or a negotiated settlement. In that case, the fee you'd pay would be a percentage of the monetary award, usually one-third to one-half. In contingency fee arrangements, you need to be especially careful of costs such as travel expenses, transcription fees, and phone bills. If you lose your case, you won't owe attorneys' fees (because your lawyer didn't recover any money). But you will often be responsible for the lawyer's out-of-pocket expenses while he or she is working on your case.

  Small business matters don't typically require contingency fee arrangements. This payment method is usually used in personal injury cases and others in which a plaintiff sues someone in hopes of winning a large money award.

- **Retainers.** Sometimes you can hire a lawyer to be more or less "on call" by paying a regular fee (usually monthly) called a retainer. This type of arrangement is useful when you have regular, ongoing legal needs such as contract review or negotiation. Based on your expected needs, you and the lawyer settle on a mutually acceptable monthly fee. Then you simply have the lawyer take care of any routine legal matters that arise. If you run into a sudden, complex legal dispute, or if your problems escalate greatly, you'll likely have to make additional payments. For this type of arrangement to work, it's important that you and the lawyer have a clear understanding of the routine services that you expect. Unless your legal needs are regular and predictable, a retainer arrangement is probably not your best option.

State laws may require a fee agreement to be in writing in some cases, such as if your lawyer estimates the total cost of legal services to be more than $1,000, or if you have a contingency fee arrangement. Even if it's not legally required, it's always a good idea to get your fee agreement in writing. A written agreement will help prevent disputes over billing and is the best way to avoid getting gouged.

Working With Accountants and Other Financial Professionals

Many of the issues that small business owners face can be solved by professionals other than lawyers. In particular, tax professionals are often indispensable in helping you deal with tax laws, which have a huge impact on your business both financially and legally. In fact, tax advice is so essential to a successful small business that we recommend that every small business owner consult with a tax expert at least occasionally, say, once a year.

Obviously, you want to manage your business and the money flowing through it so as to minimize your tax bill. But you also need to be extremely careful not to violate any tax laws—which are insanely complex—and to avoid making simple mistakes that can result in costly penalties. Complicated tax troubles may indeed call for a tax attorney, but many other more common questions can be answered by an accountant.

Matching People to Your Needs

For routine maintenance of your books, you probably don't need the experience—or expense—of an accountant (certified or otherwise). An experienced bookkeeper will be able to put in place an effective system of tracking your income and expenses and staying on top of your important bills, including the various taxes your business will owe. Depending on the complexity of your business, you may even decide to do your own bookkeeping—a job that's undoubtedly easier these days with the availability of accounting

software. As your business grows, however, an experienced bookkeeper will likely become a valuable investment.

If you find yourself seeking specific tax advice or encountering a tricky financial problem, you may need to go up a step on the professional ladder and hire an accountant who's intimate with tax laws. The top dogs of accountants are called certified public accountants (CPAs), who are licensed and regulated by the state. Uncertified accountants, called public accountants, also may be licensed by your state. Because the licensing requirements for CPAs are more stringent, they are considered to be the most experienced and knowledgeable type of accountants and, accordingly, will be the most expensive.

In addition to bookkeepers and accountants, there are other professionals out there who specialize in tax preparation. The main thing to keep in mind is that some are licensed and some are not. An enrolled agent (EA) is a tax professional, licensed by the IRS, who can answer tax questions and help you prepare your returns. Others who simply use the title "tax preparer" or "tax return preparer" may not be licensed at all. If a tax professional doesn't have a license as an enrolled agent or as a public or certified public accountant, it may mean that the "professional" has no official qualifications whatsoever.

The bottom line is that you should hire the person who is best equipped to meet your needs. Obviously, you shouldn't pay a CPA to do simple bookkeeping, nor should you use a bookkeeper for preparing complex tax returns. You'll need to decide for yourself what kind of professional to hire for your financial tasks.

Finding Good Professional Tax Help

Finding a tax professional is a lot like finding a lawyer: Your goal is to find someone both competent and trustworthy. The strategies discussed above for finding a lawyer are equally useful in finding other professionals. Getting a personal referral is the best way to find someone you can trust. Referrals from businesspeople in your field are particularly valuable. Since virtually every business has consulted a tax pro at one point or another, it shouldn't be too hard to get a decent list of names.

As with attorneys, choose a tax professional carefully, with an eye to developing a long-term relationship. Don't be shy about asking questions. Find out about the person's experience with small businesses similar to yours, and about his or her knowledge of bookkeeping methods, the tax code, the IRS, or anything else that's relevant to the work you want the professional to do for you.

Also be sure you understand the professional's fee structure up front, before any work is done. Most charge hourly fees, which vary a great deal depending on what kind of qualifications the professional has. Like your attorneys' fee agreement, your fee agreement with a tax professional should be in writing. Written fee agreements reduce the possibility of disputes over the bill.

Internet Legal Research

Some of the legal questions you may run into won't warrant an expensive consultation with an attorney but may be beyond the scope of a self-help book. For instance, you may need to look up specific consumer protection regulations on warranties and advertising, or find out what your state's rules are on hiring and firing practices. If you don't want to call your lawyer every time you have a question, you might consider doing a little legal research yourself.

Finding basic small business law is usually not difficult—much of the information you'll need can be found on the Internet. Start by visiting Nolo's website at www.nolo.com and checking under the Business Formation: LLCs & Corporations tab to see if your question has already been answered, or to get some background information in the area of the law that interests you.

Here are some other websites that offer helpful information on small business and tax law:

- National Federation of Independent Business at www.nfib.com. Here you can find small business news and practical information.
- Internal Revenue Service at www.irs. gov. You can download forms and instructions as well as a wide range of publications that do a fairly good job of explaining the tax laws.
- U.S. Small Business Administration at www.sba.gov. This site has a lot of good information on starting and financing your own business. The SBA also offers links to state websites related to business issues.
- SCORE (Service Corps of Retired Executives) at www.score.org. SCORE's association of retired executives and business owners offers email counseling and mentoring and an excellent directory of small business resources on the Web.
- At www.congress.gov, you can read small business bills pending in Congress, as well as laws that have recently been adopted.

 **RESOURCE**

Help with legalese. If, during your legal meandering, you come across strange phrases, like "blue sky," "naked option," or "commercial frustration," and you just know there's got to be a legal meaning behind them, try looking them up in Nolo's Free Dictionary of Law Terms and Legal Definitions at www.nolo. com under "Free Legal Information."

In addition to Nolo.com and other business-oriented sites, you should become familiar with your state's official website. These sites often offer valuable information for small businesses such as start-up registration requirements, state tax rules, laws on corporations and LLCs, and much more. Keep in mind that there's a lot of variation from state to state in how much info you'll find but, in general, the states have been rapidly improving their online information systems and making their sites more useful and accessible for citizens. State business- and tax-related websites are listed in Appendix A, as well as on this book's companion page on Nolo.com (see the link in Appendix A).

RESOURCE

More help with legal research.
There may be times when you'll need more guidance in researching a particular business problem. For basic advice on doing legal research and checking out federal, state, and local laws, see the Legal Research section (under "Free Legal Information") at www.nolo.com. One resource that teaches you how to find answers to your legal questions is Nolo's *Legal Research: How to Find & Understand the Law*, by the Editors of Nolo. Learning how to use legal resources online or at the law library will teach you to take care of a wide range of simple, everyday matters yourself rather than paying someone else to handle them.

Chapter 17 Checklist: Getting Legal and Other Professional Help

- ☐ Ask business associates and friends for recommendations for lawyers, as well as accountants or other tax professionals. Also check trade magazines and other industry sources.

- ☐ Try to find a lawyer who will work as a legal coach, if that approach appeals to you.

- ☐ Get your fee agreements in writing.

- ☐ Become familiar with online sources of legal information such as www.nolo.com, the IRS website, and your official state website.

Small Business Resources and State-by-State Contact Information

This appendix offers names and website addresses for various agencies that deal with businesses and taxes for each state. While every attempt has been made to direct you to the most appropriate agency or office for each topic, please keep in mind that governmental agencies often overlap and may not be organized in any logical structure. One state agency may have several offices or programs under its umbrella, and it may be under the administration of yet another office. Often, a governmental agency may provide information or laws—at its website, for instance—that are actually administered by a different agency. In other words, when it comes to state government offices, it's a jungle out there.

The goal with this appendix is to direct you to the office that not only provides the best information on the subject, but that also has some actual authority over the matter. For example, the preference is to provide a website address for an official state licensing office rather than the state's chamber of commerce, because even if the chamber offered helpful business licensing information, it wouldn't have authority over licensing matters. This appendix also directs you to specific divisions within larger agencies, such as the sales tax division within a state's tax and revenue agency, where that information is available.

Accessing the State-by-State Small Business and Resources Lists on Nolo.com

An electronic copy of the resources in this appendix is included on this book's companion page at:

www.nolo.com/back-of-book/SMBU.html

For your convenience, these lists have linked URLs. If you want to go to a website listed in this appendix, you can open the file and simply click on the URL. The URL links have been provided for your convenience. However, things change rapidly and without warning on the Internet, so there's a chance that not all the links will be current.

Small Business Start-Up Information

Alabama
Department of Revenue
Sales, Use, & Business Tax Division
 Severance & License Section
www.revenue.alabama.gov

Alaska
Department of Commerce, Community and
 Economic Development
Division of Corporations, Business, and
 Professional Licensing
www.commerce.alaska.gov

Arizona
Arizona Commerce Authority
Small Business Services
www.azcommerce.com/start-up

Arkansas
Arkansas Economic Development Commission
www.arkansasedc.com

California
Office of Business and Economic Development
www.business.ca.gov

Colorado
Colorado Small Business Development Center
 Network
www.coloradosbdc.org

Connecticut
Connecticut Economic Resource Center
www.cerc.com

Delaware
Division of Revenue
www.revenue.delaware.gov

District of Columbia
Department of Consumer and Regulatory
 Affairs
www.dcra.dc.gov

Florida
Enterprise Florida, Inc.
www.enterpriseflorida.com

Georgia
Secretary of State
www.sos.ga.gov

Hawaii
Department of Commerce and Consumer
 Affairs
Business Registration Division
www.cca.hawaii.gov/breg

Idaho
Department of Commerce
http://commerce.idaho.gov

Illinois
Department of Commerce and Economic
 Opportunity
www.illinois.gov/dceo

Indiana
Economic Development Corporation
www.iedc.in.gov

Iowa
Iowa Economic Development
www.iowaeconomicdevelopment.com

Kansas
Department of Commerce
www.kansascommerce.com

Kentucky
Cabinet for Economic Development
www.thinkkentucky.com

Louisiana
Secretary of State
Business Services
www.sos.la.gov

Maine
Department of Economic and Community
  Development
www.maine.gov/decd

Maryland
Department of Commerce
http://commerce.maryland.gov

Massachusetts
Office of Housing and Economic Development
www.mass.gov/starting-your-business

Michigan
Michigan Economic Development Corporation
Pure Michigan
www.michiganbusiness.org

Minnesota
Department of Employment and Economic
  Development
Small Business Assistance Office
http://mn.gov/deed/business

Mississippi
Mississippi Development Authority
www.mississippi.org

Missouri
Missouri Small Business & Technology
  Development Centers
www.missouribusiness.net/sbtdc

Montana
Department of Commerce
Small Business Development Center Network
www.sbdc.mt.gov

Nebraska
Department of Economic Development
http://opportunity.nebraska.gov/
  start-your-business

Nevada
Department of Business and Industry
www.business.nv.gov

New Hampshire
Small Business Development Center
www.nhsbdc.org

New Jersey
State of New Jersey Business Portal
www.nj.gov/njbusiness

New Mexico
Economic Development Department
http://gonm.biz

New York
Division for Small Business
www.ny.gov/services/business

North Carolina
Department of Commerce
www.nccommerce.com

North Dakota
Small Business Development Center
www.ndsbdc.org

Ohio
Ohio Business Gateway
http://business.ohio.gov/starting

Oklahoma
Department of Commerce
www.okcommerce.gov

Oregon
Secretary of State
http://sos.oregon.gov

Pennsylvania
Department of Community and Economic
  Development
https://dced.pa.gov

Rhode Island
Rhode Island Commerce Corporation
http://commerceri.com

South Carolina
Online Services for Businesses
www.sc.gov/Business

South Dakota
South Dakota Business Help
http://sdbusinesshelp.com

Tennessee
Business Enterprise Resource Office
www.tn.gov/ecd/section/bero

Texas
Texas Economic Development Corporation
http://businessintexas.com/start-business

Utah
Governor's Office of Economic Development
http://business.utah.gov

Vermont
Vermont Small Business Development Center
www.vtsbdc.org

Virginia
Economic Development Partnership
www.vedp.org

Washington
Department of Commerce
http://startup.choosewashington
  state.com

West Virginia
Secretary of State
Business and Licensing Division
www.sos.wv.gov

Wisconsin
Wisconsin Economic Development Corporation
www.inwisconsin.com

Wyoming
Wyoming Small Business Development Center
www.wyomingsbdc.org

State Tax Agencies

Alabama
Department of Revenue
http://revenue.alabama.gov

Alaska
Department of Revenue—Tax Division
www.tax.state.ak.us

Arizona
Department of Revenue
www.azdor.gov

Arkansas
Department of Finance and Administration
www.dfa.arkansas.gov

California
Franchise Tax Board
www.ftb.ca.gov

Colorado
Department of Revenue
www.colorado.gov/revenue

Connecticut
Department of Revenue Services
Taxpayer Services Division
http://portal.ct.gov/drs

Delaware
Department of Finance—Division
  of Revenue
www.revenue.delaware.gov

District of Columbia
Office of Tax and Revenue
http://dc.gov/page/taxpayer-service-center

Florida
Department of Revenue
http://floridarevenue.com

Georgia
Department of Revenue
http://dor.georgia.gov/taxes

Hawaii
Department of Taxation
http://tax.hawaii.gov

Idaho
State Tax Commission
www.tax.idaho.gov

Illinois
Department of Revenue
www2.illinois.gov/rev

Indiana
Department of Revenue
www.in.gov/dor

Iowa
Department of Revenue
http://tax.iowa.gov

Kansas
Department of Revenue
www.ksrevenue.org

Kentucky
Department of Revenue
www.revenue.ky.gov

Louisiana
Department of Revenue
http://revenue.louisiana.gov

Maine
Department of Administrative and Financial
  Services
Maine Revenue Services
www.maine.gov/revenue

Maryland
Comptroller of Maryland
www.marylandtaxes.com

Massachusetts
Department of Revenue
www.mass.gov/dor

Michigan
Department of Treasury
www.michigan.gov/treasury

Minnesota
Department of Revenue
www.revenue.state.mn.us

Mississippi
Department of Revenue
www.dor.ms.gov

Missouri
Department of Revenue
www.dor.mo.gov

Montana
Department of Revenue
http://mtrevenue.gov

Nebraska
Department of Revenue
www.revenue.nebraska.gov

Nevada
Department of Taxation
http://tax.nv.gov

New Hampshire
Department of Revenue Administration
http://revenue.nh.gov

New Jersey
Department of the Treasury
Division of Taxation
www.state.nj.us/treasury/taxation

New Mexico
Taxation and Revenue Department
www.tax.newmexico.gov

New York
Department of Taxation and Finance
www.tax.ny.gov

North Carolina
Department of Revenue
www.ncdor.gov

North Dakota
Office of State Tax Commissioner
www.nd.gov/tax

Ohio
Department of Taxation
www.tax.ohio.gov

Oklahoma
Tax Commission
www.ok.gov/tax

Oregon
Department of Revenue
www.oregon.gov/DOR

Pennsylvania
Department of Revenue
www.revenue.pa.gov

Rhode Island
Department of Revenue
Division of Taxation
www.tax.ri.gov

South Carolina
Department of Revenue
http://dor.sc.gov

South Dakota
Department of Revenue
http://dor.sd.gov

Tennessee
Department of Revenue
www.tn.gov/revenue

Texas
Comptroller of Public Accounts
http://comptroller.texas.gov

Utah
State Tax Commission
www.tax.utah.gov

Vermont
Department of Taxes
Agency of Administration
http://tax.vermont.gov

Virginia
Department of Taxation
www.tax.virginia.gov

Washington
Department of Revenue
www.dor.wa.gov

West Virginia
State Tax Department
http://tax.wv.gov

Wisconsin
Department of Revenue
www.revenue.wi.gov

Wyoming
Department of Revenue
http://revenue.wyo.gov

State Sales Tax or Seller's Permit Agencies

Alabama
Department of Revenue
Sales & Use Tax
www.revenue.alabama.gov/salestax

Alaska
No state sales tax.

Arizona
Department of Revenue
Transaction Privilege (Sales)
  and Use Tax
www.azdor.gov

Arkansas
Sales and Use Tax
Department of Finance and Administration
www.dfa.arkansas.gov

California
California Department of Tax
  and Fee Administration
www.cdtfa.ca.gov

Colorado
Department of Revenue
www.colorado.gov/revenueonline

Connecticut
Department of Revenue Services
Taxpayer Services Division
http://portal.ct.gov/drs

Delaware
(No state sales tax, but state gross receipts tax)
Department of Finance—Division of Revenue
www.revenue.delaware.gov

District of Columbia
Office of the Chief Financial Officer
www.cfo.dc.gov

Florida
Department of Revenue
Registration Information
www.floridarevenue.com

Georgia
Department of Revenue
Sales and Use Tax Division
http://dor.georgia.gov/sales-use-tax

Hawaii
Department of Taxation
http://tax.hawaii.gov

Idaho
State Tax Commission
www.tax.idaho.gov

Illinois
Department of Revenue
www2.illinois.gov/rev

Indiana
Department of Revenue
www.in.gov/dor

Iowa
Department of Revenue
http://tax.iowa.gov

Kansas
Department of Revenue
www.ksrevenue.org

Kentucky
Department of Revenue
www.revenue.ky.gov

Louisiana
Department of Revenue
http://revenue.louisiana.gov

Maine
Revenue Services
Sales and Use Tax Division
www.maine.gov/revenue

Maryland
Comptroller of Maryland
www.marylandtaxes.com

Massachusetts
Department of Revenue
www.mass.gov/dor

Michigan
Department of Treasury
Sales, Use, and Withholding
  Taxes Section
www.michigan.gov/treasury

Minnesota
Department of Revenue
www.revenue.state.mn.us

Mississippi
Department of Revenue
www.dor.ms.gov

Missouri
Department of Revenue
Taxation and Collection
www.dor.mo.gov

Montana
No general sales tax.

Nebraska
Department of Revenue
www.revenue.nebraska.gov

Nevada
Department of Taxation
http://tax.nv.gov

New Hampshire
No state sales tax.

New Jersey
Department of the Treasury
Division of Taxation
www.state.nj.us/treasury/taxation

New Mexico
Taxation and Revenue Department
www.tax.newmexico.gov

New York
Department of Taxation and Finance
Sales Tax Registration
www.tax.ny.gov

North Carolina
Department of Revenue
Sales and Use Tax Division
www.ncdor.gov

North Dakota
Office of State Tax Commissioner
www.nd.gov/tax

Ohio
Department of Taxation
Sales and Use Tax Division
www.tax.ohio.gov

Oklahoma
Tax Commission
www.ok.gov/tax

Oregon
No state sales tax.

Pennsylvania
Department of Revenue
www.revenue.pa.gov

Rhode Island
Department of Revenue
Division of Taxation
www.tax.ri.gov

South Carolina
Department of Revenue
http://dor.sc.gov

South Dakota
Department of Revenue
http://dor.sd.gov/Taxes/
  Business_Taxes

Tennessee
Department of Revenue
www.tn.gov/revenue

Texas
Comptroller of Public Accounts
https://comptroller.texas.gov/
  taxes/sales

Utah
State Tax Commission
www.tax.utah.gov

Vermont
Department of Taxes
http://tax.vermont.gov

Virginia
Department of Taxation
www.tax.virginia.gov

Washington
Department of Revenue
www.dor.wa.gov

West Virginia
State Tax Department
http://tax.wv.gov

Wisconsin
Department of Revenue
www.revenue.wi.gov

Wyoming
Department of Revenue
http://revenue.wyo.gov

LLC Offices

Alabama
Secretary of State
Corporate Section
http://sos.alabama.gov

Alaska
Department of Commerce, Community, and
  Economic Development
www.commerce.alaska.gov

Arizona
Corporation Commission
Corporation Filing Section
www.azcc.gov

Arkansas
Secretary of State
www.sos.arkansas.gov

California
Secretary of State
Limited Liability Company Unit
www.sos.ca.gov

Colorado
Secretary of State
www.sos.state.co.us

Connecticut
Secretary of the State
http://portal.ct.gov/SOTS

Delaware
Division of Corporations
www.corp.delaware.gov

District of Columbia
Department of Consumer and Regulatory Affairs
Business Regulation Administration
Corporations Division
www.dcra.dc.gov

Florida
Department of State
Registration Section
Division of Corporations
http://dos.myflorida.com

Georgia
Secretary of State
Corporations Division
www.sos.ga.gov

Hawaii
Department of Commerce and Consumer Affairs
Business Registration Division
www.cca.hawaii.gov/breg

Idaho
Idaho Secretary of State
Business Entities
www.sos.idaho.gov

Illinois
Illinois Secretary of State
Department of Business Services
www.cyberdriveillinois.com

Indiana
Secretary of State
Corporations Division
www.in.gov/sos

Iowa
Iowa Secretary of State
www.sos.iowa.gov

Kansas
Kansas Secretary of State
Corporation Division
http://sos.kansas.gov

Kentucky
Kentucky Secretary of State
Business Filings
www.sos.ky.gov

Louisiana
Louisiana Secretary of State
Corporations Division
www.sos.la.gov

Maine
Secretary of State
Bureau of Corporations, Elections,
and Commissions
www.maine.gov/sos

Maryland
Maryland Department of Assessments
& Taxation
Corporate Charter Division
http://dat.maryland.gov

Massachusetts
Secretary of the Commonwealth
of Massachusetts
Corporations Division
www.sec.state.ma.us/cor

Michigan
Department of Licensing and Regulatory Affairs
Corporation Division
www.michigan.gov/lara

Minnesota
Minnesota Secretary of State
Business Services Division
www.sos.state.mn.us

Mississippi
Secretary of State
Corporate Division
www.sos.ms.gov

Missouri
Secretary of State
Corporations Division
www.sos.mo.gov

Montana
Secretary of State
Corporation Bureau
http://sosmt.gov

Nebraska
Secretary of State
Corporate Division
http://sos.nebraska.gov/dyindex.html

Nevada
Secretary of State
New Filings Section
www.nvsos.gov

New Hampshire
Secretary of State
http://sos.nh.gov

New Jersey
New Jersey Department of Treasury
Division of Revenue and Enterprise Services
Corporate Filings Unit
www.state.nj.us/treasury/revenue

New Mexico
Public Regulation Commission
Corporation Department
www.nmprc.state.nm.us

New York
Department of State
Division of Corporations, State Records,
  and UCC
www.dos.ny.gov

North Carolina
Department of the Secretary of State
Corporations Division
www.sosnc.gov

North Dakota
Secretary of State
Corporations Division
http://sos.nd.gov

Ohio
Secretary of State
www.sos.state.oh.us

Oklahoma
Secretary of State
www.sos.ok.gov

Oregon
Oregon Secretary of State
Corporation Division
http://sos.oregon.gov

Pennsylvania
Department of State
Corporation Bureau
www.dos.pa.gov

Rhode Island
Secretary of State
Corporations Division
www.sos.ri.gov

South Carolina
Secretary of State
Corporations Department
http://sos.sc.gov

South Dakota
Secretary of State
www.sdsos.gov

Tennessee
Secretary of State
Division of Business Services
http://sos.tn.gov

Texas
Secretary of State
Corporations Section
www.sos.state.tx.us

Utah
Utah Division of Corporations
  and Commercial Code
www.corporations.utah.gov

Vermont
Secretary of State
www.sec.state.vt.us

Virginia
State Corporation Commission
www.scc.virginia.gov

Washington
Secretary of State
Corporations Division
www.sos.wa.gov/corps

West Virginia
Secretary of State
Corporations Division
www.sos.wv.gov

Wisconsin
Department of Financial Institutions
www.wdfi.org

Wyoming
Secretary of State
Corporations Division
http://soswy.state.wy.us

State Unemployment Compensation Agencies

Alabama
Department of Labor
http://labor.alabama.gov

Alaska
Department of Labor and Workforce
 Development
Division of Employment Security
www.labor.state.ak.us

Arizona
Department of Economic Security
http://des.az.gov

Arkansas
Department of Workforce Services
www.dws.arkansas.gov

California
Employment Development Department
www.edd.ca.gov

Colorado
Department of Labor & Employment
www.colorado.gov/CDLE

Connecticut
Department of Labor
www.ctdol.state.ct.us

Delaware
Department of Labor
http://dol.delaware.gov

District of Columbia
Department of Employment Services
http://does.dc.gov

Florida
Florida Department of Economic Opportunity
www.floridajobs.org

Georgia
Department of Labor
http://dol.georgia.gov

Hawaii
Department of Labor and Industrial Relations
http://labor.hawaii.gov

Idaho
Department of Labor
www.labor.idaho.gov/dnn

Illinois
Department of Employment Security
www2.illinois.gov/ides

Indiana
Department of Workforce Development
www.in.gov/dwd

Iowa
Iowa Workforce Development
www.iowaworkforcedevelopment.gov

Kansas
Department of Labor
www.dol.ks.gov

Kentucky
Office of Employment and Training
http://kcc.ky.gov

Louisiana
Louisiana Workforce Commission
www.ldol.state.la.us

Maine
Department of Labor
www.maine.gov/labor

Maryland
Department of Labor, Licensing,
  and Regulation
www.dllr.state.md.us/employment

Massachusetts
Labor and Workforce Development
www.mass.gov/lwd

Michigan
Department of Licensing and Regulatory Affairs
Unemployment Insurance Agency
www.michigan.gov/uia

Minnesota
Minnesota Unemployment Insurance
www.uimn.org/employers

Mississippi
Department of Employment Security
www.mdes.ms.gov

Missouri
Department of Labor & Industrial Relations
www.labor.mo.gov/des

Montana
Department of Labor & Industry
www.uid.dli.mt.gov

Nebraska
Department of Labor
www.dol.nebraska.gov

Nevada
Department of Employment,
  Training and Rehabilitation
http://detr.nv.gov

New Hampshire
Department of Employment Security
www.nhes.nh.gov

New Jersey
Department of Labor and Workforce
  Development
http://nj.gov/labor

New Mexico
Department of Workforce Solutions
www.dws.state.nm.us

New York
Department of Labor
www.labor.ny.gov

North Carolina
Department of Commerce
Division of Employment Security
http://des.nc.gov/des

North Dakota
Job Service North Dakota
www.jobsnd.com

Ohio
Department of Job and Family Services
www.jfs.ohio.gov

Oklahoma
Employment Security Commission
www.ok.gov/oesc

Oregon
Employment Department
www.oregon.gov/EMPLOY

Pennsylvania
Department of Labor & Industry
www.dli.pa.gov

Rhode Island
Department of Labor and Training
www.dlt.state.ri.us

South Carolina
Department of Employment and Workforce
http://dew.sc.gov

South Dakota
Department of Labor and Regulation
www.dlr.sd.gov

Tennessee
Department of Labor and Workforce
 Development
www.tn.gov/workforce

Texas
Texas Workforce Commission
http://twc.texas.gov

Utah
Department of Workforce Services
www.jobs.utah.gov

Vermont
Department of Labor
www.labor.vermont.gov

Virginia
Employment Commission
www.vec.virginia.gov

Washington
Employment Security Department
www.esd.wa.gov

West Virginia
Workforce West Virginia
http://commerce.wv.gov/business

Wisconsin
Department of Workforce Development
http://dwd.wisconsin.gov

Wyoming
Department of Workforce Services
www.wyomingworkforce.org

How to Use the Downloadable Forms on the Nolo Website

This book comes with downloadable files that you can access online at: **www.nolo.com/back-of-book/SMBU.html**

To use the files, your computer must have specific software programs installed. Here is a list of types of files provided by this book, as well as the software programs you'll need to access them:

- **RTF.** You can open, edit, print, and save these form files with most word processing programs such as Microsoft *Word*, Windows *WordPad*, and recent versions of *WordPerfect*.
- **PDF.** You can view these files with Adobe *Reader*, free software available from www.adobe.com. Government PDFs are sometimes fillable using your computer, but most PDFs are designed to be printed out and completed by hand.
- **XLS.** You can open, edit, print, and save these spreadsheet files with Microsoft *Excel* or other spreadsheet programs that read XLS files.

Editing RTFs

Here are some general instructions about editing RTF forms in your word processing program. Refer to the book's instructions for help about what should go in each blank.

- **Underlines.** Underlines indicate where to enter information. After filling in the needed text, delete the underline.

In most word processing programs you can do this by highlighting the underlined portion and typing CTRL-U.

- **Bracketed and italicized text.** Bracketed and italicized text indicates instructions. Be sure to remove all instructional text before you finalize your document.
- **Optional text.** Optional text gives you the choice to include or exclude text. Delete any optional text you don't want to use. Renumber numbered items, if necessary.
- **Alternative text.** Alternative text gives you the choice between two or more text options. Delete those options you don't want to use. Renumber numbered items, if necessary.
- **Signature lines.** Signature lines should appear on a page with at least some text from the document itself.

Every word processing program uses different commands to open, format, save, and print documents, so refer to your software's help documents for help using your program. Nolo cannot provide technical support for questions about how to use your computer or your software.

> **CAUTION**
>
> **In accordance with U.S. copyright laws, the forms provided by this book are for your personal use only.**

List of Forms Available on the Nolo Website

To download the following forms, go to:
www.nolo.com/back-of-book/SMBU.html

Forms in RTF format:

Form Title	File Name
Partnership Agreement	Partnership.rtf
Sample Buy-Sell Agreement Provisions	BuySellSample.rtf

Forms in Adobe *Acrobat* PDF format:

Form Title	File Name
IRS Instructions for Form SS-4	iss4.pdf
IRS Form SS-4	fss4.pdf
IRS Form 8716	f8716.pdf
IRS Form 8832	f8832.pdf
Small Business Start-Up Information	SmallBusiness.pdf
State Tax Agencies	StateTax.pdf
State Sales Tax or Seller's Permit Agencies	StateSalesTax.pdf
LLC Offices	LLCOffices.pdf
State Unemployment Compensation Agencies	StateUnemployment.pdf

Forms in spreadsheet format XLS:

Form Title	File Name
Cash Flow Projection Worksheet	CashFlow.xls
Profit/Loss Forecast Worksheet	ProfitLoss.xls
Break-Even Analysis Worksheet	BreakEven.xls
Billable Rate Worksheet	BillableRate.xls
Warranty Track Worksheet	Warranty.xls
Balance Sheet	BalanceSheet.xls

Index

 **More from Nolo**

Nolo.com offers a large library of legal solutions and forms, created by Nolo's in-house legal editors. These reliable documents can be prepared in minutes.

Create a Document Online

Incorporation. Incorporate your business in any state.

LLC Formation. Gain asset protection and pass-through tax status in any state.

Will. Nolo has helped people make over 2 million wills. Is it time to make or revise yours?

Living Trust (avoid probate). Plan now to save your family the cost, delays, and hassle of probate.

Provisional Patent. Preserve your right to obtain a patent by claiming "patent pending" status.

Download Useful Legal Forms

Nolo.com has hundreds of top quality legal forms available for download:

- bill of sale
- promissory note
- nondisclosure agreement
- LLC operating agreement
- corporate minutes
- commercial lease and sublease
- motor vehicle bill of sale
- consignment agreement
- and many more.

www.nolo.com

⚖ NOLO *Save 15%* off your next order

Register your Nolo purchase, and we'll send you a
coupon for 15% off your next Nolo.com order!

Nolo.com/customer-support/productregistration

On Nolo.com you'll also find:

Books & Software

Nolo publishes hundreds of great books and software programs for consumers and
business owners. Order a copy, or download an ebook version instantly, at Nolo.com.

Online Forms

You can quickly and easily make a will or living trust, form an LLC or corporation,
apply for a provisional patent, or make hundreds of other forms—online.

Free Legal Information

Thousands of articles answer common questions about everyday legal issues,
including wills, bankruptcy, small business formation, divorce, patents,
employment, and much more.

Plain-English Legal Dictionary

Stumped by jargon? Look it up in America's most up-to-date source for
definitions of legal terms, free at Nolo.com.

Lawyer Directory

Nolo's consumer-friendly lawyer directory provides in-depth profiles of lawyers all
over America. You'll find information you need to choose the right lawyer.

SMBU11